COLLINS
MOTORCYCLE
WORKSHOP

Consultant Editor

David Buxton

COLLINS

Published by William Collins Sons & Co. Ltd.
London · Glasgow · Sydney · Auckland · Toronto · Johannesburg

Consultant Editor: David Buxton
Book Editors: Yvonne Deutch, Randal Gray
Designer: Val Heneghan

This book was designed and produced by
Marshall Cavendish Books Limited
58 Old Compton Street
London W1V 5PA

The material in this book was first published by Marshall Cavendish Limited in the
partwork *Roadbike*

First published 1981

ISBN 0 00 411860 X

Printed and bound by
Group Poligrafici Calderara - Bologna - Italy

Introduction

There is a long standing tradition among motorcyclists that a rider does his own maintenance and minor repairs. Many manufacturers and dealers, however, are not very helpful when it comes to making workshop manuals or special tools available. Some rider's handbooks even say that simple tasks like changing a clutch cable should be carried out by a dealer, and therefore do not give instructions for the owner mechanic. Even when the workshop manual is available, it is often intended for an experienced mechanic who has worked on similar models before. Faced with this problem, what can the motorcycle owner do?

Here is the answer. A book which starts right at the beginning with the simplest maintenance and servicing tasks, and which leads on to more complex tasks like synchronizing carburettors and setting ignition timing. Not only are the maintenance and servicing details all explained in full, but the final section of the book also covers many of those inevitable tasks which occasionally crop up. Oil leaks and puncture repairs are certainly not 'maintenance' jobs; in fact regular servicing and maintenance should drastically reduce the chances of these problems occurring on a run. It is a lucky rider, though, who never has to attend to these repairs, so guidance is given both in the mechanical work itself and in the dodges that sometimes avoid the need for special tools. Help is also given with how to diagnose a problem, and ways in which the problem can be avoided in future.

The modern motorcycle is a very complex piece of machinery, and one book cannot cover the details of all the work likely to be required on the enormous range of new and second-hand machines in use today. Instead, the reader is guided through the work using typical modern machines. Where other models differ significantly from the one illustrated, this is noted in the text, and where less common machines require completely different techniques, these are explained. A Moto Guzzi clutch, for example, is very different from the one common on Japanese machines, but both types are covered in detail.

One way in which this book scores over even the most expensive workshop manuals is in the use of full colour illustrations. To a professional mechanic, already familiar with the parts concerned, a line drawing may convey the information he requires. The young rider, however, is faced with the problem of not knowing what to look for, or where to look. The combination of photography, exploded views, and sectional drawings all in full colour throughout this book can only help to remove doubts.

With this book, a reasonable tool kit, and a certain amount of common sense, any novice can start confidently down the road to becoming his own expert mechanic.

Tim Stevens

Lecturer in Motorcycle Engineering
Merton Technical College
London

Service chart

Weekly	Check/adjust tyre pressures	pages 194, 198
	Check lights, horn, electrics	pages 169 to 173
	Check all control cables	pages 22, 26, 54, 80, 193
Every two weeks	Check battery acid level	pages 37 to 39
Every 500 miles (800 km)	Check engine oil level	pages 27 to 32
	Adjust/lubricate rear chain	pages 22 and 140 to 145
Every 1,000 miles (1,600 km)	Oil all control cables	pages 23 to 27
	Check brake fluid level	pages 73 to 78
	Check disc brake pads	pages 67 to 72
	Check/adjust drum brake	pages 57 to 61 and page 191
Every 3,000 miles (5,000 km)	Check/adjust contact breaker gap	page 40
	Check/adjust ignition timing	pages 49 to 52 and page 207
	Clean spark plugs, set gaps	pages 35 to 36
	Change engine oil	page 27
	Clean/renew oil filter	page 30
	Check gearbox/drive shaft oil levels	pages 22 to 24 and page 32
	Check clutch adjustment	pages 53 to 56
	Check/adjust valve clearances	pages 99 to 110
	Check cam chain tension	page 110
	Check/adjust carburation	pages 79 to 87
	Balance carburettors	pages 85 to 87
	Check/clean air filter	pages 79 to 84
	Regrease grease points	pages 22 to 24, pages 156 to 157
	Inspect tyre condition	pages 194 to 198
	Check/adjust wheel alignment	page 150
	Check rear chain for wear	pages 140 to 141
	Decoke silencers (2-stroke only)	page 128
	Adjust oil pump (2-stroke only)	pages 94 to 98
Every 6,000 miles (10,000 km)	Change gearbox/final drive oils	pages 22 to 24 and page 32
	Renew fork oil	page 22
	Renew spark plugs	pages 33 to 34
	Clean/renew contact breaker points	pages 40 to 44
	Check compression	page 211
	Check/adjust primary chain	page 166
	Lubricate contact breaker cam felt	page 44
	Lubricate auto-advance unit	page 46
	Decoke cylinder head (2-stroke only)	pages 123 to 128
	Renew air filters	page 208
	Check for play in swinging arm	pages 166 to 168
	Check steering for play	pages 152 to 157
	Renew disc pads	pages 67 to 72
Every 12,000 miles (20,000 km)	Repack/replace wheel and steering bearings	pages 24 to 25
	Renew disc brake fluid	pages 73 to 78
	Clean carburettors/check for wear	pages 88 to 93

Contents

6

Section 1

DOWN TO BASICS

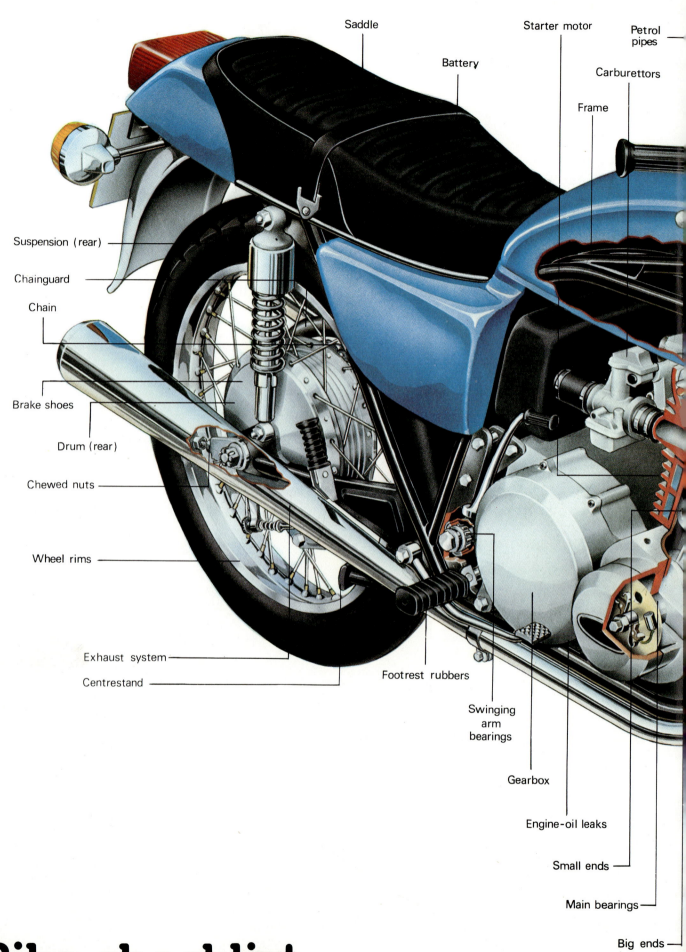

Saddle

Starter motor

Petrol pipes

Battery

Carburettors

Frame

Suspension (rear)

Chainguard

Chain

Brake shoes

Drum (rear)

Chewed nuts

Wheel rims

Exhaust system

Centrestand

Footrest rubbers

Swinging arm bearings

Gearbox

Engine-oil leaks

Small ends

Main bearings

Big ends

Bike checklist

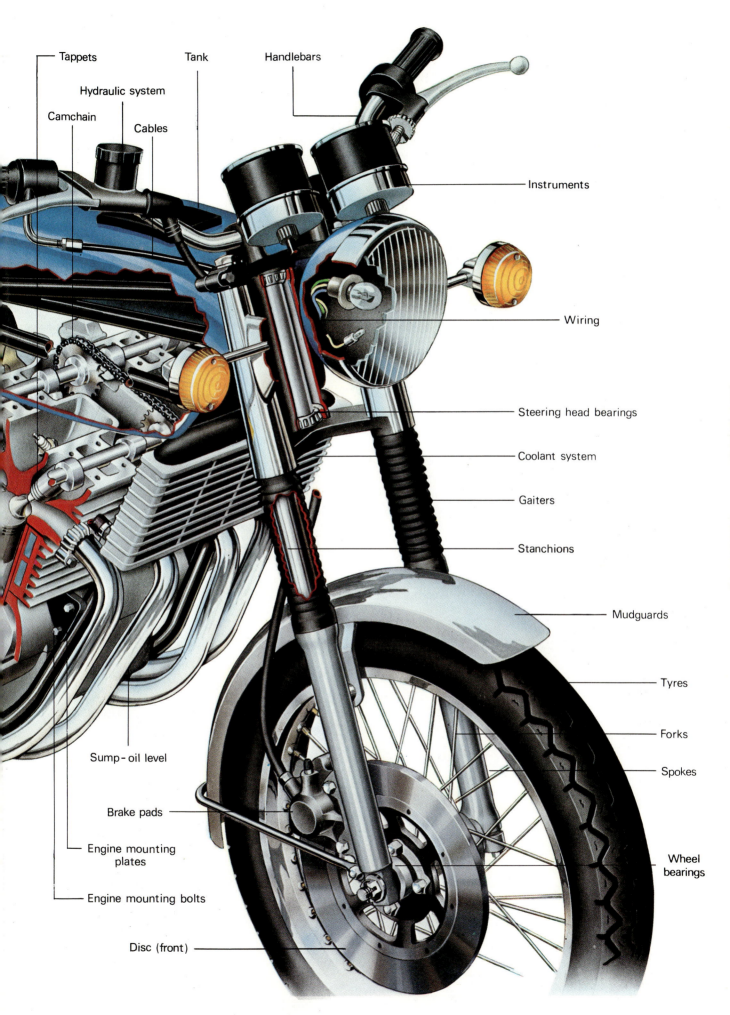

Tappets

Hydraulic system

Camchain

Cables

Tank

Handlebars

Instruments

Wiring

Steering head bearings

Coolant system

Gaiters

Stanchions

Mudguards

Tyres

Forks

Spokes

Sump - oil level

Brake pads

Engine mounting plates

Engine mounting bolts

Wheel bearings

Disc (front)

Four-stroke v two-stroke

Two-stroke or 4-stroke? The argument, like the engine designs themselves, is a hundred years old. Nowadays, the 4-stroke is 'winning' because it is a cleaner engine, avoiding the pitfalls of emission-control legislation. Does this mean that the 2-stroke is doomed for road-bike use? Or is the margin between them so narrow that just one 2-stroke breakthrough could reverse the trend?

The 2-stroke engine was originally developed as a solution to the 'inefficiency' of the 4-stroke, which produced only one power stroke for every two revolutions of the crankshaft. If a power stroke could be produced for every single crankshaft revolution, the inventors thought, the engine would produce twice as much power.

In practice, however, it is not that simple. The power that an engine produces is governed not just by the number of revolutions per firing stroke, but also by a host of other factors—the maximum speed at which the pistons can operate, the maximum number of cylinders you can usefully employ and the internal efficiency of the engine itself.

And in every one of these matters, the characteristics of 2-stroke and 4-stroke engines are quite different.

Engine power

How good an internal combustion engine is at its job—turning petrol at one end into mechanical power at the other—depends on a number of things.

The first of these is its *volumetric efficiency*. In other words: how completely does each cylinder fill with fuel/air mixture?

Ideally, the whole of a cylinder from bottom dead centre upwards would be filled with fuel/air mixture during each induction period, ready to be burned during the power stroke following. In practice, however, this cannot happen.

In a 2-stroke engine (see panel), the inflow stage begins as the upward stroke of the piston closes the transfer port. Since the intake port is not yet open, the rising of the piston creates a

Two-stroke: the Yamaha RD125

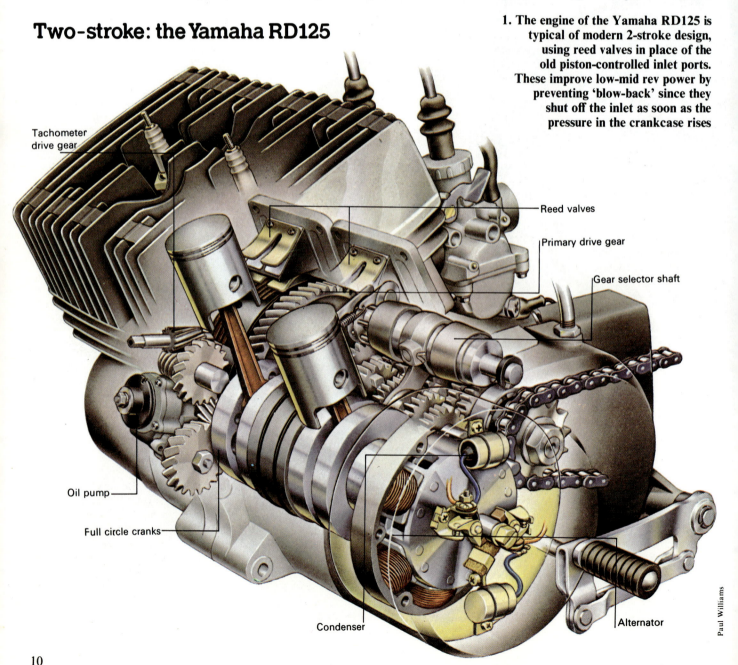

1. The engine of the Yamaha RD125 is typical of modern 2-stroke design, using reed valves in place of the old piston-controlled inlet ports. These improve low-mid rev power by preventing 'blow-back' since they shut off the inlet as soon as the pressure in the crankcase rises

Tachometer drive gear

Reed valves

Primary drive gear

Gear selector shaft

Oil pump

Full circle cranks

Condenser

Alternator

Paul Williams

partial vacuum in the crankcase. When the piston passes the intake port and opens it, fuel/air mixture from the carburettor rushes in to fill the partial vacuum. It is assisted in doing this by the 'drag' of the piston, which is travelling at its fastest as it passes the intake port.

As the piston reaches top dead centre, the mixture has been flowing in for only half a stroke. Yet from this point onwards, the mixture has only its own momentum—with no help from the piston—to keep it flowing into the crankcase.

At high rpm in a modern bike engine, this does not matter. The high-revving piston has created a strong suction, so the mixture is moving quickly. And the intake port is placed as low as possible, allowing the mixture to keep flowing until the last possible moment before the now-descending piston chops it off.

At low rpm, however, this lower-than-usual intake port works badly. Being low, the port opens early and closes late. Because it opens early, there is not so much time for the partial vacuum to develop in the crankcase. The suction is therefore weak. And because it closes late, there is time for the piston—moving more slowly at low revs—to 'blow back', that is, push some of the mixture back through the intake port as it descends.

The 2-stroke's problems do not end there. Once the mixture is successfully in the crankcase, it then has to be transferred to the combustion chamber. Since the mixture has to be ready for compression on the piston's upstroke, its transfer from the crankcase takes place at the same time as the burnt gases from the previous ignition are being removed. In fact, the new charge helps to push out the exhaust, a process called 'scavenging'.

To reduce the amount of fresh mixture which disappears through the open exhaust port instead of burnt gases, the mixture must be directed away from this port. This used to be done by shaping the head of the piston, but now it is more common to angle the transfer ports so that the mixture enters in the right direction. But some mixing of burnt and unburnt gases is inevitable.

The result of all this is that the 2-stroke engine receives nothing like a full charge of fuel/air mixture on each revolution. In the average bike engine, in fact, the cylinder is at best only about 65 per cent filled.

Flexible timing
The 4-stroke's volumetric efficiency is much better; 85 per cent to 90 per cent of the cylinder's capacity, in fact. There

The 2-stroke cycle

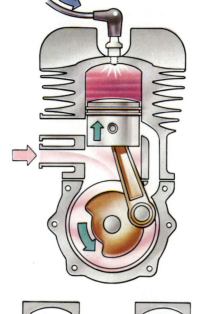
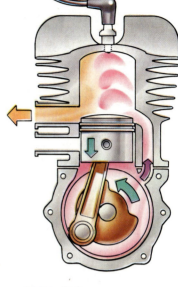

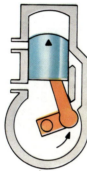
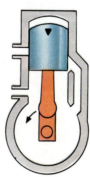
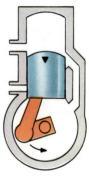

Both 2-stroke and 4-stroke cycles include four processes: intake, compression, power and exhaust. But the 4-stroke needs a separate stroke for each, while 'twos' can overlap them enough to complete the cycle in two strokes. Each cycle begins with the piston at the highest point of its travel, top dead centre (TDC) or the lowest point, bottom dead centre (BDC). In the two-stroke cycle the piston, rising from BDC, closes the transfer port causing a vacuum in the crankcase. Rising further it reveals the inlet port, and fuel/air mixture flows in to fill the vacuum.

Meanwhile, on top of the piston, mixture from the previous cycle is compressed. This expands rapidly on ignition by a spark, pushing the piston back down. As it descends, the piston reveals the exhaust port and lets out the burnt gases, and shuts the inlet port, trapping the new mixture beneath the piston. Continuing to descend, the piston opens the transfer port. The new fuel in the crankcase, squeezed under the piston, rushes up the transfer channel, pushing out the rest of the burnt gases and filling the cylinder ready to begin the next cycle

are two reasons for this.

First, the power stroke (see panel) occurs only once for every two revolutions of the crankshaft. This gives the engine more time (or degrees of crankshaft rotation) in which to suck in the fresh charge.

Second, the 4-stroke has a much more flexible intake and exhaust timing. Its system of cam-operated valves means that the intake and exhaust processes can begin at virtually any

time that the designer wishes.

Between the instant that the inlet valve begins to open and that at which fuel vapour can flow through it at full pressure, there is a delay of a fraction of a second. So the valve is made to open a little before the piston starts moving downwards on the induction stroke—a process called valve lead. This gives the incoming mixture a 'flying start'.

When the charge starts flowing, it

builds up a momentum of its own (like any other moving body) and this keeps it forcing its way into the cylinder for a while after the cylinder has filled up. To take advantage of this 'ram effect', the inlet valve is left open for a few degrees after BDC—a process called valve lag. This allows the little bit of extra fuel, and pressure, to enter the cylinder.

The same applies to the exhaust valve. This is opened a few degrees early so that the gas can begin to find its way out, and is left open a few degrees late so that the momentum of the escaping exhaust actually helps to start the new mixture into the engine.

Mixture and compression
The second thing that affects how well an engine does its job is its *combustion efficiency*. That is: how much of the fuel that enters the cylinder is actually converted into heat?

One factor is the turbulence of the mixture—the degree to which it swirls about inside the combustion chamber. The swirling of the mixture spreads the flame started by the spark rapidly into all corners of the chamber. This ensures that all the mixture is burned evenly. Turbulence is a matter of good piston and cylinder design, rather than which type of basic engine you are considering.

But another is the ratio of fuel to air in the mixture which the carburettor supplies—and it is here that, in comparison with the 4-stroke, the 2-stroke begins to suffer.

At low revs, the piston 'blow back' mentioned earlier can push the fuel

Four-stroke: the Honda CB250N

2. The overhead camshaft, high cam and twin inlet valves of this advanced engine go a long way to removing the valve problems which limited 4-stroke performance

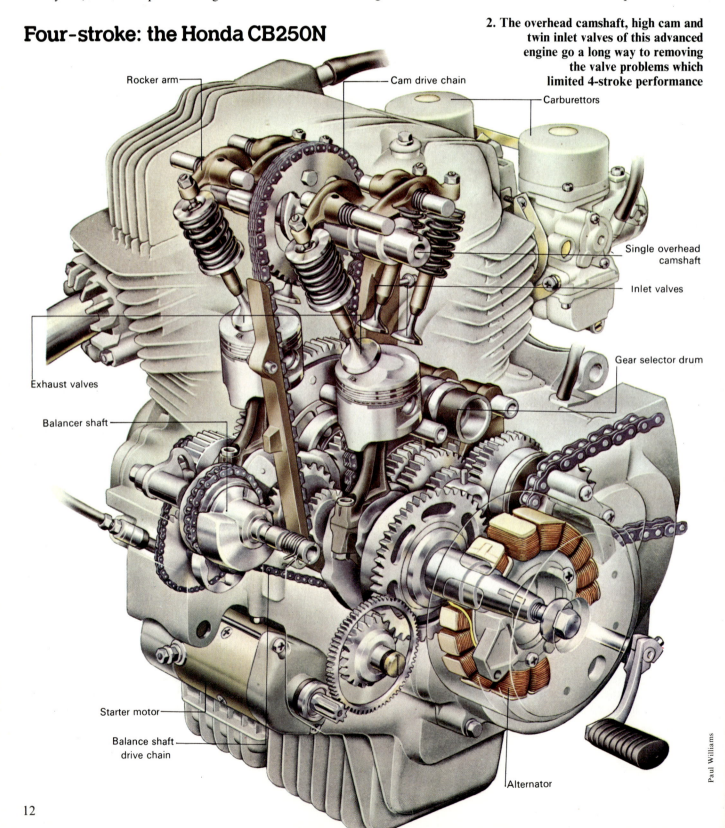

Rocker arm

Cam drive chain

Carburettors

Single overhead camshaft

Inlet valves

Gear selector drum

Exhaust valves

Balancer shaft

Starter motor

Balance shaft drive chain

Alternator

Paul Williams

12

The 4-stroke cycle

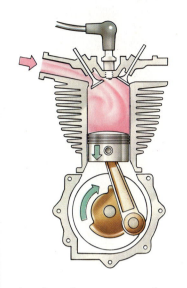  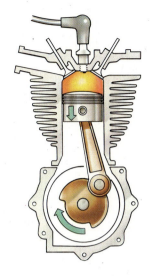 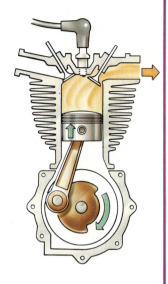

As the piston moves down from TDC on the intake stroke, fuel/air mixture is drawn into the cylinder through the inlet valve. The valve then shuts, and the piston moves up to compress the mixture (the compression stroke). As the piston nears the end of its stroke the fuel is ignited by the spark. The burning gases expand rapidly, forcing the piston back down (the power stroke). The final stroke is the exhaust stroke, when the piston returns to the top of the cylinder, expelling the burnt gases

backwards and forwards through the carburettor up to three times. The mixture becomes far too rich in the process and a lot of fuel is left unburnt.

It is, of course, possible to weaken the mixture control on the carburettor to control this but, as most 2-stroke owners know, the mixture then becomes too weak for peak performance at high revs.

The final factor in combustion efficiency is the temperature of the fuel at the instant when it is fired. Here again the 2-stroke is at a disadvantage. Petrol must not be too hot at the moment of combustion or it will detonate—'knock' —instead of burning steadily. But, short of that, the warmer it is, the better.

Everything else being equal, the higher the compression ratio of a particular engine the warmer the mixture will become. This is because, as the charge is compressed, the same amount of matter is squeezed into a smaller space and so heats up.

Theoretically, 2-stroke bike engines have a higher compression ratio than 4-strokes—typically, 12:1 compared with 9:1. But this is not a true comparison. In the 4-stroke, both the inlet and the exhaust valves are closed during nearly all the compression process. In the 2-stroke, the exhaust port is open for much of the compression stroke, so that the mixture is pushed out of the port instead of being compressed. This means that the compression ratio is much lower than the theoretical figure —in fact, about 7:1.

Losses of heat and power
The third thing that affects an engine's overall efficiency is its *thermal efficiency*. That is: how much of the heat produced by the combustion process is converted into mechanical energy?

Thermal efficiency is much lower in a 2-stroke engine, because the exhaust port opens very early. This releases— wastes—much of the pressure that would otherwise be available for driving the piston.

The fourth, and final, factor is *mechanical efficiency*. That is: how much of the mechanical energy produced at the piston is still available as usable power at the crankshaft?

All engines lose a certain amount of power through the friction involved in driving their own internal components. An average 4-stroke bike engine, for example, loses about 3 hp just in driving its valve gear and timing chain. But the 2-stroke fares even worse; it loses so much power through the effort involved in pumping the crankcase that, overall, its mechanical efficiency is only about 80 per cent of the 4-stroke's.

In terms of its ability to turn petrol into useful energy at the crankshaft, then, the 4-stroke can be seen to be a relatively efficient engine. The 2-stroke, on the other hand, is a relatively inefficient engine which compensates for its weakness by firing twice as often.

Crankshaft speed
But that is far from the end of the story. An engine's 'power' is not just the torque—turning force—it produces at the crankshaft. It is, in fact, its torque multiplied by the number of times in a minute that that torque is actually produced—in other words, its rpm.

Since power depends on crankshaft *speed* as much as on crankshaft *torque*, an engine which runs faster while maintaining the same torque will obviously be more powerful.

Here, the 4-stroke is at somewhat of a disadvantage. Its top rev range is governed by the maximum rate at which the complicated valve gear can operate. Because it is cheaper to install the camshaft down beside the crankshaft, many 4-stroke engines use pushrods to transfer the movement of the camshaft so that the valves open and shut at the right time. But the pushrods tend to flex, particularly at high speeds.

To ease this problem, some engines eliminate the pushrods and operate the valves more directly—by a chain-driven camshaft on top of the engine. Engines with these overhead camshafts can work to much higher speeds than pushrod engines. The Honda 350-Four, for example, can rev at up to nearly 10,000 rpm, while the pushrod Triumph 650 twin 'red lines' at 7,000rpm.

But even if this particular problem is overcome, the maximum speed of the 4-stroke is limited by phenomena known as 'valve float' and 'valve bounce'. At high speeds, two things can happen to a valve and its spring. Either the spring will start to wobble about in time with the valve, so that it won't have the strength to close the valve quickly enough. Alternatively, there can come a point at which the inherent strength of the spring simply is insufficient to move the valve and its operating mechanism back quickly enough. When this happens, not only does the valve timing go completely wrong, but the piston could hit the valves and wreck the engine.

Piston speed

The maximum speed of a 2-stroke is also limited, but for a quite different reason—there is a limit to the punishment that even modern pistons can stand. And the 2-stroke, with one power stroke for every revolution, has only half the time to cool down that the 4-stroke has.

On each stroke, the piston in a 2-stroke engine accelerates from stationary up to 150 km/h (90mph), and back to a dead stop again, within the space of ten or so centimetres. Even though the acceleration and deceleration are smoothed out by the rotation of the crankshaft, they are enough to impose enormous stress on the piston and other components.

Today, at 10,000rpm a piston in a typical 65 mm stroke, 400 cc 2-stroke is travelling a total distance of close to 1,200 metres (4,000ft) per minute. And that is about as fast as a mass-produced piston can go without damage.

So, among road bikes, there is little difference between the rev limits of 4-stroke and 2-stroke. But whereas laboratory 4-strokes have been pushed as high as 20,000rpm, no such figure is yet possible for the 2-stroke.

Cylinder size and number

When a manufacturer is planning a big bike, two other advantages of the 4-stroke emerge: it can have bigger cylinders, and it can have more of them without unduly complicating the carburation process.

In any engine, the size of a single cylinder can be increased only to the point where the piston becomes too big to be cooled properly. This is because a piston loses through the cylinder walls most of the heat it absorbs during combustion.

As piston size is increased, the centre becomes further away from the cylinder wall. The heat has further to travel, and the cylinder takes longer to cool. Eventually there comes a point where the cooling time necessary is longer than the interval between piston strokes.

In a 4-stroke engine, it is easy to direct oil on to the piston to reduce friction and assist in the cooling process. But in a 2-stroke, the crankcase is

not available as an oil bath. Oil has to be mixed in with the fuel, and it is almost a matter of luck whether it reaches the right place. This makes the 2-stroke harder to cool. So whereas a single 4-stroke cylinder can quite easily be of 700 cc, 2-stroke cylinders are rarely bigger than 250 cc capacity and 200 cc is the usual maximum for road bikes.

Similarly, a 4-stroke engine with six or even eight cylinders is not unduly complicated, whereas to build a 2-stroke with more than four cylinders is a fearsome task. One reason, again, is the difficulty of disposing of unwanted heat.

Another reason is that the crankcase depression—the partial vacuum which sucks in the fuel—in a 2-stroke engine is weak. So the carburettor has to be on a short and direct route to the inlet port. To site the carburettors properly in a many-cylindered 2-stroke, therefore, would require either a large number of carburettors or a very unwieldy layout. In fact, the majority of 2-stroke fours are 'square' for this reason.

Complications with the exhaust system are even worse: 2-strokes need a separate pipe for each cylinder.

Clean performance

In summary, then, the 4-stroke engine emerges a clear winner in terms of its overall performance. It operates smoothly from low revs and, in spite of the infrequency of its power strokes and the friction of its valve gear, is a far more efficient engine. It lends itself more readily to the manufacture of big bikes because it can have more and bigger cylinders. For its size, it uses far less petrol and is cheaper to run. This combination of power, smoothness and low running cost makes the 4-stroke far the better engine for a touring bike.

Today, most bike manufacturers favour the 4-stroke for another reason: emission-control laws. It is a far 'cleaner' engine than the 2-stroke, whose emissions of oil and unburnt fuel run foul of anti-pollution regulations in many countries.

Power versus weight

On the other hand, 4-stroke bikes need a lot of maintenance to keep their timing and valve gear working efficiently. They are expensive to manufacture because of the large number of moving parts. They are also heavier; a considerable amount of the 4-stroke engine's greater overall power is used simply for moving itself rather than moving the bike and rider. These limitations show up most severely at the bottom end of the bike market. Under

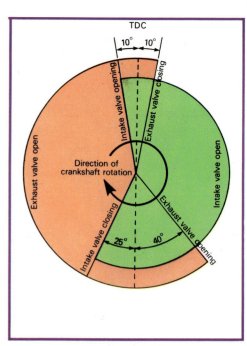

3. **Valve timing diagram for a 4-stroke, showing how valve lead and valve lag are used to improve engine breathing**

100 cc particularly, a 4-stroke costs so much to make, and wastes so much power just operating its own valve gear, that it cannot compete with a 2-stroke.

The 2-stroke engine, on the other hand, retains two great advantages over its rival—lightness and simplicity. Its light weight means that, although in nearly every respect it works less efficiently than the 4-stroke, it produces more power for its weight. Its mechanical simplicity means that it is easy and cheap to manufacture and maintain.

Innovations

In addition, designers have done much towards eliminating what traditionally has been the 2-stroke's greatest bugbear—its indifferent performance at low revs. Their innovations include reed valves and rotary valves (discussed in detail in a later article) to boost fuel induction, the Schnürle loop to improve scavenging and improvements to the design of both ports and pistons.

The 2-stroke's small number of moving parts, combined with its lightness, mean that it is easy to get moving and is far livelier than the 4-stroke. As a result, smaller, high-performance bikes all tend to be 2-strokes.

In the mid-1970s, the century-old battle for supremacy between the two engine types began to swing in favour of the 4-stroke. But, as can be seen, the margin between them is narrow. And one technical breakthrough—a cheap emission-control system for the 2-stroke, for example, or cheap, variable valve timing for the 4-stroke—could swing the contest either way.

Choosing a basic tool kit

Most machines are provided with a toolkit adequate for minor repairs and adjustment. But if you want to do any more than this, you will soon find that you need a better and more varied selection. The next step then, is to build up a more comprehensive toolkit of your own.

Usually the more you pay for tools, the better quality they will be. However 'quality' in this sense is relative to how the tools will stand up to use, as well as how well they are made. So if your aim is simply to put the odd fault right and do basic maintenance, then medium-priced tools, rather than expensive ones, will be quite adequate.

Building up a toolkit

The basic rule when building up a tool-kit from scratch is to begin by buying only what you will need and use regularly. Although it may seem wasteful, the first tools which should be bought are replacements of those in your bike's toolkit. This will allow you to use generally better quality tools, as those provided are often of poor quality.

Basic toolkits usually only cover the nuts and screws most widely used on your machine. Possessing two examples of each of the most useful tools will always come in handy. It is often essential to have, for example, two spanners of the same size. Especially when a nut and bolt needs holding from both ends at once.

Once you have bought these basic tools you should build up your kit logically until you have the equipment to tackle any job on your machine.

Choosing spanners

Before spending a lot of money, the first thing to consider is whether you are likely to stick to the machine you have (or one like it). While most bikes are fitted with metric nuts and bolts, some

British and American machines still use Whitworth or A/F sized nuts and bolts. These sizes are not interchangeable so be sure of which machine you are most likely to work on before laying out a lot of cash on a full set.

If you are going to buy a complete set of spanners in one go, as opposed to buying one at a time on a need basis, then a basic set should include a range of sizes between 10 mm to 22 mm if metric, $\frac{7}{16}$in. to $\frac{15}{16}$in. AF or $\frac{1}{8}$in. to $\frac{1}{2}$in. if Whitworth.

Open-ended spanners are, arguably, the most useful, as they have the widest application. Ideally, a matched set of ring spanners would be a valuable addition. These have a more restricted use but are particularly useful for undoing stubborn nuts and bolts as they are less likely to slip off and cause damage.

Better still are socket spanners. They

1. The ideal set of spanners will consist of open ended, ring and socket type

Nelson Hargreaves

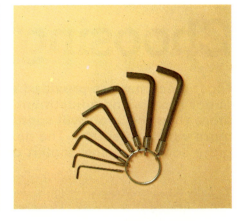

2. A torque wrench is essential if you intend to do accurate work on components such as cylinder heads

3. While not recommended for general use a set of adjustable spanners, pliers and wrenches is invaluable

4. Most motorcycles have socket screws somewhere for which you will require a set of Allen keys

combine the advantages of ring spanners but provide greater leverage and ease of use. With the variety of attachments which are available for sockets, it should be possible to reach any nut and undo it however awkwardly it is located.

Most socket sets have a $\frac{1}{2}$in. drive even if the sockets themselves are A/F or metric. This however, means that the large sockets needed to fit the drive, are often too bulky for jobs on a motorcycle, so a $\frac{3}{8}$in. drive is much better. The only drawback to buying a $\frac{3}{8}$in. drive set, is that most other tools, such as torque wrenches and impact drivers have $\frac{1}{2}$in. drives. You will therefore, require an adaptor to convert a $\frac{1}{2}$in. drive to the size you have chosen.

Apart from the basic set of spanners and sockets, it is always worth having a couple of adjustable spanners, one

large, one small. You will nearly always find at least one nut on your bike that none of your spanners fits. Adjustable spanners should only be used as a last resort, as they rarely fit precisely and can round off a nut head quite easily. For this reason, it is well worth buying the best you can afford, as the better type usually offer a greater degree of accuracy and strength.

Another essential 'spanner' is a torque wrench (fig. 2). While these are invariably expensive, they are a must if you intend to do any serious work on the engine. Torque wrenches measure the amount of force applied to a nut as it is being tightened down. Being able to measure force means components such

5. Screwdrivers tend to be one of the most abused tools – buy at least six and use the one that fits!

as the cylinder head can be tightened down evenly to the correct, specified, pressure. Many people tighten nuts by feel, but this takes a lot of experience. With the widespread use of light alloys for engine components, it is best to be accurate and do the job properly or the consequences could be disastrous.

Screwdrivers
A well equipped toolkit should contain at least six screwdrivers. Three cross-heads and three flat-blades. Although

6. Many Japanese bikes have factory tightened screws which will require an impact screwdriver

it is very tempting to try to make one size fit all, a poor fitting screwdriver will soon demolish a screw head – particularly as many of the screws used on bikes today are relatively soft metal. Having, (and using!) the widest range of sizes, will make removing and replacing screws easier, as well as reducing the chances of damaging them and the screwdrivers. For the same reason it is well worth buying the best you can afford as quality varies widely. Also be sure that the cross-head pattern is the same as that used on your machine, for Japanese, European and British cross-heads differ significantly.

Apart from the ordinary type of screwdriver you should also have an

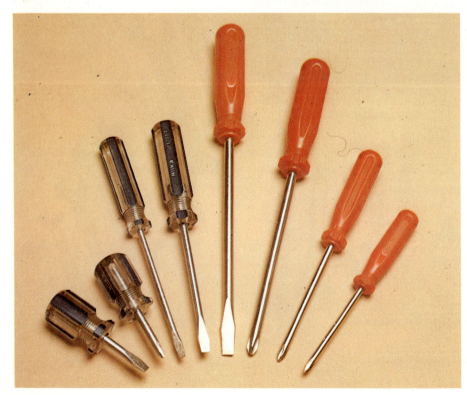

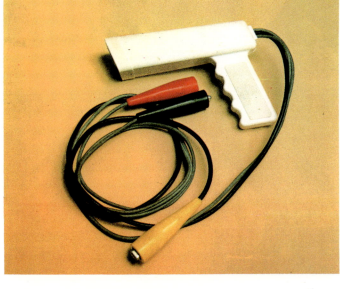

7. For accurate timing adjustment buy a strobe light. It is well worth paying the extra for a xenon type

8. A multimeter is invaluable for setting point gaps as well as testing a multitude of electrical components

Nelson Hargreaves

9. For a bike to handle well the tyre pressures must be right. It is therefore well worth having your own gauge

impact driver. This is a special screwdriver designed to twist automatically when hit with a hammer. It is an essential tool for removing the factory tightened screws on many Japanese machines, with the minimum of damage to the screw-head.

While the basic set described above should be capable of removing most screws, you may occasionally find the need for a further tool, such as a flexible screwdriver or one with a T-bar handle. But you can buy tools for special cases as the needed arises.

Other tools

Armed with a full set of spanners and screwdrivers most maintenance work on a motorcycle becomes possible. There is however, a further endless list of 'essential' tools, aside from the more obvious ones like hammers and pliers, which you will need from time to time. some are more 'essential' than others and it is often better to hire, rather than buy, an expensive tool for a special job, if it is only likely to be used rarely.

Electrical tools

With the increasing sophistication of motorcycles, the tools necessary to check and repair them are becoming equally sophisticated. For example, two lengths of wire and a bulb can be used as a test device. But a complex and often expensive multimeter is better and an 'essential' for really serious fault finding and inspection.

A multimeter (fig. 8) can be used to set and check contact-breaker adjustment, circuit continuity testing and to find out the condition of electrical components.

Another very useful tool is a strobe light (fig. 7). In fact, to check and adjust a bike's timing accurately to the standards demanded by some contemporary machinery it is essential.

There are two types of strobe available. One type uses a neon bulb, the other a xenon. The neon type which is by far the cheaper, runs solely on the HT impulse. Its main drawbacks, however, are that it only emits a faint red light which is hard to see in daylight and that it only gives accurate results at tick-over speeds. The xenon strobe on the other hand, draws power from a battery as well as using the HT impulses, and emits a white light, which is very easy to see. It also gives accurate results at high engine speeds essential when testing a motorcycles timing. Accordingly it is much dearer.

Measuring tools

The most commonly used measuring tool and one which will be required whatever machine you own, is a set of feeler gauges (fig. 11). Gauges can be bought in both metric and imperial sizes and they are so cheap you can have a set of each.

For maximum performance and economy your carburettor should be adjusted perfectly. This is fairly simple to achieve on engines with a single carburettor. But when two, three or four carburettors are used it becomes difficult to set them in balance by feel or improvised mechanical means. A vacuum gauge (fig. 10), or better still, a set of vacuum gauges, will enable the carburettors to be accurately balanced and help you get the best from your engine.

If you have a bike with overhead valves and the clearances are adjusted by shims, you will find that a micrometer or vernier gauge is indispensible.

Most shims have their width stamped on them, but after prolonged use the marks soon become illegible. Alterna-

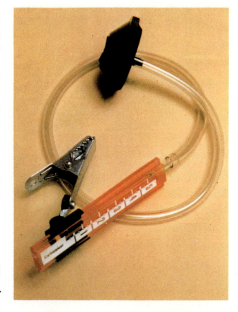

10. Balancing multi-carbs can be a very time consuming business which even a simple vacuum gauge will aid

11. Feeler gauges are essential for most adjustment jobs. They are quite cheap so buy the best you can afford

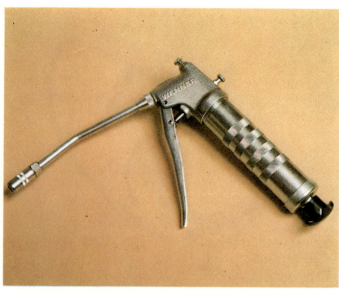

12. For lubricating parts, such as the swinging arm, you will require a high pressure grease gun

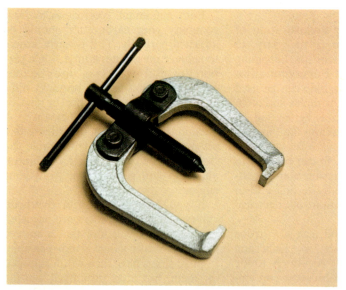

13. A general purpose puller will prove invaluable for removing such parts as flywheels and sprockets

14. With the increasing popularity of endless chains a chain splitter is an essential part of any tool kit

15. Used carefully, and at the right time, a hammer is often essential . . . particularly a copper and hide mallet

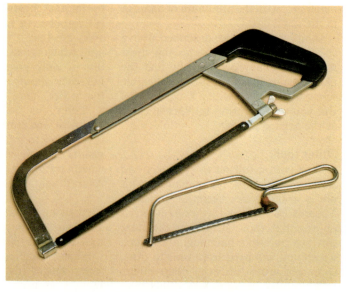

16. A pair of hacksaws will also prove useful on odd occasions, particularly for removing stubborn bolts

17. For finishing off a modification, files are invaluable. These are needle files, very handy for fine work

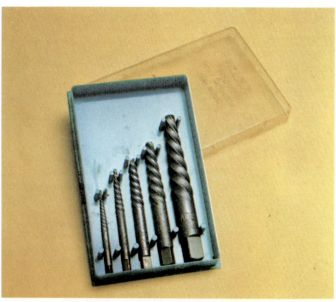

18. The tools you hope you never need. Extractors for broken studs work where other tricks have failed

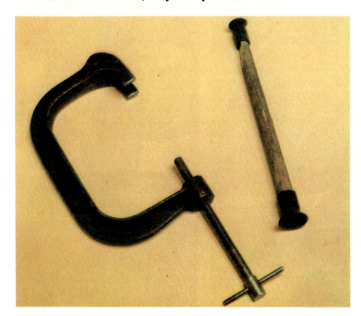

19. Valve spring compressors and valve grinding tools are essentials if you intend to overhaul an engine

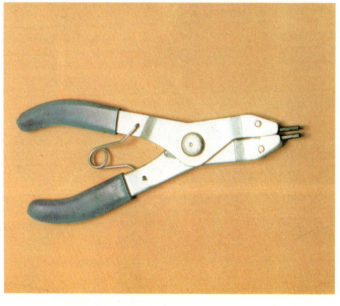

20. Circlip pliers are another essential 'extra' as it is quite easy to damage circlips using any other tool

tively, a shim can wear to a point where it is smaller than its indicated value. Clearances are critical and should never be a matter of 'near enough will do'. So a micrometer or vernier gauge is particularly useful for taking the guesswork out of adjustment. A micrometer can also have many other applications on a bike, such as measuring the amount of wear on various parts. This will also help you decide whether certain components are still useable or should be replaced.

If you own a 2-stroke, particularly a Japanese model then a dial gauge will prove vital. This tool screws into the spark plug hole and is used to check piston position when tuning the engine. Be sure to buy the correct one for your machine as sizes and types vary con-

siderably with price.

Lubrication devices

The most commonly used lubrication device is a high pressure grease gun (fig. 12). All machines have bearings, such as those on the swinging-arm, which require regular greasing.

A less essential but very valuable tool is a cable oiler. Cables can be oiled quite efficiently in many ways, but by far the quickest way of doing it is to use a proprietary cable oiler. They are reasonably inexpensive, and make throttle, clutch and brake cable lubrication less of a time consuming chore.

'Heavy' tools

The principal tools in this category are general purpose pullers.

Many components on a motorcycle, such as pedals, sprockets, gears and alternator rotors are a taper fit on a shaft. This means that they are factory-pressed into position. Consequently, they cannot be removed properly, or without damage, unless you have a special puller for the job. Bike manufacturers usually make or recommend a separate puller for each component. But you can often use a simple proprietary puller (fig. 13), or one with a universal capability, to do the job just as well.

Another 'heavy' tool which is becoming increasingly more valuable to have is a chain splitter (fig. 14). With the trend towards more bikes being fitted with 'endless' chains, the only safe way to break a chain is with a chain splitter.

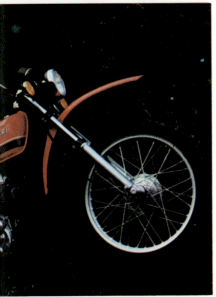

Section 2

SERVICING AND MAINTENANCE

Better lubrication

General greasing and lubrication is a straightforward job on most bikes – particularly if you know a few 'tricks of the trade'. But what many bikers do not realise is the need to use the right lubricant on every component.

Frame greasing and general lubrication once had to be done at irritatingly frequent intervals. On modern bikes this is unnecessary, but there is a trap: with service intervals so widely spaced, greasing and lubrication are often forgotten to the point where serious and unnecessary wear occurs.

The usual multi-purpose grease, such as Castrol LM or Shell Retinax, has good water resistance and is particularly useful for exposed parts of the bike.

For some jobs, however, other types of grease may be necessary. Calcium-based grease, such as Castrol CL, is runnier and more penetrating than its multi-purpose equivalent so will be easier to force through joints that are blocked with old, stale grease.

Any parts of the bike which need lubricating but which incorporate natural rubber components (gaiters, for example) require a different grease if there is a likelihood of the lubricant coming into contact with the rubber. If you have to strip a hydraulic master cylinder, for instance, silicon grease is the type to use for coating the seals and pistons during the re-build, since ordinary grease could damage the rubber components. On brakes, in fact, it pays to use only the grease recommended by the bike manufacturer – not all brake fluids are the same, and mixing two manufacturers' products could cause a reaction which would damage the brake seal.

Swinging arm

Most swinging arms have one or more grease nipples which need attention every 10,000 km (6,000 miles) or so. Force in the grease until it comes out at both sides of the swinging arm, and wipe off any excess.

Final chain drive

The chain final drive is probably the hardest-worked component on a motorcycle and, on most bikes, is totally exposed to the weather. In one week it can pick up dirt in appreciable quantities.

Putting more oil on top of this dirt will only help force the grit between the side plates, where it can attack the rollers. So before you apply fresh lubricant – usually needed at intervals of 500 km (300 miles) – you should clean the chain thoroughly.

If yours is a modern bike fitted with an endless or O-ring chain (see pages 147 to 150), the chain cannot easily be removed and should be cleaned on the bike. If you lift the back wheel and spin it you can reach all the links and work a stiff-bristled brush inside and between them. Use only paraffin (kerosene) as a cleaning agent on the sealed type, since petrol and other solvents will damage the O-rings.

Use a light coating of engine oil to lubricate O-ring chains. Do not use an aerosol spray lubricant, whose chemicals could attack the O-rings and allow the lubricant to start creeping out.

Other types of chain can be cleaned in-situ by the same method, using either paraffin or petrol. But most have, or can be fitted with, a split link enabling them to be easily removed for cleaning (see pages 144 to 146).

To lubricate this type of chain, the traditional method is to 'boil' it in a special chain grease such as that made by Duckhams – you heat the tin and immerse the chain in the molten lubricant. These days, many mechanics consider that a thorough squirting with an aerosol chain spray is quite adequate.

Final drive shaft

The components that need lubricating on final driveshafts vary from bike to bike.

On all bikes, the bevel gears operate under very high loads and usually need an EP (extreme pressure) lubricant.

Using a cable oiler

A cable oiler (fig. 1) is a worthwhile investment if you are planning regular servicing. It is reasonably inexpensive and is much more convenient for oiling a cable than other methods. They are available to fit most sizes of cable, but should you need to modify it to lubricate different sizes of cable, you can buy an adaptor kit to suit your requirements.

To use the cable oiler, unscrew the bottom ring (fig. 1) and tap the washers out. Put the threaded ring over the top of the outer cable. Now pull out the inner cable, and slot in the first metal washer under the cable nipple, and over the top of the outer cable. Fit the rubber washer on top of that, and follow it with the second metal washer. Make sure the slots in the washers are not lined up or else oil will be able to seep out. Leave part of the outer cable protruding over the washers. Screw the whole assembly back into the body of the cable oiler. Unscrew and take off the top of the oiler and fill it with fresh engine oil. Next, screw the top back on, and oil the cable by turning the handle. Hold the cable oiler away from you in case the pressure forces oil out through lined-up washer. The cable will be thoroughly lubricated when you see oil dripping from the opposite end.

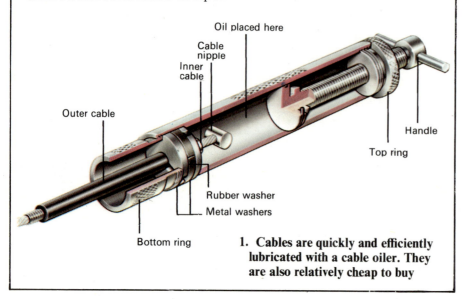

Oil placed here
Cable nipple
Inner cable
Outer cable
Handle
Top ring
Rubber washer
Metal washers
Bottom ring

1. Cables are quickly and efficiently lubricated with a cable oiler. They are also relatively cheap to buy

Lubricating cables

2. Squeeze the handlebar levers and apply a few drops of oil to the pivots and to the exposed cables

3. To oil the throttle cable, undo the two cross-head screws and split the twist grip and starter assembly

4. A drop of oil in this position will help prevent the brake light sticking. Oil all exposed cables and pivot points

5. The felt pads near the contact breakers need only a very small drop of oil. Over-oiling can ruin the contacts

6. Use engine oil to lubricate the chain as a temporary measure between scheduled cleaning and greasing

7. Lubricate the clutch actuating mechanism by applying a single stroke of the grease gun to the nipple

Lubricating the rear chain

8. Clean the chain with a paraffin moistened brush then wipe it dry and aim the spray inside the sideplates

9. Connect an old chain to the dirty chain and pull the old one on to the sprockets to facilitate re-fitting

10. Clean the chain with petrol and use a brush to remove deposits of grease and grit

11. Secure the end of the chain and lay it in the tin of grease then heat the tin until the grease melts

These come in different grades, such as EP80 or EP90, but different manufacturers may use different code names for similar products. So always consult a handbook, or your bike dealer, on the correct make and grade to use. The drain plug is below the bevel gear housing; the filler cap is on top – except on the BMW, whose filler plug is on the side of the housing instead.

Bikes needing any other driveshaft lubrication are rare. But you may find a grease nipple on the top of the driveshaft housing – as on the Honda CX500 – which should be greased with HMP. And the BMW has a separate oil reservoir for the driveshaft housing, located where this joins the bevel gear housing.

Brakes

Where using the wrong grade of oil on some components can be expensive, using the wrong grease on brake components can be fatal. So always consult a manual or dealer on the correct type.

Drum brakes need a spot of grease on their cams and spindles (page 192) to stop them sticking in the 'on' position. When you use the brakes, a lot of heat is generated. So you need HMP grease.

The same grease is used for the calipers on disc brakes (page 189). Floating calipers that stick are the cause of many disc brake problems. When the unit is stripped down, HMP grease should be applied very sparingly to the guide bolts; if the caliper isn't free to float on these bolts, the static pad will remain in contact with the disc, and brake 'grab' will result. But never over-grease any brake component; this could be dangerous.

On both types of brakes, the cables need occasional attention (see Control cables), and the pivots an occasional oiling with 3-in-1 or similar.

Wheel bearings

Wheel bearings often run in the same grease for years because they have to be stripped in order to re-pack them. But every couple of years or 20,000 km (12,000 miles) the bearings must be punched out of their hubs and thoroughly washed off in degreasing fluid.

Special wheel bearing grease should be forced into the tracks of the bearing, and into the space between the two races. Figs. 12 to 17 give a general idea of the procedure.

General Lubrication

To deal with most areas you need only a multi-purpose grease and a can of light oil such as 3-in-1. Instead of oil you can often use a dual-purpose lubricant water dispellent aerosol spray, such as WD40.

Re-packing wheel bearings

12. Lift the wheel up on the centre stand or on chocks and undo the nuts that hold the two spindle clamps

13. Undo the cross-head screw to release the speedometer cable and pull the wheel clear of the bike

14. Stop the spindle turning with a screwdriver through the hole and undo the sleeve nut on the brake disc side

15. After pulling the spindle clear, gently apply a punch and hammer to unscrew the bearing retaining ring

16. Lay the wheel on the floor and carefully punch out the bearings from the opposite sides

17. Clean the bearings in a bath of petrol, using a paint brush to remove all traces of dirt and grease

Continued

Carburettor and points·

Inner components of the carburettor take care of themselves, but all the external pivots and linkages benefit from a light oiling with 3-in-1 or similar oil.

The points need little lubrication, but a drop of light oil on the centre spindle, and on advance weight pivots, will help. Similarly, a light smear of HMP grease on the cams on which the fibre heels of the contact breakers bear will help cut down wear and prolong the interval between points adjustment. Be careful not to over-lubricate, though – you don't want oil or grease to creep between the points themselves.

Control cables

Clutch, throttle and brake cables are often sheathed in a low-friction material such as nylon and need periodic lubrica-

18. Inject new grease into the bearings with a grease gun. Reassemble in reverse order, starting with the bearings

19. Drive the bearing into the wheel housing, tapping it carefully square on with the correct sized drift

Greasing calipers

20. Remove the two clamp bolts, pull out the caliper nearest to the wheel and turn the other gently to get at the pad

21. If there is a split pin, withdraw this and take each pad from its caliper to reveal the nylon washer on the back

22. While the pad is removed, clean the back of each pad and its recess in the caliper with emery paper

23. A tiny smear of grease should be applied to the back of each pad. Replacement is simply a reversal of removal

tion. One method is to detach the top end of the cable and use a home-made paper or polythene funnel to pour in the oil. Another is to mould a lump of Plasticene into a funnel around the cable outer, fill the funnel with oil and leave it overnight to soak in.

Easiest of all is to buy a hydraulic cable oiler. This is threaded internally and has sealing rings to grip the cable firmly while you pump in the oil.

Speedometer and tachometer
If your speedometer or tachometer

needle tends to be twitchy or erratic, a little lubricant on the inner cable will probably cure it. Disconnect the outer cable from the instrument itself and extract the inner cable. Smear the inner cable with HMP grease, but leave the top 75 mm (3in.) or so clean. You risk damaging the instrument if lubricant spreads up into it.

A little care in applying the grease will save the innards of the meter from the clogging effects of misdirected grease. Tachometers and speedometers are not particularly cheap so it is worth the trouble to be careful.

As a general rule when greasing cables it is not wise to be over zealous with the lubricant. Usually, all you need is a drop or two to be effective.

Changing oil

It is often forgotten just how much work an engine oil has to do and the conditions it must cope with, for apart from providing a barrier to prevent metal-to-metal contact, the oil also has to function as a coolant. When a manufacturer advises you to put a specific amount of oil into your engine, the quantity is not determined just by the space inside the crankcase. Too much oil, and the engine may never reach its correct working temperature; too little, and it will overheat.

In a 4-stroke engine, apart from extreme temperatures, what helps to shorten lubricant life and endanger the engine is contamination. Petrol vapour, dust, carbon particles and other exhaust by-products are absorbed by the oil. If the oil change is left too long the contaminant build-up will cause premature wear of the engine bearing surfaces. This does not apply to 2-stroke engines, which operate on a 'total loss' lubricating system and do not retain oil within the engine as 4-strokes do.

Modern multi-grade oils do have a certain tolerance to abuse. As a result, some bikers stretch the intervals between changes beyond the recommended point. This is a false economy.

4-stroke systems

Two main types of lubrication are in use on 4-stroke engines – wet sump and dry sump.

The wet sump system retains the oil in the bottom of the engine directly below the crankshaft, and in most instances this oil reservoir serves the gearbox as well. This form of engine lubrication is found on the majority of modern bikes.

The dry sump system, used on most older bikes, uses a separate oil tank from which oil is passed to the engine, collected in a sump and pumped back to the tank. This type normally supplies only the engine; the gearbox has its own oil reservoir.

Filler caps and level devices

Wet sump units usually have their filler cap on the upper face of one of the crankcase covers. These caps often have a dipstick attached, although other forms of oil level check device – such as a level window in the crankcase side – are sometimes used.

Dry sump machines normally have the oil tank either on a frame side behind the engine, or beneath the saddle. Some modern dry-sump machines use the frame as the oil tank; on these, the filler is just behind the steering head or just in front of the seat. These tanks normally have a bayonet fitting cap. A few cap types have dipsticks attached, but in most instances only a visual check of the oil level is possible through the filler hole in the tank. Guide lines are sometimes marked on the outer tank casing to help.

Drain plugs

Most machines have hexagon headed drain plugs located on the sump bottom. There are, however, a few bikes where the handbook or a dealer should be consulted if you have any doubt as to which is the correct drain plug. For instance, there is sometimes confusion on the water-cooled Honda Gold Wing – this has its coolant drain plug close to the oil drain plug.

Drain plug removal

Not all drain plugs take a spanner: a few types take an Allen key instead. All you normally need to undo the plug is a ring spanner or socket wrench of the correct size. Do not use a spanner that is a sloppy fit or the wrong size, otherwise you may round off the head flats and be unable to remove the plug – particularly if the plug or sump is in a soft alloy.

Take great care when you are undoing the plug, for although they have the normal right-hand thread, it is easy to turn the plug the wrong way due to its awkward position and perhaps strip the threads through overtightening.

Drain plug fitting

A stripped drain plug can be a serious problem on bike engines and is most likely to result from careless refitting. A damaged drain plug can be replaced cheaply, but if the plug hole threads in the alloy crankcase are stripped and cannot be re-tapped a new case will usually have to be bought.

If you make this mistake, the only possible alternative is to find something like an end plug from a gas pipe and have compatible threads tapped into the sump. This doesn't always work,

2-stroke Suzuki 250 with Dunstall fairing

Changing the oil on a 4-stroke wet sump system

24. Before draining the oil on a 4-stroke wet sump bike, run the motor for a while before undoing the drain plug

25. When the oil flow stops, turn over the motor a few times with the ignition off. This will help clear out the oil

26. Next, undo the bolt or bolts on the filter cover, prise the cover carefully away and extract the oil filter

27. Being careful to identify the position and 'way up' of all components, discard the old filter and fit a new one

28. When refilling, always use the right amount and grade of oil specified for your engine

29. Next, run the engine for a minute or two, then re-check the oil level. Top up if necessary, and secure the cap

Cleaning a centrifugal filter

30. On a 4-stroke with a centrifugal filter, first remove the crankcase cover with an impact or T-bar screwdriver

31. The cover on this type of centrifugal filter is held in place by a circlip. Spring it out with circlip pliers

32. You will need a special extractor to remove the filter cover. This screws into the central hole in the cover

33. As you tighten down the extractor screw it should force the cover outwards from the body of the filter

34. Next, use a piece of rag moistened in petrol to clean out all the sediment from inside the filter body

35. Refit the filter cover by tapping it home squarely with a drift. Then attach the circlip

but is worth trying.

Because of the risk of thread stripping, it pays to obtain the specified drain plug torque setting from a dealer and to use a torque wrench. One can normally be obtained from a hire shop.

Before fitting your oil drain plug, check to see if it has a removable washer. These washers are made from soft alloy or copper, and should be renewed if there has been any sign of a leak. If you have a plug with the fixed type of sealing washer, and it has been leaking, replace the plug.

If your drain plug is magnetic – a common device on small-capacity machines with no oil filter – just wipe off the metal slivers before replacing it.

Draining the oil
Wherever possible, run the engine for a short while before draining it as this will thin the oil and help to remove all of it from the engine.

With the engine switched off, place a suitable container under the sump or oil tank to catch the old oil. Remove the oil filler cap to improve oil flow, then undo the drain plug. Avoid dropping the plug or any washer into the oil tray.

When the oil has finished draining, the plug should be wiped clean and refitted with a torque wrench as detailed above.

At this stage the engine can be cleaned out with a flushing oil. However, modern detergent oils leave very few deposits and it is up to you whether you bother. A flushing oil is best used on older bikes, or when the service has been delayed.

To use a flushing oil, pour the requisite amount into the tank or crankcase, run the engine for a few minutes, and drain it off as before. However, read the instructions on the oil can as these may differ from make to make.

When you have finished draining and flushing, pour the old oil into a sealable container. Dispose of it in a workshop waste tank or a place nominated by the local council. Waste oil should not be poured down the drain.

Sludge traps
Sludge traps incorporating a gauze strainer (fig. 39) are fitted on some bikes – often in the bottom right-hand side of the crankcase. To gain access, you will probably need to remove part of the casing, the kick-start and sometimes the exhaust pipe.

Sludge traps do not usually need cleaning at each scheduled oil change, but remember to clean them at least every other service. You just scrape them out and clean the strainer in petrol.

Disposable oil filters
Smaller capacity bikes rarely have oil filters, but most intermediate and larger machines – about 250 cc and upwards – use disposable paper element filters to keep the oil clean. These filters must be renewed at every alternate oil change, for they become blocked if left and engine wear is accelerated.

The handbook will say whether your bike has one of these filters. If so, look for a finned filter cover set underneath or in front of the engine sump. Some machines have a filter in an unusual position. They include the Norton Commando (behind the gearbox), the Moto Guzzi V twins (inside the sump) and the Yamaha XT500 and SR500 (alongside the clutch cover on the right-hand side of the engine).

Take care when undoing or refitting the cover securing nuts or bolts, and use a torque wrench when tightening. The correct torque wrench setting can be obtained from a dealer.

Having undone the filter cover, take out the old element and throw it away, being careful to identify all components and their positions ready for replacement.

If you have the type of filter with a washer and spring beneath the elements, take care not to lose the washer. If this happens and you reassemble the filter minus the washer, the spring will bear directly on to the element – and eventually will break up the rubber seal in the element bottom, causing blockages which may damage the engine.

When you install the new filter, always use new sealing rings – these are supplied with the filter. Also, when you buy a new filter, try to get a genuine manufacturer's item. There are cheaper, pattern-made filters on the market, and while some of these are good quality, others are not.

Centrifugal filters
Some bikes, particularly older ones, do not have a disposable filter but rely upon a built-in centrifugal filter. Some examples of this device are incorporated in the centre of the crankshaft and, as a result, can only be cleaned when the engine is stripped down.

Other designs have the centrifugal filter in a housing on the crankshaft end – many Hondas have this type – which is more easily reached for cleaning. The access and cleaning interval details for these are the same as for sludge traps on

Checking an oil injection system

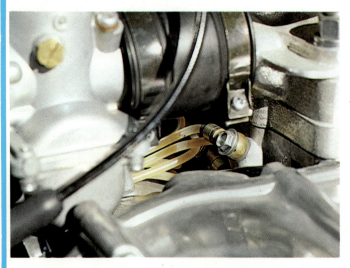

36. On a 2-stroke bike with an oil injection system, check the pipes and unions periodically for leaks and damage

37. To measure the amount of gearbox oil, detach the level plug and pour oil in until it seeps from the hole

the smaller machines.

The main problem with these units, as you will find, is removing the filter cover once it has been located inside the crankcase.

There are two different cover types. One secures the filter body by means of a screw thread and can be extracted only with a special four-pronged wrench available from dealers. The second type is a taper fit inside the filter body, and is also held by a circlip. The circlip must first be sprung with pliers, then an extractor used to pull off the cover. You may be able to avoid buying a special tool by finding a screw of suitable dimensions and thread type. If so, insert the screw into the cover's threaded hole and keep on turning it until the cover is forced out.

Tank filters
Oil tanks often have a gauze strainer inside the main outlet union. If so, it is worth undoing the union to take out the strainer for washing in petrol.

Breather pipes
Four-stroke engines have an oil breather pipe attached to an outlet either on the valve cover or on top of the crankcase. Pull off the pipe, then inspect the pipe and the outlet for any blockage. This is not a common fault, but ought to be checked.

Refilling with oil
When refilling with oil always use the specified grade, for running on an unsuitable oil will damage your engine or cause problems like clutch slip or drag. The bike manufacturer will usually recommend only one grade of oil and give a list of suitable makes. However, variations on the grade are sometimes allowed as shown in the chart.

The best method of ensuring that the oil reaches the right level is to measure out the correct amount beforehand. Most handbooks quote the engine oil capacity in cubic centimetres and often state if this includes filter capacity or not. The capacity is sometimes marked on, or near, the filler cap, too, but if in any doubt consult a dealer.

Despite the level seeming correct after filling, run the engine briefly, check the oil level again and top up as necessary – especially on engines with oil filters.

On dry sump systems the oil level in the separate tank is not quite so critical, but do make an effort to keep it correct at all times.

Topping up your oil
Between services a check must be made on the engine oil level at least once a week and before long journeys, as low

oil levels will result in engine damage.

A point to watch on some dry sump models is over-filling when the oil level is thought to be low. If the engine has a faulty oil pump or non-return valve, the oil tends to drain down into the crankcase when the bike is left standing for a few hours. If you then fill the tank and start the engine, oil which has leaked into the crankcase will pump back into the tank causing it to be grossly over-filled, probably spilling out the excess.

If you suspect the bike has this problem, start the engine and ensure that

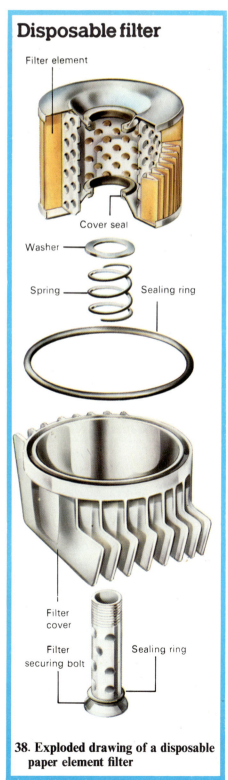

Disposable filter

Filter element

Cover seal

Washer

Spring

Sealing ring

Filter cover

Filter securing bolt

Sealing ring

38. Exploded drawing of a disposable paper element filter

some oil is returning to the tank. Then run the engine for a few minutes before checking the oil level and rectify the trouble as soon as possible. Using a system of regular weekly checks will prevent most problems.

Oil circulation
On wet sump systems there is nothing you can do to check oil circulation. The operating oil pressure in many of these engines is very low – as little as 0.63 kg/cm^2 (9psi) – and an oil pressure gauge is not a practical proposition.

On a dry sump unit, matters are slightly improved and you can often see the oil return pipe where it exits into the oil tank. A simple visual inspection of whether oil is pumping from the return pipe will show if the circulation is all right.

2-stroke systems
Unlike 4-stroke engines, a 2-stroke operates on a 'total loss' lubrication system. The oil is drawn in through the carburettor with petrol (or pumped in by a throttle-controlled pump) lubricates the engine bearing surfaces, then is burnt in the combustion chamber and expelled.

Petroil
Early 2-stroke and some modern ones use the 'petroil' system. The Puch Maxi moped and the Yamaha FSIE are examples.

Petroil is not just a pre-mix of oil and petrol in the same tank, for the ratio of oil to petrol is important and must be carefully gauged to prevent damage to the engine through poor lubrication. Also, the mix ratio often differs from one bike to another and may be anything from 16:1 to 50:1 of petrol to oil.

Although ready mixed petroil in different ratios can be obtained from a pump at some garages, it is safer to mix it yourself. Most oil companies that market 2-stroke engine oil include a 'petroil ratio guide' on the back of each translucent oil container.

All you do is place a gallon, or more, of petrol into the bike's tank, then add the right amount of oil from the container using the ratio measure marks for your engine. Rock the tank to-and-fro afterwards to make sure the oil mixes thoroughly.

Pumped 2-stroke system
The majority of modern 2-strokes use an oil injection system instead of petroil. The oil is pumped from a reservoir (tank) and fed into the engine, the oil/fuel ratio being controlled by the pump throttle linkage.

Cleaning an oil sludge trap

39. To clean the oil sludge trap gauze filter found on some 4-stroke engines you must remove part of the crankcase

40. Sump or valve cover breather tubes should be detached during servicing to check for possible blockages

Bikes with this sytem have the oil tank mounted either on the frame side behind the engine or beneath the saddle.

The majority of tanks have a window set in the side to give warning of low oil level. A few do have a dipstick, although this is not common, and some Yamahas have a low-level warning light.

The trap with this sytem is that the oil tank capacity is often large enough to allow the petrol tank to be filled many times before the oil runs out. This makes it all too easy to forget when the oil was last checked. Don't make this mistake or your engine will be one of many which are ruined every year through being run dry.

2-stroke oil

Whatever form of engine lubrication your 2-stroke has, always use the correct type of oil. Only a few types are available and the bike manufacturer will specify one of these. It may be permissible to use a different make, but a dealer should be consulted first. On no account should anything other than a mineral based oil, specifically designed for 2-stroke engines, be used.

Gearbox lubrication

All 2-stroke engines have separate lubrication for their gearboxes. A few 4-stroke motors have this, too, both the wet and dry sump types, but mainly the older-designed dry sump engines and shaft driven machines. If your bike is a 4-stroke, check gearbox lubrication in the handbook or with a dealer.

With these gearboxes the lubricant should be changed at the same time as the engine oil after running the engine for a while to warm the gear oil. The oil is drained by removing the drain plug, which will be set somewhere underneath the unit, although it will often be smaller than the main engine plug. Fill your gearbox after removing the push-in plug (2-strokes) or some form of cap, or bolt-on cover, from the top. The same fitting and removal details apply to these plugs as for the main engine items.

The level of oil is determined either by the filler hole or a separate level screw. With the bike standing level, slowly pour oil in until it just begins to seep from the hole, then replace the filler cap and level screw. Where gaskets are used on these, and are damaged, they should be renewed or leaks will occur.

Most gearboxes take the same type of multi-grade oil as the engine, but a few must have EP (extreme pressure) oils.

If your bike is fitted with automatic transmission, the method of checking and filling is the same as above. However, the grade of oil must be the one prepared for automatic transmissions, except on the Honda Dream automatic, which uses the recommended 10/40 engine oil.

Tools for an oil change, including the almost indispensible torque wrench

Know your spark plug

Apart from supplying the spark which ignites the fuel mixture in the combustion chamber, the spark plug can be a very accurate device for indicating how your engine is running. If you know how to 'read the plug' you can use it as a convenient diagnostic tool.

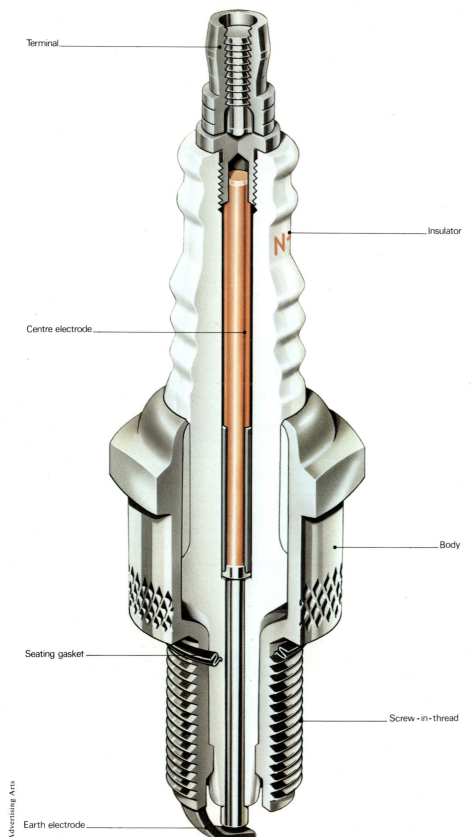

Terminal

Insulator

Centre electrode

Body

Seating gasket

Screw-in-thread

Earth electrode

Advertising Arts

Every minute the engine is running each plug has to provide up to 10,000 sparks, handle up to 25,000 volts and operate between 400 and 850 degrees centigrade, yet it is one of the most overlooked parts of a bike.

The actual life of a spark plug is difficult to predict and depends upon its use and the amount of maintenance it receives. Modern plugs should, however, last for up to 16,000 km (10,000 miles) provided that they are checked, cleaned and gapped roughly every 2,000 km (1,200 miles) or less if the bike is only used in and about town.

Periodic inspections of the spark plugs will indicate the relative health of the engine. Therefore, if read regularly, a problem such as lean running can be identified and cured before it develops into something as severe as melted pistons!

The spark plug
The spark plug (fig. 1) is basically a device for igniting the petrol/air mixture in the combustion chamber. To do this the plug is supplied with a high voltage and works under conditions of extreme heat. Modern plugs are designed to work over a wide heat range so that the motorcyle can be ridden around town and on long fast journeys without need for a plug change.

Different machines do, however, require different grades of plug. For the plug must be able to cope with the required working temperature of a particular engine. Two-strokes, for example, because they burn a certain amount of oil with the fuel, require plugs which can burn off carbon deposits, otherwise they foul-up and eventually fail.

Removing the plugs
Every toolkit supplied by a manufacturer for their motorcycles contains a plug spanner (fig. 2). They are of the box type in order to protect the ceramic insulator from damage.

Never use a ring or open ended spanner to remove a plug except in an emergency. For, if the spanner slips it may very well crack the insulator and render the plug useless.

Some spark plug spanners contain a rubber insert which slips over the insulator as the spanner is positioned. This

1. A cutaway diagram of a typical modern spark plug showing its various constituent components

33

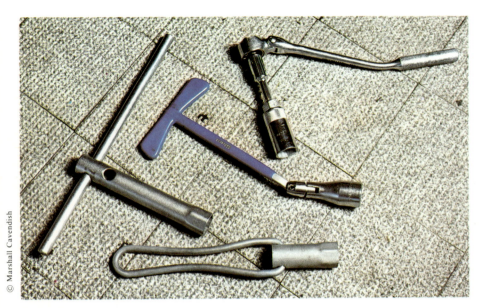

rubber serves two purposes: it protects the insulator and holds the plug in the spanner so that it can be pulled out of its hole. This is especially useful when dealing with a hot plug or one which is in an awkward position.

Before removing a plug it is a good idea to clean around its seat with a soft brush. This removes any dirt particles which may otherwise fall in the combustion chamber when the plug is removed.

On multi-cylinder bikes take care to note which cylinder each plug came from, so if you find one showing signs of oiling up or incorrect mixture you will know which cylinder is at fault.

Inspecting the plug

After removing the plug and before cleaning it, you should thoroughly inspect the firing end. Correctly reading the state of a plug can tell you a lot about the state of your engine and whether or not any trouble is imminent. If everything is running correctly then the plug firing tip should be light grey,

2. A variety of spark plug spanners. The best ones have rubber inserts which grip and protect the plug

grey-brown or brown in colour, with no excessive deposits on the electrodes (fig. 6).

Carbon fouling

If the firing end is black and sooty (fig. 4) then the plug is carbon fouled. Carbon fouling is the cause of nearly all plug trouble. The carbon build-up eventually lowers the available voltage and the spark cannot jump the gap. Carbon fouling can be caused by several problems; rich fuel mix (see pages 80–84, and also 85–87), excessive use of, or faulty choke, a blocked air filter, oil in the combustion chamber, incorrect electrode gap, ignition fault, compression loss, excessive low speed use, or plug heat range too cold.

Oil fouling

If the plug is black and wet (fig. 5) as opposed to black and sooty then it is oil fouled.

Oil fouling is relatively common on 2-strokes and is generally the result of incorrect petrol/oil mixture. This can be due either to a badly adjusted oil pump (see pages 94–98) or the wrong mix of fuel and oil in the petrol tank.

On 4-stroke machines an oiled plug indicates a worn or broken piston ring, a worn-out bore or valve guides. If the problem is only a minor one, you could try a hotter plug to burn away the excess oil, but you should on no account use full throttle or else detonation might occur.

Lead fouling

Lead fouling is indicated by a yellowish brown deposit on the nose of the insulator that occurs within about 2,000 km from the fitting of a new plug.

The only other symptom of lead fouling is misfiring under acceleration when the temperature of the plug is raised.

The solution to this problem is to change to a low lead or lead free petrol, although the fitting of a hotter plug may also be helpful.

Overheating

If the insulator tip is glazed and glossy (fig. 8) or there are signs of blistering then there is an overheating fault. Excessive overheating will eventually lead to the plug melting, followed very quickly by the piston.

There are several causes of plug overheating, these are: fuel mix too weak, over advanced timing (see pages 40–41), excessive deposits in the combustion chamber, inadequate engine cooling or insufficient lubrication, petrol octane too low or the spark plug rating too hot.

Detonation

Detonation is indicated by a cracked insulator core. This occurs when some of the petrol/air mix burns in an explo-

3. This is the type of damage which can be done to a plug if it is roughly cleaned or handled

4. The dry sooty deposits on this plug indicate that the engine is burning an over-rich fuel mixture

5. Wet oily plugs, like this one indicate that either the guides, rings, or bores are worn

6. This is what the spark plug should look like if the fuel mixture is correct and the engine running well

7. As 2-strokes burn oil with their fuel, their plugs have a much harder life and this one is well worn out

8. A white speckled plug like this one indicates engine overheating, possibly due to a weak fuel mixture

9. Overzealous cleaning can be the cause of this type of damage to the ceramic insulator

10. Lead fouling, indicated by a yellow deposit on the insulator, may be due to using a too-high octane fuel

11. This is what a spark plug will look like if it is left to carry on without any sort of maintenance

sive manner due to the excessive pressure and heat.

Commonly known as pinking, detonation usually occurs as a result of one or more of the following conditions: advanced ignition timing, petrol octane too low, weak mixture, intake manifold leaks, combustion chamber deposits which raise the compression ratio, intake manifold too hot, or running for too long in too low a gear. If you ignore this condition serious engine damage will follow.

Mechanical damage
Very rarely the firing end of a plug will be damaged but will not be showing any signs of overheating or melting.

This is usually due to some foreign body in the combustion chamber or may occur following the fitting of a plug with an incorrect reach.

Plugs can become damaged through improper use of a gapping tool which can break or bend the side electrode and possibly even crack the insulator core.

Core and gap bridging
Core and gap bridging occur when combustion particles become wedged be-

tween the electrodes or between the core and the shell.

The particles originate from the piston and cylinder head surfaces and occur under one or more of the following circumstances: excessive carbon in the cylinder, using the wrong oil, opening the throttle quickly after a prolonged spell of very low speed riding, 2-stroke mix not correct.

Cleaning
After you have thoroughly inspected the plug(s) and made notes on any engine faults requiring attention, the plugs should either be replaced or cleaned.

Oily plugs should be cleaned with a solvent (fig. 12) such as petrol or white spirit and a stiff brush. Once clean the plugs should be left to dry.

Plugs which are covered with hard deposits can be left to soak overnight in household vinegar. This will soften the deposits and make them easier to remove. If this does not get the electrodes clean, you will probably need new plugs. You could try taking the old ones to a garage to have them sand

blasted (home sand blasters are available but expensive). Sand blasting is a thorough process which removes all the heavier carbon, dirt and oil deposits. Get a price for the job first, as it might be cheaper to buy new plugs.

Do not use a wire brush on the electrodes. Bits of the wire will adhere to the ceramic insulator and cause earthing.

Once the plug is clean you should use a small points file to clean and square off the side and centre electrodes. While

12. If your spark plugs do not require replacement, clean them in white spirit with a stiff brush

this is a perfectly straightforward job on most plugs, great care should be taken if you are working on a plug which has a centre electrode made of precious metal. These electrodes are much softer and bend easily.

Once the electrodes are clean they should be filed perfectly square. To facilitate this the side electrode can be bent back slightly. A plug with square electrodes requires 25–40 per cent less voltage to fire than one with rounded electrodes.

Finally, wipe the outside of the ceramic insulator clean as excessive amounts of dirt here will result in shorting and lead to misfiring.

If a screw cap is fitted to the end, check to see if it is tight, or, again, misfiring could occur.

Incorrect cleaning or inadequate cleaning are the main reasons why a plug fouls again very quickly after a service. A little extra time taken to do the job properly could save you a lot of time and money in the long run.

Gapping

In order to ensure optimum performance the plug electrodes must be set at the recommended gap.

A narrow gap causes poor running at low speeds while an over wide gap impairs running at higher speed as the voltage is not great enough to keep jumping the gap.

Opening or closing the gap should be performed as carefully as possible. It is quite easy to damage both the electrodes. Special gapping tools are available but a knife blade used carefully is almost as good.

The gap should be measured with feeler gauges and is correct when the specified thickness of feeler is a sliding fit, between the electrodes.

Buying new plugs

When replacing old or worn out plugs you should always buy the recommended grade (or equivalent). Manufacturers take a great deal of care to match engine performance with plug performance and a great deal of damage could be caused if the wrong plug is used.

The various letters and numbers used by manufacturers to describe their plugs refer to heat range, thread length, thread diameter and structural features. Most manufacturers provide comparison charts so you can be sure that you get the right one.

Generally speaking, it is not necessary to choose a different heat rating from the one recommended for your engine, even for adverse conditions or different driving circumstances, provided that the engine is in a good state of tune and you are using the correct grade of petrol.

Thread length (reach)

The thread length of a plug is critical. If it is too long the firing end will reach too far into the combustion chamber with the possibility of damage from the piston or valves. The firing end might also overheat with the resultant engine damage. If this does not happen then it is almost certain that carbon will build up on the projecting threads and make the plug very difficult or impossible to remove.

Using a plug with too short a reach causes other problems. Engine performance will suffer and the thread in the cylinder head will clog with carbon and make it very difficult to refit the correct plug.

Heat range

The firing end of a plug is exposed to very high temperatures and the amount of heat it retains is largely governed by the length of the projecting nose core. The longer the core the hotter the plug.

Hot plugs

The insulator nose on hot plugs is kept long to provide a longer heat path and so keep the firing end at a temperature high enough to burn off oil and carbon deposits.

Cold plugs

The short nose of cold plugs provides for faster dissipation of the heat thus avoiding pre-ignition and excessive temperatures at the firing end.

Cold plugs are used in machines which are consistently used under heavy loads or are run at high conpressions.

Refitting the plug

If you find that the new plug will not screw into the head freely, do not try to force it home. First, try cleaning the threads. This is easily done by cutting three or four slots across the thread of an old plug. Apply some grease to this plug and carefully screw it into the hole making sure that it goes in square. The grease and slots should remove any particles of dirt in the threads and make refitting the new plug easy.

Once the plug is finger tight, give it no more than $\frac{1}{2}$ to $\frac{3}{4}$ of a turn with a spanner.

13. Once clean check that the electrode gap is correct with a feeler gauge of the recommended thickness

14. If the gap is not correct then alter it with a knife blade or one of the special tools available

15. If the electrodes need to be filed smooth, first carefully bend out the side electrode

16. Filing the plug electrodes so that they are square reduces the voltage required by the plug by 25–40%

Keeping the battery charged

A flat battery is the most common single cause of keeping a bike out of action. This faultfinding guide shows how to check the battery and the charging system so that you can get back on the road as soon as possible.

Under normal conditions, the battery's charge is restored and maintained, when the engine is running, by the bike's charging system. Even if the bike is not used for several weeks, the battery should hold its stored-up charge and not go flat.

Depending on the fault, a flat battery may occur either while the bike is running or while it is not being used. These two conditions may indicate different types of fault which can be traced accordingly.

The cause of a flat battery, especially if it occurs unexpectedly is likely to lie somewhere in the bike's charging system, but you should first make sure that the battery itself is not defective.

Defective battery

By a careful visual examination you may be able to determine whether a flat battery is ruined and needs replacing, or just recharging.

First remove the battery from the bike and hold it against a light source. Bike batteries are usually made with a transparent case, so you should be able to see inside quite easily. On no account expose the battery to a naked flame as the gas it gives off is explosive.

If the electrolyte (sulphuric acid and distilled water) level has been allowed to remain consistently low, the internal plates may have grown a thick, white or blue/green sulphate deposit (fig. 2) which you should be able to see. Badly sulphated plates impede the chemical action of the electrolyte and eventually ruin the battery. Similarly, a battery that has not been topped up regularly could short circuit itself and will not hold a charge. A charged battery gives off a gaseous mixture from the internal

chemical reaction which causes the distilled water to evaporate from the acid mixture. The result is a concentrated acid solution which, if it is not diluted by topping up, becomes strong enough to eat away the battery plates. Eventually, metal sediment is deposited at the bottom of the battery and causes a short circuit between the plates. The battery must be replaced if you can see such a deposit or evidence of badly corroded plates.

If the battery appears clean and clear you can test its condition, before recharging it with a hydrometer or multimeter.

A hydrometer (fig. 3) is used to find the specific gravity of the electrolyte solution in the battery. And from the specific gravity reading you should be able to establish the battery's condition. The correct specific gravity of the electrolyte is predetermined at an optimum level by the manufacturers.

Each cell of a fully charged battery should show a reading of about 1.280 on the hydrometer scale at 20°C (68°F). But as a battery discharges the specific

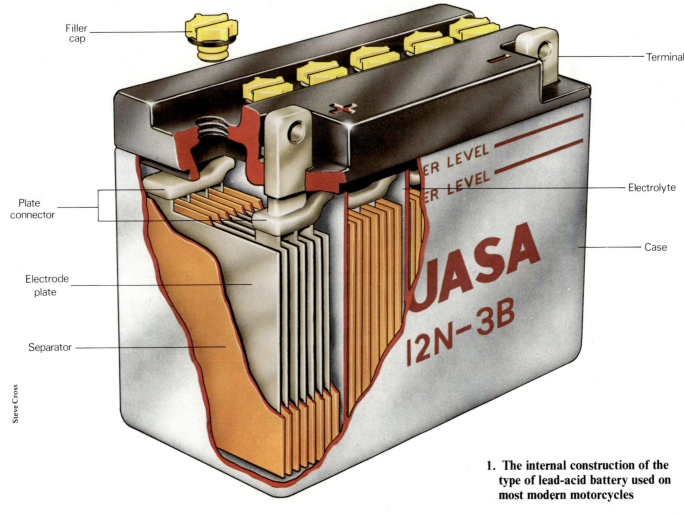

1. **The internal construction of the type of lead-acid battery used on most modern motorcycles**

37

Checking the battery's condition

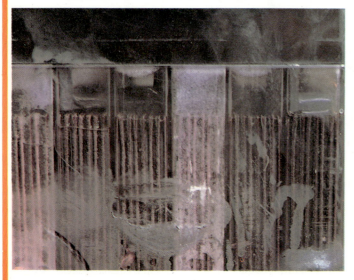

2. Look first at the battery's plates. Notice the badly sulphated plates in two of the cells

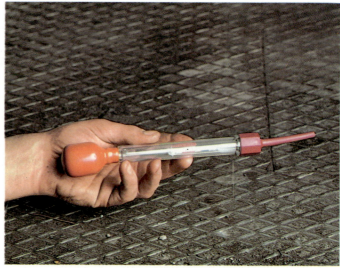

3. Use a hydrometer to test the battery's condition and its state of charge by sampling the electrolyte

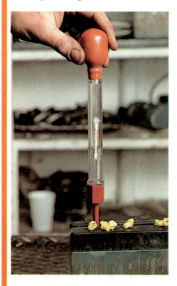

4. Insert the hydrometer into one of the cells and draw off some electrolyte. Read off the SG on the float scale

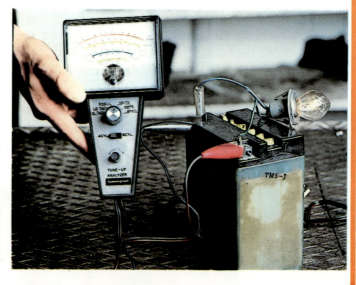

5. To test the battery with a multimeter, connect the meter with a headlight bulb in parallel with the battery posts

gravity of the electrolyte goes down.

Insert the hydrometer into one cell and draw off some of the electrolyte (fig. 4). If the reading shows the electrolyte to have a specific gravity of about 1.100 the cell is fully discharged. Repeat the operation on the other cells. If some cells show a charged reading but others are discharged, the battery may have an internal fault. Examine the battery carefully as described above making sure it is not damaged and replace if necessary.

A hydrometer test will only be accurate if you know beforehand that the electrolyte is of the correct solution. If, for example, the electrolyte has been spilled and topped up with dilute acid in the wrong proportion, the reading

you take with a hydrometer could be misleading. The readings could show a high specific gravity even though the battery is flat. If you are in any doubt about the history of the battery, test its state of charge with a multimeter instead.

Set the multimeter to a range of 20 volts (or 10 volts for a 6V battery) and connect the positive lead of the multimeter to the positive terminal of the battery. The test will give a more accurate indication of the battery's condition if you introduce a load in to the circuit. A headlight bulb of the same voltage as the battery is ideal for this. Join two lengths of wire to the bulb contacts, or use the bulb's holder with its leads and connect the leads to the

battery terminals (fig. 5) in parallel. Connect the other (negative) lead of the multimeter to the negative battery terminal. If the battery is in a low state of charge, the meter should show a sustained reading of less than 12 volts, on a 12V battery, or under 6 volts on a 6V battery. The headlight bulb will also only light with a dull glow.

If the battery is flat but otherwise in good condition, there is probably a fault somewhere in the charging system. To assist the troubleshooting procedure the battery must be recharged and put back in the bike.

With the battery fully charged, begin fault finding by looking for an earth leak in the wiring.

An earth leak occurs when the current

from the battery is going to earth via a short circuit.

Wiring earth leak

The battery's charge could be leaking to earth if the insulation of a live wire wears through and touches an earth point. It may happen while the bike is standing or while it is being ridden.

This type of electrical leak can cause the battery to go flat extremely quickly due to the heavy discharge of current directly to earth. For the same reason such a leak is unlikely to go un-noticed for long as the discharge will cause the wire's insulation to smoke and melt. The violent sparking of the bare wire may also be clearly audible when the engine is switched off.

Tracing the cause of the leak should be fairly simple. Look for burned or blackened insulation, especially where live wires run close to the frame or a moving component. The source of the leak will usually be evident as a length of bare wire where the insulation has completely melted away. The wire should be replaced or a new length inserted. If several wires run together near the leak point make sure that they have not become fused together. If this has happened, you should strip out the old wires, and join in new pieces. These should be well insulated.

Charging a battery

First remove all dirt from the battery with water and ensure that the terminal posts are clean. Pull off the cell caps or strip and make sure that the electrolyte level is topped up to the lower level mark.

Connect the positive and negative leads of the charger to the corresponding posts on the battery before switching on. Most modern chargers adjust the rate of charge automatically over the charging period. In this way the battery is fed with a high initial rate of charge which then drops to a low trickle charge spread over several hours. This slow, steady method of charging ensures that the battery charges properly under the best possible conditions.

You can calculate the approximate time it will take to charge a completely flat battery if you know the charging rate of the charger and the capacity rating of the battery.

Batteries are rated in ampere hours (AH). And the rating of batteries varies between bikes according to the demands of a particular bike's electrical system. A battery rated at 14 AH would take about 10 hours to charge if the trickle charge rate is set at 1.4 amps.

If the battery charger is not the fully automatic type it is important not to set and maintain the charge rate at too high

a level over the charging period, otherwise the battery could be ruined. The maximum prolonged charge a battery will stand can be calculated as just under one third of its AH rating. The maximum charge rate of a 14 AH battery would, therefore, be about 4 amps.

Check the battery frequently while it is being charged as the temperature of the electrolyte rises under a high charge rate. If the battery begins to feel hot, switch off the charger or reduce the rate of charge and increase the charging period. Failure to do this could result in damage to the battery.

Battery care

Battery care is vital to maintaining easy starting and the correct operation of all associated electrical components under all conditions. A regular check should be made weekly to keep the battery in peak form.

Check first the electrolyte level in the battery cells. Most modern battery casings are transparent so you should be able to see the level. If you allow the electrolyte level to remain consistently low, lead sulphate forms and this can do irreparable damage to the plates, and the battery will become impossible to charge.

If the electrolyte is below the level line, top it up with distilled water. Do not use ordinary tap water as the lime content of it will eventually coat the internal plates with a deposit reducing the efficiency of the battery. If too much distilled water is added the electrolyte will expand when the battery gets warm and force an acid mist out of the breather. The result is a soft, white powder-like substance, iron sulphate, which can attack the battery clamps and terminals. The condition of the battery terminals and clamps is important because, if they are corroded (or loose), they may prevent the bike from starting. To remove sulphation, dirt or rust, scrape the worst of it off with a knife, then pour hot water over the affected part. Dry the part off, then smear it with a protector such as No Crode or Vaseline.

Make sure also that the battery is secured firmly in position. A loose, shaking or vibrating battery will soon break down. Put a piece of foam or a block of rubber underneath it to reduce vibration.

6. You can often determine a battery's condition simply by looking at it. This one is completely ruined

Maintaining your points

Keeping the contact breaker points in good condition is a simple yet vital job if a bike is to perform well. Furthermore, on 4-strokes, it is essential that the auto-advance unit is serviced regularly to ensure that the spark occurs at the right time relative to engine speed.

Keeping points correctly adjusted is only possible while the condition of the contact faces is within certain limits. Once wear reaches a certain point replacement of the contact breaker assembly becomes essential.

Inspecting the points
The simplest way to check the condition of the points is to make a visual inspection. But unless you know what to look for, the contact faces may actually appear a lot worse than they really are. In order to make a proper evaluation of the condition of the points you should understand exactly what they do.

Contact breaker points, when closed, control the time, in terms of crankshaft rotation, that current has to build up in the ignition coil. As the points open coil voltage collapses producing a spark from the high tension circuit. To prevent a discharge occurring between the point faces a capacitor (condenser) is fitted in parallel to them. But some discharge does occur and eventually it erodes or 'pits' the faces. The faces can also blacken if oil gets onto them and burns. Ideally the points' faces should be smooth so that the gap can be accurately measured and consequently the current build up time determined. Some wear is, however, inevitable but severe wear will affect the dwell angle and spark strength. To avoid this the contacts themselves are made from tungsten, a metal with a very high melting point, and which is also very hard. Filing has almost no effect other than wearing out the file, and for a professional job an engineer's stone must be used. Once the surfaces are free of pitting, polish with a fine grade of wet and dry paper to get back the original factory finish.

Another way the points can be examined is by how freely the current flows from one contact to the other. This can be checked with a resistance meter across the points. On energy transfer systems disconnect the coil, on battery systems be sure that the ignition is off. Resistance should be close to zero.

Even though the contact faces may look in good condition and show acceptable resistance they should be replaced at regular intervals as recommended by the manufacturer. This is because the spring which returns the moving contact weakens with age. While the ignition timing may be correct at low engine speeds, at higher speeds an old spring may 'bounce' and considerably affect the dwell.

Using feeler gauges
To check and, if necessary, adjust the points gap with feeler gauges, start by removing the spark plug(s). Next remove the points cover, or in the case of those machines with flywheel magnetos, the engine cover.

Bikes can have one, two or three sets of points, but the method of adjustment is exactly the same for each and is quite straightforward. Difficulties usually arise only on those bikes with flywheel

1. Bikes with flywheel magnetos have elongated slots in the flywheel for gapping and adjusting the points

magneto arrangements where the points have to be gapped and adjusted through elongated slots in the flywheel (fig. 1). The procedure is the same; it is just that the job is more 'fiddly'.

As already mentioned all contact breaker points are basically the same and similar to those in fig. 2. They comprise one fixed contact and another which is free to move. This contact has a heel which bears on the points cam and, as the cam rotates, the contact opens and closes the low tension circuit which generates the high tension spark. On many bikes there is a mark on the cam (fig. 7) which, when aligned with the heel of the movable contact, will open the points to a specified gap. If there is

no reference mark provided then the points gap should be measured at its widest.

To rotate the cam to open and close the points, you will have to turn the engine over. This can be done in one of several ways. If the bike has a kickstart then this is perhaps the easiest method – gentle hand pressure on the lever will allow the cam to be turned very slowly, allowing precise alignment. Alternatively, if there is no kickstart or if it is on the opposite side of the bike to the points, then there is often a bolt head on the end of the crankshaft or alternator rotor which can be turned to rotate the engine. Lastly, if none of these methods is suitable, then with the bike on its centre stand you can engage a high gear and rotate the rear wheel.

Having turned the engine over so that the marker on the cam is aligned with the heel of the movable contact breaker or so that the points gap is at its widest (if there is no reference mark) the gap can be measured. Before doing this, however, check that the faces of the contacts are clean and not pitted. For if the contacts are uneven you will not get a true reading. Unless the points are really bad a few strokes with a points file should be sufficient to clean them up.

Nearly all bikes have a specified contact breaker gap of between 0.3 and 0.4 mm (.012–.016in.) and this can be used as a roadside rule of thumb. But in the workshop, check with your manual for the exact setting.

If the feeler of the correct width is a loose fit between the points, or alternatively is so tight that it moves the points apart, then the gap will have to be reset. Do this by first loosening the contact breaker base-plate screw. This will allow the fixed contact to be moved. The breaker plate can be moved either by twisting a screwdriver in a slot between two posts on the base-plate or by turning an eccentric screw.

Once the gap is correctly set so that the feeler gauge is just a sliding fit, the base-plate screw can be retightened. If you leave the feeler in place as you do this you should avoid the possibility of altering the gap, but just to be sure rotate the engine a few times and re-check the gap.

If the bike has more than one set of points, turn now to the next set and repeat the operation. Once the points are correctly gapped the engine timing can be checked.

Using a dwell meter

While setting the contact breaker gap with feeler gauges can be quite accurate if done carefully enough, the most precise means of adjusting the points is to use a dwell meter. The only drawback of this method is that such meters are quite expensive.

A dwell meter does not measure the gap between the points, but the time period or 'dwell' for which they are closed. The dwell is measured in terms of degrees of rotation of the cam and thus can be calibrated very precisely. Dwell meters give readings either in degrees or in percentages, or both, and the only other thing you may have to do is to halve or double the reading if you are, for example, using a dwell meter calibrated for 4-cylinder machines or a twin.

To check the points dwell, remove the points cover and attach the negative lead of the meter to a suitable earth and the positive lead to the contact breaker terminal (fig. 8). Start the engine and, when it is running smoothly, read off the figure on the meter.

If the reading does not correspond to that specified in your manual, the points will require adjustment. This is done in exactly the same way as described above. Loosen the contact breaker base-plate screw, and adjust the points gap until the meter registers the correct dwell. If you are careful, you can do this with the engine still running, but

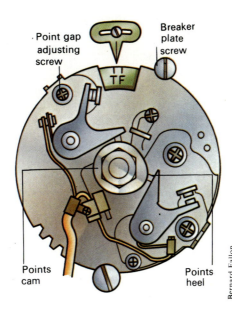

2. A typical double contact breaker set as found on the Yamaha XS500

take care not to catch yourself on any of the moving parts, particularly if the mechanical advance weights are positioned above the points. Once you have the correct dwell registering on the meter, tighten the base-plate screw.

If more than one set of points are fitted, simply repeat the operation on the other sets until they are all set correctly. With the points now accurately adjusted the timing can be checked.

Overhauling the points

Once you have established that the points require replacing the next step will, obviously, be to remove them. Access is basically a simple job on most machines you will come across, the exception being those bikes which have flywheel magnetos such as mopeds. On these machines the flywheel has to be removed from the end of the crankshaft before the points can be reached.

Flywheel removal

Flywheels are most usually located onto the crankshaft by a taper lock and keyway. Before it can be removed the locking nut must first be undone. To do this you will have to either use a strap

Adjusting the contact-breaker gap

3. Before the points can be examined the cover must be removed. You may find an impact driver is essential

4. With the engine turned over so that the points are open at their widest, check the gap with a feeler gauge

5. If the points gap is incorrect, then the next step is to slacken off the fixed contact's securing screw

6. Using a screwdriver as a lever in the slot provided, open or close the points until the gap is correct

7. On other bikes the points are set not by a slot and post arrangement but by turning an eccentric screw

8. A more accurate way of checking the points is to measure the 'dwell' by wiring a meter across the contacts

Removing the flywheel

9. Access to the flywheel is usually easy. Lock the engine, then remove the fixing nut with a ringspanner

10. If recommended, use a special tool to remove the flywheel, or a three legged puller which fits securely

11. When the flywheel has been removed, the points will be revealed, and can be adjusted in the normal way

wrench around the rotor or else put the engine in gear and the rear brake on.

Undo and remove the flywheel central fixing bolt or nut. You will then require a puller to break the flywheel's taper lock. In most cases you should use the recommended special tool which screws into the centre of the flywheel. Proprietary two or three legged pullers should only be used if they have legs small enough to fit securely through the elongated inspection slots. No attempt should be made to force the flywheel off the crank with levers from behind. This would only damage the crankshaft or the crankcase housing. Similarly you should only tap the shaft gently to break the taper seal or else you could do more harm than good. Many 2-strokes have very accurate pressed-up crankshaft assemblies and a hard blow from a hammer can knock a crank out of line, or even press the crank pin into the flywheel and wreck the big-end assembly.

Once the flywheel has been removed the points can be changed in the same way as for any other machine.

An electronic ignition system can take the sweat out of setting up the ignition timing and points though its installation and adjustment may require patience

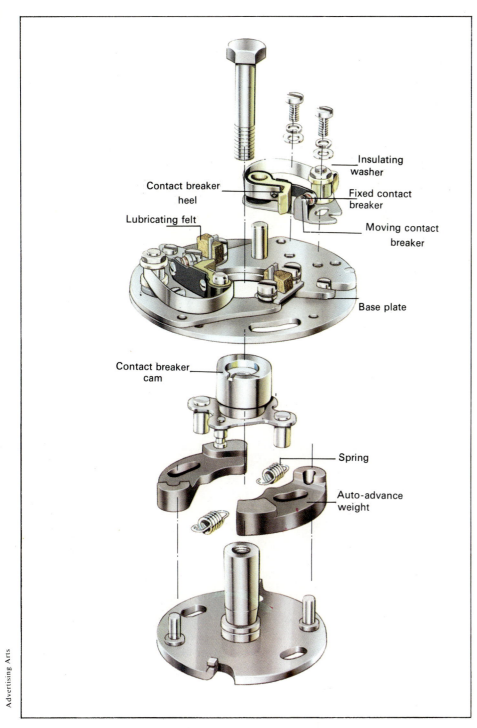

Contact breaker
heel

Lubricating felt

Contact breaker
cam

Insulating
washer

Fixed contact
breaker

Moving contact
breaker

Base plate

Spring

Auto-advance
weight

12. An exploded view of the auto-advance unit and contact breaker assemblies as found on the Triumph Bonneville T140V 750cc twin

Removing and replacing the points

Contact breaker replacement is basically the same for all machines. For those bikes with more than one set of points the procedure is simply repeated for each set.

To remove the points, first unscrew the retaining screw (fig. 18) which secures the fixed contact. In some cases before this can be done the coil and capacitor leads have to be removed from the spring blade of the moving point. The leads are usually retained by a nut and have insulating washers (fig. 17)– note their position by laying them out in the sequence as they are removed.

The moving contact is secured to its post by a circlip. Remove this and pull off the contact, again noting the position of any insulating washers.

This operation should then be repeated for any other set of contacts.

Once the points have been removed give them one final inspection. If they are not too bad then they may be worth keeping as an emergency spare set.

Refitting the new set is simply the reverse of the dismantling procedure. It sometimes helps to fit new capacitors too, as over a period of time these components break down and cause the

points to wear quicker making the machine harder to start. Once reassembly is complete the points gap should be adjusted as described on pages 40 to 41.

Auto-advance unit overhaul

If you are working on a 4-stroke machine and have just renewed the contact breaker assembly, it is worthwhile carrying the job one step further by checking the auto-advance unit.

While most 2-strokes can run at all speeds with the same ignition timing, 4-strokes must have the timing of the spark advanced for higher engine speeds. Automatic timing advance is usually achieved by means of sprung weights attached to the points cam. As engine speed increases the weights move outwards, due to centrifugal force, and pull on the points cam, rotating it by a small amount, so that it opens the points marginally sooner. As engine speed drops the springs pull the weights back, and the points cam returns to the fully-retarded position.

Obviously, the operation of this unit is quite critical if the bike is to run well at all speeds and periodic maintenance is therefore essential.

To gain access to the auto-advance, the first step is to remove the points base plate (fig. 15) By doing this you will, however, upset the bike's ignition timing. Therefore before going any further be sure that you are familiar with the procedure for timing your bike as described on pages 47 to 52. To make retiming the engine a little easier it is a good idea to mark the relative position of the base plate and any sub plates to a convenient point on the engine.

The contact-breaker plate is usually secured by two screws and can be taken out once these have been undone. With the contact breaker plate removed the auto-advance weights will be exposed, ready for dismantling.

Dismantling the auto-advance weights

Auto-advance weights are attached to the points camshaft by means of a single bolt (fig. 17) which passes through the centre of the shaft. Remove this bolt, and its washer, and the auto-advance assembly can be pulled free.

All auto-advance units are basically the same and are composed of spring loaded weights located on pivot posts (fig. 18). To dismantle the assembly, simply lift the weights off the posts and unhook the springs.

Due to the relatively small distance that the weights move, wear is seldom appreciable. The springs, however, do occasionally stretch or break and it is a

Advertising Arts

Dismantling and adjusting the points

13. Use your handbook to locate the points, then undo the crosshead screws and lift off the cover

14. Some bikes, like this Honda Gold Wing, have two sets of contact breakers activated by two lobes on the cam

17. Make sure you know the exact position of all the washers before you undo the retaining nut to release the lead

18. The contacts are usually mounted separately, be careful not to lose the retaining screws when you undo them

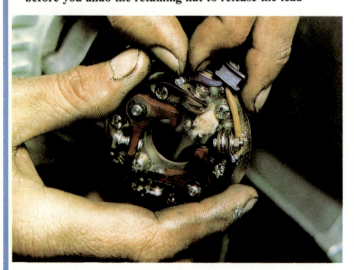

21. Make sure to replace the lead in the correct position, after fitting the contacts back to the base plate

22. Lubricate the felt pad with a light engine oil, but do not get it on the points as it will hinder performance

15. If it is difficult to adjust the points when they are still attached to the bike, unscrew the base plate

16. With the retaining screws in the base plate removed, the points should slide out as a complete unit

19. Inspect the condition of the contact faces. If they are badly pitted, they should be replaced

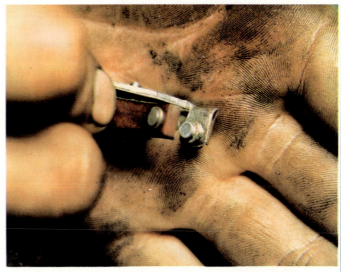

20. If the points are in reasonable condition, clean off any pitting with a stone and abrasive paper

23. Set the gap with a feeler gauge when the moving contact is resting on the highest point of the cam

24. The capacitors are often mounted near the points and should be renewed if you doubt their effectiveness

good idea to renew them. Some manufacturers such as BMW offer the choice of fitting stronger springs which delay advance and improve low-speed running.

The most common cause of trouble with auto-advance units is sticking. This is usually due to the weights rusting slightly and not moving smoothly in their pivots. The remedy is simple – thoroughly clean all the components and then lightly grease them.

Rusting is seldom caused by water directly penetrating the points cover, but mostly through condensation within the assembly. A small breather hole drilled in the points cover, not the engine casing, is often all that is required to cure the problem. As long as the hole is no larger than 3 mm ($\frac{1}{8}$in.) there will be no chance of rain getting in.

Once all the parts have been inspected they can be replaced in the reverse order to dismantling.

Stripping the auto-advance mechanism

25. When the points have been removed, undo the nut or bolt which retains the auto-advance mechanism

26. On dismantling the auto-advance, be ready to catch the circlips as you prise them off with a screwdriver

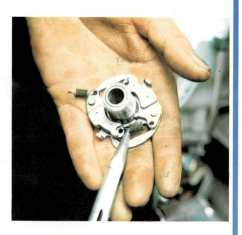

27. Equal care should be taken when removing the springs, so that the weights can be detached

28. Take the cam off the auto-advance unit, then clean and lightly grease the post on its base

29. Do not forget to replace the shims (if fitted) before fitting the cam back to the auto-advance mechanism

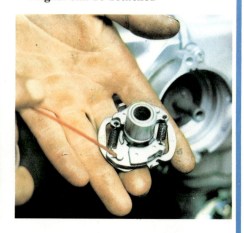

30. Add a drop of oil to the pivot pins for the weights on the auto-advance before replacing the circlips

31. Check the operation of the weights and springs, when the auto-advance unit has been completely reassembled

32. Align the mark on the cam with the corresponding mark on the base, or the timing will be out by 180°

33. A peg on the end of the camshaft locates in a groove in the base of the auto-advance mechanism

Strobe timing

The importance of correct ignition timing to a bike's performance cannot be overstressed.

Timing with a strobe light

There are two ways to check the accuracy of an engine's ignition timing: the static method and the dynamic method. The most accurate of the two is the dynamic test using a stroboscope. Nearly all bikes have some provision for strobe timing, but if your machine does not, see the accompanying panel.

The only drawback with strobe tim-

Dynamic timing

1. To check the timing with a strobe, first locate the timing marks. On this machine they are on the rotor

ing is that it requires the engine to be running. So it is obviously useless if you want to check the timing to find out why your machine will not start. If your timing has altered to the point that the bike will not start, refer to part two of this article which deals with static timing and adjustment.

A strobe light uses a neon, or similar high voltage, bulb that triggers a flash of very short duration virtually instantly it is triggered. This flash is triggered by current in the high-tension lead to the spark plug. So each time the plug fires the bulb lights up.

To use a strobe light, you shine it on the timing marks (on the flywheel or alternator) while the engine is running. Since the strobe flashes only when the plug fires, it makes the timing marks appear stationary. So when the two marks align, the engine will be firing at the correct number of degrees, in terms of crankshaft rotation, before TDC.

There are two different types of strobe light on the market. Cheapest by far is the neon strobe. This type is powered entirely by the bike's high ten-

sion impulse; most emit a red coloured beam. The principal disadvantage of these strobes is that they emit a very faint beam and are only really satisfactory if the timing marks can be chalked so that they show up more clearly, and the job is done in subdued light.

Better, but usually two or three times as expensive, are xenon or power strobes. These not only receive the HT impulse, but also draw additional power from the bike's battery. These strobes emit a powerful white light which is easy to see even if you are working in sunlight.

Checking the timing

Before you can check the timing with the strobe you will first have to find the location of the timing marks for your machine. Figs. 4 to 7 show a variety of timing marks and their locations. As there is a limit to where these marks can be placed you should have no difficulty in finding them.

If you are going to use a neon strobe light then, once the marks have been located, the next step will be to chalk the marks so that they will stand out more clearly. To connect a neon strobe, remove the spark plug cap and fit one of the strobe's leads to this and the other to the spark plug. If you are using a xenon strobe, attach the red and black leads to their respective terminals on

2. With the strobe connected in the HT circuit, start the engine and hold the light close to the marks

3. On this bike the F-mark should line up with the engine at idle

4. A common location for the timing marks is on the alternator rotor

5. A plastic plug usually covers the timing marks on this BMW's flywheel

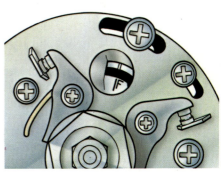

6. On this Honda the timing marks are visible through the contacts plate

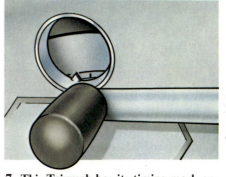

7. This Triumph has its timing mark on the timing cover under a plug

Bernard Fallon

47

the battery. The third lead then fits on to a special connector which is placed between the spark plug and its cap.

All you need to know now is the engine speed at which the timing marks are supposed to align. This is because on many machines, whether with mechanical contact breakers or electronic ignition, the timing of the spark advances as engine speed increases. So the timing marks are set to align either when the timing is fully retarded (which it will be when the engine is idling), or else when the timing is fully advanced (which it will be above a certain rev range). Some machines have two separate marks so you can check the operation of the advance mechanism at the same time as the timing is done. But if your machine has only one, check in your manual to find out the specified engine speed at which the timing should be checked.

Also note that most multi-cylinder machines will have more than one timing mark. Consequently, when you come to strobe checking a particular cylinder, refer to your manual or dealer to make sure that it is the correct timing mark which is aligning with the fixed reference point.

All that remains to be done now is to run the engine at the suggested speed and point the strobe light at the marks. If they align, the timing is correct. If the moving timing mark passes the fixed pointer, the timing is over-retarded; if it falls short then it is over-advanced. If the timing is found to be incorrect, refer to the next chapter (pages 49 to 52) for the method of adjustment.

Scribing your own timing marks

While most bikes today have timing marks which allow the timing to be checked dynamically with a strobe light, there are still quite a few machines on the road which do not. If you have one of these machines it may be possible for you to make your own timing marks. For this to be possible there are two basic requirements. First, you must have easy access to part of the engine which rotates, such as the flywheel or alternator rotor. Second, you must know at what point before TDC, in degrees or millimetres, the engine is supposed to fire.

Once you have this information the next step is to set the engine at its firing position. This can be done with either a timing disc or a dial gauge and adapter.

Using a timing disc

A timing disc is simply a circle of plastic, calibrated around its edge in degrees. This disc is fitted on the end of the camshaft to which the points are attached. As a pointer to go with it, use a screwdriver attached to a convenient point (fig. 8) such as the exhaust header pipe.

Next, you find TDC. On some machines there is a special provision made for this. On Triumphs there is a plug behind the cylinders which, when removed, gives access to the flywheel. A special tool (or home-made equivalent consisting of a socket and screwdriver) can then be fitted over this hole. When the machine is at TDC a slot will be felt in the flywheel. On machines which do not have this facility you will have to use a plunger gauge. This tool is basically just a threaded cylinder which replaces the spark plug and through which a metal rod is free to slide. To find TDC with this tool simply rotate the engine until the plunger rod is at its highest position.

With the engine set at TDC, rotate the timing disc until the pointer is at zero. Then rotate the engine again until the pointer registers the specified number of degrees before TDC at which the engine is supposed to fire.

The engine is now set up and the timing marks can be scribed (see below) on a suitable rotating part of the engine.

Using a dial gauge

If you have a dial gauge the job is a lot easier. This time, you fit the gauge in place of the spark plug (fig. 9) and rotate the engine until the highest reading is achieved—this will be at TDC. At this point adjust the gauge to zero. Next rotate the engine until the gauge reads the specified number of degrees or millimetres before zero at which the engine is supposed to fire. The engine is now correctly set, and the timing marks can be made.

Scribing the timing marks

Once you have the engine correctly set up you can scribe your timing marks. One must be on a rotating part of the engine and the other on an adjacent piece of casing. Usually either the flywheel or alternator rotor will be accessible and both are suitable locations for the marks. Use a steel ruler and a sharp scribing tool and be sure to mark the lines as accurately as possible. They do not need to be particularly large or deep, as they can always be chalked to make them clearer under the strobe.

Finally, if you used the figures provided for static timing to set the engine at its firing point, then the marks you will have made will represent fully retarded ignition timing. So when you check them with a strobe, run the engine at idle.

8. A timing disc fits on the end of the points camshaft. A suitable pointer should be taped nearby

9. At TDC, zero the dial gauge. The engine can then be rotated to the correct number of degrees BTDC

10. With the engine correctly set up scribe the timing marks—the flywheel is an ideal location

Chris Ridley

Timing by the static method

How to check the ignition timing by the static method is something that every biker needs to know. It can get you moving if, for some reason, you do not have a strobe light to check the timing dynamically. And if your engine will not run at all because of bad timing, you need a method of adjusting the timing—however roughly—before a strobe can be used.

Once you have discovered that the timing is out, by whatever method, the next step is to correct it.

Checking the timing statically

Checking the timing statically is, in principle, exactly the same as checking it with a strobe light—you relate the position at which the points open to the position of the piston(s). The difference is merely that, this time, the engine is not running.

The job falls into two parts. The first is to set the engine so that the piston is at the position at which ignition should

1. When timing 4-stroke singles, make sure that the piston is on its compression stroke by observing the inlet valve (arrowed)

occur. The second is to check the contact breaker to ensure that it is just on the point of opening.

Setting up the engine

Setting the engine at the position at which it should fire can be done in one of several ways. The most usual way is to align the timing mark—which, on almost all machines, will be found on either the flywheel or the alternator rotor—with the adjacent reference mark. First locate the timing marks, which are usually behind the points or alternator cover (fig. 2) and rotate the engine by hand. Turn the engine over

either by using the kickstart, rotating the rear wheel with the bike in gear and spark plugs out, or turning the bolt head (if any) on the end of the crankshaft, until the timing marks align.

If there is more than one timing mark, you will have to refer to your manual (or bike dealer) to find out which one should be aligned. On multicylinder machines there will be separate marks for each set of points, so make sure that you know which mark relates to which set of points.

On 4-stroke singles, one further complication is that it is possible to align the timing marks with the piston on its exhaust stroke instead of on its compression stroke. To make sure that you do not make this mistake and set the timing 360° out you will have to check the position of the inlet valve. To do this remove the valve clearance adjuster

cap (fig. 1) from the inlet valve. Rotate the engine clockwise and note the movement of the valve. When the valve has just finished opening and closing (moving downward and returning upward) continue rotating the engine until the timing marks align. The piston is now correctly positioned on its compression stroke.

If your machine does not have timing marks, you will have to set up each cylinder in turn using either a dial gauge or a timing disc as described in the panel on page 50.

If you have a large 2-stroke, it is well worth using a dial gauge anyway, even if timing marks are provided. On these machines the timing must be set very accurately and, often, the manufacturer's marks are not particularly precise.

Checking the points

With the piston set at the position at which the engine should fire, the points should just be starting to open. This is, however, difficult to check visually. So you will need either a test lamp, a buzzer box or an ohmmeter (set to the ×1 ohm range) to check it. The test lamp or buzzer will also require a

Triumph fitted with day lamps

49

Static timing with a test bulb

2. The timing marks are usually behind the points plate or, as on this Honda 250, on the alternator

3. With the ignition on, a bulb connected across the points will light up when they open

4. Loosen the mounting plate screws and adjust the plate so that the points open when the timing marks are in line

5. On bikes with more than one set of points, repeat the operation for the other set or sets

battery if you are working on a bike with a flywheel magneto, energy transfer or AC ignition. Whichever device you use, the procedure is roughly the same.

If you are working on a multi-cylinder machine which has more than one set of points, make sure that you are working on the set which corresponds with the timing marks you have aligned, or the cylinder you have just set up.

Whether you are using a test lamp, a buzzer or an ohmmeter, the next steps are the same. The first is to connect the test device across the points you are checking (fig. 3). Next, rotate the engine back so that it is several degrees before the firing point. If you are using a test lamp or buzzer now turn the ignition on—but do not do this if you are using an ohmmeter. At this point the light or buzzer should be off while the ohmmeter will read zero.

With the test device connected, rotate the engine as slowly as possible towards its firing point, carefully watching the tester as you do so. When the timing is correct then, as the timing marks align (or the dial gauge or timing disc indicates that the engine is at its firing point), the test device will indicate that the points are just opening. If you are using a bulb it will glow, while a buzzer will start to buzz and an ohmmeter needle will jump. If the ohmmeter needle does not appear to move try isolating the circuit by disconnecting the LT lead. This should result in the meter giving a more positive reading.

If you have to pass the point at which the engine should fire before the tester registers that the points are just about to open, then the timing is over-retarded and will require adjustment.

If the test device does not register anything, first check the connections and second check that the ignition

circuit is live. If the test device still fails to register, rotate the engine back past the timing marks until it does—what's wrong is that the ignition is seriously advanced and the points will require adjustment.

Adjusting the timing

The timing should be corrected if it is incorrect by even the slightest amount. If your machine has contact breaker points, the procedure is basically the same for all machines. Some bikes which have electronic ignition can also have their timing adjusted, but this depends on the system fitted—some units can only be replaced if they are found to be faulty.

Bikes with contact breaker points

To adjust the timing on a machine with contact breaker points, first set the engine at its firing point as described above. Then, with a test device connected across the points, loosen the contact breaker mounting plate screws (fig. 4). With these screws loose, the plate can be rotated (fig. 8) using a screwdriver in the pry points. Rotate the points plate until the test device registers that the points are just beginning to open. With this done, carefully tighten down the retaining screws. Rotate the engine a couple of times with the tester still connected to check the accuracy of your adjustment. Repeat, if necessary, until you have spot-on accuracy.

On bikes with more than one set of points, next repeat the operation for the other set(s). Take care that, as you adjust each set, you align the correct timing mark or that you are working on the cylinder which corresponds to the set of points which you are adjusting.

You must make the adjustments as accurately as possible, particularly if you are working on a high revving 2-stroke where even the slightest amount of error could have serious consequences.

Bikes with electronic ignition

The varying types of electronic ignition can be divided into two for adjustment purposes: those which are factory fitted as standard and those which are bought as replacement units for machines originally fitted with points.

Adjustment of the replacement type is possible as, obviously, the units have to be correctly set up when they are

Static timing with an ohmmeter

6. On many bikes, such as this Suzuki 250, the timing marks can be seen through an aperture in the points plate

7. With the ignition off, an ohmmeter connected across the points will read 0 when they are closed

8. Align the timing marks and loosen the mounting plate screws. Adjust the plate until the points just open

9. The ohmmeter needle will swing back to the left when the points open

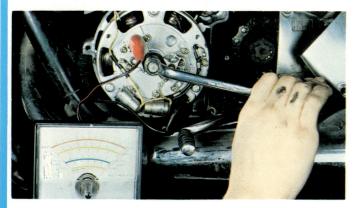

10. Where there are more than one set of points, connect the meter to the other set and align the other timing marks

11. Adjust the other set of points so that they open when the appropriate timing marks are aligned

George Wright

installed. Adjustment is usually simply a matter of moving the stator plate as you check the timing with a strobe. If there is not enough available movement of the stator plate, the rotor can be repositioned, following the instructions supplied by the manufacturer.

Timing adjustment on machines which have factory fitted electronic ignition, if it is possible at all, is basically the same. This is because all systems work on roughly the same principles. Before going any further, check with your local dealer to find out if adjustment is possible. If so, the first step is to locate the unit, which will usually be quite accessible and behind the plate which carries the timing marks. In some cases this 'plate' will be the flywheel, in which case the flywheel will have to be unbolted. With the ignition unit exposed, the pick-up or pulser coil plate will be visible (fig. 14). It is this plate which should be loosened by undoing its securing screws (fig. 15). With the plate loose, it can be rotated either way depending on whether the timing, when strobed, is found to be over-advanced or over-retarded.

As the unit usually does not move very much, you should rotate it only a little each time before rechecking the timing with the strobe.

When you do this rechecking, remember to rev the engine to the recommended speed. As with all electronic systems, only one adjustment is necessary, even on multi-cylinder machines.

Timing electronic ignition

12. On the Suzuki GT250X7 the ignition fires when one of the two O-shaped elements passes beneath the sensing coil

13. This is how *not* to remove your flywheel – obtain the proper puller for your model

14. With the flywheel removed the electronic ignition stator plate can be reached for adjustment

15. The stator plate is held by three screws fitted through elongated slots. Loosen the screws and adjust the plate

16. Tighten the stator plate screws and replace the flywheel and its nut. Check the timing with a strobe

17. Do not be confused by timing marks on the back-plate – these are for factory use

Adjusting the clutch

Clutch slip and clutch drag, both symptoms of a badly adjusted clutch, are often overlooked until a major problem develops. But regular adjustment of the clutch linkage is not difficult, and helps to prolong the life of the clutch and maintain the efficiency of the engine.

A bike clutch is in constant use and is subject to extreme stresses. Its components, including friction plates, pressure plates, clutch springs, cables and levers, inevitably wear down. So regular adjustment is necessary to maintain its efficiency and keep running costs down.

A faulty clutch shows up in one of two ways—clutch slip or clutch drag.

Clutch slip, as the name implies, occurs when the clutch plates slip against one another and the clutch does not engage fully. A symptom of clutch slip is the engine racing when you are pulling away from a standstill, even with the clutch lever released, or when the engine is under load—for example, when climbing a hill.

If not rectified quickly, clutch slip will cause the clutch to overheat rapidly. The result: glazing of the friction pads, loss of their friction properties, possible distortion of the plates, and eventual loss of the springs' springiness.

Clutch drag occurs when the plates do not separate enough and the engine power cannot be fully disengaged from the transmission. One symptom is the bike's creeping forward at junctions with the clutch disengaged but still in gear. Another is difficulty in engaging a gear from neutral, so that when the bike finally 'clonks' into gear it jumps forward.

Types of clutch

Two types of clutch are used on modern bikes with manual gearboxes. Most common is the oil-immersed multiplate clutch found on all machines of below 250 cc and on most larger machines. The other design is the dry-running single- or twin-plate clutch found mainly on shaft-driven, larger capacity machines. This type is based on car clutch design and contains fewer parts than the multi-plate variety.

The multi-plate clutch (fig. 1) consists of the clutch housing or outer drum, the centre driven drum and the friction plates. The complete unit is located on the gearbox mainshaft, but the clutch housing is bearing-mounted so that it can turn independently of the mainshaft. The clutch housing is linked by primary gears or chain to the crankshaft and rotates in relation to the crankshaft speed.

The centre driven drum is located on the gearbox mainshaft by splines and turns at the same rate as the mainshaft. This driven drum retains the friction plates inside the clutch housing and

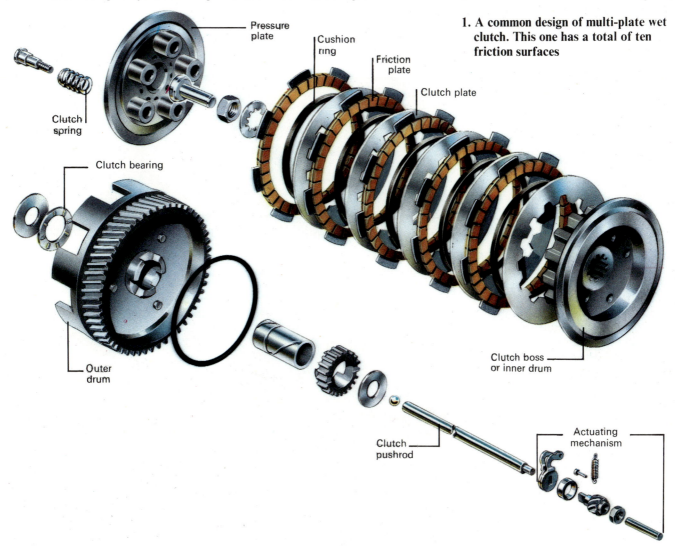

1. A common design of multi-plate wet clutch. This one has a total of ten friction surfaces

Pressure plate

Cushion ring

Friction plate

Clutch plate

Clutch spring

Clutch bearing

Outer drum

Clutch boss or inner drum

Clutch pushrod

Actuating mechanism

these are compressed by the clutch springs to form the friction bond when the clutch is engaged.

The dry clutch (fig. 11), similar to a car clutch design, is used on a number of large-capacity bikes. In this type, the clutch is mounted directly on to the end of the crankshaft, and consists of a flywheel on the crankshaft, one or two friction plates and a spring loaded pressure-and-drive plate. The springs can be ordinary coil springs or a conical diaphragm spring.

Clutch adjustment

When your clutch is correctly adjusted there should be from 4 mm to 6 mm ($\frac{1}{8}$ in.-$\frac{1}{4}$ in.) of free play at the clutch lever (fig. 2) before it begins to 'bite'.

To carry out the adjustment, you first use the cable adjusters (figs. 3 to 6). Depending on your bike, you will find up to three of these.

2. The correct amount of free play at the clutch lever. It is between 4 and 6 mm ($\frac{1}{8}$ in. to $\frac{1}{4}$ in.)

When you have used up all the adjustment possible on these, the next stage is to slacken them all off and use the screw adjuster on the pushrod (fig. 10). —or, on some bikes, thrust bearing—to gain the required free play at the lever. The cable adjusters can then be used again for fine adjustments, and to compensate for progressive wear.

Once all possible cable and pushrod adjustment has been used up, the worn clutch parts must be renewed. This will involve the more drastic process of stripping the clutch.

Tools required for clutch adjustment include an open-ended spanner for the cable adjuster locknuts, ring or box spanner for the pushrod screw locknut, flat-bladed screwdriver and pliers.

Checking the cable

Before attempting to adjust your clutch, check the condition of the clutch cable to see that it is running smoothly.

Check the outer casing for signs of

Adjusting the clutch

3. First, screw the large adjuster right out. It should not be stiff, so finger pressure will do

5. At the crankcase end, slide the dust cap clear, undo the lock nut and screw it back up the cable

7. It is a good idea to grease the mechanism when exposed. Use a high melting point grease

9. While holding the outer lock nut, screw the adjuster in until some resistance is just being felt

4. Then screw in the small inner adjuster all the way. This gives you the necessary free play

6. Having screwed the adjuster into the crankcase, remove the panel for access to the actuating machanism

8. If adjustment is needed at the pushrod, undo the outer lock nut so that the adjuster can move freely

10. Screw the adjuster out between $\frac{1}{4}$ and $\frac{1}{2}$ a turn and keep it there while doing up the lock nut

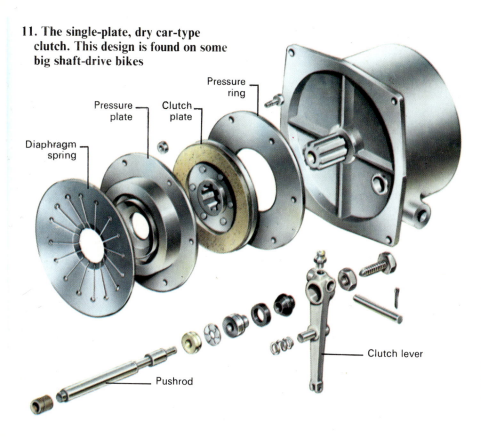

11. The single-plate, dry car-type clutch. This design is found on some big shaft-drive bikes

Diaphragm spring

Pressure plate

Clutch plate

Pressure ring

Clutch lever

Pushrod

with oil (fig. 15).

Hydraulic cable oilers which force the oil through the whole length of the cable are also available.

Nylon-lined cables should not be lubricated, but just cleaned with paraffin (kerosene) or a water-repellent aerosol such as WD40.

Renewing a cable

Renewing a cable is simply a reversal of the removal procedure. But if you are fitting a new one, make sure it is long enough around the steering head not to foul when the forks are turned, and to avoid any over-tight bends.

New cables can sometimes be bought

12. The end of this cable is in good condition. If one is even slightly frayed, replace it

chafing, especially at the clutch lever. Next, depress the lever and at the same time watch the other end to see that there is an instant response when the lever is pulled and released. If the cable is running smoothly, the pressure needed on the lever should be steady and not jerky, and when released it should spring back freely.

With the lever pulled in, the wire ends of the cable will be exposed and their condition can be checked (fig. 12). There should be no wear signs—burrs or flat spots where the cable passes through the lever guides—and no dry spots, rust spots, or broken wires.

If the cable is sticking and the reason is not obvious, remove it for examination and lubrication or, if necessary, replacement.

Removing the cable.

To remove the cable, first screw in all the cable adjusters to get maximum free play at the lever. Pull the outer casing out of the lever cable guide and push the inner-cable nipple out of the retaining hole in the handlebar lever. At the lower end, the nipple can now simply be pulled out of the retaining slot. On some bikes, you may have to remove a cover plate to do this; you may also find it necessary to remove the petrol tank.

Lubricating the cable

The easiest method of lubricating the cable is to suspend it while you slowly drip oil down the inner wire. Occa-

sionally pull the inner wire up and down through the casing to help the oil penetrate down the whole length (fig. 14).

A variation on this method which wastes less oil is to make a funnel of greaseproof paper or Plasticene around the top of the cable and fill the funnel

Dunstall converted Honda CBX

with an oiling point, similar to a grease nipple, fitted to the outer casing. This allows proper lubrication without having to remove the cable.

Adjusting the cable
Cable adjustment can be carried out at up to three points, depending on your bike's design.

Begin with the lever adjuster (fig. 3). This is designed for adjustment with your fingers. Slacken off the knurled locknut and screw out the adjuster to take up any slack in the cable. When the amount of free play in the lever is correct, tighten the locknut.

If a mid-cable expander (fig. 16) is fitted, it is normally in one of two places: where the clutch cable loops down by the bottom fork yoke before it is routed under the tank, or where it re-emerges between tank and crankcase. This adjuster is of the expanding variety, with one half screwed into the other.

First, slacken off the clutch lever adjuster. Undo the locknut on the expander, and screw or unscrew the knurled adjuster nut until you have the required slack at the clutch lever. Finally, tighten up both locknuts.

The same basic procedure applies to the crankcase cable adjuster (fig. 5). If one is fitted, you will find a threaded cable stop where the cable enters the crankcase. Again, the locknut must be undone, the cable stop screwed out until the slack is taken up, and the nut retightened.

That is the standard procedure. On some machines, for example the Suzuki 750 three-cylinder, the use of a feeler gauge is recommended (although not mandatory) between the adjusting screw and the pushrod to measure the end float. The end float on this machine should be 0.5mm (0.018 in). If adjustment is required, you first have to slacken off the cable adjusters and then undo the locknut. Then you set the adjuster at the required gap, and re-tighten the locknut.

Clutch pushrod adjustment
The position of the clutch pushrod adjuster varies from bike to bike and can be on the left-hand or right-hand side of the engine. Sometimes it is accessible from outside the crankcase; sometimes you need to remove a rubber bung on a screwed-on alloy cover plate.

If in any doubt, remove the clutch cover and look for the pressure plate with its four or six spring screws. On multi-plate clutches, the adjusting nut and screw are usually directly in line with the centre of this plate, at the other end of the pushrod, or in the centre of the clutch plate itself.

Before starting work, screw in all of the cable adjusters so they can be adjusted later.

First, slacken off the locknut with either a ring or a box spanner (fig. 8). Turn the screw anti-clockwise a couple of turns to clear any pressure that is on the screw. Then slowly screw in the adjuster until pressure is felt (fig. 9). This point is easy to miss, so if in doubt repeat the procedure a couple of times to make sure. Once you feel the pressure, back off the screw by a quarter-turn and re-tighten the locknut (fig. 10).

Check that the free play at the clutch lever is the required 4 mm to 6 mm and, if necessary, adjust the cable adjusters.

On one or two bikes there are slight variations to this procedure. You may have to align the lever which operates the pushrod with a mark on the crankcase, for example, or 'aim' the end of the clutch release lever at a V-mark on the drive chain cover. But such variations are usually given in the manual—and can anyway be resolved by experiment.

This 'if it works, use it' approach will not work on Velocette singles, however. Their clutch adjustment procedure is complex, and should not be undertaken without a rider's manual.

Road testing
After adjusting the clutch linkage, a

13. Some machines have a mid-cable adjuster. Use it to give plenty of adjustment at the handlebars

road test is needed to check that the adjustment is correct. If possible, do the test in town traffic, where constant use of the clutch will heat it if clutch drag persists. To check for clutch slip, try 'dropping' the clutch when taking off from a standstill.

If you notice a juddering as the clutch takes up, this is caused by a defect inside the clutch itself—not the linkage. Regular care and lubrication of your clutch will certainly help to prevent problems from occuring.

Clutch linings
Clutch plate facings have an immensely difficult task to perform. They must be capable of transmitting a large amount of torque efficiently and consistently at all times; when engaged, the clutch should be able to transmit all of the torque delivered by the driving side of the clutch. Yet it must not generate so much friction that the plates will not slip over each other and the clutch snatches when drive is being taken up.

Clutch facings must be able to withstand tremendous heat without losing their frictional properties and conduct this heat away from the mating surfaces. They must also survive the contamination of the oilbath.

In almost all situations, the best solution is a combination of one surface of metal to provide rigidity and one surface of organic material. With dry metal to metal, the amount of friction between the two surfaces is excessive because the retention of heat means that the two surfaces tend to weld together. With wet metal to metal, the layer of oil keeps the plates apart so well that the torque transmitting capacity of the clutch is low. Where metal to metal plates are used, as they were in some Moto Guzzi racers of the fifties, a large number of plates is needed to compensate for this reduction.

Over the years many substances have been used for clutch linings. The first linings were made of leather, which gave a good grip but tended to char or even catch fire. Cork was an improvement, but suffered from the same problems. It is not surprising, then, that asbestos linings became popular in the twenties. However oilbaths allowed cork to become popular again since they withstood oil contamination better and the oil cooled the cork well and provided a quieter action.

After the war, synthetic rubbers such as Neoprene were introduced. These worked well, but tended to swell under the influence of oil. An improvement was the Neolangite mixture of granules of cork set in a Neoprene base used first by Triumphs.

Nowadays clutch facings can be a variety of thin segments stuck to the driving plate by strong adhesives. They can be made of anything from bonded resin mixed with sintered (powdered and reformed) metal – typically bronze – to rubber and cork.

Adjusting drum brakes

Considering that you trust your life to the braking system of your bike every time you ride, it is vital to give it regular attention. It is quite an easy job to maintain your drum brakes at peak efficiency.

Until comparatively recently, all bikes had drum brakes front and rear. Many modern machines still retain this kind of system, especially on the rear wheel. Compared with a hydraulic disc brake, a good drum brake can be cheaper to produce and can give almost equal braking performance.

There are two main types of drum brake both of which operate in a similar manner. These are the single-leading shoe (SLS) and the twin-leading shoe (TLS) types.

SLS and TLS systems

On both SLS and TLS systems, two shoes located on a stationary brake plate, are made to move apart from each other and expand to bear against a drum that rotates with the bike wheel. Usually, this drum forms the hub or centre of the wheel. As the shoes rub against the drum the friction retards the revolution of the wheel and the bike slows

down. The shoes are made to expand against the drum by a cam located on the inside of the brake plate.

On the outside of the brake plate, the cam is attached to an arm. As this arm is moved, the cam turns and either moves the shoes apart or lets them come together. The two shoes are held together with one or more springs, which automatically close the shoes when the cam is not forcing them apart.

In practice, the difference between the two types of drum brake is the number of operating cams.

With one cam, as the brake shoes are forced apart, one of the shoes is forced against the drum by the rotation of the wheel and the other is forced back against the cam by the drum (fig. 1). With two cams, both brake shoes are forced on to the drum (fig. 2). The shoe that is forced on to the drum is called the 'leading' shoe. So when a brake has one cam it is known as a single-leading shoe brake, and when it has two cams, it is

1. Typical SLS brake design. Drum rotation helps the cam's action for the leading shoe, here the left

Paul Williams

2. With this TLS design, both shoes are helped by drum rotation, two pivots and two cams being required

Kawasaki KH125

3. This SLS brake is of the floating shoe type. Metal thrust pads allow the shoes to move on to the drum

known as a twin-leading shoe brake.

On most SLS brakes, the ends of the brake shoes opposite to the cam pivot on a spindle. Some, however, in an effort to achieve greater braking efficiency, are designed as 'semi-floating' types (fig. 3). Here the threads of the brake shoes farthest from the cam have small steel thrust plates attached which allow the brake shoes to move about slightly as they are applied to the drum. The theory is that the force of the brake shoes being pushed against the drum will increase if the shoes are free to slide into the drum. But in practice, however, the system is not all that effective when compared with the TLS design.

The arm attached to the brake cam is operated by a rod or cable. All front brakes are operated by a cable from the brake lever to a cable stop on the brake plate or the fork leg. The cable has an inner and an outer part, the outer acting as a sheath for the inner which is always made of steel cable.

With many rear brakes, a rod is used to operate the brake directly instead of a cable. Whether a rod or cable is used, the principles of operation and method of adjustment are very similar.

Removing the rear wheel and brake

4. The rear brake of this bike is well within the 'usable range' shown by the pointer on the scribed mark

5. Start to remove the rear wheel by taking out the split pin from the castellated nut on the wheel spindle

6. Undo the spindle nut. If it has not been undone for a while, you may have to tap the spanner with a mallet

7. Remove the spindle from the rear wheel. You may find you have to knock it through with a hammer

8. If there are any spacers between the brake plate and the swinging arm take them out and keep safely

9. Take the spring clip out of the brake torque arm castellated nut. Keep it carefully for re-use

10. Having removed the bolt, catch any washers and spacers and free the torque arm from the brake plate

11. Remove the brake adjuster nut from the brake rod. You will have to hold the rod with pliers

12. Finally, the wheel can be taken from the bike and the rear brake should just pull easily from the drum

Removing the front wheel and brake

13. Slacken off all the cable adjusters so that you can remove the brake cable from the front brake arm

14. If the speedometer drive is on the front wheel, remove it by undoing the screw. A push fit on some models

15. If your bike has a front brake torque arm, remove the split pin and undo the nut to remove

16. Remove both the spindle clamps on the front wheel to free the wheel spindle prior to wheel removal

17. On this Honda 250 K4, the spindle splits in two to release the brake plate, unscrew the two halves

18. One some bikes, the plate is held by a nut on the spindle. Undo this nut and remove the brake plate

Wear and tear

On all drum brakes the most severe wear takes place on the leading edges of the shoe friction pads or linings. Although the linings are made from a heat resistant material, the high temperatures and frictional stress incurred under braking eventually wears them out.

The linings may be bonded or rivetted to the brake shoe. If the linings are allowed to wear right down, the shoes or rivet heads could make contact with the drum and ruin it. This necessitates an expensive replacement. For this reason, as well as safety, the condition of the linings should be checked and maintained at regular service intervals.

Wear on the linings will rapidly increase if the shoe return springs break or stretch after prolonged use.

Some components wear very slowly. For example, the drum itself, the activating cam and its spindle or bush. Gradual wear on these items may hardly be noticed but will eventually reduce the overall efficiency of the brake.

Tests for wear

If you get on a bike for the first time and the braking is really poor, it is a simple matter to see that the brakes need adjusting. However, after riding your own bike around for a long time the gradual deterioration in braking performance

19. Always give the brake a visual examination for any obvious signs of wear and tear

can go unnoticed, until it is too late.

The external signs to look for before removing the wheel and stripping the brake are mostly rather obvious. If your bike has a 'useable limits' mark scribed into the brake plate it is easy to know when it is time to examine the brake linings for wear (fig. 4). If there is no more adjustment left at either end of the cable, or if there is any sudden deterioration in the braking performance coupled with any unusual noise, you should strip the system.

Before you start

You should not need any special tools for the wheel removal or stripping the brake drum. But for absolutely accurate examination of the lining thickness and for measurement of the spring free length, it is useful to have a vernier caliper. If you cannot get hold of one, a transparent plastic ruler will do.

Both the front and the rear wheels need to be removed for a complete drum brake strip.

Spring and lining checks

20. On this type of drum brake, the shoes are held firmly in each hand and removed in a V shape

21. Measure the free spring length with a Vernier caliper if you have one. Examine it for general wear

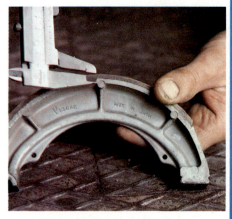

22. With the Vernier caliper measure the lining thickness at the sides at several points. A ruler will do

Continued

Rear wheel removal

If your bike's rear wheel spindle is held by a castellated nut and a split pin, start by removing it (fig. 5) and undo the spindle nut (fig. 6). If your bike has a knock through spindle, you may have to take off the exhaust on the side from which the spindle is withdrawn. If your back wheel comes out with the spindle still in place this will not be necessary.

Generally though, wheel removal varies widely from bike to bike.

Easiest wheels to remove are those on bikes with a shaft drive. All you do is remove the spindle nut and clamp bolt, then knock out the spindle. The wheel can then be pulled clear of the splines, which are the machined grooves that transfer the drive from the final drive unit to the rear wheel. On some bikes, you will have to compress the rear shock absorbers to free the spindle, then hinge back the rear section of the mudguard releasing the rear wheel from under the back end of the bike.

On bikes with chains, the procedure is a bit more complicated. A lot of bikes have continuous chains. If they are designed so the rear wheel sprocket is a part of the wheel, and this is not quickly detachable, the chain will either have to be split, or removed by taking it off one or other of the sprockets. Slacken off the chain tensioners located on the left and right of the wheel spindle first if this is possible. Move the wheel forward in the swinging arm spindle slots until the chain can be taken off. Alternatively you may be able to free the wheel and get the chain off by moving it forward as far as it will go and slipping the chain off the sprocket. If the chain must be split, remove the split-link with a pair of pliers (see page 141).

Some chain-driven bikes have quickly

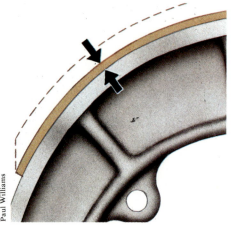

Paul Williams

23. The depth of the lining should be more than 3 mm (⅛ in.) throughout the length and width of the lining

detachable (QD) wheels. In this case, the sprocket is not a part of the rear wheel. With this type of wheel, you should be able to remove the spindle (fig. 7) and then undo the bolts that hold the hub to the sprocket.

With the chain out of the way, and the spindle removed, disconnect the rear brake drum from the bike. Start by undoing the torque arm from the brake plate. Remove the spring clip (fig. 9), undo the castellated nut and then remove the torque arm (fig. 10). Now undo and remove the brake adjuster nut (fig. 11). Put the nut to one side, along with any washers attached.

With the brake drum disconnected, you can now remove the rear wheel. You might need an assistant to help steady the bike while you remove the wheel out from under the mudguard.

As the rear wheel comes out, the drum should be free to be removed (fig. 12) if your bike has a knock out spindle, or should come out after you have un-

done the brake plate retaining nut, in cases where the spindle is retained in the wheel hub.

Front wheel removal

It should not be at all difficult to remove the front wheel for access to the front brake drum. Start by disconnecting the brake cable (fig. 13) from the brake arm. Then remove the speedometer drive cable (fig. 14) if it is driven from the front wheel. If the bike has one, undo one end of the brake torque arm. Next undo the spindle clamps (fig. 16). The wheel will now drop out from between the forks. If your bike's wheel is held by a clamped spindle, undo the nut on the end of the spindle first, then undo the clamp on the fork leg opposite to the spindle nut. Now knock out the spindle to free the wheel.

Next, remove the brake plate from the hub. You may have to remove a nut from the spindle, or unscrew an extension from the spindle (fig. 17). Lift the brake plate out of the wheel hub (fig. 18).

Dismantling and examination

Drum brakes on both the front and rear wheels are very similar, the only real difference being between the two types of brake (SLS and TLS).

The entire brake mechanism is attached to the back of the brake plate (fig. 19). First remove the shoes from the plate. This is best done by holding both shoes firmly, one in each hand, and lifting the outside edge of each shoe so that they come up into a V-shape (fig. 20). Pull them off the brake plate, being careful not to trap your fingers. Try not to get any grease from dirty hands on to the lining material in case they are still in good enough condition to be returned.

Some TLS brakes are secured at both

24. With rivetted linings, there must be adequate lining depth above the head of the rivet

25. The top shoe has plenty of lining left. The bottom shoe has not much left and needs replacing

26. Before taking the arm off a splined cam, make two punch marks for alignment on reassembly

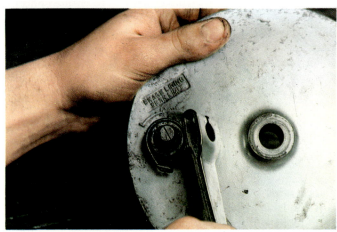

27. Undo the pinch-bolt and take the arm off. The cam can now be taken out from the other side and checked

ends. In this case, each brake shoe will have an eye which slides over a spindle. To remove this, you have to take out a split pin from the spindle, remove the washer and then take off the shoes by easing them off the two spindles.

You can now pull off and check the springs. To examine the springs, open the vernier gauge and measure their length (fig. 21). Some springs have hooks that can slip down into the coil. Be sure that the hooks are fully extended and taken into account when measuring the spring. The precise limits for the individual bikes can be found in a manual. But as a rough guide ensure that the springs are both the same length. If they are of the closed-coil type, none of the coils should be opened up. If you are in any doubt as to the correct functioning of the springs, buy a new set as they are inexpensive. If you do not, the brakes could stick on if the springs fail to close the shoes.

Next, check the shoe linings for wear. If you have a vernier gauge, measure the thickness of the lining over the entire surface area. The thickness of the lining

at all points should be greater than 3 mm ($\frac{1}{8}$in.) at the very least. If the linings are rivetted to the shoe, clean out the dust from the head recesses and check that there is more than 3 mm ($\frac{1}{8}$in.) between the top of the lining and the top of the rivet (fig. 24).

Rivetted linings can sometimes be bought separately from the shoes. But they are best replaced as complete shoe and lining exchange units. It is not advisable to try and rivet linings to the shoes yourself.

The cam should be removed from the brake plate to check it properly for wear. But first mark the position of the brake arm where it fits on the splines of the cam spindle with a punch (fig. 26). In this way the arm and cam can be fitted back together in exactly the same positions on reassembly.

If the cam has been well greased, there should be little sign of wear. But if you are in doubt as to the tightness of the fit of the cam in the brake plate, you must decide whether it is the cam or the plate itself that is worn. Take the cam and plate to a dealer. If possible borrow a

new cam and compare the faces. Then insert the cam spindle into the plate. If the fit is still sloppy, it is the plate that is worn and must be renewed.

If your bike is of the semi-floating type, the small thrust pads on the ends of the shoe must be examined for wear or grooving. If the grooves on them are not too deep, the pad can be re-used. If they are deep the thrust pad must be replaced.

If none of the items in the brake itself are worn to the limits described above, but the brake is still inefficient the cable may be rusty internally, or the shoes could be contaminated with grease. The procedure for checking the brake drum wear is described on page 193. Part replacement, reassembly and adjustment are all fully covered in the following chapter.

Drum brakes are very reliable providing that they are regularly inspected. Maintenance is the gentle art of prevention and there is nothing more vital to your safety than braking. This includes maintaining the cables and linkages that operate the brake assembly.

Brake reassembly

After dismantling your drum brakes we show you how to replace, reassemble and adjust them for peak power, performance and reliability.

The previous chapter showed how to dismantle and examine your bike's drum brake assembly. The second part of this procedure involves replacing and re-assembling the components.

If you are in doubt about replacing a particular item do not be tempted to take any risks. Take the old part to a dealer for comparison with a new one, it should then be clear whether or not it needs renewing. When buying a new part always tell a dealer the exact model, year and if necessary, the engine or frame number of the bike. This will enable him to find the part you want, and ensure that no mistakes are made.

Before reassembly

In addition to the tools for reassembling the brake, you will also need a flat file. The best type is one that has its cutting teeth quite close together which gives a smooth finish to the workpiece.

If you have had your drum skimmed to reduce ovality or scoring you may have to buy and fit oversized shoes for your bike. Normal replacement shoes may not give good performance when fitted into an enlarged skimmed drum. Oversized shoes will have to be turned on a lathe so that they just fit into the drum after the brake has been fully assembled. If you think this might be necessary, the shoes must be turned when assembled on the brake drum to ensure concentricity.

To lubricate parts of the braking mechanism you will need a can of high melting point grease such as Castrol LM.

All parts to be reassembled must be scrupulously clean. This applies especially to the brake shoe linings. Try to handle them as little as possible, and if you have to touch them make sure your hands are completely clean and free from grease.

Reassembling the brake mechanism

Start by putting the cam or cams back in place in the brake plate. Put a small smear of grease on the part of the cam that bears against the brake plate (fig. 1), and put back any rubber O-rings on the end of the cam (fig. 2). If the end of the cam has a nipple for greasing, make sure this is clean and that the 'grease-way' in the cam is clean.

Push the brake arm back on its splines making sure that the punch marks you made when taking it off are aligned and that any return springs are in place. If you have a TLS brake, attach the linkage between the two splined cams.

With the cam or cams in place, you can put the shoes back on. If they are new, you must 'chamfer' the ends of the lining, this can also make an old shoe work better. If the shoes are not chamfered, the brake will probably grab and snatch, which could be dangerous especially when the roads are wet.

Put the shoes in a vice, and rub each end of the lining with the file (fig. 3) to give a smooth sloping bevel (fig. 4). With an ordinary SLS brake it is only necessary to chamfer the end of the shoe nearest to the cam. But it is a good idea to chamfer both ends so that you can assemble the shoes either way into the brake drum.

If you are putting old shoes back into the drum, examine them to see which end is most worn. With SLS shoes, do not put them back in reverse position so that the worn part fits at the opposite end to where it was. If the unworn end becomes the leading part of the shoe the brake lining could cause snatching.

When the brake shoes have been carefully prepared, they can be put on to the brake plate. First, attach the springs to the underside of the shoe, making sure that the springs are correctly positioned on their retaining hoops or hooks. Put a thin smear of grease on the part of the shoe that bears against the operating cams (fig. 6). Replace the thrust pads on the non-cam end of the shoe if the brake is the 'floating' SLS type.

If your brake shoes turn on a spindle at the non-cam end, the replacement procedure is different to the type which are simply put back with the shoes in a V-shape. Reassemble the non-V shoes by pushing the spindle ends halfway on, then levering the other ends on to the cam (fig. 8). You can now slide the other ends all the way on to the spindle. A small smear of grease on the cam and spindle will help the procedure. Finally, replace the washers in place on the spindle (fig. 9), and secure them with split pins (fig. 10). Use new split pins, do not attempt to re-use the old ones.

When you have reassembled the shoe mechanism to the brake plate, try to operate the brake manually before you put it back into the drum. Pull the brake arm and make sure that the movement is smooth and that both the brake shoes

900SS Ducatti and Moto Guzzi California

Brake reassembly

1. Lightly grease the brake cam spindle where it bears in the brake plate. Use high melting point grease

2. If there is an O-ring acting as a dust seal or grease retainer on the outside of the cam, always put it back

3. Proper chamfering of the brake shoes will accelerate the bedding in process and reduce snatch and grab

4. This shoe has been well chamfered and has a gradual slope at the end of the lining

5. Put a small amount of grease on the actuating cam to assist replacement of the drum shoes and brake operation

6. A small smear on the part of the shoe that is rubbed by the cam will make brake actuation smoother

Mike Sheil

Continued

7. With one of the shoes half on and over the spindle, the other one can be manoeuvred into the correct position

8. Now pull against the springs and lever it over the retainer and on to the spindle

Mike Sheil

9. Place the retaining plate over the spindles. This Z 400 Kawasaki has one plate, others have one per spindle

10. Be sure to put back the two pins. If they are of the split pin type, new ones must be used every time

move outwards evenly. If it functions properly you can put the brake plate back into the drum. This is the reverse to the removal procedure. Be sure that the brake plate nut, which retains the brake plate on the spindle is fully tightened if one is fitted.

Install the wheel back into the forks. If the brake plate of the front wheel locates into a lug or slot make sure it is lined up and in place before tightening the wheel spindle clamps. Similarly fit the torque arm bar (fig. 12), if one is fitted, on to its bolt or stud on the brake plate. Make sure the spindle clamps are tight on the front wheel, and check that they are done up correctly. Some clamps are closed at one end and other types have even gaps at each ends.

If you are replacing a rear brake and the rear wheel is chain driven, adjust the chain first of all before you attach the brake rod or torque arm.

On some rear torque arms, the bolt head locates in a recessed hole to prevent it slipping. With the torque arm on (fig. 13) tighten the spindle clamps, attach the cable or rod to the brake arm and adjust the brake.

Adjusting the brakes

Although adjusting the front and rear brakes is similar in principle, the methods differ slightly in detail.

Front brake adjustment

Attach the cable brake arm in the reverse way to which it was removed. If there are two cable adjusters, undo both before putting the nipple into its holder in the brake arm, Locate the cable outer into the cable stop either on the brake plate or on the lower part of the fork leg. Take up the play with the cable

adjusters at the handlebar lever (fig. 15), and at the cable stop (fig. 16). Turn the adjusters until there is about 3 mm (0.125in.) play in the cable before the brake begins to bite (fig. 22).

If you have renewed the brake cable, route it so that there are no kinks along its length or so that it does not stick out from the bike.

The angle between the cable and the arm must not be more than 90 degrees with the brake fully applied (fig. 22). If the angle is greater, you have reassembled the arm on the splined cam incorrectly. If the angle is not correct, the mechanical advantage of the system starts off low and is reduced by wear. In addition the machine will not pass a roadworthiness test.

Adjusting a TLS brake

Most TLS brakes have the two oper-

11. An ideal chamfer on the brake shoe is the only way to ensure that a brake beds in quickly

12. The brake torque arm must be put back into place with a new split pin through the castellated nut

ating cams linked by an adjustable steel rod. When the brake is properly adjusted, the two cams should cause both brake shoes to come into contact with the brake drum simultaneously. If the rod or cams have been disturbed in any way, re-adjustment will need to be made. Also, if new brake shoes are fitted, it is probable that the relative points

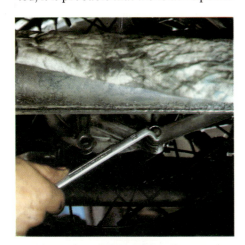

13. The rear brake torque arm must be attached to the brake plate before the wheel spindle is done up

at which the cams open will need to be altered in consequence.

There are several different methods of adjustment. The simplest way is to slacken off the locknut on the rod adjuster and pull one brake arm on. Alter the rod's length by screwing the barrel adjuster in or out until the pin connecting the rod and the non-cable brake arm tightens to show that the other lining is just beginning to bite. At this point, tighten the locknut (fig. 19), securely.

An alternative method of adjustment can be made by turning both cams simultaneously so that both shoes come in to contact with the drum, Then adjust the rod so that it is pulling both arms by the same amount.

You can measure the distance between the cam centres and the rod linkage centres on some bikes (fig. 20). Adjust the rod linkage to be equal in length to the distance between the cam centres when measured with a ruler. This will give an approximate setting, ready for fine adjustment.

Rear brake adjustment
On some models, the rear brake is operated by a cable similar to the front brake and adjustment is made in the same way.

14. The split pin or spring clip that secured the rear brake torque arm must not be forgotten

With rod operated types, simply screw the adjuster nut up until the required play is obtained at the brake pedal. It is a good idea to have about 10 to 25 mm (0.5 in. to 1 in.) of free movement at the pedal. In this way the brake light should come on just as the brake starts to bite (fig. 18).

If, after adjusting the brake the brake light switch fails to operate with the brake on, adjust it by undoing the locknut and moving the switch until it comes on immediately the pedal is depressed, and then doing up the lock-nut.

Riding with new brake shoes
Before setting off with rebuilt brakes,

15. The front brake cable is adjusted at the handlebar lever by screwing the cable stop out of the lever

16. On some bikes such as this Norton, there is an additional adjuster at the other end of the cable

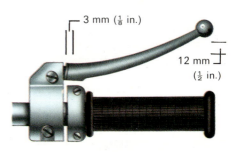

17. Adjust so the lever moves 12 mm ($\frac{1}{2}$ in.) at its end and 3 mm ($\frac{1}{8}$ in.) at the cable before the brake bites

whether front or rear or both, give the bike a quick test by rocking it backwards and forwards at walking speed. If all appears to be in order, ride off gently, gradually finding out the capabilities of the brake. There will inevitably be a period of running in until the brakes reach peak efficiency. Do not expect your brakes to be too good until the shoes have had time to bed in and conform to the shape of the drum. This may

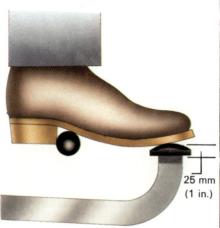

18. Leave about 25 mm (1 in.) of travel in the brake pedal before the rear brake bites, to operate stop lamp

19. To set up a TLS brake, adjust the rod linkage so both shoes contact the drum at once then do up lock-nut

20. As a rough measure, use a ruler to check the effective rod length against the cam separation

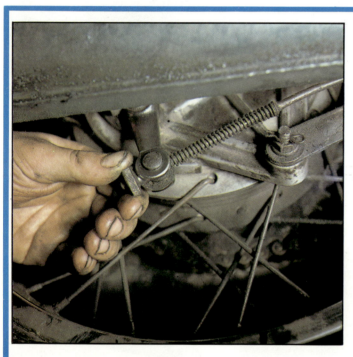

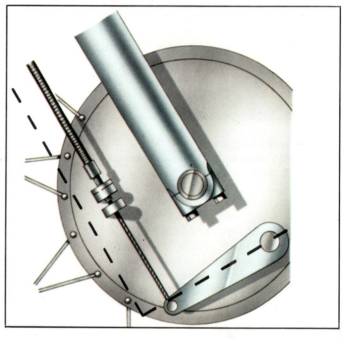

21. The rear brake adjustment is obtained with the knurled knob or nut on the brake rod

22. The angle (dashed lines) should not exceed 90 degrees when the brake is applied or efficiency is reduced

23. As part of your regular maintenance schedule, lightly grease the cams through any nipples provided

take several days of riding.

If a brake grabs and feels very fierce, it is probably due to inadequate chamfering of the linings. The brake should be stripped and dealt with as soon as possible. Ride carefully until the brakes are smooth and powerful in operation.

Regular brake maintenance

Apart from using occasional adjustment, the only regular maintenance a brake needs is light lubrication of the external moving parts. It is most important to keep cables free, so either drip oil down the cable inner, or use a cable oiler if you have one. Grease the lever where it pivots in the handlebar control, and the pedal shaft where it is attached to

the frame. Oil the linkages on a TLS brake and the points where the rear brake rod pivots to transmit movement. If your bike has a grease nipple on the cam, grease it periodically (fig. 23) with a single stroke of a grease gun.

The importance of correctly adjusted and well maintained brakes cannot be overstressed.

The difference between good and bad brakes can be the difference between a safe journey and a broken leg, or worse.

It is all too easy to get used to a gradual deterioration in the performance of the brakes, until disaster happens.

Make a point of servicing the brakes at regular intervals.

Renewing disc pads

Disc brakes normally provide powerful and reliable stopping. But to maintain their condition, the disc pads must be inspected and replaced at regular intervals.

Disc brakes consist of a metal disc, attached to the wheel hub, surmounted by a caliper that is fixed to a part of the chassis.

Inside the caliper are usually two friction pads set opposite each other. The disc rotates between the pads. At least one of the pads is moved out of its housing and on to the disc by a hydraulic piston operated by a slave cylinder in the caliper body. Fluid is prevented from passing between the cylinder and the piston by rubber seals.

Application of the brake lever generates hydraulic pressure in the master cylinder. Pressure is passed on through the system to the slave cylinder and the piston is forced toward the disc along with the brake pad. The disc is squashed between the brake pads, and when it is rotating is literally dragged to a stop (figs. 1 and 2).

If the brake is fitted to the front wheel, the caliper is mounted to a fork leg, or, on twin disc designs, both legs. The fluid reservoir and master cylinder are mounted on the handle bars. Some bikes have disc brakes fitted at the rear as well as the front. Both systems are usually completely isolated from each other and should be treated as separate entities. One exception is the integrated braking system used on Moto-Guzzi machines, where one front caliper and back brakes are joined into a single system.

Generally, the main differences between hydraulic disc brake designs are in the detail design of components, particularly the caliper mechanism. There are three types of caliper, the fixed type (fig. 2) and the floating type (fig. 1) which are both hydraulically operated, and the cable operated type (fig. 3).

Fixed calipers have two slave cylinders, one on either side of the disc. Both pads are rammed against the disc by hydraulic pressure.

Floating calipers have two brake pads, but only one moves. The caliper is mounted so that it slides or swings sideways. Applying the brakes causes the piston to push on one side of the disc and this action pulls the caliper across, until it comes into contact with the second, static pad and pulls this onto the disc.

Floating calipers are used on many modern machines and have the advantage over fixed types of fewer moving parts and cheaper production.

A variation of the floating caliper is the cable operated unit often used for light duties on small capacity bikes such as the Yamaha FS1E and the Honda CB125J. The principle of operation is similar to the hydraulic type but the moving pad is carried on the front of a guide-screw mechanism that winds the pad onto the disc (fig. 3). A self-adjusting ratchet built into the mechanism keeps brake lever travel constant as the pad wears down. Between the caliper and brake lever, the system is virtually identical to conventional cable operated drum brake systems.

Servicing disc brakes

Maintaining and servicing disc brakes falls into two sections: inspecting or changing the brake pads and bleeding or changing the fluid in the hydraulic system. This chapter deals with how to change brake pads on different disc types. The following pages 73–78 covers bleeding hydraulic systems and stripping and servicing calipers.

Hydraulic brakes should be progressive in operation and allow the rider to control the exact amount of braking force. Worn pads or contaminated brake fluid not only reduce braking efficiency but are extremely dangerous.

Many manufacturers specify service intervals for their brakes though these are bound to vary widely from rider to rider depending on how a bike is used. If you ride your bike very regularly you should check the condition of the pads at least every 3,000 km (2,000 miles).

Changing disc pads

Changing the pads is an easy job and should only take a few minutes to complete. A small screwdriver and a pair of long-nose pliers are helpful for extracting the pads and an essential item is silicone brake grease. This must be used to the exclusion of all other types of grease because it does not attack rubber seals or hydraulic system components. Some replacement brake pad kits include a sachet of silicone grease (fig. 13). Access to the pads for inspection, removal or replacement depends on the method used to hold them in place. A similar method may be common to different types of caliper. Access to the pads sometimes involves either removing the caliper (fig. 35) or taking the

Kawasaki KH100 EL

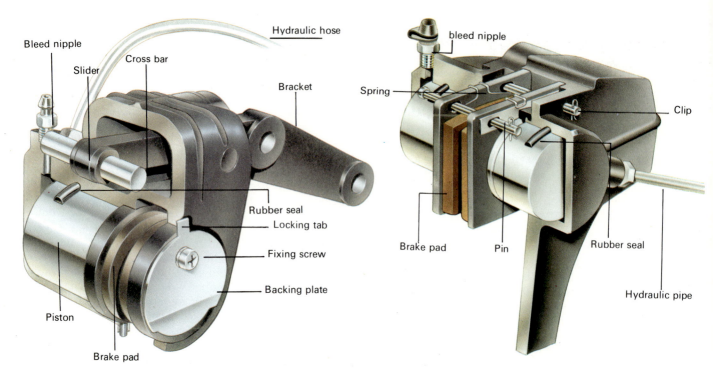

Bleed nipple
Slider
Cross bar
Hydraulic hose
Bracket
Rubber seal
Locking tab
Fixing screw
Backing plate
Piston
Brake pad

bleed nipple
Spring
Clip
Brake pad
Pin
Rubber seal
Hydraulic pipe

1. The floating caliper works by jamming one pad against the disc so that the caliper swings across to engage the other

2. The twin piston type uses hydraulic pressure to apply both pads to the disc simultaneously

wheel out (fig. 5).

If you unbolt the caliper make sure that you support it to avoid straining the pipe hoses or unions. Suspend the caliper from a convenient point with a piece of soft wire.

If your hydraulic pipes are metal you must be careful to release the end of the metal pipe to avoid bending it. If you

disconnect the pipes at the union the hydraulic system will have to be bled later. Alternatively, you can take the wheel out and leave the caliper in place.

Side access type
Calipers with side access to the disc pads are used on most Yamahas over 500 cc, nearly all Suzuki machines above 125 cc

and Kawasaki 650 cc, 750 cc, and 1,000 cc machines.

Use a crosshead screwdriver to undo the single screw retaining the convoluted backing plate on the inner wheel side of the caliper (fig. 36). The inner brake pad should then fall out. The outer pad can be pulled out with your fingers. If the pad is recessed into the slave cylinder bore, give the brake lever a gentle squeeze to bring the pad out. Do not squeeze the lever too hard or the entire piston assembly may pop out of the cylinder and necessitate bleeding the hydraulic system.

Hatch type
Access to the disc pads is gained by removing a hatch or inspection cover on top of the caliper body. Both floating and fixed caliper units employ this method but there are several variations in pad removal procedure depending on whether the pads are retained by crossbars, a spring loaded keeper or split pins.

To remove pads retained by crossbars, undo the single screw which holds the hatch cover in place over the pads. Pull off the spring clip on the end of each crossbar. Withdraw the crossbars complete with the pads from the caliper housing. Pull the pads from the crossbar unit and note which way round the anti-chatter plates fit (fig. 20).

Brembo brakes fitted to Moto-Guzzis, Laverdas and Ducatis have pads held by keeper pins. Undo any screws holding the inspection cover and lift it away. Remove the pads by depressing the spring-loaded keeper pin

Spring
Rubber cover
Slotted trunnion
Cable adjuster
Locknut
Pivot
High tensile bolt
Caliper cover
Self-adjusting mechanism
Nipple
Worm mechanism
Brake pad
Dowel

3. The cable operated caliper swings on a pivot, so that the unit is free to swing sideways when the pad is forced against the disc by a worm device

Changing the disc pads on a cable operated disc

4. Use a car jack to lift the bike up so that the wheel will clear the mudguard as it is removed

5. Release the speedo drive from the wheel hub. Undo the wheelnut and pull out the wheel spindle

6. Pull back the rubber cover, screw in the adjuster with a spanner to relax the tension on the cable

7. Undo the bolts holding the caliper cover in place, it will fall off leaving the mechanism exposed

8. Lift up the mechanism and push out the pad. Do not lose the dowel pin that fits in to the backing plate

9. The other pad is a press fit, prise this away from the housing with a screwdriver or long-nose pliers

Rupert Watts

and release the pins one at a time. Lift out the spring clip and draw out the central taper pin. Finally pull out the brake pads from the unit.

Some Triumphs use split pins to secure the brake pads (figs. 22 and 25). First unscrew the hatch cover to reveal the brake pads hung on split pins. Use long-nose pliers to straighten the pins. Pull them out from one side. It is essential that new split pins are fitted on reassembly and that the pins are re-located firmly so that they cannot rattle.

Clam type

Clam type calipers (such as used on the Honda CX500 and Norton Commando) contain pads which are removed from below the caliper unit. Such calipers are best removed from the bike to change the pads. But on the Norton the caliper can be left in position. Remove the front wheel and withdraw the pads with the aid of a small screwdriver (figs. 26 to 28).

Each pad has a lug which locates into the caliper body and a spring clip holds each pad firmly in place. Take the

spring pressure off the pads by easing them open with a small screwdriver, then pull the pads out.

It is a good idea to use long-nose pliers to do this properly.

Cable-operated discs

Several small capacity machines are fitted with cable operated discs. To take out the pads for inspection or replacement you must remove the caliper unit

Inspection and Renovation of Disc Pads

10. If the pad has a rubber seal see that it is intact; in this case one of the pads is badly chipped

11. A red wear line is scribed on the edge of the pad; this shows the minimum margin of safety

Continued

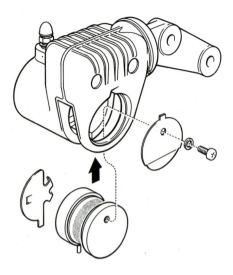

14. **Access to the pads is gained by removing the convoluted backing plate that screws into the pad**

from the bike.

Start by pulling back the rubber boot on the brake cable. Screw the adjuster right in so that the cable becomes as slack as possible and makes it easier to remove. Undo the bolts that hold the

caliper cover and remove it. Detach the brake cable from the brake arm by sliding the nipple out of its slot. With the caliper cover removed, the pad actuating mechanism can be withdrawn from the caliper unit. The moving pad is located on the end of the actuating mechanism by a locking ring. The ring should be a loose push fit, but is prevented from turning during operation of the brake by locating lugs. Pull off the ring and push out the pad. Take note of any positioning marks on the pad which indicate which way round it should be fitted.

The backing pad is simply a press fit in the caliper body and can be pulled straight out.

Inspecting the pads

Nearly all pads are marked with a line indicating their minimum operating thickness (fig. 11). Even if only one pad is worn down to, or below the line, both pads must be renewed as a matched set. If a wear line is not marked on the pads, measure their thickness (not including the backing plate), with a vernier caliper or ruler. The minimum thickness should

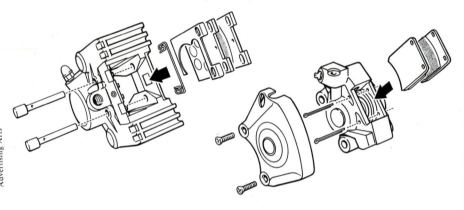

15 & 16. **Honda and Triumph calipers. The pads are inserted through the top of the unit, and are held in position by two cross pins**

12. **If the old pad is going to be put back in, clean up the face of the pad on a piece of emery cloth**

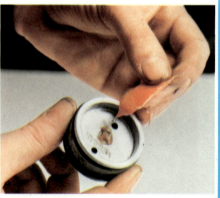

13. **Smear the sides and the rear of the pad with silicone brake grease. Use sparingly, keep away from the face**

Hatch caliper

17. **Access is through a hatch on top of the caliper. Undo the single screw that holds the cover in place**

18. **Remove the spring clip that locates through holes in the end of each of the keeper pins**

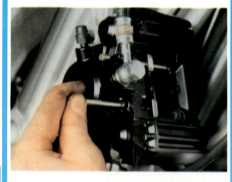

19. **Withdraw the keeper pin with a pair of pliers and pull out the pads together with the metal shim**

20. **The new pads have slotted surfaces to help bedding in. Remember to insert the shim next to the piston**

Advertising Arts

be about 3 mm (0.12 in.).

The pad should have a smooth flat surface. If part of the pad is scored or unevenly worn the disc may be running out of true. Check the disc before replacing the pads. This procedure is shown on page 69. If the surface is badly pitted (fig. 10) or chipped, renew the pads. If the surface area of the pad is reduced in any way, heat generated under braking will be concentrated over a smaller area and cause local burning. Abnormally high temperatures affect the efficiency of the whole system.

If the pad is contaminated with a small amount of oil or grease, it can be cleaned with a volatile solvent like white spirit. Inspect the caliper for tell-tail runs of hydraulic fluid from the slave cylinder or the fork seals. If the pads are to be used again, rub faces on a piece of emery paper laid on a flat surface (fig. 12).

Wipe out the inside of the caliper with

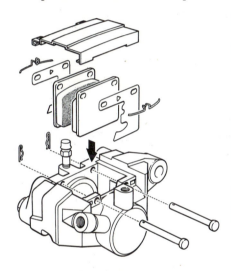

21. **A twin piston caliper used on the rear disc of a Suzuki GS1000. Note the arrangement of the shims**

Lockheed hatch-type caliper

22. **Take off the chrome cover by removing the screws at the top and bottom of the caliper**

23. **Lift off the cover. You can inspect the pads in situ. If they need to be replaced then continue dismantling**

24. **Straighten the split pins with a pair of pliers and pull them out. Remember to fit new split pins**

25. **Take out the old pads. Push on the piston so that it makes room for the new brake pads**

a clean dry cloth. Smear the back and side of the brake pad with a thin film of brake grease but use the grease sparingly. An alternative lubricant is brake fluid which can be lightly dabbed on the back of the pad plate (fig. 13).

Refitting pads and calipers
Fit the pads to the caliper by a reversal of the removal procedure.

Use a screwdriver to push the piston carefully back into the slave cylinder so that the caliper can be slotted on to the

Norton Lockheed clam-type caliper

26. **Release the wheel nut and tap out the spindle. Drop the wheel clear of the forks and mudguard**

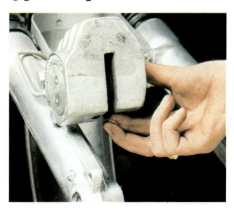

27. **The pads are located in circular slots in the caliper and they can be reached from underneath**

28. **The pads are a press fit. Prise them out with the aid of a small screwdriver or pliers**

Rupert Watts

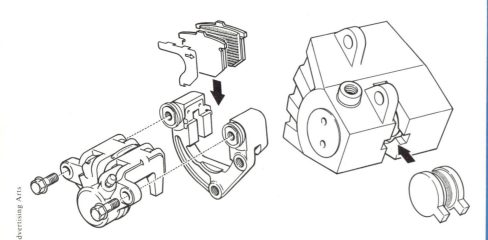

29. On the left is a Honda clam caliper showing the piston unit detached from the bracket. Access to the Norton caliper is from the underneath and there is no need to remove the inspection cover on the side

disc. With everything reassembled, lift the front of the bike and spin the wheel to make sure it runs smoothly without snatching. Before you move the bike, pump the brake lever several times so that the slave cylinder is properly positioned. Take the bike out for a slow run to test your handiwork. If new pads have been fitted, use the brakes gently to help bedding in for 80 km (50 miles).

Twin piston Hatch caliper

30. Take off the plastic inspection cover on top of the caliper, it comes off with finger pressure

31. Pull out the clips that pin through the centre of each of the cross pins

32. Use your fingers to press down the springs that hold the pins and draw the pin out with pliers

33. Remove the brake pads and the shims behind them. Reassemble the shims with the arrow pointing forwards

Side access type

34. The caliper must be removed from the forks in order to inspect the condition of the pads

35. Unscrew the bolts that fix the unit to the front forks, cup your hand around the unit as it falls free

36. Turn the caliper upside down, undo the single screw in the centre, the pad should fall out

37. Use a screwdriver to jiggle the other pad until it will clear the piston and drop out

Bleeding disc brakes

The life blood of a hydraulic braking system is the fluid it contains. If the fluid escapes or becomes contaminated the system will suffer a dangerous loss of pressure that could leave you without brakes when you need them most. Aim to keep your brakes in peak condition by thorough maintenance.

Hydraulic disc brakes, with their superior braking capabilities over drums are fitted, on the front wheel at least, to the majority of modern bikes. There are slight variations in different manufacturers' designs but the basic principle of operation is shared by all systems.

Basic operation

Two main components are common to every hydraulic disc brake, the reservoir (or master cylinder) which is normally mounted on the handlebar, and the brake caliper containing the brake pads, which is mounted on the front fork or on the swinging arm. Operating the brake lever forces the hydraulic fluid from the master cylinder towards the wheel cylinder. Because hydraulic fluid is virtually incompressible, lever pressure is transferred, via the specially constructed brake hoses to the brake caliper, and brings the brake pads to bear on the disc.

There are several basic variations in hydraulic brake caliper operation. A common system uses a fixed caliper containing two pistons and friction pads which bear on either side of the disc. Alternatively, there may be only one moving piston and pad and the caliper moves. (This floating caliper type is shown in fig. 1.) Less common is a disc that floats sideways (floating disc).

Whatever the variations in design, regular maintenance of the hydraulic link between the handlebar lever and the brake caliper is essential if the brake is to function efficiently.

The essence of the hydraulic system is the pressure under which the fluid operates. If the hydraulic pressure is not sustained, effort between the handlebar lever and brake pads will be lost, along with braking power. A typical hydraulic disc brake system operates at about 15 kg/cm^2 (200 psi).

Two conditions are necessary to maintain hydraulic pressure, a fluid-tight system and an incompressible fluid.

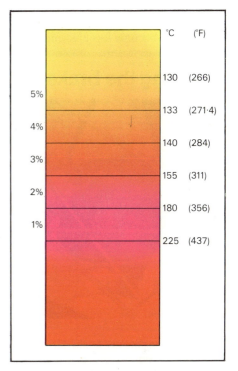

	°C	(°F)
5%	130	(266)
4%	133	(271·4)
3%	140	(284)
2%	155	(311)
1%	180	(356)
	225	(437)

2. As the percentage of brake fluid contamination increases the boiling point of the fluid will fall

The fluid-tightness of the system depends on various seals which are

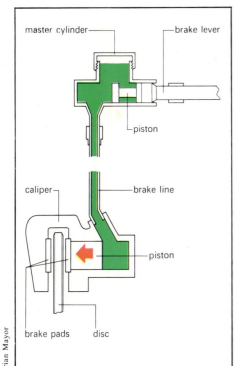

Brian Mayor

1. A typical hydraulic disc brake master cylinder and caliper set-up. This is a floating caliper type

Testing a trail bike – Kawasaki KL250

designed to keep the fluid inside and the air outside. They must be maintained in perfect condition. Faulty seals will show up by a trickle of fluid at the leak point, or a consistently low level of fluid in the reservoir.

Fluid will become less efficient or fail altogether under pressure if it becomes contaminated. Contamination can arise from water vapour, dirt or air entering the system.

Hydraulic brake fluid is hygroscopic (absorbs moisture), and has a finite life due to the phenomenon of 'vapour lock'. This occurs when enough water is absorbed by the fluid to lower its effective boiling point (fig. 2). If the fluid does boil when the brakes get hot the brakes will fail. Brake fluid can be tested for water content but this is a job best left to a specialist. In any case,

Bleeding the brakes

3. First fit the spanner to the bleed valve and then push the plastic bleed pipe over the nipple-like protrusion.

4. Place the free end of the bleed piping into the glass container and fill with enough fluid to submerge it

5. Pump the brake lever several times to build up pressure in the system before opening the bleed valve

6. Open the bleed valve one complete turn. Do not release the brake lever once you have opened the valve

7. Press the brake lever fully against the handlebar and watch for air bubbles escaping from the bleed piping

8. Replenish the brake fluid reservoir as necessary during the operation to stop air entering through it

Rupert Watts

brake fluid is inexpensive and should be renewed if you suspect contamination.

Different brake fluid manufacturers specify different working life spans for their products and their recommendations should be followed carefully. But unless symptoms of brake faults occur or periodic visual checks show no trace of leaks it should not be necessary to change the fluid more often than every two years or 28,000 km (18,000 miles). Similarly the piston assembly in the master cylinder and caliper need not be disturbed unless they develop a fault or their service is due.

Dirt in the hydraulic system may well damage the fragile seals. If by any chance mineral oil enters the system the seals will swell, jamming the brakes in the on position. In cases of oil contamination renew all the seals, the flexible hoses and the fluid.

Air may get in to the hydraulic system either through a leaky seal or through the reservoir if the brake fluid is allowed to drop below the supply duct opening. The operation of removing air and contaminants from the hydraulic system is called bleeding. And the brake system should be bled whenever the action at the front brake lever feels spongy, when brake fluid is changed or if a brake line fitting has been loosened or disconnected.

Bleeding the brakes
Bleeding the brakes is a simple operation and should only take a few minutes from start to finish. But before you start you will need to obtain a few pieces of equipment to assist with the bleeding procedure and to observe some simple precautions.

A small flat ring spanner is needed to open the caliper bleed valve. Find a glass jar, an old coffee jar will do, to bleed the fluid into. Make sure that the jar is scrupulously clean beforehand. Do not use a plastic container as brake fluid will dissolve some types of plastic. Buy a length of clear pipe – about 30 cm (12 in.) should be enough. This is sold at most accessory shops specifically for brake bleeding. Failing this you can use a piece of fuel line pipe or a car's windscreen washer tubing. Depending on whether you are going to bleed out all of the hydraulic fluid or just some of it, you will need an appropriate size can of fresh fluid. Ensure that you buy the recommended type. As a rough guide you will need about 250 ml for a 'light' bleed, 500 ml to change the fluid completely on a single disc system, and about one litre for three disc systems.

As a precaution against introducing contaminants into the system carry out the bleeding procedure paying strict attention to general cleanliness. Before starting, wash the machine to clear away road dirt and particles of grit. Brake fluid is very corrosive and will attack plastic and paintwork if allowed to come into contact with them. It is a good idea, therefore, to cover the petrol tank and instruments with a piece of polythene sheet or absorbent rag. Keep a bucket of water on hand to wash off any fluid spilled accidentally.

Start the bleeding operation by fitting a spanner on to the bleed valve (fig. 3). The valve should be evident as the nipple-like protrusion on the brake caliper. Push the bleed piping over the bleed valve (fig. 3) and put the free end into the glass container. Fill the container with enough fresh brake fluid to keep the free end submerged (fig. 4). This stops air from passing back into the hydraulic system during the bleed-

Renewing master cylinder brake seals

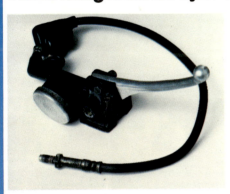

9. A typical hydraulic brake master cylinder. Remove it from the handlebar before dismantling it

10. Undo the brake lever pivot bolt using a suitable spanner, then remove the lever

11. Prise the dust cover retaining clip off with a small screwdriver and pull off the dust cover

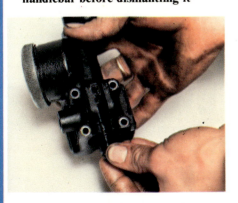

12. Pull the piston assembly out of its bore. Note the order of the parts as they are removed

13. Use an air line or bicycle pump to blow out the primary cap spring and the secondary cap

14. The component parts of the master cylinder ready for inspection. Renew all seals and O-rings

ing procedure. Before opening the bleed valve remove the fluid reservoir cap. Check the brake fluid level and top it up if necessary. Throughout the bleeding operation the reservoir must not be allowed to empty. Keep it at least half-full. If the reservoir runs dry during the operation bleeding must be started again as air will be sucked into the system.

Squeeze the handlebar lever fully and release it rapidly in a pumping action to build up pressure in the system (fig. 5). Now open the bleed valve one complete turn whilst continuing to maintain pressure on the handlebar lever (fig. 6). Pump the lever several times until air bubbles are visible, rising from the fluid in the jar. Keep pumping the lever using long slow strokes until no more bubbles appear. On the final stroke at this stage keep the lever pulled firmly against the handlebar as far as it will go and tighten the valve (fig. 7).

On some systems quicker results may be got by tightening the bleed screw lightly when the lever is released. This will stop any bubbles in the outlet pipe being drawn back into the system as the seals relax. Finally, fill up the reservoir to the upper level indicated on the master cylinder and replace the cap. In the case of those reservoir caps which are secured by four cross-head screws, care should be taken not to overtighten the screws.

If twin discs are fitted, repeat the operation on the other caliper. If an integrated braking system is used, such as fitted to some Moto Guzzis, start on the front calipers first, then bleed the rear. Where two bleed valves per caliper are found, the procedure is straightforward. You just bleed each one in turn.

When bleeding is being carried out after parts of the hydraulic system have been removed, fill the master cyclinder and pump fluid through it with the brake lever. Continue until air bubbles stop coming up through the relief port in the bottom of the reservoir. The system can then be bled normally from the caliper end.

Servicing hydraulic components

Hydraulic components should need servicing only at major intervals. Servicing usually involves dismantling the master cylinder and caliper to replace the seals, and removing the hydraulic hoses to check the condition of the unions.

It may be tempting not to strip the hydraulic components especially if they show no signs of leaking. But if the recommended working life span of their seals has run out, it could be dangerous to leave them. A deteriorating seal will usually allow fluid to weep past it. Regular inspection should reveal the tell-tale trace giving you plenty of warning and time to rectify the problem. Occasionally, however, seals may break down with no warning – often with disastrous results, as the brakes suddenly fail.

Servicing the master cylinder

Before the master cylinder can be removed for inspection the brake system must be drained of brake fluid. Attach a pipe to the bleed valve, open the valve one turn and pump out the fluid by repeatedly squeezing the brake lever. When the system is empty, unscrew the banjo bolt to free the brake hose from the master cylinder.

On nearly every bike the master cylinder is fixed to the lever unit on the

Renewing caliper seals: floating caliper

15. Split the brake caliper after the through bolts have been removed. Renew them if at all corroded

16. Remove the dust seal by simply pulling it away from the caliper. Renew it on reassembly

17. Prise the spring band off the brake caliper with a pointed tool or thin screwdriver

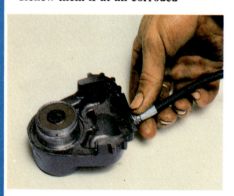

18. Blow the piston out of the cylinder with an air line or bicycle pump. Do not let it fly out

19. Prise the piston seal out of the cylinder with a pointed tool. Take care not to scratch the bore

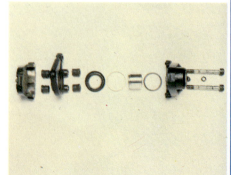

20. The component parts of the brake caliper ready for inspection. Renew all the seals and O-rings

Renewing caliper seals: fixed caliper

21. A typical fixed brake caliper removed from the fork leg. There is no need to remove the brake pipe

22. Unscrew the piston cap to gain access to the pistons. Use two small bolts held in a vice

23. Push the first piston out of the brake caliper with a screwdriver. Protect the end with a piece of rubber

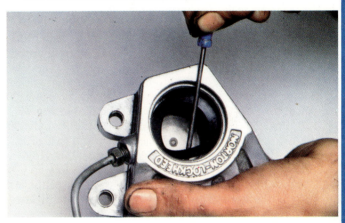

24. Prise the piston seal out of the cylinder with a small screwdriver

25. Blow the second piston out of the brake caliper with an air line or bicycle pump

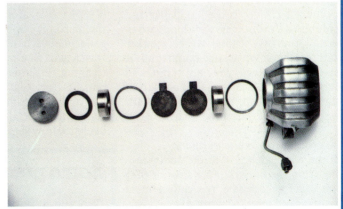

26. The component parts of the caliper ready for inspection. Renew all seals and O-rings

Rupert Watts

handlebar, and is removed by undoing the clamp bolts. However on some bikes the master cylinder is located under the petrol tank and is operated by a cable from the brake lever. Disconnect the cable and unbolt the master cylinder. Dismantling is then dealt with in exactly the same way as conventional types.

With the master cylinder off the machine undo, the lever pivot bolt and remove the lever (fig. 10). The master cylinder piston should now be visible though it may be covered with a rubber dust cover or shroud. If the cover is retained by a spring clip or a circlip, pull it off with circlip pliers (fig. 11). The piston assembly can then be withdrawn easily (fig. 12).

On some models, such as the Moto Guzzi V-twins, you will have to push out the piston by inserting a short smooth rod into the brake hose fluid outlet hole.

Before further dismantling, note the position of the piston assembly components and place the assembly carefully to one side. Use a bicycle pump to blow out the primary cap spring and the secondary cap (fig. 13). Going back to the piston, prise off the seals from the piston rod taking great care not to scratch the piston. Clean all components with fresh brake fluid or alcohol. Do not use petrol, paraffin or abrasive or you may damage the delicate components. After cleaning carefully examine the components.

Worn seals usually show up as dull areas, possibly with scratches around the tips where the sealing surface has been abraded by the cylinder wall. Signs of swelling could indicate a poor or incorrect seal seating on the piston rod or oil contamination of the brake fluid. Ideally the working surface or seats of the piston should be highly polished with no scores or corrosion. If signs of corrosion are noticed the piston must be renewed or it will rapidly destroy the new seals. The inside of the master cylinder should be similarly inspected for scratches, rust or pitting and renewed if badly marked.

Before fitting new seals on the pistons, soak them in fresh brake fluid. Assembly is the reverse of the dismantling sequence.

Most master cylinder assemblies feature a dished washer in the piston assembly. Make sure that the washer is installed the right way round, that is with the hollow side of the washer facing into the bore. Throughout the reassembly operation conditions of ultra cleanliness must be observed; the slightest speck of dirt could ruin all your careful work.

Once reassembled fit the master cylinder back on to the handlebar and reconnect the brake hose, taking care to install the two sealing washers either side of the hose as the banjo bolt is installed. Unless you are going to service the brake caliper, the final part of the operation is to fill the cylinder with brake fluid and bleed the system.

Servicing the brake caliper

If there is evidence of brake fluid weeping from the brake caliper seals or they are due for a service, the caliper must be removed and dismantled.

Start by disconnecting the brake pipe from the caliper. Unscrew the caliper gland nut and pull the pipe out. Wrap a piece of polythene over the end of the pipe and secure it with an elastic band; this prevents dirt entering the system and brake fluid from escaping. Take precautions to stop the brake fluid from coming into contact with paintwork or plastic surfaces as described on page 75.

Remove the caliper from the fork leg. The caliper can be split by undoing the through bolts (fig. 15). Badly corroded bolts should be renewed using only genuine parts when the

Brake lines

27. Bend and twist the flexible brake hose to check for splits. Renew it if there is any sign of damage

28. Make sure that the hose does not rub against any adjacent part and that it follows its proper route

caliper is split. Look for a dust seal and a circlip or spring band (fig. 16), which in some cases must be removed before the piston will come out. But on some types of caliper, the piston has to be removed first (fig. 23). Blow the piston out of the cylinder with the air pressure from a garage air-line or a bicycle pump (fig. 25). Hold a clean rag over the piston to stop it flying out.

If the piston is seized, free it by soaking in methylated spirit. Such a seized piston however is unlikely to be serviceable and really should be replaced. With the piston out of the caliper, prise out the oil seals from the cylinder with a pointed tool such as a thin screwdriver (fig. 24). All piston seals and O-rings on the through bolts and in the fluid gallery between the caliper halves should be renewed as a matter of course. After cleaning, examine the caliper components for wear in exactly the same way as described for the master cylinder components. Caliper bores are least likely to show signs of wear or corrosion

damage, but if corrosion or damage is evident you should renew the complete caliper unit. Reassemble and reinstall the brake caliper on the bike, then make a check of the brake pipes or hoses.

Checking brake hoses

Check the flexible hoses for splits or scuffing by bending and twisting them (fig. 27). If they are damaged (fig. 27), make no attempt to repair them, they must be renewed. Change hoses every second year as a matter of course because they perish over time. Metal pipes should be checked for cracks around the union connections. When replacing the hydraulic hoses or rigid pipes, it is important to ensure that they are positioned to prevent rubbing against any adjacent part. This can be achieved by making sure that the hose or pipe takes the route which the manufacturer intended it to do. When tightening a union nut or banjo bolt, thread the pipes through all retaining brackets or arms before bolting them back.

Some precautions

Work in ultra-clean conditions with hands free from grit and only use rag that will not fragment or deposit fluff when cleaning components.

Never re-use old brake fluid.

Do not use brake fluid that has been stored in an unsealed container. Transfer any small amount of brake fluid that may be left over into a smaller can.

Use only the correct brake fluid and do not mix brand types. Universal brake and clutch fluid labelled DOT 3 or SAE J1703 should be used.

Never shake the brake fluid can.

Use fresh brake fluid or alcohol for cleaning brake parts. Petrol, paraffin or engine oil will cause deterioration of the rubber parts.

Be careful not to spill brake fluid on the disc pads. Wash them in methylated spirit if this happens

If any of the brake line fittings are disturbed or the bleed valve is opened at any time, the air must be bled from the brake.

Keep brake fluid off paintwork or plastic parts.

Carburettor maintenance

Carburettor cleaning and adjustment is part of a bike's routine maintenance every 3,000 to 5,000 km (2,000–3,000 miles). But if, between services, you notice any engine roughness, difficult starting, an erratic tickover or a tendency for the engine to cut out when it should be idling, the carburettor may need immediate attention.

The function of the carburettor is to atomize the petrol into a mist of liquid fuel and to mix it with air before it enters the combustion chamber. This mixture must be in the proper proportions to suit the operating conditions of the engine.

Bike manufacturers set the carburation of each model to obtain the best balance between good performance and fuel economy, and the object of the carburettor adjustments at the stipulated service intervals is to maintain this balance. These regular adjustments compensate for the vibration and wear which gradually affect the accuracy of the carburation settings.

If the bike is used for a period of time at the wrong idle speed or mixture, it can lead to problems such as sooty plugs and difficult starting or slow-speed running which can be annoying on cold mornings or if the bike stalls in traffic. Such a situation could be dangerous.

Preliminaries

Certain preliminaries have to be carried out before adjusting any carburettor. These are most important and should not be omitted in any circumstances, because the carburettor is extremely sensitive to other engine conditions, and its adjustment is the *last* job of all when you are servicing the engine.

First, before adjusting the carburation, the rest of the engine must be in perfect condition. The spark plug must be in good condition with the correct gap between its electrodes. The contact-breaker points must be clean and gapped according to the manufacturer's specification, the ignition timing must be accurate and the automatic advance working correctly. The valve clearances must be set, the camshaft chain (if fitted) must be set correctly, the air filter fitted and clean, and the exhaust system in good condition. The fuel pipes and filters must also be free of leaks and

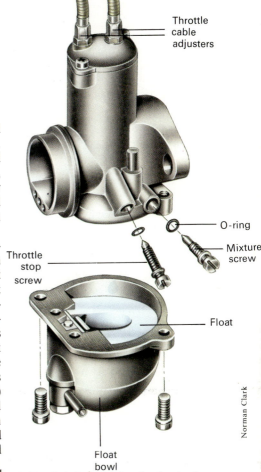

1. **Exploded view of a simple single slide-type carburettor, showing the adjustment points**

obstructions.

Next, the carburettor itself must be free of petrol leaks and blocked jets, and the inlet manifold free of air leaks.

Finally, make sure that all throttle cables, choke cables, and throttle linkages run smoothly, do not bind, and are in good condition. And check the choke control to make sure it is fully open or in the 'off' position. If the choke is on, or even partly on, this will ruin your carburettor adjustment.

Cleaning the float-bowl

The float bowl must be cleaned at the specified service interval. Dirt, sediment and water gradually accumulate at the bottom of the float bowl, and if left there, may eventually enter the carburettor jets and block them, causing fuel starvation, and perhaps flooding the carburettor by jamming open the float needle.

First, you need to identify the float chamber. Most recent bikes have it directly beneath the main body of the carburettor. But the float chamber on

Yamaha RD 400

2. The Amal on a Triumph 500, showing (1) cable adjuster, (2) throttle-stop screw and (3) mixture screw

3. Mikuni on a Yamaha RD200, showing (1) cable adjuster, (2) throttle-stop screw and (3) mixture screw

4. Keihin carburettor on a Honda CB175 showing (1) cable adjuster, (2) throttle-stop screw and (3) mixture screw

5. The Dell'Orto carburettor on a Garelli 50 moped, showing (1) the mixture screw and (2) the throttle-stop screw

Nelson Hargreaves

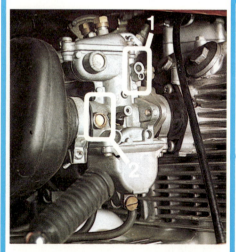

6. Keihins on a Honda CB400, showing (1) master throttle-stop screw and (2) mixture screw with plastic limiter cap

the Amal monobloc, as on most British machines of the 1960s, is located on the side of the carburettor.

The float bowl can be retained in several ways. On the Amal concentric, there are two or four screws. The commonest Dell'Orto has a single large screw on the bottom of the float bowl. Keihin carburettors on most Hondas have a large retainer clip that clips tight underneath the float bowl.

Next, make sure the petrol taps are in the 'off' position, and have a container handy to capture the excess petrol from the float bowl. Then free the float bowl and gently pull it straight downwards to avoid damaging the floats or the main jet.

Pour the petrol into the container, and clean the sediment out of the bottom of the float bowl with a clean, non-fluffy cloth, making sure the bowl is completely clean. Rinse the bowl through with petrol.

Replace the float bowl, making sure that the float bowl gasket is not damaged and that the floats are not disturbed.

Finally, turn on the petrol, and check that petrol is not leaking from the float bowl joint. If it does leak, undo the float bowl, check the condition of the gasket, and repeat the procedure, making sure that the bowl seats squarely against the carburettor body.

Adjusting the carburettor(s)
On all bikes except those fitted with emission-control carburettors, the adjustment procedure is much the same.

First you have to get the mixture setting right, or very close, by turning in the mixture screw until you feel a resistance and then turning it out again. On most bikes the amount needed is about two turns, but requirements may vary depending on individual makes of carburettor. Then you must adjust the throttle stop screw until the engine idles at the correct speed of about 1100 rpm.

This doesn't always work at the first attempt. If it doesn't, and the engine sounds rough, you have to adjust the mixture screw very slightly – varying, by no more than one-eighth of a turn, the amount by which you turn it out.

On emission-control carburettors the procedure is much simpler. A plastic blanking plug prevents your getting access to the mixture screw, which has been pre-set by the manufacturer, and all you can do is adjust the throttle-stop at this stage.

So before you can begin work, you need to identify which type of carburettor you have.

Two basic types of carburettor design are used on motorcycles:
1. The sliding-piston throttle-valve type, known for short as the 'slide' type.
2. The constant-vacuum butterfly-valve type, usually known for short as the CV carburettor.

The rest of the chapter deals with the first of the two types. The CV carburettor, its adjustment and balance is covered in the next chapter (pages 85 to 87).

Slide carburettors

Slide-type throttle-valve carburettors are used on most English bikes, most older bikes (English and foreign), some 4-cylinder Japanese bikes such·as the Kawasaki Z1 and Honda 750s, most Japanese singles and many twins. They are also used on nearly all 2-stroke machines.

The slide-type carburettor (figs. 1 and 17) can be identified by its tall, thin appearance. The body of the carburettor is usually tall, round and thin, although

some of the Dell'Orto range have a square-shaped body. If the throttle cable enters the carburettor at the very top of carburettor it is always a slide type.

Usually the choke cable will also enter at the top. But some Hondas, like the CB200 and CD175, have a piston-type throttle valve with the choke operated by a lever at the side of the carburettor.

Most modern twins, threes and four-carburettor bikes have their throttle valves operated by a common linkage with individual rockers on each carburretor. On these, twin throttle cables are often used, one to open and one to close the throttle valves.

The CV carburettor is quite different in shape, much shorter and fatter with

How to use a Colortune kit

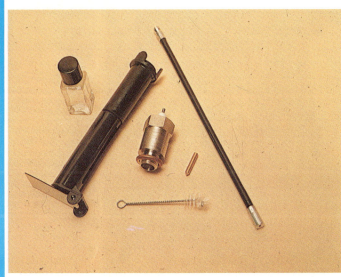

7. A Colortune kit has a glass-topped spark plug which shows you the colour of the combustion chamber flame

8. With the engine thoroughly warm, remove No. 1 spark plug from the engine and fit the Colortune plug in its place

9. Next, screw the plain end of the black adaptor lead on to the centre electrode of the plug

10. Now fit the viewerscope. Its lower half slides over the lead; the claw end goes over the flats of the plug

Nelson Hargreaves

Continued

11. Slide the adaptor lead up the slot in the upper half of the viewerscope, pushing it on to the lower half

12. Clip the free end of the adaptor lead into the plug cap, and adjust the viewerscope mirror

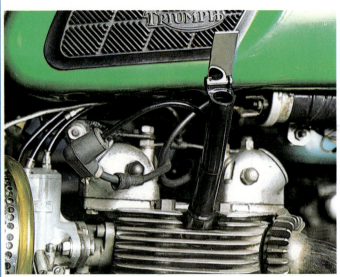

13. The viewerscope is included to help you see any 'awkward' plugs. It need not always be used

14. Start the engine, warm it up, and let it tick over at idling speed – around 1,200 rpm for most bikes

15. Adjust the mixture until the flame glows blue in the glass. Bright orange indicates too rich a mixture

16. To remove the Colortune, loosen it with a plug spanner and unscrew it by the adaptor lead or viewerscope

no cables entering at the top of the carburettor.

Having identified your carburettor as a slide type, you must now locate the throttle stop screw and the mixture screw.

Adjustment screw

The throttle-stop screw regulates the idling speed of the engine. The mixture screw regulates the fuel-air mixture used by the engine when it is idling, by varying either the amount of air or the amount of fuel in the mixture.

On carburettors whose throttle cable enters at the top, such as the Amal Concentric on the Norton Commando or the Keihin on the Honda CB200 and CB175, the throttle stop screw is situated on the main body of the carburettor in line with the neck of the carburettor, and screws into the carburettor. The mixture screw is situated to the left or the right of the carburettor, and *below* or in front of the throttle stop screw – never above it.

The mixture screws on some carburettors, like the sliding throttle valve Bing, may be situated underneath the inlet mouth of the carburettor, next to the air filter.

On a multi-cylinder bike with a bank of carburettors, there is only one master throttle-stop screw, situated at the top of the carburettor on the central linkage mechanism. On these, the mixture screw is usually beneath the main body of the carburettor. Early Suzuki 380 and 550 2-stroke triples have three carburettors with a separate throttle cable entering the top of each carburettor, without any throttle linkage. The throttle-stop screw adjustments on these have to be done individually.

Single carburettors

Before adjusting any of the screws, make sure that the engine has reached its normal running temperature. Then make sure that there is plenty of play in the throttle cable by loosening the cable adjuster on the handlebars. This ensures that the throttle valves (or throttle valve linkage) are fully closed against the throttle-stop screw.

Next you must adjust the setting on the mixture screw. Every carburettor has a specified setting for this screw, but if you have no handbook you can try $1\frac{1}{2}$–2 turns out from the fully-in position. So carefully screw in the mixture screw until you feel a very slight resistance. The engine should falter and 'die'. Then unscrew the mixture screw the specified amount $1\frac{1}{2}$–2 complete turns), start the engine again and let it settle. It may now be running too slow or too fast. (Too fast will be about 1500 rpm, too slow about 600 rpm.) So swap to the throttle-stop adjuster, and turn it in or out to find the best, and smoothest, tickover at about 1100 rpm.

If the tickover is not satisfactory, adjust the mixture screw by turning it out a little more or a little less than the recommended figure, and adjust the throttle stop screw accordingly.

When you are satisfied, remember to take up any excess slack in the throttle cable until you have between zero and 2 mm of free play at the handlebar adjuster.

Twins with separate cables

On twin-carburettor bikes, without a linkage between the carburettors, adjust the carburettors separately, but using the same procedure as for a single carburettor. To make sure they are idling at the same speed, let the engine run on one cylinder at a time while you compare the idling speeds. (To do this, detach the spark plug and lead from one cylinder and allow it to earth by laying it on its side on the cylinder head so that it makes metal-to-metal contact.) If they are different, adjust the throttle stop screws to make them even. Then replace

the plug cap you have just had off. You will probably find that the engine runs too quickly, now that both cylinders are firing. So turn both throttle adjuster screws back by *exactly* the same amount to get the tickover right.

Readjust the throttle cables as described above, and waggle the handlebars to make sure there is no tight spot in the cable that will make the engine race. Then check the throttle response by 'blipping' the throttle. If the engine revs are slow to drop, either the engine is running on too lean a mixture or the automatic advance is stuck in the open position. Turn the mixture screws in or out slightly, and by an equal amount, then adjust the throttle stop screw accordingly.

Twins with linked carburettors

Adjusting an engine with twin, linked carburettors involves much the same procedure as a carburettor with separate throttle cables, except that the throttle-stop screw will be on the linkage mechanism at the top of the carburettor.

The best procedure is to screw in the mixture screws on both carburettors until you feel the small resistance, then unscrew them by the specified amount, and finally adjust the idling speed by turning the master throttle stop screw.

Four-cylinder models

On 4-cylinder models it is difficult to adjust the mixture – but unlikely that it is much out. Slacken off the opening throttle cable, and adjust the master throttle-stop screw situated at the top of the carburettors on the linkage mechanism to find the correct idling speed (approximately 1100 rpm). Then adjust the throttle cable to 2 mm free play at the lever; make sure there is no tight spot along the run of the cable.

Balancing a twin

Once the throttle-stop and mixture screws are at their correct setting, the next stage on a twin- or multi-carburettor bike is to synchronize the carburettors – that is, to make sure the throttle valve in one carburettor opens at exactly the same moment as the throttle valve in the other. If this does not happen the bike feels rough and flat during acceleration.

Non-linked twins

On twin carburettors without a linking mechanism, first make sure that there is the correct amount of play, 2 mm, in the throttle cable at the twistgrip. Then

17. Multiple slide-type carburettor, as found on many large Japanese bikes, showing throttle adjustment points

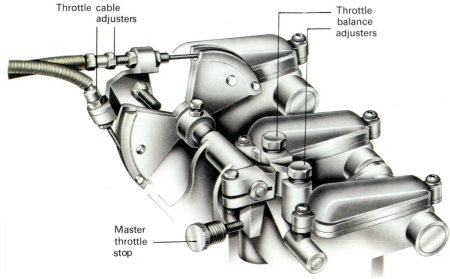

Throttle cable adjusters

Throttle balance adjusters

Master throttle stop

Norman Clark

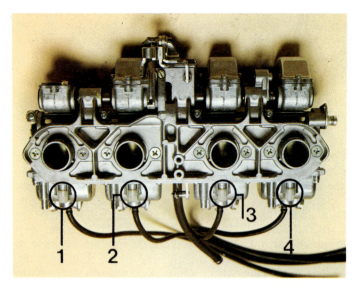

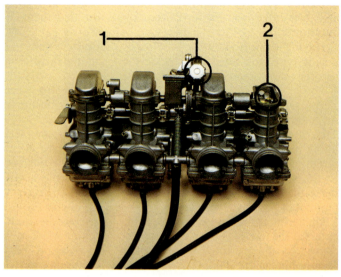

18. The backs of four Mikunis for a 4-cylinder Kawasaki with the rather inaccessible mixture screws (1, 2, 3 and 4)

19. The same carburettors from the front, showing (1) the master throttle-stop screw and (2) the balance adjuster

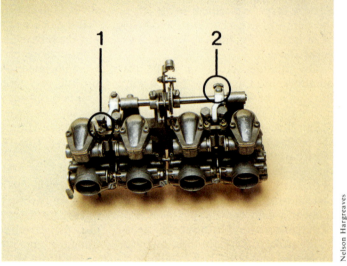

20. Small Keihin, with (1) mixture and (2) throttle-stop screws

21. Bank of four Keihin carburettors for the Honda CB500. (Left) one mixture screw. (Right) the balance adjuster screw (1) and master throttle-stop screw (2)

peel back the rubber gaiter that leads from the air filter to the carburettor.

For the next stage you will need a friend to help you. Put one finger down one carburettor intake until you can feel the throttle valve. Put another finger down the other. Then ask your friend to open the throttle slowly. You will feel the throttle valves moving upwards. Ask your friend to repeat the procedure until you are sure that both are moving together.

If they are moving together the carburettors are synchronized, and you can replace the rubber bellows in their normal position. If the carburettors are not opening at the same time, ask your friend to open the throttle slowly until he has full throttle. Make sure he does not let the throttle shut suddenly. The edge of the throttle valve should now be flush with the top of the chamber.

If you have felt one carburettor open before the other, the 'later' carburettor will not be flush with the top of the chamber. So let the throttle slowly close again, this time making sure that the carburettor that opens first closes fully. If it does close fully you must adjust the other carburettor. Undo the locknut at the top of the carburettor where the cable enters, and turn *out* the cable adjuster.

Now feel the throttles again. This procedure must be repeated until you are satisfied that the two throttle valves open at the same time. Finally, check that both valves open fully, and close fully. Then make sure that the locknut is fully tight. Check the throttle by blipping the engine. It should feel clear and smooth, and the exhaust noise from each cylinder should be about the same.

Linked twins

The same procedure as for non-linked twins is used on twins with the linked system. But here the rockers on the top

of the carburettors will have to be exposed by undoing the rocker covers. Then the adjustment is made by undoing the locknut and turning the adjuster.

Some linked carburettors may have an adjuster mounted externally on the linkage. Here, the procedure for synchronizing the carburettors is the same. The importance of balancing carburettors cannot be overstressed. It will make the bike an efficient convertor of fuel into mechanical energy and keep petrol consumption down.

The carburettor is one of the most precision turned devices on the bike and adjusting it properly requires care and great attention to detail.

If in doubt as to the correct settings for any given type of carb, refer to the instruction manual where manufacturer's specifications for carb settings should be clearly laid out.

Treat your carburettor with care and give it the respect it deserves.

Better carburation

Adjusting and balancing your carburettors can transform the power characteristics of your bike by smoothing out the power delivery of initial acceleration, by cutting out mid-range harshness and by eliminating an erratic tickover.

The previous chapter dealt with adjustment procedures on piston-type carburettors, and with how to balance carburettors of this type on twin machines. This chapter describes the adjustment of CV carburettors and with their balancing on twins. It also deals with balancing problems of multis of all kinds.

CV carburettors

Constant depression carburettors—usually referred to as constant vacuum (CV) carburettors—are more complex than piston-type carburettors. But this does not mean that the CV type carburettor is more difficult to adjust. In fact, the basic procedure for adjusting the idling speed and mixture is the same in both types of carburettor, although the more modern design of the CV carburettor often means that the mixture cannot, and should not, be touched unless the mixture is obviously incorrect. In many cases the mixture screw has a plastic limiter cap covering it to dissuade the owner from making his own adjustments.

The CV carburettor can be identified by its shape. It is fairly bulky, with a short, fat neck that is always circular, and the top is round and flat. Unlike the majority of piston-type carburettors, there are no cables entering the carburettor.

The CV carburettor has a disc-shaped throttle valve—called a butterfly valve—that is located inside the mouth of the carburettor next to the inlet manifold. This butterfly valve is actuated by an operating arm that sits on the side of the carburettor.

Non-linked twins

Non-linked twins with CV carburettors have the throttle cable attached directly to the operating arm. Examples are the Bing carburettor on the larger capacity BMWs and the Keihins on the early Honda CB250 and CB360. There is a throttle cable and a throttle-stop screw for each carburettor.

Finding the adjusting screws

On twins whose CV carburettors are not linked, the throttle-stop screw is completely external, and is located right next to the operating arm. The screw acts against the arm to vary the amount by which the butterfly opens. This controls the idling speed for the one cylinder. Both carburettors, obviously, have the same arrangement.

The mixture screws on these twins are usually located in the side of the carburettor near the inlet manifold, or underneath the mouth of the carburettor in the same area.

On twins whose CV carburettors are linked, and on all multi-cylindered machines, the linkage is arranged so that the throttle cable actuates a connecting spindle which, in turn, actuates the operating arm of the butterfly valve on each carburettor.

The exact location of the throttle-stop screw in this design often varies. The spindle is situated behind the carburettors, about half-way down the neck.

The throttle cable meets the carburettors between carburettors 2 and 3 on a 4-cylinder machine, or between the two carburettors on a linked twin. On the Yamaha XS750 triple, it meets the carburettors between the left-hand and centre ones. The cable fits into a pulley mechanism which then operates the long spindle or a series of short ones.

On most multiple CV designs, as with piston-type carburettors, there is

Harley Davidson FLH-80

1. **Mikuni on a Yamaha XS650, showing (1) the mixture screw limiter cap aad (2) the throttle-stop screw**

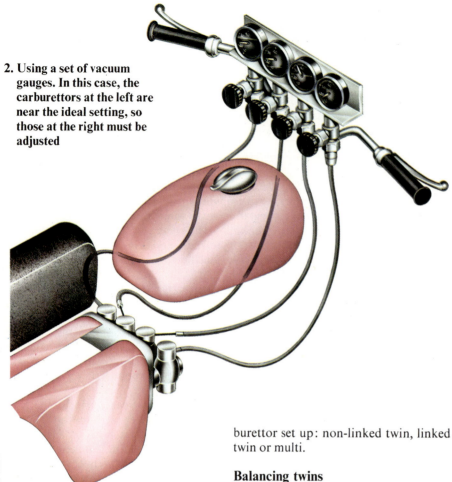

2. Using a set of vacuum gauges. In this case, the carburettors at the left are near the ideal setting, so those at the right must be adjusted

Norman Clark

one master throttle-stop screw which acts upon the pulley mechanism or on the spindle. It is located between the two central carburettors. Some makes have this screw pointing downwards; others have it pointing upwards. It is often difficult to see, but the head is plastic and knurled (that is, ridged around the edge).

Each carburettor has its own mixture screw in the side of the main body of the carburettor, but these are very difficult to get at, and should not be touched unless you have reason to believe that your idling mixture is incorrect. Setting the idling correctly does not automatically mean that the mixture also needs adjustment.

Adjusting a CV carburettor
Before adjusting CV carburettors, make sure you have carried out all the necessary preliminaries on the engine (see pages 79 to 84). This is most important. If the recommendations are not carried out, your carburettors will be incorrectly set up.

The procedure for adjusting the tickover is identical to that used on piston-type carburettors (pages 79 to 84). Just make sure you refer to the correct section for your own car-

burettor set up: non-linked twin, linked twin or multi.

Balancing twins
Balancing twin CV carburettors is done by a different procedure from that used on the piston-type carburettor. So do not attempt to balance the carburettors by feeling for the throttle valves.

The butterfly valve on each carburettor must open at the same time to obtain an even and smooth response when accelerating. The valves must also open fully.

On a non-linked CV carburettor the adjustment for balance is made on the throttle cable, where it joins the operating arm. There is an adjuster nut and locknut there for this purpose.

On a linked twin, like the Yamaha XS250 and XS400, adjustment is made through the adjuster screws on the operating arm. The Yamaha adjuster brings the butterflies together, adjusting one against the other at the same time; there is no separate adjuster for each butterfly.

There are two methods of balancing CV twins, both done by 'feel', but you will need a friend to help you.

For the first method, start the engine, and make sure it is warm and that the cables are not taut. Place a hand at the end of each silencer and ask your friend to open the throttle slowly. If the carburettors are badly out of balance you will feel the exhaust pressure exit from one silencer as being much stronger than the other.

Alternatively, place a hand gently under the operating arm of each carburettor, and again ask your friend to open the throttle slowly. You can feel which arm begins to move before the other. Make sure that one butterfly is not opening early because of a tight cable. Now use the adjuster on the cable for the non-linked twin, or the adjuster on the operating arm for the linked twins, to balance the carburettors properly.

Balancing multis

Whether the carburettors are the piston type or the CV type, there are two methods of balancing them on 4-cylinder triples and fours. One method is to take the carburettors off as one unit, manipulate the spindle while you watch the throttle valves open and shut, and then adjust accordingly. But for real accuracy a vacuum gauge must be used.

A vacuum gauge measures the vacuum created by the engine the instant that the throttle is opened.

A set of vacuum gauges, or one gauge with a set of adaptors and leads each with an off-on tap, can be bought from a large accessory shop. Although it is easier to use a complete set of vacuum gauges, they are expensive. One vacuum gauge will do the job, despite taking longer. Vacuum gauges are quite simple to use.

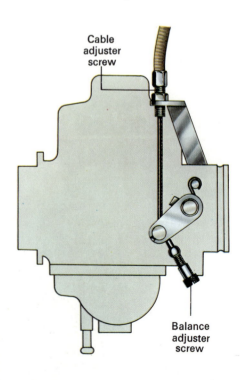

3. Typical balance adjuster screw as found on multiple CVs. It is used to adjust the butterfly valve

4. Twin Keihins for some Honda 250s and 360s, showing (1) the mixture screw and (2) the master throttle stop screw

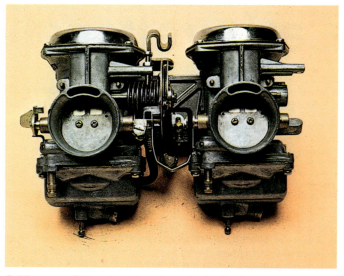

5. The same CV carburettors from the back, showing the balance adjuster screw and locknut

Using a vacuum gauge

If your bike has a vacuum operated petrol tap, make sure this is in the 'prime' position, and that the engine is at its normal running temperature. Unscrew the short cross-head screws in the inlet manifolds. On some bikes the tester plug screws may be in the body of the carburettor itself. Fit the adaptors into the hole vacated by the tester plug screws and connect the hoses to the vacuum gauge.

Next set the engine for a fast idling speed (1500rpm) by adjusting the master throttle-stop screw. Damp out the fluctuations in the needles of the gauge by kinking the rubber tubes. If you are using a separate gauge for each carburettor, each gauge should give a reading of between 18 and 23 cm Hg. Do not worry if the gauges read slightly under or over that recommendation—the important thing is to make sure that all the gauges have the same reading. If

they have, then your carburettors are synchronized.

If the readings are different, like those in fig. 2, use the individual adjuster screws to bring all the carburettors into line with whichever one is reading nearest to 21 cm Hg.

Some new machines with a multi-carburettor set-up have one 'static' carburettor that cannot be adjusted. In this case the other carburettors must be brought into line with the static one.

Whereas CV-type multi carburettors have individual adjuster screws on the operating arms, the adjustment on piston-type throttle valve multis is made at the top of each carburettor. Here, the adjuster screw and locknut are located off the common spindle, but beside the carburettor covers—as, for example, on the Honda CB500-Four. You loosen the locknut and turn in or out the adjuster screw to equalize the balance between the carburettors.

On some bikes the adjusters are concealed. On the early Honda CB750, for example, it is necessary to lift up the rubber gaiters at the top of the carburettors, loosen the locknuts, and rotate the individual throttle valve adjusters. On some modern carburettors, like those on the Suzuki GS550, GS50, and GS750, and Kawasaki Z1000, the adjusters are beneath the covers on the top of the carburettors. You release the two nuts to release the cover; this reveals the locknut and adjuster screw.

If you find it impossible to get all the carburettors exactly equal, they must at least be within 3 cm Hg of each other. Once the correct balance has been established, it may be necessary to re-adjust the idling speed by adjusting the master throttle stop screw.

Finally, snap open the throttles once or twice to see if the readings remain constant at idling speed.

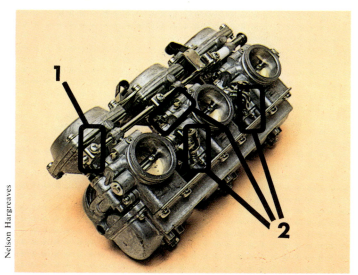

6. Bank of three Mikunis for a Yamaha triple, showing (1) mixture screw and (2) balance adjuster mechanism

7. The same carburettors turned over to show (1) the master throttle-stop screw and (2) the balance adjuster screws

Carburettor strip

If you own a Yamaha, Suzuki or Kawasaki machine, it is very likely that you will have occasion to strip and service a piston-slide or constant vacuum type of Mikuni carburettor.

Mikuni carburettors normally require very little maintenance apart from the occasional readjustment of tickover or a check to ensure that none of the fittings have worked loose. But about every 16,000 km (10,000 miles) the carburettor should be removed from the machine, stripped down for examination and cleaned thoroughly.

Removing the carburettor

Carburettor removal is basically the same whether you have the piston-slide type or constant vacuum type fitted to your machine. But some differences do occur between linked multi-carburettor assemblies and separate or single units.

On some bikes with multi-carburettors where access is limited you may find the removal procedure is made much easier by taking off the petrol tank first.

Fuel tanks are usually secured in place by a combination of rubber blocks and bolts located either under the seat or the rear underside of the tank. Switch off the fuel tap, then undo and remove the tank bolts. Disconnect the carburettor fuel lines by opening up the spring clip and easing the pipe from its connection using the end of a screwdriver.

If a negative pressure pipe is fitted, remove it by freeing the spring clip with a pair of pliers, and pulling it off its stub.

To gain sufficient working clearance for carburettor removal on most bikes you must also separate the air cleaner from the stub on the carburettor. Undo the hose clip and pull the air cleaner hose free. Next, undo the carburettor retaining nuts from the inlet manifold or slacken the clips around the flexible connectors. Before removing the carburettor the control cables must also be detached.

On most multi-cylinder machines the carburettors, whether piston-slide type or CV, are mounted together as a block unit on a plate, usually with a linked actuating mechanism. In this case disconnect the throttle cables by loosening the cable adjusters and rotating the operating pulley until the inner cable nipple can be pushed out of the anchor point. Single CV carburettors can be dealt with in exactly the same way.

If the carburettor is directly operated by the throttle cable the mixing chamber cap will have to be unscrewed to free the cable. Take care as you unscrew the cap as the slide return spring lies compressed beneath the cap. With this done pull upwards on the cable to withdraw the slide and needle assembly. Place the

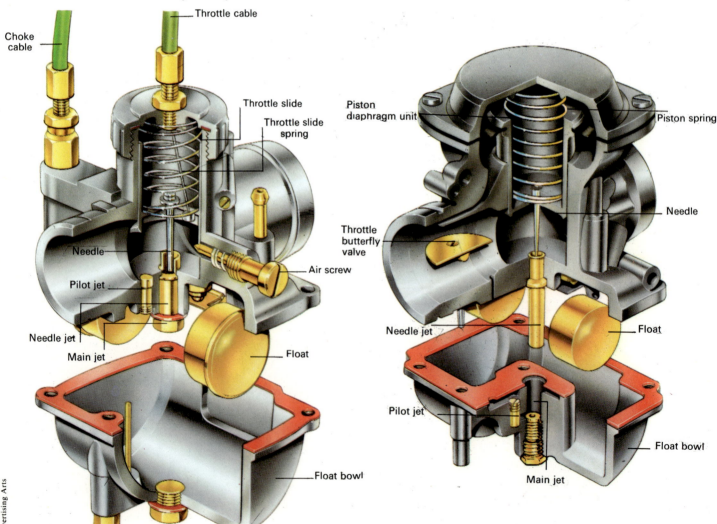

1. A variable-venturi, needle jet type Mikuni carburettor. The throttle piston controls the size of the venturi

2. A constant partial vacuum type Mikuni carburettor. The butterfly valve controls the vacuum operated piston

Separating multiple carbs

3. **Remove the screws securing the carb to the lower bracket. You may need an impact screwdriver**

4. **Undo the retaining screws holding the upper bracket, then remove it from the carburettor**

5. **Remove the pivot screw securing the choke lever. Detach the lever and note the sequence of washers**

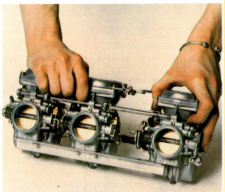

6. **Prise the fuel cross-over pipe off one stub, separate the throttle clamps and remove the right carb**

cable with the slide still attached to one side and leave it for the moment.

Finally pull the carburettor or block assembly towards the rear of the bike and off its mounting studs or inlet manifold.

The innards of a multi-carburettor assembly are best investigated by separating each carburettor from the mounting unit. But if the carburettor assembly has not been dismantled before, you may notice that various screws and nuts

are marked with yellow paint. If the bike is fairly new and still under warranty you should make no attempt to break the paint seal or obliterate the marks, otherwise you will invalidate the bike's guarantee. First, remove the throttle and choke shaft linkage which are secured with clamping screws or bolts. Next remove the mounting bracket by unscrewing the (usually very tight) cross-head screws. To split some CV type multi-carburettors such as found on the GT750 Suzuki, prise down the spring loaded rod on the lower half of the linking clamp. Now slide the carburettors apart. On reassembly prise the clamp apart and slide them together again. After separation the individual carburettors are dealt with in exactly the same way as non-linked or individual types.

Stripping the carburettor
Before starting to strip the carburettor tip away any fuel still left in the float chamber. Give the outside of the carburettor a thorough clean with an oil solvent such as Gunk or Jizer. Use a fine wire brush or a stiff bristle brush to remove deposits on the carburettor body.

At each stage of dismantling make a note of the correct position of all the components in order to facilitate correct reassembly. Note that on the underside of some Mikuni piston-slide carburettors, the pilot air screw is marked with yellow paint (fig. 7). This is the pilot screw and should not be disturbed, having been pre-set at the factory with a flow-meter.

Removing the float exposes the float needle so lift it out with your fingers.

Once the carburettor is clean, remove the float bowl by undoing the four

Dismantling the float bowl

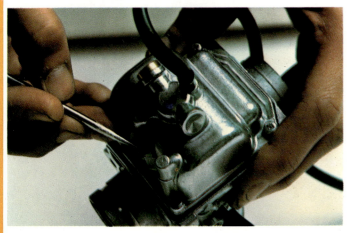

7. **Pilot air screws are factory set and marked with paint. Do not remove the screw if the bike is under warranty**

8. **Unscrew the four cross-head screws securing the float bowl to the carb body**

Continued ▪

Jake Wynter

9. Removing the float bowl cover reveals the float assembly. Take care to work in ultra clean conditions

10. Slide out the pivot pin to free the float and lift it away. Then take out the float needle

and may be withdrawn on some models such as the BS34 from the float chamber and on others such as the YM28SC from the venturi. Remove the pilot jet by unscrewing it from the float bowl. The float needle seat can be simply unscrewed from the float bowl.

With all the jets removed and placed carefully to one side, attention can be focused on dismantling the top part of the carburettor. At this stage differences between the piston-slide type and CV types of carburettors will become apparent.

Piston-slide types

In the case of a directly linked type carburettor the piston-slide will already have been removed before the carburettor was taken off the bike but you can now free the slide from the cable. Free the throttle cable from the slide by compressing the slide return spring against the cap, and grasping the cable between thumb and forefinger. Push the cable down until its nipple is clear of its locating niche in the slide. Now pull the cable sideways to free it.

cross-head screws (fig. 8). With the float assembly exposed pull out the hinge pin that locates the twin float assembly (fig. 10), lift away the float and put it carefully to one side.

Remove the main jet by unscrewing it carefully with a spanner. The needle jet will normally unscrew with the main jet. Separate them by holding the needle jet with a spanner around its hexagonal body and removing the main jet with a screwdriver. On some Mikuni carburettors, the needle jet may be a push fit, secured by a rubber O-ring,

Removing the jets

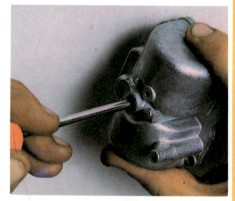

11. Use a screwdriver in the slotted head of the main jet to remove it. The needle jet will come away with it.

12. On some carbs remove the bolt on the base of the float bowl to gain access to the main jet

13. The main jet can be reached with a thin screwdriver. Unscrew the jet carefully, it is easy to damage

14. The needle jet is usually a push fit and can be withdrawn either from the float bowl or venturi

15. The pilot jet may be hidden below the bowl gasket. Undo it with a small screwdriver

16. Remove the float needle seat from the float bowl by unscrewing it from its housing with a spanner

Remove the needle by simply pushing it through the throttle slide. Note the position of the small spring clip so that it can be replaced in the same groove on reassembly. Altering the needle height changes the air-fuel ratio and if you have any doubt about the correct position, start on a rich setting (that is with the spring clip in the lowest groove) and work down to the best one.

On linked multi-carburettors the piston-slides are mechanically opened and closed; a single slide return spring may be found outside the carburettor on the operating linkage so remove this first. Undo the piston slide cap, undoing the retaining screws (fig. 17). Then simply withdraw the throttle slide with its actuating mechanism (fig. 18). To separate the throttle slide, remove the cross-head screw securing the actuating mechanism to the throttle slide. Push the needle out to detach it from the throttle slide (fig. 19).

Remove the starter unit (choke) by unscrewing the plunger unit nut with a spanner (fig. 20), then pull it out.

Do not remove the air screw without first making a note of its exact position. Mark the relative position of the screw and the body with a light scratch. Failure to observe this precaution will make it necessary to resynchronise the carburettors on re-assembly. Multiple models have a rocker linkage from the top of the carburettor rather than the more familiar screw-throttle-stop.

Next, carefully check for wear.

Constant vacuum types

Access to the slide and needle is gained by removing the slide cap. First remove the four cross-head screws on the top of the carburettor (fig. 21). Dismantling calls for great care, otherwise the sealing diaphragm may be damaged. Lift out the piston spring followed by the integral piston/diaphragm unit, together with the needle (fig. 23). Invert the piston to allow the needle and needle seat to drop out (fig. 24).

Do not disturb the 'butterfly' throttle valve assembly as the components are not prone to wear and in any case are not serviceable.

Inspecting the components

As with all mechanical assemblies, an imperfection in one component produces corresponding wear in another; bear this in mind when examining the carburettor for wear and deciding whether to renew components.

Examining the slide needle

Examine the slide valve needle for scoring or polishing of its surface, or 'stepping' near the needle point. Roll the needle on a flat surface to check it for straightness. If the needle is found to be worn or bent it must be replaced along with a new needle valve which will also have been affected. The needle jet often becomes oval after much use. If the fixed jet tube, through which the needle passes, is worn and cast integral with the carburettor, the body will have to be renewed.

After checking the needle examine the exterior surface of the throttle slide, as well as the inner face of the carburettor bore in which it slides (fig. 25). Usual indications of wear are scoring of the sliding parts and half-moon shaped

Dismantling the top end: piston slide type

17. On the mechanically linked type carb remove the cap by unscrewing the three cross-head securing screws

18. Simply withdraw the throttle slide. To separate the actuating mechanism remove the securing screw

19. Push the needle out to detach it from the throttle slide and make a note of the spring clip position

20. Remove the starter unit (choke) by unscrewing the choke plunger nut-head then pull the unit out

Dismantling the top end: constant vacuum type

21. Unscrew the four cross-head screws securing the cap to the top of the carb

22. Remove the carb cap taking great care not to damage the fragile sealing diaphragm

marks on the slide. Put the slide back into the carburettor and see if it is a sloppy fit. If wear is apparent the slide should be renewed. Be sure to replace the slide with the correct amount of cutaway (this should be stamped on the top of the slide).

Examine the piston and bore in the CV type in the same way. The air slide in a CV carburettor will become defective even with slight wear, so the sealing mechanism must be scrutinised very carefully. Inspect the throttle return spring for efficiency and check for a loss of compressive strength against a new spring. Do not forget to check the diaphragm for signs of perishing or splits (fig. 26). Renew the piston/diaphragm unit if any damage is evident.

Inspecting components for wear

25. Examine the exterior surface of the throttle slide as well as the inner face of the carb bore

26. Check the diaphragm for signs of perishing or splits. Renew the unit if damaged

27. Examine the needle, float needle, air screw and spring for signs of wear or damage

28. Inspect the choke tip for stepping. If any part is defective or broken the entire unit must be replaced

Examining float bowl components

Check the float first. Pick up the float and shake it; if you can hear petrol splashing inside, the float is punctured and must be replaced. Check the float spindle for straightness by rolling it on a flat surface and then refit the spindle and make sure the float moves freely on it. Inspect the float needle for wear. This usually takes the form of a ridge or step in the conical tip. Blow through the float needle valve to check that it is clear then push the needle on to its seat and blow through the valve again. The needle should seal the valve completely – if it doesn't it is worn and must be replaced. Finally check that the valve is not sticking; hold the carburettor body in one hand and push the needle into the valve with a finger. Release the valve and it should drop out. If it sticks persistently renew the needle or valve.

Setting float height

Float height determines the level of fuel in the float chamber and should be checked when all the float bowl components have been reassembled. The measurement is critical and made with the unit inverted. Refer to the workshop manual for the correct height. Use an engineer's rule to measure the distance between the inner face of the float chamber body, with the gasket removed, and the bottom edge of the float (fig. 29). If adjustment is necessary bend the float tongue, to either lower or raise the float. Once the float is at the correct height the float bowl can be refitted.

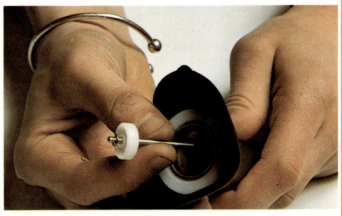

Jake Wynter

23. Carefully lift out the piston spring followed by the integral piston/diaphragm unit and the needle

24. Invert the piston to allow the needle and the needle seat to drop out, note the spring clip position

Examining the control screws

Inspect the control screws visually for a ridged or damaged point. Examine the springs (if fitted) for loss of compressive strength. Sealing O-rings may be fitted on the screws which serve both to retain the screws and to prevent induction air leaks. Renew defective items.

Examining the choke mechanism

Most Mikuni carburettors feature a plunger type choke fitted within the carburettor body, operated by a rod and fork actuating mechanism. Attention to the choke is rarely required as wear is limited. Make sure that the choke returns properly on those models that rely on spring pressure. The mechanism and linkage requires only occasional light lubrication of the moving parts. If any part is defective or broken the entire plunger assembly must be replaced.

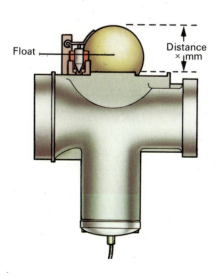

Float — Distance × mm

Bernard Fallon

29. To check the float height measure the distance between the float base and the chamber face

Cleaning the components

Before reassembling the carburettor and components they should be thoroughly cleaned. Clean the float chamber of any sediment by washing it out with clean petrol. Avoid using a piece of rag because particles may find their way into airways or jets. Allow the parts to drain and blow through all the jets and airways with an air-line, or a tyre pump.

If a jet is found to be blocked do not try to clear it with a piece of wire or any pointed metal object. It is very easy to enlarge the delicate jet orifices. A stiff bristle from a toothbrush will do.

Rebuilding the carburettor

Reassembly of the carburettor is exactly the reverse of the stripping procedure. Exercise great care, however, when replacing jets as the threads in the light-alloy carburettor body are easily damaged and will strip before the stronger threads on the brass jets.

Renew all gaskets and O-rings unless they are in perfect condition. These include the float chamber gasket, the carburettor top gasket (if fitted) and the control screw O-rings. Also, any gaskets on the inlet manifold stubs that were disturbed on dismantling should be checked and renewed if necessary.

When refitting the throttle slide and needle (with the clip correctly positioned) make sure that the slot in the slide fits on the 'runner' inside the carburettor and makes a good solid 'thud' sound when fully home.

In the case of the CV type carburettor ensure that the projections on the diaphragm locate with the recesses on the carburettor body. Then replace the carburettor top and tighten the four cross-head screws evenly.

If for some reason you disturbed the adjustment of some CV multi-carburet-

tors, such as the BS40 assembly, the valves can be synchronised as follows. Back off the throttle stop screw so the 'butterfly' valve is completely shut. Back off the lock nut and adjusting screw on the actuating clamp and then tighten both screws on to the metal tongue which operates the adjoining carburettor. Then do up the lock nut. The 'butterfly' valves on all the carburettors will now be synchronised but the tickover will have to be re-adjusted by the throttle stop screw to the recommended idling speed.

If the control screws have been disturbed they should be set roughly to enable the bike to be started for fine tuning. Screw in the throttle stop screw roughly half way. Then screw in each air screw fully (not so hard as to damage the point). Back it off one turn.

Before refitting the carburettor assembly check for distortion of the inlet flange on the carburettor face and the inlet stub by laying a straight edge across it. Distortion can usually be removed with abrasive on a flat surface.

Adjusting multi-carburettors

After reassembly refit the carburettors to the mounting plate or bars and re-install the throttle and choke linkages. It may be necessary to set the throttle linkage so that the throttle valves on all the carburettors are synchronised. This is usually a simple matter of backing off all the adjustment on the linkage and then tightening the throttle slide actuating lever on to the linkage shaft.

For adjustment and synchronisation refer back to pages 79–84 and 85–87. If there is any doubt about carburettor specifications you should consult your dealer or the bike manufacturer, quoting the machine model and engine number.

Adjusting 2-stroke oil pumps

Most 2-stroke engines rely on oil metered out by an oil pump for correct lubrication. If the pump is allowed to go seriously out of adjustment the result could be an engine seizure. Aim to protect your engine by careful and regular servicing of this vital component.

Direct lubrication of 2-stroke crankcase and cylinder components is difficult due to the very nature of the engine design. The traditional solution to this problem is to mix the oil with the petrol in the fuel tank. But the inherent inadequacy of the system is that the oil and petrol is delivered to the engine in the same proportion at both high and low speed. Premix lubrication was then superceded when the mixing was made automatic and the oil kept in a separate tank. Most modern 2-stroke machines, however, use a more sophisticated method by which oil is sprayed into the inlet manifold under pressure. Oil is stored in a separate tank and is gravity fed to a pump located behind one of the engine casings. The pump delivers oil under pressure, to nozzles in the inlet manifold, where it mixes with the passing stream of air and petrol. Suzuki and Silk both modify this system with CCI injection, in which the main bearings are lubricated as well.

Whatever system is used, however, its heart is the oil pump and it is this component which usually requires maintenance. Before going any further it is worth knowing exactly what the pump does and how it does it.

Two stroke oil pumps

Two-stroke oil pumps consist of a cylindrical casting with a central bore. Within the pump body are two principal components, the plunger and its follower. The two are an interference fit

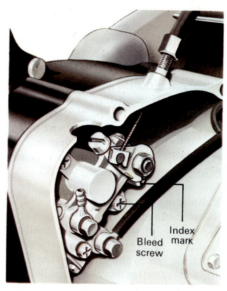

2. **Thin body pumps have the cable on a quadrant on the side of the unit underneath the adjuster in the cover**

and move up and down in unison. Moving components in the pump are driven by the crankshaft, through reduction gears. The final gear engages in slots machined into the plunger. At the base of the pump is an eccentric cam on which the plunger sits. Rotational motion of the cam is converted to an up and down pumping action by the plunger. As the plunger moves down, oil is sucked in and as it moves up oil is driven out. While pumps are often a good deal more complex than this, they all operate on this simple basic principle.

Apart from simply pumping oil into the inlet manifold, the pump also has to meter the volume of oil it passes to match the demands of the engine. The amount of oil the pump delivers depends on two factors, the length of each stroke and frequency of the strokes. Pump speed is directly related to the crankshaft and hence engine speed, but the pump stroke can be altered by adjusting the profile of the elliptical cam at the base of the pump. In fact, the cam profile adjustment is directly linked to the throttle, enabling the displacement of the pump to be increased as engine power is increased.

Maintaining the lubrication system
Maintaining this system falls into three separate areas. First, you must ensure that the oil in the tank is kept well topped up. Check it weekly or every 300 km (200 miles). Second, the whole system should be inspected monthly or 650 km (400 miles) and third you should service the pump every three months or at intervals of 1,000 km (700 miles).

Inspecting the system
Regular inspection of the lubrication system will often show a slight fault which, if left, could become serious.

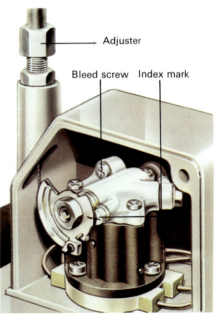

3. **The jelly mould type is mounted on top of the motor, the adjuster fits in the housing that covers the unit**

Start the inspection procedure by checking the oil level. Many bikes have a sight window in the side panel to make the job easier. If your machine has not got one of these then check the level in the usual way with a dipstick. It is a good idea to keep the tank topped up as a high oil level improves the gravity feed to the pump.

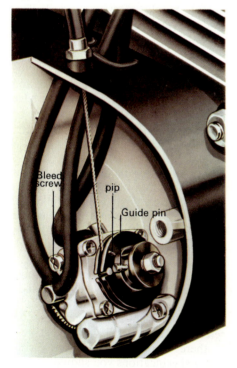

1. **The fat body pump has the alignment pip on the face of the cable pulley which matches up with the guide pin**

After filling up the tank, give the outside of it a good clean with a rag soaked with a degreasing agent such as Jizer. If the tank is clean you have a better chance of spotting tell-tale leaks which often occur along the welds of metal tanks.

Next, examine the condition of the rubber tank hose. Check that the rubber is not perished or torn around the clip. This is particularly important. If the pipe is damaged near the clip, try cutting back the pipe before you decide to buy a new one. There is often enough excess pipe to make a repair possible.

After checking the hose at the tank end, follow it down to the point where it enters the engine casing. This is probably the most vulnerable area as the pipes tend to harden, due to heat from the engine. A cracked pipe will often allow air into the system without

Servicing a fat body pump

4. The pump is on the right hand side of the engine. Remove the set screws that hold the crankcase cover in place

5. Adjust the pump by using the cable adjuster to align the index pip on the pulley with the engine guide pin

6. Turn the engine over with the kickstart so that the gap between the end plate and the pulley is at its maximum

7. Use a feeler gauge to measure the width of the gap. It should fall between 0.20-0.25mm (0.008-0.010in.)

8. If the gap is outside these limits undo the nut on the end plate and remove the shims on the stud

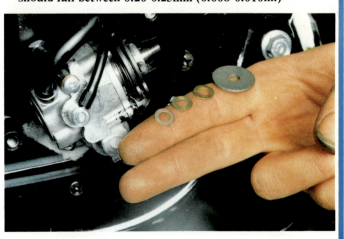

9. Subtract the correct value from the one you measured and add the correct shims to make up the difference

Continued

Rupert Watts

allowing oil to escape. This can stop the oil flow as the pump will not pass air through it.

Once the external inspection checks have been made you can check the pump.

Servicing the pump

As all the moving parts of the 2-stroke oil-pump continually run in oil, its components should prove to be among the longest lived of any on the bike. Consequently maintenance is minimal and usually this simply amounts to periodic adjustment. If, however, a hose breaks or you run out of oil, and air gets into the system, then the system must be bled. Certain pumps also require periodic shimming to set the pump stroke.

Pump adjustment

Pump adjustment basically involves synchronising the pump action with the throttle. Adjustment is first set by the manufacturers but over time the cable wears and so the pump should be checked at regular intervals.

There are three basic types of pumps, fat bodied, thin bodied and jelly mould (figs. 1 to 3). Adjustment is slightly different for each.

Fat bodied pumps

Fat bodied pumps are used by Yamaha, NVT and CZ/Jawa. There are small differences between them but from the point of view of adjustment they are all very similar.

On Yamaha machines the pump is located on the right side of the engine (fig. 4). It is controlled by a cable which runs from the throttle to a pulley on the pump. With the engine cover removed you will be able to see the cable wrapped around the pulley (fig. 1). The pulley has a pip on one side which should align with a slotted guide pin on the right of the pulley.

Whether the pip should align with the pin when the throttle is fully open or closed, depends on the model you are working on. Such differences were introduced on machines in a rather haphazard fashion so you will have to check with a dealer to find out which type you have. But the marks should not be too far out of alignment, however, and it should not be difficult to find which type you have, as they are all quite different.

To adjust the cable, pull the rubber boot off the adjuster where it enters the casing above the pump. Release the locknut and turn the adjuster to alter the quadrant setting until the pip and pin align (fig. 5). If you are making this adjustment with the throttle closed, make sure that any slack in the cable has been taken up, before you begin. Failure to observe this can lead to the

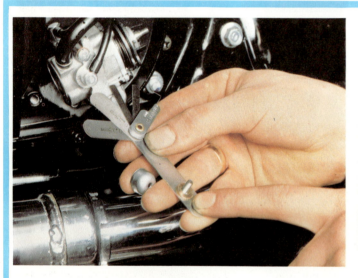

10. **Yamaha market a feeler gauge that is designed for this job and includes an assortment of shims in the handle**

11. **Remove any air bubbles that are blocking the pump by undoing the bleed screw with a screwdriver**

12. **Turn the engine over with the kickstart and watch the bleed hole until a continuous stream of oil trickles out**

13. **Clear the feed tube by pulling it off the manifold then priming it with oil until all the air is expelled**

Servicing a jelly mould pump

14. Undo the cross-head screws holding the inspection cover in place; normally, a rubber plug fits into the porthole

15. Synchronise the pump with the throttle linkage; start by removing the brass plug in the slide chamber

16. Line up the mark on the slide with the top of the plug hole. Next, check the reference marks on the oil pump

17. The marks which must line up can be seen right of the large brass nut retaining the operating arm

Rupert Watts

pump being over advanced and the engine will oil-up. The best way of eliminating slack is to warm up the engine, let it idle, and then slowly twist the throttle until the revs rise. Just before this point, lock the throttle by wrapping adhesive tape round the twistgrip and handlebar, then switch off the engine.

Fat bodied pumps on Jawas and CZs are fairly similar to the Yamaha pump. On this type, however, the throttle cable runs to the pump first, goes around a pulley and then to the carburettor slide. Adjust the pump so that the notch on the inner face of the pulley lines up with the horizontal seam on the casing. If the notch does not align, undo the locknut on the throttle cable and turn the knurled adjuster until the marks match. With this done the carburettor and its cable must be set. All this entails is ensuring that there is 1 mm (0.04in.) of play in the cable where it enters the top of the carburettor. Undo the locknut and turn the screw adjuster until the play is correct.

Shimming a fat bodied pump

While nearly all oil pumps are adjusted simply by means of the cable quadrant the fat bodied pump also employs shims to further control stroke length. To check whether the pump needs shimming, turn the engine over until gap between pulley and housing is at its largest. With a feeler gauge, measure the gap between pulley and adjusting plate (fig. 7). It should be between 0.20–0.25 mm (0.008–0.010 in.). If the gap is larger than this, a shim of the corresponding size must be fitted. Yamaha produce a workshop tool (fig. 10) which carries both feeler gauges, and an assortment of shims in the handle.

Shims simply fit onto the pulley spindle once the locking bolt has been removed (fig. 8).

Thin bodied pumps

Thin bodied types of pump as used by some Kawasakis are equally simple to adjust. Usually located behind the right-hand side cover (fig. 18), adjustment is just a matter of aligning the

reference marks using the cable adjuster. On these pumps there are often two marks on the cable quadrant (fig. 19), one should align with the throttle open and the other with the throttle closed. If you cannot reconcile the two positions, set the pump with the throttle closed mark aligned, as this is the more accurate setting of the two.

Jelly mould pumps

On the jelly mould type of pump, as found on many Suzukis, problems of synchronizing the carburettor are reduced. These pumps have a hole in the carburettor slide chamber which is aligned with a punch mark on the slide (fig. 16). The window is normally blocked off by a small screw and this should be removed (fig. 15).

Access to the oil pump is usually gained by removing the right-hand side engine cover (fig. 14). Twist the throttle and observe the slide through the window (fig. 16). Secure the twist-grip when the punch mark on the slide is aligned with the top of the window.

Now check that the mark on the cable quadrant lines up with the one on the pump body (fig. 17). If they are out, then adjust the cable until the marks align.

On machines which have a mechanical linkage instead of a cable, adjustment is made with the throttle closed. Turn the threaded linkage on the end of the rod nearest the carburettor until the reference marks on the pump align. No carburettor synchronization is necessary.

Bleeding the oil pump

If air gets into the lubrication system then it must be bled out as it will prevent the pump from working properly. Usually you will only discover that there is an airlock in the system after the engine has blown up. But if, for example, you have replaced a hose or even the pump, the system must be bled before the engine is started. As with adjustment, the method for bleeding the various types of pump differs slightly for each type of pump.

Bleeding fat bodied pumps
Figure 12 shows the location of the bleed nipple on a typical fat bodied pump. To bleed the pump, simply unscrew the bleed screw (fig. 11) and turn the engine over by hand. On Jawas, CZs and older Yamahas a wheel is provided on the pump for this purpose. Once oil gushes out the hole replace the bleed screw. Then remove the oil pipe from where it joins the carburettor and operate the pump or turn the engine over, until oil flows out of the pipe.

Bleeding thin bodied pumps
Bleeding thin bodied pumps follows a two-stage procedure. First slacken the bleed screw (fig. 21) and operate the pump manually by pulling the quadrant until oil flows out, then close it immediately. Bleed the outlet hose by starting the engine. With the motor idling, hold the pump quadrant fully open. Do this until the oil that passes through the pipe is free of air bubbles. If the bubbles persist, check the tightness of the bleed screw and the condition of the sealing rings around the pipe's banjo connection.

Bleeding jelly mould pumps
On the jelly mould type of pump the bleed screw is located on the top of the unit, just above the cable quadrant. Bleeding procedure is the same as for thin bodied pump types.

Bleeding other models
Many non-Japanese bikes including Harley-Davidson and Cagira 2-strokes, have Japanese pumps. Most of them are very similar to those already described here.

If the adjustment is not clear, or your attempts at bleeding do not remove the air, it may be better to get professional help rather than risk wrecking your engine. Generally, you should not have any trouble.

Servicing a thin body pump

18. Remove the front portion of the crankcase cover, undo the cross-head screws on the periphery of the cover

19. Close the throttle and check that the mark on the cable quadrant lines up with the index on the pump body

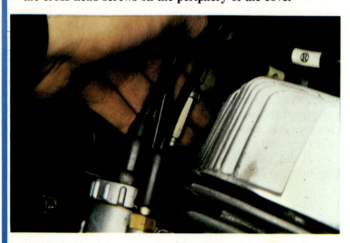

20. If the pump proves to be out of adjustment, correct it by turning the adjuster in the middle of the pump cable

21. Bleed the pump by removing the bleed screw and turning the engine over until clean oil dribbles out of the hole

SOHC valve clearance

Correctly-adjusted valve clearances are vital for the efficient running of a 4-stroke bike engine. They will maintain the engine's mechanical efficiency, prevent excessive engine noise, reduce fuel consumption and increase the life of the engine. All you need to adjust the valves are a few tools and – once you have the knack – an hour or two.

Each cylinder in a 4-stroke engine has at least two valves – an inlet valve to permit the entry of the fuel/air mixture and an exhaust valve to permit the escape of exhaust gases.

A number of different mechanisms – it depends on the design of the engine – are used to open the valves at the correct intervals as the crankshaft rotates. All such mechanisms are designed to bear on the valve stem (fig. 14). All are operated by the camshaft, whose pear-shaped cams are designed to hold the valves open for a pre-determined period.

And all have one problem in common: in the extreme temperatures at which a valve operates while the engine is running, the metal in the valve and associated components expands. So a pre-set clearance, to allow for this expansion, is essential.

Although this clearance is measured only in hundredths of a millimetre or thousandths of an inch, it must be correct. If it is too large, the valve will open too late and close too early. This will result in excessive noise, loss of power and greater wear.

If the gap is too small, the valve will not be able to seat properly in the cylinder head. Eventually, both the valve and valve seat will burn out and serious engine damage could result.

Under normal running, the valve clearances in any bike gradually increase or decrease through ordinary 'wear and tear'. This is why all camshaft -to-valve systems have some means of adjusting the gap at stated intervals.

Normally, valve clearances are adjusted every 3,000 to 5,000 km (2,000–3,000 miles), or as specified in the bike manufacturer's handbook. But naturally, if engine performance suddenly falls, or there is a gradual increase in engine clatter from the vicinity of the valves, the valve clearances should be checked at once.

It is possible to identify and locate certain engine noises without the need to dismantle part of the engine. One method of doing this is to use a screwdriver or long metal bar as a simple stethoscope. Start the engine and warm it up until it reaches its normal running temperature. Place the blade of the screwdriver on the part of the engine you wish to listen to (fig. 2). Vibrations from the moving parts will travel along the metal directly to your ear. This has the effect of amplifying various noises, and by moving the blade over an area until a particular sound frequency becomes loudest, you can pinpoint the exact source of the noise.

This simple device is particularly useful for identifying the characteristic rattle which signifies an out of adjustment tappet.

Types of valve gear

Valve gear on bikes can be divided into six types:
1: Pushrod-operated valves with screw-type adjusters.
2: Single and double overhead camshafts with screw-type adjusters.
3: Single and double overhead camshafts with eccentric adjusters.
4: Double overhead camshafts with adjusting shims *above* the tappets.
5: Double overhead camshafts with adjusting shims *below* the tappets.
6: The desmodromic valve gear used on Ducati engines.

The methods of adjusting valve clearances on the first five of these are dealt with in this and the following chapter (see pages 104–110). The Ducati system, for which part of the engines must be dismantled, is best adjusted using the manufacturer's handbook.

Tools and spares

Before you begin, make sure you have the correct tools for the job and any spares that may be necessary.

You will certainly need a feeler gauge of the right size to measure the gap. Traditionally, British bikes' dimensions are given in thousandths of an inch, while Japanese and Continental bikes' are in hundredths of a millimetre. Examples:

Norton Commando 850 cc: Inlet, 0.006in. ('six thou'); exhaust, 0.008in. ('eight thou').
Kawasaki Z400: Inlet, 0.08 mm; exhaust, 0.13 mm.

If the rider's manual does not give the required valve clearance figures, ask a main dealer. To measure the gap, you can use either a single feeler gauge, or two that together make up the required

NUT Rambler 175

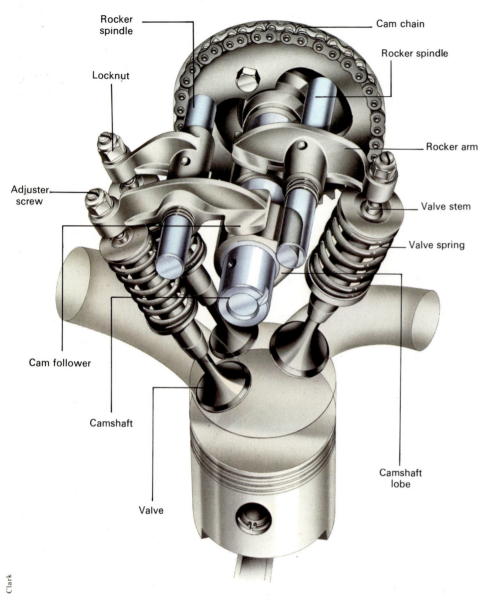

Rocker spindle
Cam chain
Locknut
Rocker spindle
Adjuster screw
Rocker arm
Valve stem
Valve spring
Cam follower
Camshaft
Camshaft lobe
Valve

Norman Clark

1. Valve layout on the Honda Dream – a typical single overhead camshaft engine with rocker-arm adjusters

thickness.

You will also need ring spanners, screwdrivers, and a small adjuster tool (usually supplied in the bike's toolkit) with which to make the adjustment. If you do not have the adjuster tool, you can use a pair of pliers, provided there is enough space within the confines of the rocker box.

If your bike has a gasket between the rocker cover and cylinder head, this must be replaced when you reassemble. So have a new one ready. You will also need a rag to deal with oil spillage.

Preparations

Valve clearances should be checked with the engine cold, unless stated otherwise in the owner's manual.

Put the bike on its centre stand and remove the petrol tank. Remove the

spark plugs to make the engine easier to turn over.

The next job is to remove the rocker box cover or caps. As well as giving access for the job, this will enable you to find out – if you don't know already – which type of valve actuating mechanism your bike has.

Some bikes have a rocker box cover, held on by nuts and bolts. Some, like most Hondas and early Triumphs, have a cap or caps that thread into the cylinder head. To remove either, a firm tap with a soft hammer may be necessary to break the gasket seal (fig. 3).

With the cover or caps removed, the valve gear will be exposed. Unless the valve clearance is the same for both inlet and exhaust valves, you will need to establish which is which. This is easy: the exhaust valves line up with the exhaust manifold, while the inlet valves are on the opposite side of the cylinder(s) (fig. 5) and line up with the carburettor inlet tract.

The basic procedure for adjusting valve clearances is the same for all 4-stroke engines.

Order of work

First you bring No. 1 piston to top dead centre on the compression stroke and adjust both its inlet and its exhaust valves.

Then, on a twin- or multi-cylinder machine, you turn the engine over until the next cylinder is at top dead centre on the compression stroke and adjust both its valves.

On a 3- or 4-cylinder machine, this procedure is repeated until all the valves have been adjusted.

On a 4-cylinder machine, you can save time by bringing the next cylinder to fire up to top dead centre. If your engine fires 1,2,4,3, for example, you adjust in this order – which means that you need turn the engine over only by 180° between one cylinder and the next. But obviously you must have the correct firing order to do this, so check it in your manual.

Finding TDC

To turn the engine over, make sure the rear wheel is off the ground, then engage the engine in top gear. By turning the rear wheel you can now rotate the engine.

To make sure that it is the compression, and not the exhaust, stroke on which you make the adjustment, put your thumb over the hole vacated by the spark plug and turn the rear wheel in a forward direction. You will eventually feel a strong pressure of air against your thumb and at the same time the wheel will become difficult to turn (fig. 6).

This means that the piston is compressing the fuel/air mixture because the relevant combustion chamber is gastight. To make sure, look at the inlet and exhaust valve stems – both should be in the same position.

Now you must bring the piston exactly to TDC. To do this, carefully insert a clean metal rod or long screwdriver into the hole. Keep it plumb vertical and make absolutely sure that neither the tool nor any part of it can drop down the hole – an error here could mean having to strip down the engine.

Turn the rear wheel very slowly forwards so that the rod or screwdriver slowly rises – forced upwards by the piston – until it reaches its highest point. This is TDC (fig. 7).

If the rod or screwdriver starts dropping again, the piston has travelled past TDC. So you will have to pull the rear wheel backwards until the piston has just passed TDC, then forwards again until you have the exact spot.

On some Japanese bikes, the procedure for finding TDC is simplified. They have TDC marks scribed on the alternator rotor that align with a pointer alongside it. All you have to do is to find the compression stroke as before, and then align marks and pointer (fig. 13).

On four-cylinder Hondas, you can save time if you wish by following the manufacturer's procedure. First you get No. 1 cylinder on to the compression stroke. Then you set the T1.4 mark on the rotor behind the contact breaker against the stationary scribed line. With the marks lined up, you adjust these clearances: No. 1 inlet and exhaust; No. 2 exhaust; No. 3 inlet. Then you rotate the crankshaft a full turn until the T1.4 mark lines up again, and adjust the other clearances: No. 2 inlet, No. 3 exhaust, and No. 4 inlet and exhaust.

Adjusting valve clearances with screw-type adjusters

2. Identify excessive or unusual tappet noise by placing a screwdriver between your ear and the rocker-box

3. A sharp tap with a soft-headed mallet will help free the rocker-box from its gasket by breaking the oil seal

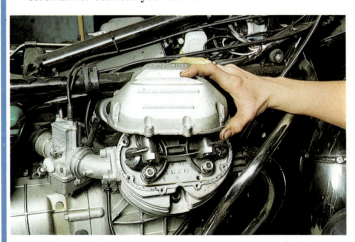

4. To gain access to the valves, remove the rocker-box cover. Have a rag ready to wipe up any oil spills

5. On this Moto Guzzi T3 you can clearly see all the OHV components, including the adjuster screw and locknut

6. To find TDC, put your thumb over the spark plug hole and feel for compression while rotating the engine

7. Next, carefully insert a screwdriver in the plug hole and rotate the engine. Highest point of lift indicates TDC

Nelson Hargreaves

Continued

Checking the clearances

The valve clearances on the cylinder you have just lined up may now be checked. To do this, insert the appropriate feeler gauge between the adjuster screw and the valve stem or pushrod head. (On BMWs and the Moto Guzzi V-twins, the adjuster is on the pushrod end of the rocker, but the clearance is measured at the *other* end.) The gauge should just slide in, with a very slight 'nip' if the gap is currect (fig. 80).

If the gauge will not enter the gap, or does so with difficulty, the gap is too small and must be altered. If the gauge is a sloppy fit, or if there is perceptible movement when the rocker is pulled away from the valve and pressed down while the gauge is there, the gap is too large.

To re-set the gap, you next need to

8. Having found TDC, measure the valve clearance by placing a feeler gauge between the valve stem and rocker arm

9. To adjust the clearance, slacken off the locknut and turn the adjuster screw until it just nips the gauge in place

10. Then keep the feeler gauge in place and hold the adjuster tool steady while tightening the locknut

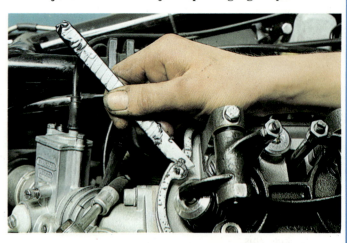

11. After adjusting the next valve, clean the mating surfaces between the rocker-box and cylinder head

12. Re-check the clearances, then fit a new gasket with a smear of grease, and replace the rocker-box cover

13. On the rotor of a Honda CD175, the letter T lines up against the static pointer to show TDC

Nelson Hargreaves

When trouble persists

Valves that consistently lose their adjustment are either damaged or are suffering from a degree of damage or wear somewhere in the valve train.

If the ends of the pushrod, rocker or valve stem are curved or worn a false reading will be obtained as the feeler gauge rests on the unworn parts.

If wear is excessive, or the case hardening has worn from the end of the rocker arm, then the removal of the parts concerned is the best remedy.

In more severe cases there may be pitting or scoring on the surface of the cam follower and the cam itself. This necessitates immediate renewal to protect the engine against further damage.

A bent valve or pushrod will also upset the valve clearance, so remove these items for examination if you are in the slightest doubt.

determine what type of adjuster is used on your bike.

Screw-type adjusters

Three types of engine use screw-type adjusters:

In the *pushrod* engine (fig. 14), the camshaft is situated low down in the engine, near the crankshaft. Running on each cam is a cam follower – traditionally called a tappet – which takes the form of a foot, a bucket or a rocker. And bearing on the cam follower is a steel or light alloy pushrod that runs up through the cylinder block to the head, where it makes contact with one side of the rocker. This rocker pivots on a shaft in the cylinder head so that one of its arms meets the pushrod and the other bears on the valve stem.

In the *single overhead camshaft* (SOHC) engine (fig. 1), the camshaft is situated at the top of the cylinder head alongside the rockers. The pushrod is dispensed with, each cam bearing directly against one arm of the rocker. Some double overhead camshaft (DOHC) engines – notably the Yamaha XS500 – have a similar arrangement, one camshaft operating the inlet valves and the other operating the exhaust valves.

In all these engines, the adjustment screw (where used) is threaded through one end of the rocker arm – it can be at either end – and is held in place by a locknut.

To re-set the gap, loosen the locknut and turn the adjuster screw until it nips

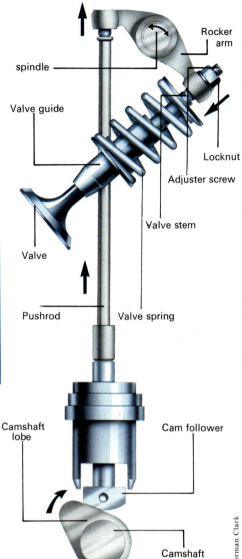

14. Valve layout of the Triumph Twin, showing the pushrod actuated valve and its adjuster screw and locknut

the feeler gauge in place (fig. 9). Then slowly loosen the adjuster, keeping a gentle pull on the feeler gauge. The moment that the adjuster releases the gauge is the right one – so hold the adjuster steady with the adjuster tool (fig. 10) and tighten the locknut.

Then re-check the gap and, if necessary, repeat the procedure, making sure that the gap does not widen while you tighten down the locknut. Make sure the locknut is fully tight.

When you are satisfied with one cylinder, move on to the next one in the firing order.

Eccentric adjusters

Eccentric adjusters are used on some SOHC engines, notably the Honda CB250 K2/3/4 and CB350 K4 and the Kawasaki Z400 up to about April 1978

and on some DOHCs, notably the Honda 450 and 500 twins.

In these engines, the rocker rotates on an eccentric spindle (fig. 15) and adjustment is made by means of the screw that locks the spindle to the head.

First you check the clearances as described above. Then you slacken off the screw in the side of the head so that the eccentric spindle can be rotated. Insert a thick screwdriver in the end of the spindle and rotate it until the desired clearance is obtained, then tighten the locknut. Again, re-check the clearances before you go on to the next cylinder.

On Honda engines, there is an important extra point to watch. There is a single scribed line radiating outwards from the screwdriver slot on the spindle. On the inlet valve rocker spindles, this line must point towards the carburettors, while on the exhaust rocker spindles the line must point towards the exhaust manifolds. Otherwise the rocker will not seat correctly on the spindle.

Replacing the cover
Once you have set the clearances for all the cylinders, clean the mating surfaces of the rocker cover and cylinder and replace any old gaskets with new ones. Before fitting the new gaskets, smear a thin coating of LM grease on both sides

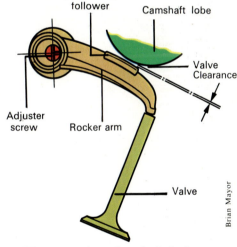

15. The eccentric rocker shaft design used on the Honda 500T, showing the eccentric spindle and the adjuster

of it. This will hold the gasket in place while you refit the rocker cover, and will make it easier to remove when you service the valves again.

Finally, replace the rocker cover(s) or caps.

Once having finished and checked the work you should not have to touch the valve clearance until the next service. However, if there still appears to be a rattle coming from the valve gear after adjustment, either your work is at fault or there is something more serious wrong with the mechanism.

DOHC valve clearance

Double overhead camshaft engines are designed to give high engine performance at high rpm. Because the camshafts bear directly on the valves – one on the inlet valves, the other on the exhaust valves – a method of adjustment different from that used on pushrod and SOHC engines has to be used to maintain correct valve clearances on most DOHCs.

This is done by the use of shims – small steel discs that take the form of spacers and come in different thicknesses. When the clearance is found to be too great, a thicker shim is used to replace the old one to keep the gap according to the manufacturer's specification.

Although the procedure for checking and adjusting valve clearances on this design is more complicated than the screw and locknut device used on push-rod and SOHC engines, it has certain advantages: first, the shim arrangement keeps the clearance correct over a longer period of time because of a much lower wear rate; and second, as there are fewer moving parts, it is more accurate and reliable.

SOHC systems

In a 2-, 3- or 4-cylinder SOHC engine the camshafts are mounted at the very top of the engine, the exhaust cam at the front of the engine, and the inlet cam at the back near the carburettors. So that the camshaft lobes do not directly hit the valves, there is an inverted bucket type cam follower (tappet) sitting on the top of the valve stem, and this does away with the need for the traditional rockers

As the camshaft rotates, the lobe on the camshaft bears against the follower, pushing the follower down against the pressure of the valve spring, and so forcing the valve open. As the camshaft rotates further, the follower comes off the cam lobe, and the valve spring pulls the valve back into a closed position.

When the camshaft lobe is pointing directly away from the cam follower, the valve should be completely closed. At this moment there is a small gap between the cam lobe and the cam follower, and this is the clearance that should be measured, according to the manufacturer's specification.

The more popular design, as in the Suzuki GS400 and the Yamaha XS750, has a small recess at the top of the cam follower in which the all-important adjuster shim is placed. Access to this shim is helped by the use of a special tool which can sometimes be purchased from a bike dealer or manufacturer. If not, it is possible to have one made up by a small motor engineering workshop. The tool depresses the cam follower, and allows room for the shim to be removed with a magnetic screwdriver or a pair of tweezers.

Suzuki GS850

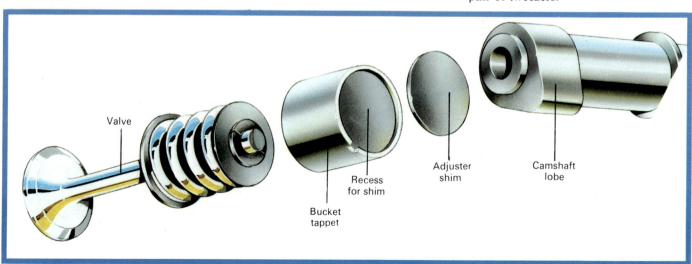

Valve

Bucket tappet

Recess for shim

Adjuster shim

Camshaft lobe

The other design is used on sporting bikes like the MV Agusta and Laverda triples, and on a few popular bikes such as the Kawasaki Z650. In this design, the adjuster shim is held in a cup in the valve retainer, beneath the tappet, so that the shim bears on the valve tip.

This design has long wearing capabilities, which means long servicing intervals and longer life. This is just as well, since both camshafts have to be taken out before the shims can be replaced, although the measurement of the gap is made before removing the camshafts.

On either type, if the valve clearance is too small, the valve does not close fully against its seat, power and compression are reduced, and the valve and its seat are burned by the hot exhaust gases swirling past. In addition, there is increased wear on the adjusting shim or the cam follower, and the cam itself.

Too great a gap, on the other hand, results in a noisy valve clatter, and a lack of performance because the valve does not open fully.

So most manufacturers recommend checking the valve clearances every 10,000 km (6,000 miles) or every six months. Some even recommend a check at 5,000 km (3,000 miles) intervals. This information, and the correct clearances for both inlet and exhaust valves, is given in the owner's handbook.

It is advisable to check the clearances before buying shims, as this way you buy only what you need.

Shims above the bucket

To adjust valves clearances where the shims are *above* the bucket, first remove the petrol tank and all the spark plugs. Then remove the two camshaft covers. The procedure is to measure the clearance of each valve in turn.

Using the method given in the previous chapter (pages 99 to 103), rotate the engine until the cam lobe is pointing away from the cam follower. Then place

Nelson Hargreaves

1. Cutaway of the valve arrangement on a double overhead camshaft engine, the Yamaha XS750. The camshaft lobe is pressing on the shim to open the valve

DOHC valve with shim below the tappet

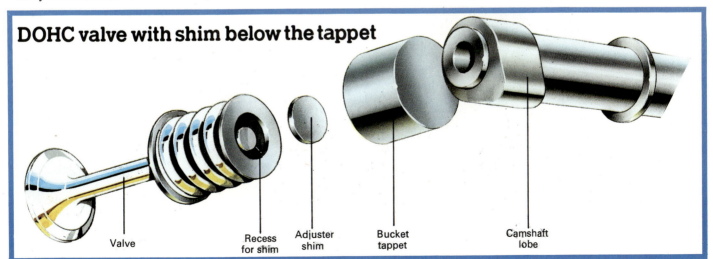

Valve Recess for shim Adjuster shim Bucket tappet Camshaft lobe

How to calculate shim thicknesses

Typical calculations showing how to work out the required thickness of shims in shim-adjusted engines are as follows:

When the clearance is too great

Take actual thickness of shim	0.100 in.
Add actual measured clearance of	0.018 in.
To give a total of	0.118 in.
Subtract recommended clearance of (say)	0.008 in.
To give a new shim thickness of	0.110 in.

So you should install a 0.110 in. thick shim.

When the clearance is too small

Take actual thickness of shim	0.090 in.
Add actual clearance of	0.004 in.
To give a total of	0.094 in.
Subtract recommended clearance of	0.008 in.
To give a new shim thickness of	0.086 in.

So you should install a 0.086 in. thick shim.

Adjusting the clearances with the shim above the tappet

2. The DOHC layout of the 3-cylinder Yamaha XS750, showing the inlet camshaft nearest the carburettors

3. Start off by removing all three spark plugs; then make sure you locate all the camshaft cover retaining screws

6. Turn the engine so that the camshaft lobe points away from the valve bucket. The adjuster shim is now visible

7. Now measure the clearance between the cam and the shim by inserting the feeler gauge. Measure all gaps in turn

10. Now turn the engine so that the cam comes off the shim. With the valve compressed, you have access to the shim

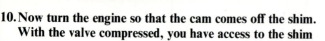

11. The adjuster shim can now be extracted by using a magnetic screwdriver and a pair of tweezers

a feeler gauge of the correct thickness between the cam follower and the cam and measure the clearance.

Check each valve gap in turn, making a note of what the existing clearances are. If the clearance is incorrect, the adjuster shim must be removed (and a small calculation made) so that you know what thickness of shim to install to correct the gap. To do this, you will need to rotate the engine so that the special tool can be inserted; this will hold down the valve to provide access.

So first rotate the engine until the cam is at full lift with the valve fully open. Fit the holding tool so that the curved end makes contact with the raised edge of the cam follower, but is not touching the adjuster shim. Now rotate the engine back through 360°, so that the back of the cam is nearest the tappet, and the lobe is pointing away from the tappet. The tappet should remain depressed by the tool, away from the cam. Now you can prise the shim out through the slot in the tappet wall.

Do not allow the cam lobe to touch the special tool, as this could result in the cylinder head casting being damaged. To avoid this happening, the *exhaust* cam must be turned *anti-clockwise* only and the *inlet* cam *clockwise* only, if viewed from the left.

The old shim may have a number stamped on the underside – for example 200, which means 2.00 mm. Theoretically, if the clearance is 0.15 mm too great then the old shim must be replaced with one 0.15 mm thicker – in this case No

4. Release all the camshaft cover retaining screws – not forgetting one behind the cam chain – and remove the cover

5. Camshaft detail of the Yamaha XS750, showing the inlet and exhaust camshafts and the camshaft chain

8. You now need a special tool to compress the valves. Shown is the factory tool, but you can have one made

9. Turn the engine to compress the valve. Then fit the special tool so that it rests on the edge of the bucket

12. Now measure the thickness of the shim, using a micrometer for accuracy. Refer to the panel for shim calculations

13. Now select the shim of the appropriate thickness to correct the gap to the manufacturer's specification

14. Fit the new shim in the bucket. Turn the cam, extract the tool and check the gap. Now adjust the other valves

15. The layout of the Suzuki GS750 shows the basic similarity in the design of DOHC valve arrangements

Nelson Hargreaves

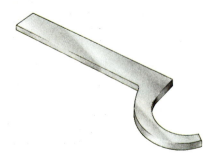

16. Suzuki issue a special tool for their DOHC engines. This speeds up the shimming operation but only works on Suzuki engines

17. (right). The tool in position

215 or 2.15 mm. But that assumes that the wear is on the valve seat; if in fact it is on the shim, the number given will be wrong. So to be on the safe side, measure the thickness of the shim with a micrometer.

Each manufacturer produces a table of shim selections that is well worth consulting. But if you do not have access to this kind of table for your bike, refer to the panel on page 106, which tells how to calculate for both thicker and thinner shims.

After consulting the panel, select the appropriate shim to restore the clearance to the manufacturer's specification. Insert it in the top of the cam follower, with the figures (if any) facing downwards. Rotate the engine until the cam lobe comes onto the shim, then release the tool. Rotate the engine to make sure that the shim is seated properly, then check the clearance you have just adjusted.

Now repeat this procedure with the remaining valves, making sure that all gaps are according to the manufacturer's specifications.

Shims below the bucket

On bikes that have the adjuster shim *beneath* the tappet, you first measure the clearances in the manner described above. Then you have to remove the camshafts to make any adjustments to the valve clearances.

But beware! When you come to replace the camshafts after doing the job,

they must go back in exactly the right place. If this is not done – even if the chain is 'out' by one or two teeth – the valve timing will be wrong. And you will run the risk of bent valves and damaged pistons.

So, before you begin, use nail varnish (or something similar) to mark one tooth on the camshaft sprocket and the chain link which fits it. And as you remove the chain, ensure that it cannot slip off the crankshaft sprocket. (You can do this by securing each side of the

chain with a twist of wire.)

Now you can slacken off the chain tensioner. The technique for this varies from bike to bike; on some, it may be necessary to split the chain by taking off the split link. To release the cam chain tension on the Kawasaki Z650 it is only necessary to remove the jockey wheel that the chain runs under (fig. 20). This gives enough slack for the chain to be lifted off the camshaft sprockets. Then slacken off the bolts retaining the camshaft bearing caps, lift off the caps, and slide out the camshaft (fig. 23). This will reveal the tappets.

Lift out the tappets – carefully, so that you do not lose any shims, and making sure you know which valve each tappet belongs to.

With the tappets out, the shims will be clearly visible. Remove the ones that need replacing and insert new shims of the correct thickness after first doing the relevant arithmetic (see panel). Once the shims have been installed, replace the tappets on their original valves, then replace the camshafts.

Some bikes have marks to help you position the camshaft correctly. On the Kawasaki Z650, for example, the T14 mark on the auto-advance mechanism behind the generator cover must be lined up with the static pointer. At this point, the arrow marked T on the inlet camshaft must be lined up so that it points directly to the carburettors, but parallel to the cylinder head.

The T mark on the exhaust camshaft must have the arrow pointing towards the exhausts and parallel to the head. When refitting the camshaft bearing caps, the camshaft will try to twist, against the pressure of the valve springs. There is nothing you can do about this, so getting the marks correctly lined up is a matter of trial and error.

Adjusting the clearances with the shim below the tappet

18. The 650 Kawasaki DOHC layout, showing the camshafts, cam chain, jockey wheel and camshaft bearing caps

19. The clearance is measured between the camshaft and the tappet, with the cam lobe pointing away from the tappet

20. First check all the valve clearances, then release the jockey wheel by undoing the four retaining bolts

21. If it is necessary to release both camshafts, undo the 16 bolts that hold the retainer caps to the camshafts

22. Then release the caps in sequence, making sure you do not mix them up. They must be replaced in the same order

23. Pull the chain off the sprocket and remove one camshaft. If removing both cams, support the chain with some wire

Bob Taylor

If in the slightest doubt, contact your dealer; if the timing is out by only a couple of teeth it will result in damage to the pistons and valves.

With the camshafts installed in the correct position, refit the camshaft bearing caps. Then refit the chain. Adjust the chain to its correct tension, and check all the valve gaps.

After you have run the engine for about 400 km (250 miles) it is as well to recheck the valve clearances – they should not have altered, but it is better to be on the safe side. You may also find that it is necessary to adjust the camchain tensioner at the same time.

It can be a good idea to keep a record of any alterations in the shimming you have had to carry out, for future reference. This way you will know how much shimming there is on each valve so that you do not have to peer at indistinct numbers stamped on the shims, with the possibility of getting it wrong.

24. Now remove the tappets, using a magnetic tool. Do not disturb the valves that do not need adjusting

25. Next extract the shim from its seat. Because of the magnet the shim will usually come out with the tappet

26. Refer to the panel to calculate the shim thickness. Then select the correct shim and place it in its seat

27. Refit the tappet on the valve it originally came from. Then replace the camshafts in their original positions

28. Remove the contact breaker cover. For correct valve timing, turn the engine so that the T14 mark appears on the auto advance unit in the hole behind the contact breakers. Now turn your attention to the camshafts

29. The T mark on the exhaust camshaft sprocket must point forwards. Count 36 links back from here on the cam. This aligns the T mark on the inlet cam sprocket. Now refit the cam bearing caps and other components

Bob Taylor

110

SOHC cylinder head

Removing and replacing the cylinder head on a 4-stroke bike because the head gasket has blown is a task which a bike owner will face only rarely. But knowing how to handle this job is an essential preliminary to a complete engine strip.

The head gasket is usually made of either asbestos fibre or solid copper or aluminium. Its purpose is to form a gas-tight seal between the cylinder head and the barrel. Replacing it is not a difficult job in itself, but on 4-stroke engines is complicated by the work that has to be done before the head can actually be removed.

SOHC engines

In SOHC engines the valves are actuated by a chain-driven camshaft moun-ted in the head. This means that, before the cylinder head is removed, the cam chain must be detached and this disturbs the valve timing. It is vital that it is reset exactly, otherwise serious damage can be done to the engine. If the chain is only one tooth out, at least the valve will collide with the piston. So do not undertake this job without an illustration of your bike's timing marks – either from the manufacturer's technical department or a manual – or, alternatively, unless you have the experience to interprete the timing marks as you dismantle the pieces which make up the camshaft.

Preparations

If you do this job over a weekend you will have time to road-test the bike to make sure all is well. Try to use a shed or garage so you can work on the bike under cover. Clean it up in advance – there is nothing worse than groping around in the dirt and waste looking for the nut you have just dropped.

The stage at which many do-it-yourself mechanics run into difficulty is re-assembly, because they cannot remember how the components came apart. So use a systematic approach to dismantling. Set up a workbench – it need only be a piece of chipboard resting on crates – and cover it with paper. Lay out

Removing the cylinder head on a SOHC engine

1. Carburettors, exhausts and ignition leads have been taken off this Honda 400/Four. Now remove the breather cover

2. Underneath the breather plate you will find the bolts which secure the camshaft cover. Remove them

3. Lift off the cover and the gasket. Clean out the head with degreaser and smear oil over the rocker gear

4. Inspect the rockers for signs of wear and tear. This one is beyond its working life and must be replaced

Continued ▶

George Wright

a tray containing a cleaning fluid such as Jizer or paraffin (kerosene), with an old toothbrush. Next to it, have a jar of oil and a paintbrush. Finally have an assortment of luggage tags and sticky labels available.

The system works like this: you remove a part of the engine, clean it, smear oil over it, and label it, stating how and where it fits into the engine. Obviously there is no point in slapping oil over parts like the contact breakers or external fittings. But components such as the camshaft are precision-made and this method not only ensures their correct assembly but also protects them from damage in the meantime.

As well as the contents of the bike's toolkit, you will need a socket set, a torque wrench (see below) and either an impact screwdriver or – much less expensive – a T-bar screwdriver and hammer. Ask for a T-bar to suit your own bike, since their heads are not uniform.

If you cannot borrow a torque wrench you can hire one from a tool shop; you will need a few pounds as a refundable deposit.

Some bikes – the Yamaha 650 is one – are supposed to require a special cam-chain splitting tool. But many workshop mechanics modify nut-splitters to push out the relevant chain rivets, or use a power drill to 'waste' the rivet heads. If you use this method, pad the chain well with rags to catch the swarf.

You will also need electrical screwdrivers, possibly a wooden mallet (in case the head proves stubborn) and a length of wire to secure the camchain.

When you come to reassemble, the cylinder head will have to be tightened to the torque setting recommended by the manufacturer. So before you begin, ring the maker's technical department and ask for a list of the torque settings for your bike.

A gasket set is essential. This will

contain all the O-rings, seals and inserts that are necessary. Additional items such as new chain rivets or an exhaust port seal will have to be bought separately.

In Britain, a number of pattern gasket sets are available for the more popular models. These are often about half the price of the manufacturer's own spares, but they contain only those seals that require regular replacement.

Gaining access

First, put the bike on its centre stand or, if this is missing, on a stout block. Leave the sump plug accessible; you may need to remove it later. Clean the engine thoroughly with petrol, washing off all the grit to ensure that it does not get inside the barrel when you remove the head.

Some bikes are designed so that the cylinder head can be removed without taking the engine out of the frame. In

5. The camchain tensioner is held by a small plate behind the camchain sprocket. Undo the bolts to release it

6. With the cam caps off – they must be released slowly and evenly – undo the bolts that hold on the chain sprocket

7. Wire the camchain to the top tube. Lift out the camshaft, clean it up with paraffin and smear the faces with oil

8. Take out the camchain tensioner. This is a press fit in the well. Unhook the chain guide which is opposite

Continued

9. Inspect the camchain tensioner for wear. Most makers give a minimum thickness at which it must be replaced

10. This cylinder head is held by 12 nuts. Release these, starting at the edge and working towards the centre

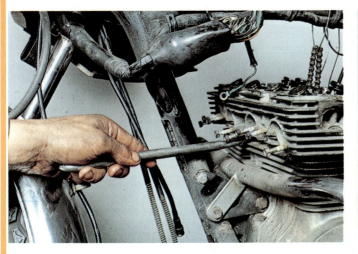

11. Now try to lift off the head. If it proves stubborn, use a screwdriver to pry at the reinforced lifting point

12. Slip a bar in under the camchain to stop it falling into the well. Now you can untie the wire from the top tube

Continued

this case it is only a matter of taking off the fuel tank, exhaust pipes, carburettors, plugs and plug leads to gain access to the rocker covers and head bolts or studs.

But on some bikes the engine must be removed before you can dismantle the head. This is because the head is retained by very long studs and, although the head can be shifted, the top frame tube will not allow it to be lifted clear of the barrel. On bigger bikes, such as the Honda 750 four, engine removal is a two-man job.

Removing the ancillaries
First disconnect the battery, remembering to take off first whichever terminal is earthed to the bike. If this job has to be done during winter, take the opportunity to clean up the terminals with a wire brush and have the battery recharged.

Next, remove all electrical connections between the engine and the frame – usually a job simply of unplugging the connectors. Either make a note of the connections and their colour codes, or attach labels to the wires as you pull them apart. Tape back all loose wires out of harm's way.

On smaller engines, the carburettors can be left in place and just the fuel lines disconnected, but with larger models they should be removed to make lifting the heavier engine easier. Bear in mind that, although twin or multiple carburettors may look identical, on a few bikes – notably Suzukis – the internal specifications may differ. So label them to ensure that they are refitted in the correct order.

Removing the engine
If the engine has to be removed – and only experimenting will tell you – start by draining the oil on wet sump machines, or run off the oil tank on dry sump models. Once this has been done, tie up the oil supply pipes out of the way.

While the oil is draining, remove the tachometer drive from its housing – normally it screws anti-clockwise. Disengage the clutch cable at either end. Remove the exhaust pipe or pipes (page 188). Finally, disconnect the rear drive chain (page 141). If the machine is fitted with shaft drive, you will need to consult a manual on the best place to separate it from the rocker.

With all its ancillaries stripped, the engine should by now be secured only by its mounting brackets.

Try to get someone to help with the next stage, as the bike may fall over while you lift the engine. As the engine is removed, take care to note the positions of any spacers which fall out when the brackets are dismantled.

Removing the rocker arms
On most SOHC bikes the rocker cover is on top of the engine. There are exceptions, however, such as the Honda mopeds and Kawasaki SOHCs, where access to the camshaft is gained through a cover on the side of the head.

The rocker cover (or covers) is usually

13. Timing marks on an engine rotor – this one is from a Honda moped. The T aligns with a notch on the casing

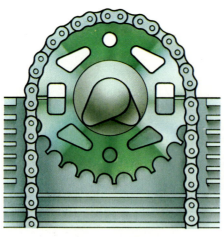

14. On this Honda SOHC, the camshaft sprocket timing marks have to be aligned with the top of the head

held on with cross-head screws. Expect these to be stubborn, particularly if the bike is new, since they will have been tightened with compressed air tools. You *must* use either an impact screwdriver or the correct make of T-bar screwdriver.

The rocker arms may be mounted either in the rocker cover or in the head itself. In the first instance the rockers lift off with the cover. Usually the design of the cover means that you cannot replace it – and hence the rockers – wrong way round. But just in case, look for an arrow on the cover which tells you which way it should go back.

If the rockers are in the head, they may be held in place by rocker caps. In this case, the camshaft has to be positioned so that no valve spring load is taken on the rockers you are removing. So turn the crankshaft over until the rocker you are taking off is released.

You can now release the rocker spindle clamp bolts and lift out the spindles. These items must be labelled so they are returned to their original positions. Each follower will match one of the lobes on the camshaft.

Some bikes – notably the Honda CB185, CB200 and K2/K3/K4 250s – have rockers which are a sliding fit. These have to be pushed out with a screwdriver or a long bolt.

Dismantling the camshaft assembly

Removing the rockers exposes the camshaft assembly. The next job is to dismantle this – and this is the stage at which great care is needed, since every component must be returned to exactly the right position if the timing is to be correct.

The camshaft runs in two or more bearings, so the next task is to loosen the bolts holding the bearing caps in position. Now loosen the camchain tensioner – usually a spring-loaded slip-

per arrangement which bolts between the cylinders.

If the camshaft sprocket is detachable, it is not necessary to split the camchain. Start by stuffing clean rag around the chain well. Next, pass a length of wire through the camchain and fix the other end to the bike frame. This precludes any possibility of the camchain falling down into the crankcase when the sprocket is removed. Undo the bolts holding the camshaft sprocket in place.

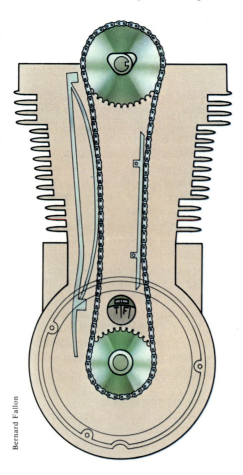

15. This timing system, used on some Hondas, aligns a notch on the sprocket with the top of the head

Once free of the chain, the sprocket should slip off the end of the camshaft without any difficulty.

Note carefully the position of the sprocket fixings. Some Hondas, for example, have one bolt and one set screw. If you mix them while reassembling they can shear while the motor is running under load.

On some models, like the Yamaha 650, it is not possible to lift the head without splitting the camchain. To do this you will need some help – you must not let the chain slip to the point where it disengages with the sprocket on the other (crankshaft) end. One of the chain links has a soft rivet with a slotted head; turn the engine over until you find it. While your helper holds the chain, remove the rivet with a pin rivet extractor (obtainable from a motorcycle spares shop). Then secure both ends of the chain with wire.

Now the camshaft can be removed. This is held in place by split bearing caps. This means that each cap must be replaced with its respective mate on the cylinder head. The caps are normally numbered or marked for identification during rebuilding, but check on this point before allowing the caps to get mixed up.

The camshaft carriers can now be unbolted, once again taking careful note of the bolts' respective 'homes'. On some bikes, located under the camshaft carriers you will find several rubber seals and some metering jets for the oil feeds. These must be removed and kept in a safe place. If they are not refitted during the rebuild the oil feed to the camshaft will be adversely affected.

Along with the oil seals and the metering jets there may well be some locating dowels. These are often loose in the head and should be removed rather than left in place.

Removing the head

Now, at last, you can remove the actual bolts or studs holding the cylinder head in place. On a twin- or multi-cylindered engine you should start with the outer nuts and work your way towards the centre. You 'crack' each nut by giving it a half turn anti-clockwise and then release the nuts slowly and evenly. This is to ensure that the head is not placed under stress which could cause it to warp.

Watch out for any hidden bolts or nuts down in between the cylinders. These may be covered with rubber plugs, tucked away out of sight among the cooling fins. Only when you are sure that all the nuts have been removed should you attempt to break the head seal and then very carefully.

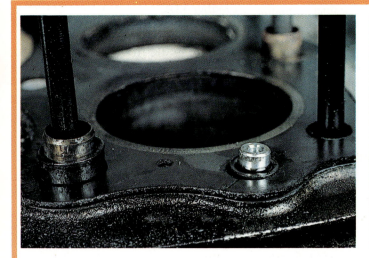

16. Note the position of the oil restrictors. The stud seals should be renewed every time the head is disturbed

17. Scrape off the carbon deposited on the head and barrels. Clean the faces with paraffin and blow out oil restrictor

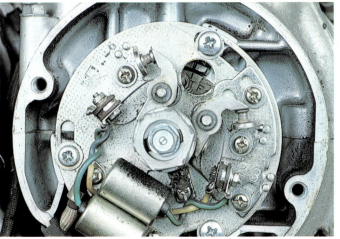

18. To set the motor to TDC use the window in the breaker plate to align the T mark with the mark on the casing

19. Refit the camshaft so that the timing lines are level and exactly parallel to the joint faces

Actually removing the head may prove something of a problem, since modern fibre gaskets can stick the head solidly to the barrel. If you have trouble, try turning the engine over, using either the kickstart or a spanner on the central bolt of the alternator. The compression should push the head off. If this fails, you may find leverage points, either in the form of a solid lip or bracing bars located between the fins. You can try using a heavy screwdriver or tyre lever here – but not on the cooling fins, which may snap.

If everything else fails, you may have to resort to clouting the head with a mallet to free it, again taking care not to hit the fins.

Once the head is off, slide a bar or screwdriver across the cam chain well; this will prevent the chain from slipping into the crankcase while the head is being removed. Untie the wire which is holding the chain to the bike frame, pass it out of the head and tie it up again. Now you can lift the head clear.

Cleaning the head and block

With the head removed, there will be particles of gasket stuck to both the mating surfaces. Also, where an oilway passes through the head gasket joint, there will be rubber O-rings. Remove these rings before you clean the head. Plug the oil gallery with rag to stop debris falling in and blocking the passage.

The best tool for scraping off the remanants of gasket is a plastic car windscreen wiper. Workshop mechanics often use a dull knife, but this is risky, because it could score the soft alloy. But ensure that every bit of the old gasket is removed, scrubbing it off with a nylon pan scourer and a degreasing solvent such as Jizer

The surface of the cylinder block should be cleaned in a similar manner, but taking extra care not to spill too much degreaser into the cylinder bores. Before you begin, turn the engine so that all the pistons are half way up their bores, and stuff clean rag into the cyl-

inders to protect them.

Next, inspect the oil galleries to make sure they are clear – if not, blow out the muck – and clean all the surfaces with a paraffin-soaked rag.

Inspect the faces of the valves to see that they seat properly. If there are signs of pitting at the edges, the valves will need regrinding or replacement. You can test the efficiency of each valve seal by turning the head upside down and filling each chamber with paraffin. If it runs away, the valve is leaking and must be reground.

Check both mating surfaces again to see there is no distortion. Lay a steel straightedge across each surface. If you can slip a 0.05 mm (0.002in.) feeler gauge under the straightedge at any point the head is beyond maximum tolerance. It can be skimmed flat again by a local engineering firm

Finally, check that the threads of the head bolts or studs are in good condition. If you can see silver slivers of metal, this means that the thread has stripped and the whole item may need to be replaced.

A common occurrence with studs is for a whole stud to unscrew. Because it is under tension, this damages the alloy threads in the crankcase – and, once they are stripped, the unit must be replaced or drilled out and helicoiled (fitted with a threaded insert) by an engineering firm. To prevent this happening, a precaution when you are reassembling is to apply a thread-lock fluid to the bottom set of threads and smear high-melting-point grease on the top of the stud.

Fitting the new gasket

When both the mating surfaces are clean and flat, the new gasket can be fitted. Check that it is right way round, as well as right way up. Any rubber O-rings should be fitted at this stage; they can be held in place with a small dab of grease. Make sure that any locating dowels you removed are also back in place.

Do not use gasket cement on the cylinder head joint. Provided the surfaces are clean and flat, and you have not omitted any O-rings, the head gasket will not leak oil or engine compression.

The head can now be lowered into position and the retaining nuts or bolts fitted hand tight. For the final tightening of the bolts, you must use a torque wrench set to the figure specified by the bike manufacturer. A manufacturer's manual will also give a correct sequence for tightening the bolts, but provided that you work diagonally, and from the inside outwards (see charts on page 126), this is not vital.

Reassembly and timing

Once the head has been torqued down, the cam carriers can be refitted. Do not forget to replace any dowels, O-rings or oil-feed jets that locate under them.

If you have split the chain during dismantling, the next job is to repair it with a new link. With the link inserted, fit its side plate and rivet it home, supporting it against the thrust of the riveting by a hammer head held behind it – obviously you will need some help while doing this. Use a nail punch to spread out the rivets, and make sure the link is secure.

To make sure the timing is accurate, all of the following marks must be aligned as you reassemble the engine:
1. The T mark on the engine rotor with the mark on the crankcase. (If there is no such mark, the engine must be brought to TDC by another method
2. The scribed line on the end of the camshaft with the split of the end bearing cap; or – depending on your bike
3. The timing mark on the camshaft sprocket with the fixed mark on the cylinder head.
The procedure is as follows: (see next column).

Finding TDC

Before you replace the camshaft assembly, the engine must be brought to top dead centre (on No. 1 cylinder, if there is more than one). On many bikes, you can align a T mark on the rotor with a corresponding mark on the crankcase. Otherwise, use the procedure described on pages 40 to 41.

Trial assembly

Next, feed the cam chain sprocket on to the camshaft.

The camshaft can now be fitted into its carriers (check that it is right way round), and the split caps re-fitted. Tighten the caps to the recommended torque.

Do not fix the cam sprocket to the camshaft yet; the timing must be set first. With the engine at TDC, turn the camshaft and sprocket until the timing marks (see above) line up. Next, check that the camshaft is right way up, and not 180° out.

To do this, see that the lobes on the cylinder from which you are setting the timing are 'on the rock' – that is, if the cam followers were fitted one valve would just be opening while the other was just closing. (You may have to do some trial assembling at this stage to check this point.)

Now, *without* moving either the engine or the crankshaft, you must turn the sprocket in the cam chain until its bolt holes line up exactly. Then fit the sprocket to the camshaft.

Next, the cam chain tensioner must be refitted, and tension applied to the chain as described in the workshop manual.

Once you are satisfied, rotate the engine until the lobes on one side of the camshaft are in the 'closed' position, and refit the cam followers on that side. Lock the cam follower spindles in place.

Next, slacken the tappet adjusters right off (page 100) and rotate the engine until the cam lobes on the opposite side of the engine are in the closed position. Fit the cam followers on that side, and again slacken off the adjusters.

If the engine you are working on has the cam followers fitted into the camshaft cover, the tappet adjusters should be backed off before the cover is refitted. Next, adjust the tappets (pages 99 to 103).

Refit the exhaust, making sure that new gasket sealing rings are used in the exhaust ports. Double check that the old seals have been removed – one extra seal on one port will pull a four-into-one exhaust system out of line.

The carburettors can now be refitted, the fuel lines hooked up, and the engine oil replaced or topped up.

20 (below). Two arrangements of camshaft timing marks. Note that in these types the contact breakers are fitted on the end of the camshaft, so the crankshaft timing marks are stamped on the generator rotor.

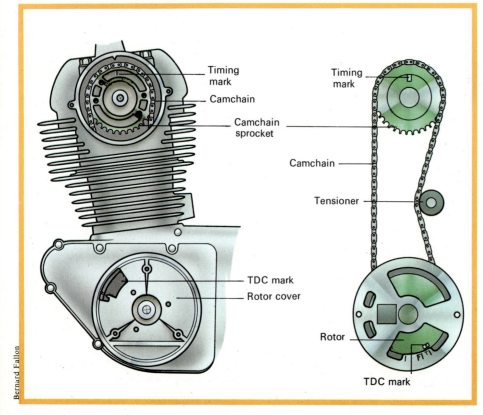

Bernard Fallon

DOHC cylinder head

Cylinder head removal on double overhead camshaft engines 'DOHCs' follows the same principles as on SOHCs. The difficult bit is to rebuild the camshaft assembly without disturbing the valve timing—a job that is complicated by there being two camshafts instead of one.

As with SOHCs, you gain access to the head by removing the engine ancillaries and camshaft covers, slackening off the camshaft chain tensioner, and dismantling the camshaft assembly. With the cylinder head removed and all traces of the old head gasket cleaned off—jobs described in detail on pages 111 to 116 – you then have to reassemble in reverse order and make sure that the timing is correct.

Since correct timing is so vital to the engine's operation—and a camchain which is 'out' by one link on the cam sprocket can produce an error of 20° in the timing—two things are essential in tackling this job:

1: That you get from the manufacturer's technical department, or from a manual, an illustration showing how the timing marks align (or alternatively that you have enough experience to interpret the marks correctly as you dismantle the camshaft assembly).

2: That, having done the job, you turn the engine over by hand several times to make sure that, for example, none of the valve stems is hitting the top of a piston.

The same thing applies to pushrod engines, incorrect valve timing on a OHV engine can result in a valve colliding with the piston with disastrous consequences.

DOHC engines

The DOHC engine is an extension of the SOHC principle, with two camshafts operating the valves where one was used before. One camshaft opens the inlet valves; the other opens the exhaust valves. Both are usually driven by a single chain running off the crankshaft.

Double overhead camshafts are usually fitted to large capacity bikes, typical of which are the Kawasaki Z650 and Z1000. Suzuki compete in the same field with their GS range of bikes. Both these makers use the archetypal DOHC design—that is, a transverse in-line four, with the camshafts acting directly on inverted, bucket-type cam followers. The camchain runs up through the centre of the motor to a sprocket in the middle of the camshaft.

Lifting the head on a double-overhead-camshaft engine

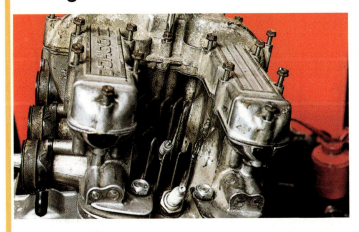

1. Use an impact driver or a T-bar screwdriver to undo the bolts holding the camshaft cover. Remove the cover

2. Lift off the gasket and remove the rubber plugs on the end of the camshaft. Clean the joint faces with Jizer

3. Remove the camchain tensioner. Lock the spring in place and undo the bolts that hold the assembly in position

4. Clean the tensioner assembly with degreaser and check the action of the spring, making sure it moves freely

Nelson Hargreaves

Stripping down

The stripping procedure is similar to that for an SOHC engine (pages 111 to 116). But the DOHC engine is more complicated, so there are certain additional problems to be overcome.

To save time, it is best to work on the engine in the frame, which is possible on the larger models. But if you have to work on the bike out of doors it may be worthwhile taking out the engine so that it can be cleaned and worked on in comfort.

To get the engine out of the frame you will need help—at least one other person, and preferably two. First strip off all the ancillaries. Use a jack to support the engine as you lift it; do not jack directly on to the casing. Spread the load by fitting a wooden block on top of the jack. Loosen the engine mounting bolts and slip a stout rope sling under the engine. As a precaution against scratching the frame, tie rags around the most vulnerable parts. Raise the jack and lift the engine out to one side between two people, while a third person steadies the bike.

The next stage is to take off the camshaft cover, usually held down by conventional screws or bolts. The exception is Yamaha, which uses Allen screws; you will need a metric Allen key to fit. Whichever type is used, slacken the bolts as evenly as possible.

Lifting the cover reveals the camshafts and chain assembly. Turn the engine over, by aligning the marks on the ignition plate behind the right-hand chain case cover, until it is at top dead centre.

Slacken the cam chain tensioner (see page 116. Now release the camshaft bearing caps. On most bikes this should present no difficulty, but Suzuki recommend clamping the camshaft in position with vice grips while the caps are released. On most models releasing the camchain tensioner allows the camshaft to be slid out. Make sure the camchain does not fall down into the crankcase by wiring it to the frame.

On the Honda 500T and Yamaha models it will be necessary to split the camchain using the special tool already mentioned (page 112).

As you remove any parts, label them so they can be replaced in their original positions, right way up and right way round. This applies especially to cam followers and cam bearing inserts, both of which can fall out when the head is lifted.

Loosen the head bolts a little at a time, and working diagonally outwards from the middle (page 126). On the Yamaha XS500, which uses metric Allen bolts for the head, long series Allen key's are available.

When removing the nuts look out for special copper sealing washers. These are to prevent oil which is forced up under pressure from leaking from the studs.

Make sure you have released all the nuts and bolts securing the head. It is quite common to have two or more bolts to locate the head on the block. These are sometimes hidden at the side of the head, so check carefully before attempting to lift off the head.

Reassembly

Reassembly is the reverse of the

5. Undo the Allen bolts which pin the chainwheel in place. Pull off the assembly, including the rubber pads under it

6. Release the bolts that hold the camshaft bearing caps. Do this evenly to minimize the stress on the shaft

7. To ensure that the bearing caps are returned to their original positions, they are marked with a number

8. Slip the chain off the sprocket and lift out the shaft. Clean it with degreaser and coat the lobes with oil

Continued

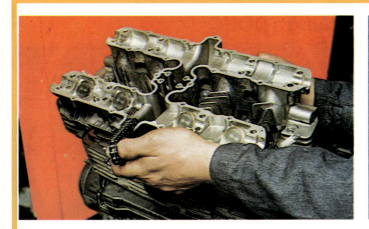

9. Slacken the head bolts in a diagonal sequence so that the head is released evenly. Pry off the head

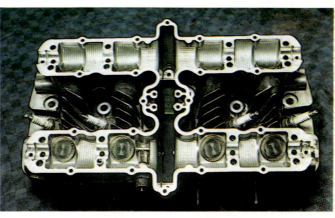

10. Clean the top of the head with a pan scourer dipped in Jizer or degreaser. Wipe the casting dry with a rag

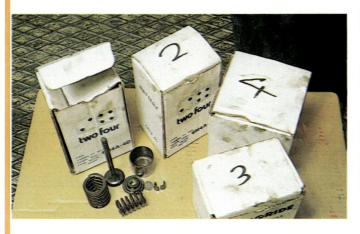

11. The cam followers are a press fit and not interchangeable. They should be removed and tagged for easy assembly

12. Now turn the head over and clean off the carbon deposit with Jizer. Remove the valves only if it is necessary

13. Remove the old gasket and clean up the face of the block. Use a spanner to hold the chain out of the way

14. The chainwheels are a press fit in the block. Be careful that the rubber blocks do not topple into the crankcase

Nelson Hargreaves

stripping procedure. The most important thing to remember when refitting the head is to tighten the bolts a little at a time and in the correct order. When you fit a moving part like the camshaft or camshaft sprocket, lubricate it thoroughly. Many mechanics use a thin smear of molybdenum disulphide paste such as Molykote, on the cam lobes and bearings. This lubricates the surface for the first few miles until the engine oil galleries have primed themselves.

To ensure that the timing is correct, assembly must be carried out in a specific order. First, one camshaft is set in position with the engine at TDC. Then the second camshaft is installed. If it runs off the same chain as the first, its position is established by counting the correct number of pins—not links—between the two sprockets.

Always start with whichever camshaft is driven directly from the crankshaft (if both are, start with either). Loop the

camchain over the sprocket, making sure that the timing marks line up. On Yamahas, each cam sprocket has a punch mark which aligns with a similar mark on the cam cap. On most Hondas, the timing marks run across the sprocket and align with the top of the head. On some other bikes, the sprocket marks align with those on the casing.

Now thread the camshaft through the sprocket—make sure you have it right way round—and bolt on the sprocket

'Superbike' timing marks

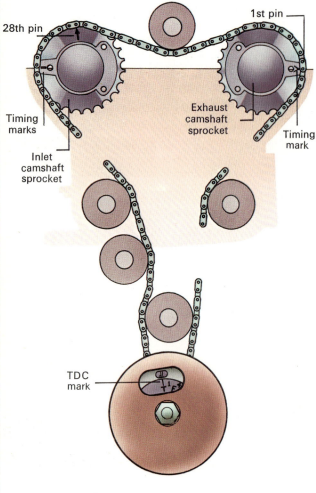

28th pin

1st pin

Timing marks

Exhaust camshaft sprocket

Timing mark

Inlet camshaft sprocket

TDC mark

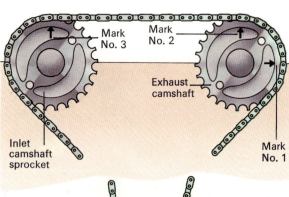

Mark No. 3

Mark No. 2

Exhaust camshaft

Inlet camshaft sprocket

Mark No. 1

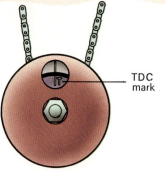

TDC mark

15. Timing on the Kawasaki Z1000 and the Suzuki GS1000 is done in a similar way. With the engine at TDC, a V-mark (or arrow) is used to align the exhaust camshaft with the top of the head. Then the correct number of pins is counted off to align the inlet camshaft—on the Kawasaki, 28 pins from the V; on the Suzuki, 20 pins between marks

Timing a DOHC

16. Turn the engine to TDC, using the marks behind the contact breaker plate. Make sure they align precisely

17. Refit the exhaust camshaft with the timing mark level against the lip of the cylinder head. Bolt down the caps

18. Starting with the first pin above the arrow, count off the correct number of pins—not links—for your bike

19. Fit the chainwheel and torque the bearing caps to the maker's recommended settings. Tighten the head bolts

Bernard Fallon

120

Lifting the head on a pushrod engine

20. Take off the exhausts and the carburettor, including the dripshield. Remove the inspection covers

21. Take off the head-steady brackets. Make sure these are replaced when the motor is assembled

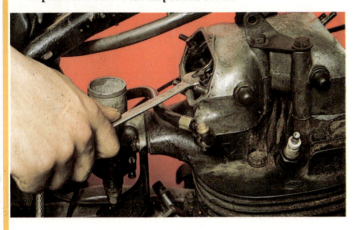

22. Undo the rocker cover bolts. Note that two of them are situated inside the casing

23. Lift off the rocker cover, which should come off without difficulty. There is no need to remove the rocker arms

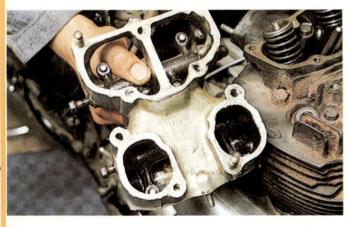

24. Clean the old gasket off the lip of the casings. Inspect the rocker arms for signs of wear and play

25. This shows the original arrangement of the pushrods. Make sure that you label them as they are removed

to the correct torque setting.

Assemble the second camshaft by the same method, making sure it is correctly spaced from the first. Now release the camchain tensioner while you re-check that all the timing marks align.

Complete your reassembly by the same methods as for an SOHC. When you replace the camshaft covers, use a new gasket and seal it with a clear silicone gasket compound such as RTV to seal down the plate.

Pushrod engines

The overhead valve engine is much simpler to work on than the more recent overhead camshaft designs.

Stripping down

Start by taking off the exhaust pipes.

These are held either by clamps or threaded roses and you may need to gently hammer these off with a mallet and drift. Next, detach the carburettors, which should come off as one unit. Turn off the petrol, remove the fuel pipe and detach the carburettor from the block. Lift off the carburettor with the cables still attached.

Remove the engine-steady brackets if

26. Inspect the valve spring assembly for wear and tear, paying particular attention to the collets

27. Start to release the head bolts, working inwards from the side of the engine. Leave the centre ones until last

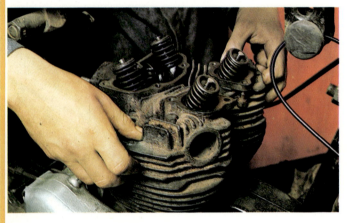

28. Straddle the bike and pull upwards on the cylinder head. If this fails, insert a pry bar between head and block

29. Remove the copper gasket carefully. This may be used again providing it is re-annealed

they are fitted. Undo the bolts holding the rocker cover in position and lift it out of the way. Turn the engine to release each pushrod from the rocker arm and remove the pushrods one at a time.

Since each pushrod must go back in its correct position and the right way up, this must be recorded. The easiest way is to take a cardboard box, turn it upside down, punch holes in it and insert the rods in the same order that they came out of the engine. This procedure is of particular importance on Morini V-twins, which use pushrods of different length, the rear cylinder pushrods being 2 mm longer than the front.

Inspect the pushrods for signs of wear or cracking. Sometimes you can see a hairline crack in the rod before it fails in use. Pay particular attention to the tips of the rod, looking for signs of galling and for discoloration from overheating. Roll the rod on a flat surface like plate glass, to see that it is straight, because a rod that is bent will rob the motor of power by failing to open the valves properly.

Now you can begin to slacken the cylinder head bolts. On singles like the Honda PC50 and angled twins like the Morini V-twins, Honda CX500 and BMW, the head bolts are arranged in a symmetrical pattern. The nuts should be slackened in a diagonal sequence (see page 126). On the big twins like the Triumph, BSA and Norton make a start by releasing the bolts on the outside and progressing inwards. Leave the central bolts until last.

Straddle the bike and gently pull the head upwards. Remove the gasket and decarbonize the chambers as described on pages 114 and 115.

Reassembly
On those models that have a copper gasket, the old one can be used again providing it is annealed. This is necessary to soften the metal and involves heating the cut-out with a blow torch and then quenching in a water bath.

To keep the gasket in position while you install the head, smear it with grease. Fit it in position. Next install the pushrods so that they are properly

engaged in their followers. Turn the engine until the pushrods are 'off the rock' so that they will engage the rocker arms without difficulty. Grease the threads on the studs and fit the cylinder head in position. Slide the head down on to the barrel and engage the pushrods in the rockers. This is a bit fiddly, so once you are sure that they are in place push the head home and fix it with a couple of bolts. Now turn the engine over and check the operation of the pushrods. Now fit the rest of the head bolts and tighten them all to the maker's torque settings.

Squirt oil over the rocker assemblies and valve gear and replace the rocker cover minus the two inspection covers used to set the tappets. Bolt on the head steadies and reset the tappets. This operation is left until last, as tightening a head bracket can throw out the clearances.

Take the bike out for a road test. Ride gently for the first few km, watch out for oil leaks that show that the gasket is blowing. If this occurs retighten the head bolts.

Decoking a 2-stroke

A carbon-clogged 2-stroke will lose both mileage and performance. However, regular decarbonizing of the engine and exhaust will prevent this. And decoking is a job which any bike owner can undertake from stripping down to reassembling without special training or tools.

As a 2-stroke has to burn all its lubricant within the engine, or expel it through the exhaust, it is more liable than a 4-stroke is to suffer from an excessive build-up of carbon.

Oil burns comparatively slowly unless subjected to intense heat. So in a 2-stroke, where the temperature rarely reaches the point at which the oil is totally evaporated for perfect combustion, some oil partially burns to form carbon, and carbon compounds like tar, while the rest is exhausted as vapour.

As the combustion residuals pass through the complexity of tubes and baffles in the exhaust system, some condense to mix with particles of carbon and form a black, sticky substance which, over a period of time, will clog the system.

Fortunately, 'ash-free' 2-stroke oils and advances in engine design—whereby oil is metered into the motor according to demand or throttle opening—have helped to reduce the problem.

So you no longer have to strip the top end of the motor and dismantle the exhaust system every 1,600 km (1,000 miles) to recapture performance lost by carbon build-up. A unit can now be left for anything between 5,000 km (3,000 miles) and 8,000 km (5,000 miles) between decokes.

This deals with the decoking of air-cooled 2-strokes. Decoking 4-strokes is covered in the next chapter.

Tools for the job

With the exception of a torque wrench, which may be needed to tighten the cylinder head nuts or bolts, the bike's toolkit may suffice, although a good socket wrench, combination spanners and screwdrivers are preferable.

To carry out the decoke sharp plastic scrapers are very good for alloy components. A soft wire brush on an electric drill is also an effective decarbonizing tool, particularly for cylinder heads.

Fine glass-paper may be used to remove stubborn deposits such as piston lacquering, but the item must be washed off with petrol afterwards to remove any abrasive particles that may have become embedded in the alloy. Steel wool can also be used for the same purpose, but care must be taken, as before, not to leave any particles behind on the component. A slower, but more satisfactory, means of cleaning scorch marks and lacquer off is with a proprietary metal polish, for this imparts a very smooth finish.

Steel scrapers of some kind, such as a ground-down hacksaw blade or feeler gauge, will be needed to decarbonize the exhaust ports. You will also need a wire brush and perhaps a blowlamp to clean the exhaust baffles.

Decoking a single

1. Having detached the HT lead and removed the spark plug, slacken the exhaust flange with a C-spanner

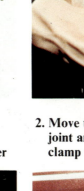

2. Move to the exhaust pipe/silencer joint and slacken the securing clamp with a cross-head screwdriver

3. Unclamp and release the carburettor from the air-filter pipe, then unbolt it from the barrel flange

4. Release the head bolts one full turn each, working in diagonal order, then undo them completely

5. Ease the cylinder head from the barrel. If it won't budge, tap round the joint to break the seal

6. While removing the cylinder head, take careful note of the gasket position and way up for reassembly

Continued

7. Remove the exhaust pipe from the engine, then prise the sealing ring out of the exhaust port

8. If necessary, free the barrel from the crankcase by light taps with a soft mallet or hammer handle

9. Pull the barrel squarely off the crankcase studs, then proceed to decoke all components

Before starting you must also first obtain a complete decoke gasket set of cylinder head gasket, cylinder base gasket, exhaust port gasket seal and, sometimes, carburettor flange gasket or O-ring(s). Also, in case the pistons are to be removed, buy the necessary set of gudgeon pin circlips.

Removing the ancillaries

First, you must remove or disconnect all ancillary components such as the HT lead, spark plug and the carburettor.

The carburettor is usually either attached to the cylinder barrel by a metal strap around a rubber induction stub (fig. 22) or bolted direct to the barrel on a flange which incorporates a neoprene O-ring (fig. 3).

If the engine is of the disc inlet valve type, the carburettor feeds directly into the crankcase and therefore need not be disturbed.

Where the carburettor is bolted directly to the cylinder barrel, ensure that the O-ring is in good condition and not pinched on reassembly.

On certain machines, the air filter box and manifold to the carburettor(s) may have to be removed. This is straightforward and normally a cross-head screwdriver is all you'll need to loosen the various clamps.

Removing the exhaust

Next remove the baffle from the silencer while it is still firmly attached to the machine.

A small bolt or cross-head screw normally retains the baffle tube (fig. 11) and, after this is removed, a pair of pliers can be used to grip the bar across the centre of the baffle tube to pull it out (fig. 13). If it is stuck in the silencer a twisting motion should help to free it.

Next, undo the exhaust pipe retaining clamp or bolts on the cylinder barrel. Some models require a C-spanner (fig. 1) to release the threaded exhaust

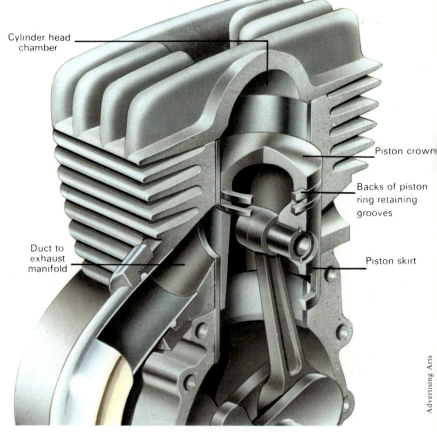

Cylinder head chamber

Piston crown

Backs of piston ring retaining grooves

Duct to exhaust manifold

Piston skirt

Advertising Arts

flange which screws into the barrel. Others simply have two or three nuts which hold the exhaust pipe clamp on studs in the barrel (fig. 20). Use plenty of penetrating oil before undoing the nuts.

With silencer bracket bolts removed, you should now be able to lift off the entire system. Note that inside the exhaust port, where the exhaust pipe presses internally, there is normally a copper/asbestos O-ring sealing gasket (fig. 7). If this does not drop out, it should be hooked out and renewed on reassembly.

If the silencer has become so blocked as to make removing the baffle tube difficult, detach the system and try

10. A representative view of a 2-stroke engine showing the areas that need to be decarbonized

soaking the silencer in a strong solution of caustic soda to free the baffle (figs. 14–15).

To do this, stand one end of the silencer in a small tin of molten candle-wax, which will solidify and seal the end of the silencer. Mix a caustic soda solution and pour it into the other end of the silencer. Leave it overnight. Take care not to get the caustic soda on your hands or clothes. Do this job out in the open on concrete, where there is drainage and a good supply of running water.

Twenty-four hours later, pour away

Dealing with a gummed-up exhaust

11. To remove a silencer baffle, first undo its securing screw from the silencer body at the tailpipe

12. Feed some cable round the baffle cross-bar, hold it firmly with pliers and knock out the baffle

13. If the baffle is loose enough, just grip the cross-bar with the pliers and pull it out with a twist action

14. If the baffle will not come out by either of these methods, detach the silencer and seal the tailpipe

15. Stand the silencer upright, pour in a solution of caustic soda and leave it 24 hours to free the baffle

16. To clean the baffle, burn it off with a blow-lamp and then use a wire brush to remove the dried carbon

the soda solution, rinse out the silencer with clean water from a hose and remove the baffle tube. If the baffle still won't come out take the system to your bike dealer who may have the equipment to remove it, or renew the silencer completely.

Note that caustic soda dissolves aluminium and should not be used if the baffles are made of this metal (e.g. some Puch models).

Removing the cylinder head

To remove the cylinder head is perfectly straightforward on a 2-stroke and should not even require petrol tank removal, unless access to the head nuts or bolts is badly restricted.

On a 2-stroke motor usually both the barrel and cylinder head are retained by cylinder head nuts, screwed on to crankcase-located studs that pass through the head and barrel. However, the barrel and head may be located on separate studs, or use a combination stud and bolt arrangement.

Initially, each head securing nut or bolt should be slackened one full turn, working in the correct removal sequence. This sequence should be in

diagonals which, on a single cylinder engine, simply means working from corner-to-corner as you release the bolts. On a one-piece cylinder head fitted to a two- or three-cylinder engine the 'diagonals' sequence still applies, but you should work from the middle of the head outwards (fig. 17) when releasing the bolts to avoid possible head distortion. After releasing the head, lift it off the barrel.

At this stage you can check whether the barrel needs to come off or not by examining the exhaust port for excessive carbon deposits. Inspect the port both from outside and inside the cylinder. You may have to move the piston down the barrel to do this and care should be taken on the 'through stud' type not to unseat the barrel, possibly breaking the gasket, while doing so.

If the port is only lightly covered with deposits (less than 2–3 mm) there is no need to disturb the barrel.

If necessary ease the barrel from the crankcase, after undoing any securing nuts ('base stud' type—fig. 23). Sometimes the barrel becomes stuck fast with the base gasket and needs a gentle

tap with a hide mallet to free it.

As the barrel is lifted clear of the crankcase, wrap some clean rag round the con-rod (fig. 24), tucking it well into the crankcase opening so that no dirt, pieces of grit or circlips can drop into the crankcase.

Inspect the piston to see if it needs to be removed for further attention. If the rings don't appear to be sticking in their grooves and no excessive lacquering on the piston below the rings is present (caused by ring wear allowing 'blow by'), you may be able to decoke the piston crown without removing the piston from the con-rod.

Removing the piston

If you do have to remove the piston, a pair of circlip pliers may be required to compress the pin circlips (fig. 27) and lift them out of their grooves. Some circlips have no 'plier ears' and these will need a pointed metal rod, such as a ground-down pop-rivet to pry them out of their grooves. Note that, for safety, all piston circlips should be renewed on reassembly. Before you start, check that the top of the piston has a direction arrow (see Rebuilding the engine, below). If not, mark one on, pointing forwards, so that it will be refitted the correct way round. On twin and multi-cylinder engines, also number each piston so that they are replaced in their original bores.

With the circlips removed, you can sometimes just push the gudgeon pin out of the piston with a suitably sized rod (fig. 28). But if this is not possible, in no circumstances take a hammer or mallet and try to knock the pin out with a drift, as this will probably damage the connecting rod.

Instead, use a proper gudgeon pin extractor or simply heat the crown of the piston with a blowlamp for 30 seconds or so. This will expand the metal and the pin will then easily push out.

Most modern 2-strokes have caged needle roller small-end bearings so, after lifting off the piston, take the cage out of the connecting rod small end (fig. 29). At this stage, the bearing can be cleaned and inspected for damage; the cages sometimes crack and break up.

Decoking the head and barrel

Place the cylinder head on a bench and line up your scraping tools. To clean the cylinder head, using a sharp hardwood or plastic scraper, scratch off all carbon, rub lightly with steel wool or fine glass-paper, then wash the chamber out with petrol. A faster method of de-carbonizing is to use a soft wire brush on an electric drill (fig. 30). If you wish to be really meticulous, the combustion area can be finished off by polishing with ordinary metal polish.

The only section of the barrel which needs attention is the exhaust port. The port can be scraped clean with an old hacksaw blade (fig. 34) and finished off with wire wool or a brush on a drill. Also, pay attention to the base of the barrel where it joins the crankcase (fig. 35). There may be parts of an old base gasket stuck to the mating surface and this should be cleaned off and replaced.

While on the bench, the barrel can be checked for bore wear. If a distinct groove or wear ridge can be felt with the fingernail about 6 mm ($\frac{1}{4}$in.) down from the top of the bore, a rebore may be needed.

Decoking the piston

Look at the piston next. If it is still on the engine, the crown should be scraped clean (fig. 24) and then 'polished' with fine wire wool or a fine grade of wet-and-dry and washed off in petrol.

If there is excessive lacquering or the rings are stuck in the grooves, more detailed work with the piston out will be necessary.

Decoking guide

A 2-stroke needs decoking as soon as it shows the slightest symptoms of carbon build-up. Loss of power, pre-ignition and excessive smoking indicate that your bike needs attention.

On a moped, loss of power will mean having to use the pedals to assist the bike up hills which it normally pulls unaided. On a light-weight motorcycle, the need to change down to save a flagging engine, where the bike normally pulls well in the higher gears, indicates a clogged engine.

On some sports 2-strokes, there will also be 'pinking' or pre-ignition —a high-pitched, metallic clicking or pinging noise emitted by the motor when pulling hard at low engine revs with the throttle wide. The noise is made by pockets of gas igniting due to glowing carbon particles in the combustion chamber. In extreme cases, pre-ignition can cause serious damage to the motor.

Although manufacturers' manuals recommend decoking at stated intervals, two identical bikes can in fact have widely different decoke periods.

If one machine is used around town daily for short trips to the office or factory, with little more than half throttle being used for any length of time, the motor never reaches its optimum operating temperature. Eventually, you will see a thick, black sticky mess dripping out of the exhaust silencer. It will probably need decoking every 2,000 km or 1,250 miles.

But if an identical machine is used every day on longish trips on main roads or dual carriageways, where wide throttle openings are used most of the time, the tailpipe has a smooth grey or coppery brown appearance, with no black, oily deposits. So the owner can often ride for up to 8,000 km (5,000 miles) without problems.

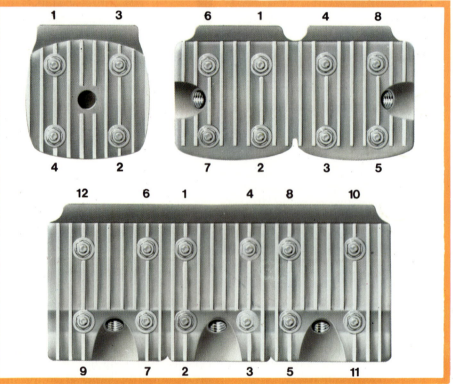

First remove the piston rings from their grooves by springing them outwards using both thumbnails (fig. 26). If they are stuck, try sliding a feeler gauge behind each one to free it (fig. 25). If they are badly stuck they will probably break and need replacing.

Behind the piston rings, there may be expander rings. Hook these out of the way and scrape the piston ring grooves clean (an old broken piston

17. View of the heads from single, double and triple cylinder 2-strokes, showing nut removal sequences

ring makes an ideal scraper tool). Finally, clean the grooves using a piece of string dipped in metal polish pulled back and forth. Gently rubbing with metal polish will also remove all but the heaviest lacquering on the piston. Fine glass-paper will also do, but do not use

Decoking a twin or multi

18. Disconnect and remove the fuel tank for access purposes, then unscrew and remove the cylinder head cover

19. Remove the spark plugs, undo the head nuts in the correct order and lift off the one-piece head

20. Soak each exhaust pipe-to-manifold clamp stud with penetrating oil, then undo the securing nut

21. Working under the saddle, undo the bolts that hold the air-filter box to the bike frame

22. Slacken off the manifold clamps, then detach both the carburettor and the air-filter box

23. Using a ring spanner, release the nuts holding each barrel to the crankcase and lift off one barrel

24. With a cloth round the con-rod to stop bits falling into the crankcase, clean the piston crown

25. If the rings are stuck in their grooves, run an old feeler gauge behind each one to free it

26. Remove each ring by carefully prising it apart, lifting it out of the groove and off the piston

27. If the gudgeon pin circlips have no ears, prise out the clips with needle-nose pliers or a sharp nail

28. Push out the gudgeon pin with a drift by hand. Heat the piston crown first if the pin is stiff

29. Lift off the piston and extract the needle roller bearing from the con-rod 'small-end'

Continued

30. Decarbonize the cylinder head with a scraper or drill and brush. Also scrape off any old gasket remains

31. Clean out the ring grooves with a sharp nail or pop-rivet, remove any lacquering and finish off with polish

32. Wash off the needle roller bearing in solvent and examine it for wear. Replace it if defective in any way

33. Prise out the exhaust manifold sealing ring and replace it with a new item when rebuilding

34. Clean out the carbon from the exhaust port with an old feeler gauge or a sharpened hacksaw blade

35. Clean any old gasket remains from the mating faces of each barrel, then rebuild the engine

36. Method of checking a cylinder head for distortion with a straightedge and a feeler gauge

any steel scrapers, files or other hard metal for working on the piston.

Cleaning the silencers

The last and most messy stage in the decoke is to clean the silencer system. Removing the deposit from the baffle tube is best done with a blowlamp. With the baffle standing on bricks, out in the open, simply keep heating it with the blowlamp until all the grease has burned off leaving dry carbon (fig. 16). This may then be scraped off and the baffle tube wire-brushed clean. Also, poke clear all the baffle tube holes with a nail or the tang of a file.

Rebuilding the engine

Before you start, check the mating face of the cylinder head with a straightedge and feeler gauge as in fig. 36. Bike heads rarely warp, but if they do they must be corrected—a job for a specialist workshop.

If fitting new piston rings, note that the grooves are pegged to stop undue rotation of the rings. The open ends of the rings are curved to fit around the pegs and this dictates which side up they should be fitted. This is important, as the rings will go on the wrong way up, but will not compress sufficiently to allow the cylinder barrel to slide over the piston.

If the piston has been removed, note that the arrow should point towards the exhaust port when refitting the piston and small-end bearing to the connecting rod. If not, serious engine damage could result. Also be sure to lubricate the bearing and gudgeon pin with fresh engine oil before reassembly.

Make sure that all the base gasket stuck to the crankcase mouth is removed and that the mating surface is thoroughly clean. If the motor has a positive feed oil system, check if there are oilways in the barrel (as on Suzuki bikes). Clean such oilways by blowing or flushing with petrol, but do not use any hard substance which might enlarge them. And watch that you do not block them by fitting the new base gasket the wrong way round.

When refitting the barrel, lubricate rings and barrel with 2-stroke oil first.

Some cylinder head gaskets, usually the copper type, have to be fitted the correct way up. This is usually with the 'compressible' groove uppermost.

Cylinder head nuts normally have a specific torque setting. The nuts should be tightened down diagonally (fig. 17) with a torque wrench and re-checked after the motor has been run for a couple of hours.

Always take care not to overtighten head or barrel nuts.

Decoking a 4-stroke

Four-stroke engines suffer from a progressive power loss as deposits of hardened carbon build up on the piston, valves and head. Carbon affects combustion efficiency, but you can rejuvenate an ailing engine by giving it a decoke and top end overhaul at 32,000 km (20,000 mile) intervals.

After prolonged use, the combustion chamber of a 4-stroke engine becomes encrusted with a layer of hardened carbon. Carbon is an unburnt residue of the fuel mixture which enters the cylinder from the carburettor. Most of the residue is expelled with the exhaust gases but particles are deposited and take root on the piston crown, the combustion chamber, the exhaust ports and the valve gear. Once the first fine film has been laid down, it becomes progressively easier for further, heavier deposits to build up as the gas passage out of the cylinder becomes increasingly restricted. Modern cylinder heads operate at such high temperatures that the deposits take on a hard, ceramic-like appearance. Eventually, if left unattended, all the combustion chamber components will 'coke up', resulting in poor engine efficiency.

But carbonization is not a sudden process, it may take many months to affect the engine seriously. Consequently, you may not notice the gradual deterioration in the bike's performance.

The first clues to the 'coked up' state of the engine are a heavy fuel consumption and an audible 'pinking' caused by the overheated carbon deposits pre-igniting the combustion chamber mixture. But the condition of the spark plug is quite an accurate indicator. If the plug is fouled with carbon it is more than likely that the head needs a decoke.

However, if you know the bottom end of your engine to be badly worn, there is little point in undertaking a decoke. Resulting power increase from an overhaul could greatly speed up wear or even destroy a weak bottom end.

Decoking involves removing the cylinder head and cleaning the carbon from the affected parts to restore the engine to peak working efficiency.

Preparation

Before starting the decoke, you will need to buy a new cylinder head gasket set and obtain a few tools to make the job easier. A valve spring compressor,

Removing the cylinder head and rocker assembly

1. On a few bikes you will have to remove the engine from the frame. The remaining procedure follows

2. With some machines the camchain or the complete camshaft must be removed before the head will come off

3. Then remove the cylinder head nuts and withdraw the cam chain tensioner bolt if one is fitted

4. Remove the cylinder head by carefully lifting it off the long through bolts

5. The rocker assembly is released by removing the rocker shaft retainer screw and withdrawing the retainer

6. Pull the rocker shaft out with a pair of pliers, and extract the rocker from the cylinder head

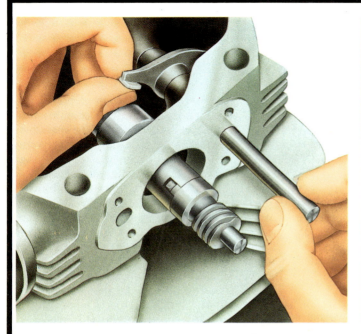

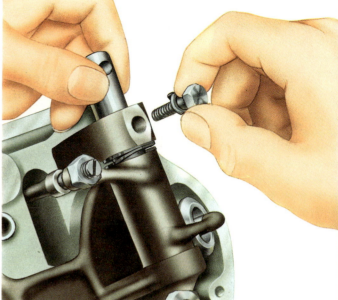

7. The Honda CB175 rockers can be extracted after removing the camshaft housing and withdrawing the rocker shafts

8. On the Moto Guzzi V-twins, you must remove the locating screw and slide out the shaft to free the rocker

a valve grinding tool, some grinding paste, a hardwood scraper and a strong metal scraper with a chisel edge are essential, and an electric drill with a selection of brass wire brush attachments will make cleaning the cylinder head a lot simpler than doing it by hand.

Removing the cylinder head

Decoking procedure involves removing the cylinder head and rocker or cam assembly. This operation varies enormously from one machine down and there is not space here for us to detail all possible variations.

Figures 1–9 (pages 129 to 130) show some of the variations found on different models. The main snags involve detaching the camchain without allowing it to fall into the crankcases and on pushrod machines manoeuvring the head to extract the pushrods.

Removing the rocker assembly

To dismantle the rocker assembly, first remove the spark plugs and set the engine to TDC. This releases spring pressure on the rockers and makes their removal easier. On some bikes, such as Triumph twins, the rockers and their spindles are housed in the rocker box top, which is bolted on top of the head. In this case the housing is removed as a unit by releasing the bolts that hold it in place. Once the rocker box is removed the head can be unbolted and the valves extracted.

To remove the rockers on other

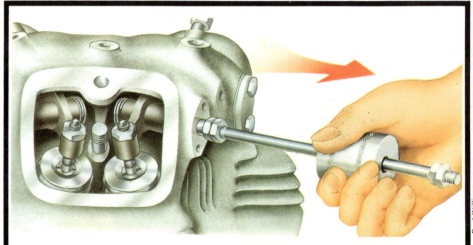

9. The Norton Commando needs a special tool to extract the rocker shafts; the tool is a sliding hammer with one end screwed into the rocker shaft

machines, like Moto Guzzis, the rocker spindles have to be taken out to free the rocker arms (figs. 7 and 8). The spindles are held in place by mounting posts and located by screws. Remove the screws and carefully pull out the spindles, noting which way round they come out. Catch the rocker arms, the coiled spacing spring and any small washers as the spindles are freed.

A different type of rocker assembly, found on some Norton vertical twins, employs rockers running on a spindle that locates directly into the cylinder head. The spindle must be extracted from the head to take the rocker arms off. Spindle and rocker removal can be left until the head has been taken off but it may be found easier to perform the job with the head in place. You will

need a special tool to pull the spindle from its mounting as it is an extremely tight fit (fig. 9). If the tool is not available, find a bolt of the correct thread size and screw it through a T-bar and into the end of the spindle. Hold the T-bar firmly and pull the spindle out.

Once the rockers have been taken out, remove the pushrods from their tubes in the head. Mark each rod as it comes out so that it can be replaced in the same location on reassembly.

With the rockers and associated components removed, unbolt any remaining stud nuts or bolts holding the head and pull it clear of the barrel (fig. 4). If the head is stuck firmly in place, break the seal by tapping it very gently with a mallet.

Some Japanese bikes have pry points

Extracting the valves

10. A valve spring compressor is needed in order to remove the valves; make sure it fits

11. Fit the compressor and turn in the handle to compress the springs until the valve collets are free

12. After removing the valve compressor, the valve can be withdrawn sliding it out from the cylinder head

13. You can now remove the valve springs and the valve retainer cap; remember the order in which they come out

14. Keep each valve spring assembly and its valve together so that there is no chance of mixing them up

15. If you have a multi-cylinder engine, it helps to mark each valve so that it is replaced in its original guide

between the head and the barrel, and in this case, pressure with a screwdriver can separate the two. However, if your bike does not have pry points do not try to separate the head from the barrel with a screwdriver between the fins, or between the mating surfaces.

You can now extract the valves from the head.

This is a complex procedure.

Extracting the valves

Valves must be removed from the head so that the combustion chambers and the valves themselves can be cleaned. Extracting the valves requires the use of a valve spring compressor (fig. 10) and the procedure is virtually the same whether you are working on an OHC or pushrod engine.

On DOHC machines, a bucket and adjusting shim fits on to the top of each valve stem. Remove these before fitting the spring compressor.

Compress each spring in turn by placing the forked end of the tool over the valve stem, so that it rests on the spring retainer. Fit the screw plate on to the valve head in the combustion chamber. Then screw in the adjusting bar to compress the spring (fig. 11). Compress the spring so that it moves down the valve stem far enough to reveal the two small split collets (fig. 16). Hold the tool securely then remove the collets from their grooves with a small screwdriver with a dab of grease on the end, or a magnet. Slowly unscrew the compressor and remove it from the head. Pull the valve cap, the springs, the spring base plate and any oil seals off the

valve stem. The valve should then drop out of the head from the combustion chamber side (fig. 12). Make a note of the order in which the components came out ready for reassembly.

Remove the other valves in exactly the same way and make sure that each assembly is kept separate from the rest by marking them with tape so that they can be returned to their original position (fig. 15).

Parts to be decoked can now be dealt with as three separate units: the pistons (still in the barrel), the combustion chamber and the valves. Arrange the parts so that each cylinder unit can be cleaned in turn.

Decoking the piston crowns

In order to clean a piston crown the piston must be positioned at the top of its stroke in the cylinder (TDC). With the bike on its centre stand, put the engine in gear and turn the rear wheel until one, or (on multi-cylinder machines), two pistons are at TDC. Note how much you have to turn the wheel and in which direction. This will help you when the valve timing is reset.

Place a piece of rag in the bores of the pistons that are not being worked on so that as little dirt as possible enters the cylinders.

Clean the piston by rubbing the edge of a wooden scraper over the crown. You can use an electric drill fitted with a soft wire brush attachment, but do not apply too much pressure (fig. 21). Rub the crown carefully using a circular motion. On no account use emery cloth as it can scratch the piston. Localized scratching on the crown can act as heat points, which concentrate heat during

combustion, and could severely damage the piston. If the carbon still refuses to budge, use some fine, or medium-fine wet-and-dry with some engine oil, and gradually rub the coke down using a circular motion. It is also possible to use a large screwdriver with squared, chisel edges and rounded corners. Take great care not to scratch the piston crown.

If your engine is fairly old or has covered a high mileage, do not remove the ring of carbon which has formed at the edges of the piston and the top of the cylinder bore (fig. 22). The ring acts as an oil and compression seal and removing it could reduce the efficiency of an old engine.

Once the piston is clear of carbon, polish the crown with some metal polish applied with a soft rag. This will help reduce the rate at which the piston picks up carbon. After polishing, turn the rear wheel round so that the piston moves slightly down the cylinder, and wipe out dirt or dust from the bore. If you have access to an air line use it to blow out the dirt.

Finally, squirt a little engine oil on to the top of the crown and the cylinder walls. This will help to pick up any particles of dirt left in the cylinder as well as replacing the lubricant that has been rubbed off during cleaning. The oil will cause the exhaust to smoke when the bike is first started, but it will burn off quickly after a short while.

This is quite normal and a short ride should be sufficient to clear the oil.

Decoking the combustion chamber

Before cleaning the combustion chamber, slot the valves back into place to stop the seats from being damaged. This is just a precaution; if you are extremely careful, it is not necessary to replace the valves. As your bike has an alloy head, handle it with care as they are very soft and damage easily.

Use a hardwood scraper or some wet-and-dry abrasive paper with some engine oil to clean the combustion chamber. Alternatively, use an electric drill fitted with a rotary, soft-brass brush. Once all the heavy deposits have been cleaned off, complete the job by polishing the chamber with metal polish.

Polish the inlet and exhaust port channels with some metal polish after carefully cleaning any carbon from the area, as this will aid the gas flow through the chamber and increase the efficiency of the engine. When the head has been fully decoked, take the valves out and clean off all dirt and swarf with paraffin.

Split collets
Inner valve spring
Valve spring compressor
Valve spring retainer cap
Outer valve spring

Steve Cross

16. The compressor in place with one end over the valve head and the other over the spring cap

Removing the carbon

George Wright

17. Now inspect the piston crown with the piston at TDC. This piston has a good crust of carbon

18. Then inspect the cylinder head; this head does not have too much carbon, but it must be cleaned

Continued ▶

19. The neck of the inlet valve is usually well coated with carbon and this must be removed to improve the gas flow

20. If in any doubt about the condition of your valves, compare them to a new set and replace them if necessary

21. Whatever method you use to clean the piston crown, take extreme care not to scratch the metal surface

22. If your engine is well worn, leave a ring of carbon round the top of the piston; if not, remove it

23. Again with care, a soft rotary brush can be used to clean the head; an alternative is oiled wet and dry

24. Clean all the carbon off the valve neck by using a metal scraper. Finish by polishing the cleaned parts

George Wright

Decoking the valves

Valves, particularly exhaust valves, build up heavy deposits of carbon on the head face and the lower part of the stem. Do not be tempted to put the valve in a vice while dealing with stubborn deposits – you will probably bend the stem and ruin the valve.

Use a metal scraper to remove the worst of the carbon (fig. 24) and finish off by polishing with metal polish or emery cloth.

After prolonged exposure to combustion chamber temperatures, the valves may show signs of heavy pitting on the seat area of the head. Exhaust valves, though made of extremely hard metal, may even crack or chip under the heat.

Test the valves for wear by replacing each one back into its guide in the cylinder head. Hold a valve head between finger and thumb, pull it about 1.27 cm (0.5in.) out from the seat and try to move it sideways in the valve guide. If there is even a small amount of lateral movement, the valve and possibly the guide will have to be renewed. If much movement is evident, it is likely that both the valve and its guide has worn out. But rather than replace a guide unnecessarily, fit a new valve into the guide and make another check for lateral movement, if none is felt then only the valve need be renewed.

Fitting new pistons

Piston kits are manufactured for specific machines. Make sure that you are choosing the correct kit for your bike.

Start by removing the cylinder head and gasket following the instructions given on pages 111–122.

Remove the push rods (if there are any) or secure the camchain so that it cannot fall into the crankcase.

Removing the barrels

On some machines slots are cut at the base of the barrels where you can insert a screwdriver to help lever them up. In no circumstances insert a screwdriver between the barrels and crankcases in

1. Loosen the barrels by tapping them very gently with a soft object such as a hide hammer or block of wood

2. Another way of loosening the barrels is by turning the engine with a spanner on the end of the crankshaft

5. Carefully remove the gudgeon-pin circlip with a pair of long-nosed pliers or a pointed scribing tool

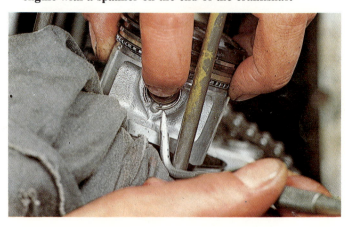

6. Be very careful not to drop the circlip down into the crankcases, as this could mean a complete strip-down

9. With all the pistons removed, and the con-rods laid against the casings, the base gasket can be removed

10. Don't forget to remove any dowels locating the barrels on the crankcases

any other place, as this will damage the mating surface and cause oil leaks. If the barrels do not lift off easily, try turning the engine over (fig. 2), or tapping them very gently with a hide mallet or an ordinary hammer on a block of wood (fig. 1). Be very gentle – it's very easy to break a fin and they are difficult to repair.

As you raise the barrels up the studs you will have to feed the camchain through and secure it hanging over the side of the crankcases (fig. 3). When the barrels are about halfway up the studs, stuff the crankcase mouths with rags around the con-rods to prevent any loose particles falling down into the cases, or the con-rods falling heavily against the sides of the crankcase mouths and damaging them. Remove the barrels completely and place them with the head gasket surface downwards (fig. 4). This is because the part of the cylinder liner which protrudes below the barrel block can be quite fragile and easily cracked.

Removing the pistons

To remove the pistons themselves, it is necessary to take out the gudgeon-pin circlips and then the gudgeon pins. The circlips may be of two varieties. There are Seeger circlips which must be re-

3. Feed the cam chain through and secure it over the sides of the crankcases, and stuff the openings with rags

4. Place the barrels with the head gasket surface downwards to prevent damage to the protruding liners

7. The gudgeon-pin can usually be removed by pressing it with your fingers, supporting the piston as you do it

8. Be careful not to allow the con-rod to fall heavily against the crankcase mouths as this will damage them

11. Remove the gasket carefully, not forgetting to thread the camchain through and secure it over the side

12. Scrape all remains of gasket off using an old blunt knife so as not to damage the gasket surfaces

George Wright

Continued

moved using proper circlip pliers or wire rings which are removed using ordinary long-nosed pliers or a scribing tool (fig. 5). Be very careful not to drop the circlips into the crankcases – in fact, throw them away, as they must not be used a second time.

The gudgeon-pin can often be removed merely by pressing it out with your fingers (fig. 7). If it seems stuck, do not force it but try wrapping the piston in a rag soaked in boiling water. This will expand the piston but not the pin, so it should then slide out easily. If it still won't move, you will have to try and get hold of a gudgeon pin extractor. You may be able to borrow one from your dealer or a local garage. Lift the piston off carefully. The hole this reveals in the end of the con-rod is called the little-end, which will contain one of two types of bearing. The simplest is just hardening on the inside surface of the eye, which bears directly on the gudgeon-pin. If this is so you have already dismantled it by removing the pin. Some little-ends contain pressed-in bushes. These can usually be removed by gentle heating with a hot rag followed by gentle pressure on the bush with a

metal tube of the same diameter. Do not hit it with a hammer as this will damage the big-end bearings.

Try the gudgeon-pin in the hole: it should slide smoothly in but not have any perceptible up and down movement.

If the eye has worn out, the entire con-rod must be replaced.

Remove the old base gasket carefully not forgetting any dry locating dowels (fig. 10) and scrape off any of it that has stuck to the crankcases with a blunt knife – a sharp one will damage the mating surfaces and cause oil leaks (fig. 12). Clean the underside of the barrel block in the same way and finish off by wiping the surfaces with methylated spirits or petrol to thoroughly degrease them. Fit the new base gasket using a gasket compound such as Hylomar (fig. 13) closely following the instructions on the packet.

Piston, ring and cylinder wear
Major wear of these components usually manifests itself in continuous piston slap when the engine is under load, a condition which should not be apparent in a sound engine once it has warmed up. In addition, wear leads to high oil consumption (in a 4-stroke), indicated

by blue smoke from the exhaust, and eventually to a noticeable loss of compression and power.

The piston itself wears relatively little, especially in the ring-belt area above the gudgeon pin. In contrast, the bore wears most severely at the top, front and rear where the pressure exerted by the piston is transferred from one face to the other as it passes through top dead centre.

Wear investigation should start with the cylinder bore and necessitates the use of an internal micrometer or the careful use of calipers and a vernier gauge. If the maximum fore and aft diameter measured just below the top of the ring travel is more than about 0.2 mm (0.008in.) greater than that at the bottom of the bore, a rebore or reconditioned cylinder is required, plus, of course, a new oversize piston/ring assembly.

Should the bore wear be a bit below that limit, but the engine has piston slap or an excessive thirst for oil, renewal of the piston and rings should alleviate matters. Even if the bore is quite lightly worn, and the piston shows no signs of scuffing and no rings have broken, it is

13. Carefully apply gasket compound to the underside of the new gasket, following the manufacturer's instructions

14. Fitting the piston rings is a difficult job when done by hand, and great care must be taken

15. A piston ring expander makes this job much easier and reduces the likelihood of breaking a ring

16. Slide the new gudgeon-pin through the piston and little-end making sure the piston is the right way round

George Wright

Piston assembly wear

17. Piston skirts should be checked for signs of scuffing as this may indicate cylinder bore wear or damage

18. Piston ring side clearances should be checked with feeler gauges. Excessive clearances can lead to ring failure

19. Gudgeon pin wear, if it is very bad, will be easy to spot. This gudgeon pin should definitely be replaced

20. Where the wear is less obvious use a micrometer to check the pin's diameter at both ends and in the centre

Jake Wynter

worth checking the rings for side clearance in their grooves and end gap, with feelers.

The side clearances of new rings are usually between 0.05–0.08 mm (0.002–0.003in.). If, when you check these in the piston, you discover a side clearance in excess of 0.15 mm (0.006in.) then new rings are needed. Overlarge side clearances can lead to ring failure through hammering fatigue, and a greater tendency to pump oil up to the combustion chamber.

End gaps clearly increase with bore and ring wear, and can be measured with feelers after the ring has been fitted squarely into the empty bore at a position near the top of the piston's travel. Gaps of new rings are normally 0.03–0.04 mm per 10 mm (0.003–0.004in. per inch) of bore diameter; 0.1 mm per 10 mm (0.010in. per inch) should be treated as the maximum. Excessive gap clearances could well mean that the

ring will fail to do its job.

Fitting the piston rings

The next part of the job – fitting the rings to the new pistons – requires great care as it is very easy to break a ring. The safest and easiest way is to use a piston ring expander (fig. 15) but if you can't find one you will have to do the job by hand (fig. 14). On a 4-stroke piston there are usually three rings and the lowest one is sometimes actually composed of three separate rings itself, so make sure you know which ring goes where. Don't open out the rings too far or they will break as you fit them.

The upper two rings will probably have different cross-sectional shapes, so be certain that you are placing them in the correct grooves. They will also have a mark on them at one end to show which side is uppermost. When they are seated correctly, turn them so that the gaps are 120° apart – if they are lined up

with each other there is a risk of oil blow-by and compression loss. Finally, smear the pistons and rings with clean engine oil of the type you are going to use in your engine, or 2-stroke oil if you are modifying a 2-stroke engine.

Fitting the new pistons

You are now ready to fit the pistons. You should already have fitted new little-end bushes or bearings where necessary. Place the piston on the conrod so that the little-end eye lines up with the gudgeon-pin bosses in the piston. Make sure you are fitting the piston the right way round – there is often an arrow marked on the crown showing which side is the front, that is, the exhaust side. Otherwise, the smaller of the two valve cut-outs should be at the front (fig. 16). Oil the new gudgeon-pin and slide it in, then insert the new circlips, one each end of the pin. Make sure they are properly seated in their grooves

– if one comes out while the engine is running it can result in total disaster.

Fitting the barrels can be a fiddly job, so exercise a lot of patience or you may break a piston ring or crack a barrel liner. First, smear the inside of the bores with oil, and slide the barrels on to the studs, with at least one piston at TDC. Halfway down you will find that they come to a full stop against the top rings of a piston. Some barrel liners have a tapered lead-in at the bottom and this will help you to feed in the piston rings (fig. 25). But the job will be made much easier by the use of a piston ring compressor (fig. 22). To make your own, find an empty tin can of about the same diameter as the piston. Cut a slice out of it with a small hacksaw and cut it to shape (fig. 26). Place the compressor around the piston so you are holding the rings flush with the surface, then ease it into the cylinder, releasing the compressor when all the rings have been inserted. If you have two pistons at TDC at the same time, you will need two compressors (fig. 23). To insert other pistons which are at a different position, you must carefully turn the engine, keeping the pistons you have already inserted inside the cylinders, and repeat the process. Using strips of wood underneath the edges of the pistons to hold them while the barrels are lowered makes this much easier. When all the pistons and rings are safely inside the barrels, feed the camchain up the tunnel and secure it, apply gasket compound to the upper surface of the base gasket and seat the barrels fully on the crankcases.

Finally, you can replace the head gasket and cylinder head following the instructions on pages 115 to 116.

Running in

New engine parts must always be run in and, if you do this correctly, you can double the life of the new parts you have fitted.

The first time you start your engine

21. With the new pistons fitted, you must then apply gasket compound to the top surface of the base gasket

22. On the left is a proper ring compressor, on the right a home-made one from a tin can

23. Two ring compressors are necessary if two pistons are at top dead centre at the same time

24. The new pistons must have a good coating of clean engine oil before the cylinder head is fitted

after the rebuilt, do not use the electric starter. The kickstart is a much gentler way of starting, and your engine will repay the kindness you show it while it is still 'tight'.

New pistons and rings should be run in for about 1,600 km (1,000 miles) to be on the safe side. For the first 800 km (500 miles) don't run the engine at more than half revs, or $\frac{1}{4}$ throttle then in the second 800 km (500 miles) gradually increase the revs and throttle opening until you are using the entire range, but even then full throttle should only be used for short bursts for a while. It is also a good idea to change the oil at 800 km and 1,600 km (500 and 1,000 miles),

after which you can revert to the normal oil change intervals for your bike. Make sure your tappet clearances and ignition timing are correct, because with the high-compression pistons any faulty adjustment could lead to rough running and possibly a holed piston. If you can hear a strange pinking noise from the engine as you open the throttle it is suffering from detonation, so try a higher grade of petrol.

25. The inside of the cylinder liner is tapered at the bottom to help in inserting the pistons and rings

26. You can make a ring compressor by cutting an empty tin can to this shape with a hacksaw or tin snips

25 mm

50 mm

Circumference of piston

Replacing split-link chains

Driving a bike with a worn or badly adjusted chain and defective sprockets is dangerous, for it may affect handling and will wear other components. But with care and commonsense, you can check for drive wear and renew the parts yourself.

There are two main things to check when inspecting a drive chain: adjustment and wear.

Checking the chain for adjustment is normally undertaken during a service, or more frequently in some cases, but it is not always possible to use the amount of chain adjustment left as an accurate indication of chain wear. In some instances it is better to detach the chain and check it.

If your bike has wheel adjuster marks on the swinging arm ends and the spindle has come to the end of these, as well as the chain tension being beyond 'limits', just renew the chain without further checks.

If, on the other hand, there still seems to be adjustment left but the chain won't tension properly, it should be taken off and checked accurately. Examples of the latter fault are where the chain tension varies widely when the back wheel is rotated, or when the chain requires adjustment every 160 km (100 miles) or so.

Where a bike has no wheel adjuster marks on the frame, it is not so easy to check chain wear on the machine. All that can be done is to see how far the wheel spindle has already been moved back in the swinging arm fork and whether there is sufficient room left for it to come back any further. This is checked in conjunction with chain free play. Tensioning problems, as detailed previously, should also be looked for.

A quick check for chain wear, without removing the unit, is to pull the chain away at the rear of the sprocket in the middle. If it is possible to insert a pencil between the chain and sprocket when this is done the chain is worn out.

If there is any doubt on either type as to there being sufficient adjustment left at the spindle forks to tension the chain correctly, the chain should be removed for cleaning and accurate wear measurement.

Adjusting the chain

Once any new chain has been fitted, or an original unit put back, the chain must be correctly tensioned, otherwise rapid wear of chain and sprockets will take place.

But since all chain, sprocket and wheel alignment adjustment is controlled by the same means, you may not obtain 'spot-on' adjustment and instead have to balance out the inaccuracies among the three items. In practice, the simplest thing to do is to set up the chain tension and wheel adjustment at the same time, then make any minor adjustments for misalignment of the sprockets.

On most bikes the chain tension is determined by the amount of movement at the middle of the lower chain run (fig. 1). The correct amount of chain deflection at this point is usually between 18 mm and 25 mm ($\frac{3}{4}$in.–1in.), but it is worth checking.

On most machines the chain tension also has to be measured when the swinging arm is at the mid-point of its travel with the rear suspension compressed. This is because the rear suspension configuration on these bikes causes the chain tension to vary as the suspension moves, the tightest point usually being at the half-way mark. If this applies to your bike, have a second person sit on the rear of the saddle to compress the suspension while you check the tension.

Paul Williams

1. The chain tension on most bikes is measured at the midway point of the lower chain run

The means of adjusting the chain tension on some bikes is by screw adjusters at the rear wheel spindle. You just back off the locknuts and turn the adjusters by equal amounts so that they pull or push against the spindle forks and draw the wheel backwards (figs. 4–5). When the right chain tension is achieved, secure the locknuts.

Another form of adjuster is the eccentric cam. This is mainly used on racing or off-road bikes and is found on only

2. Lean across the bike in order to compress the suspension then check the rear chain tension

3. Screw the rear chain adjusters in to tighten the chain then tighten the spindle nut and re-check the tension

John Carr

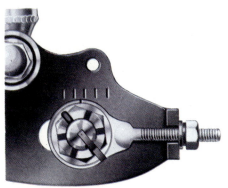

4. A typical wheel adjuster where the bolt pushes against a spacer to pull the wheel backwards

5. Another common form of adjuster. Adjusting the nut pulls the wheel spindle back in its fork slot

6. If the chain is loose on the rear sprocket like this, it should be renewed and the sprockets checked

a few road bikes.

A modern example of a machine with this type of adjuster is the Ducati 860. The advantage of this type is that it gives a simpler and more positive means of adjustment than the screw type, as well as eliminating the possibility of misaligning the rear wheel, which can easily be done with the screw type of adjuster.

Measuring chain wear

Before checking most chains for wear they should first be cleaned off in a paraffin wash. Do not do this with a sealed chain though, or you will wash away the lubricant from inside the rollers. The sealed chain is usually only found on larger machines, and is similar to the endless chain (see the description on pages 147–151). You may have to take the chain off for a wear check (see know-how on 147–151). Split link chains are the easiest to remove.

When the chain is clean, place it flat on a bench in a straight line. Hold the link at one end firmly in place, then push the first dozen or so links at that end carefully in towards each other so that the line of links is still straight but fully compressed. Take a ruler, place it beside the links and measure a certain number of them – say ten – from the end. Still holding the end link in place, stretch the ten links fully out then check their length against the ruler once more. If the length differential between the ten links being compressed and extended is more than 2% ($\frac{1}{4}$in. for a 12in. length, 12 mm in 300 mm) the chain is worn out and should be renewed (fig. 7).

The measurements used here are only a guideline and manufacturers' figures for determining wear by this method will differ according to the chain size. Therefore you will have to consult a workshop manual or a dealer for the chain wear specifications on your bike.

Lubricating the chain

If a chain has been removed for a wear check and is to be refitted it must be lubricated.

A chain does not slide around the sprocket. Each chain roller fits between the sprocket teeth and then rotates around the pin in the centre of the chain. This is where the lubricant is needed, between the pin and its bush.

Lubricating the chain is normally a service job and entails spraying oil on

from the outside, which does little to lubricate the chain inside, although special oils have been formulated which will 'creep' between the rollers and pins, then turn into a form of light grease.

While the chain is 'off' it can be lubricated in another way. This is to clean it and place it in a special grease bath obtainable from most bike accessory shops. The grease is heated in its container until it melts and the chain sinks through. The chain is then taken out and hung up until the grease that has worked its way into the links has solidified.

A couple of drawbacks with the latter method are that it is very messy fitting a grease covered chain, and that much of the grease squeezes out from the rollers after running for a few miles and encourages dirt to stick to the chain, which will abrade and wear it.

Another way of lubricating the chain is to liberally apply heavy weight engine oil between each roller and its link

7. Chain wear is measured by the difference in link length between expansion and compression

plates, then to wipe off the excess oil. This is simple, effective and cleaner.

Removing rear wheel

If the rear sprocket has to be removed the wheel will have to come out after detaching the chain.

Once the chain is off or free of the sprocket, removing the wheel is done in one of two ways. The simplest is where the wheel spindle is held in 'open ended' forks on the swinging arm. This type merely needs the wheel spindle securing nuts to be slackened off, any adjuster 'stop bolts' and spacer blocks removed, the brake drum linkage released and the wheel pulled straight out. Should a rear disc brake be fitted, either slacken the caliper clamp or detach the caliper completely if the disc fouls when pulling out the wheel. Whether or not the caliper has to be moved, a block of wood should be inserted between the pads to prevent accidental ejection of the piston while the disc is out.

The second type is the so called 'quick release' wheel. This features sealed-end wheel spindle forks and the wheel cannot be pulled straight out. Instead

Fitting a new chain to a Honda 'step-through'

8. Place the bike up on its centre stand and detach the chain guard. This may be held by nuts, bolts or screws

9. The nut is near the end of its travel, showing that the rear chain is worn

12. Slacken the rear brake adjuster nut, then undo the wheel spindle lock nuts and push the wheel forward

13. To reach the gearbox sprocket, just take off the cover using some form of impact screwdriver

16. To fix a new chain when the rear sprocket cover is still on, leave the old chain on and fit the new item to it

17. Pull the old chain round on the sprockets (in neutral) so that the new chain gradually feeds on

the wheel spindle must be extracted first and then the wheel removed. There again, this type comes in two different forms: those wheels which come out with the sprocket attached and those which come out leaving the sprocket still attached to a separate shaft on the swinging arm.

With the first type, disconnect the brake mechanism, the remove the split pin and single nut from the spindle (fig. 20). The spindle can now be extracted from the hub (fig. 22) by first tapping it through at the threaded end, then pulling from the 'boss' end. Following this remove any spacers fitted between wheel and fork, then pull out the wheel and sprocket.

The second type requires much the same procedure except that the sprocket is secured to the swinging arm by an inner spindle nut and this should be left in place until the wheel has been detached. Once the spindle has been extracted, pull the wheel sideways to separate it from the cush drive that locates it on the sprocket (fig. 23) then remove the wheel. The sprocket assembly is released from the swinging arm after undoing its retaining nut (fig. 24).

10. Using a suitably sized ring spanner or socket, undo and remove the castellated nuts from the spindle

11. As the rear wheel will have been adjusted back to take up chain wear, slacken off the adjusters

14. This chain was badly worn and should have been changed earlier. Despite this the sprockets were serviceable

15. To remove the chain, undo the split-link with pliers after turning the link to the bottom chain run

18. After fitting it to the gear cog, feed the chain round the rear sprocket and secure it with a split-link

19. Refit all components, tension the chain with the sprockets aligned, secure the wheel and adjust the brake

143

A couple of points concerning quick-release wheels are that you should take note of the position of any spacers fitted on the wheel spindle for when rebuilding, and that difficulty may be experienced in removing the spindle on those machines where a silencer restricts clearance. Rather than detach the silencer, take off the top or bottom fixings for the suspension units. This will allow you to raise or lower the wheel to gain clearance for the wheel spindle. It may help to tie the fork up to the frame while you remove the wheel.

Renewing rear sprocket

No matter whether the sprocket is attached directly to the wheel hub or a cush drive assembly it will be held either by a circlip, bolts and lock straps, or both.

The circlip type merely requires the clip to be spread with the proper pliers and lifted out of its groove (fig. 33) then the sprocket pulled off. With the bolted pattern, knock back the lock tab ears undo the bolts and detach the sprocket (fig. 34).

The new sprocket is fitted in the reverse order, any bolts being tightened down evenly and the lock tabs turned over. If any tabs broke off while being undone, replace the relevant strap.

Once the new sprocket has been fitted, you can replace the rear wheel.

Removing gearbox sprockets

On modern machines the gearbox sprocket is reached after detaching an outer—and sometimes an inner—cover plate from the engine (see panel). This may also entail unbolting the gear lever and pulling it off its splines and possibly detaching the footrest or kick-start on that side.

The sprocket itself is normally retained on a coarse splined shaft by a single nut (fig. 27). However, it may be held by a ring with three securing bolts (fig. 26) or a plate with two bolts. Note that after removing the bolts from the latter type, the plate has to be rotated on the shaft until the splines line-up before it can be removed (fig. 29). What they all have in common though is lock tabs, and these have to be flattened away from the bolt head(s) using a hammer and screwdriver or chisel.

Whatever the number of bolts used to secure the sprocket, you will probably have to use a socket wrench and extension bar to reach them. Then put the engine into gear to stop the engine from turning over and undo the bolt(s). Where the bike has an automatic clutch/gearbox or the engine turns over despite being in gear, try to jar the bolt free by holding the sprocket firmly in place and

Removing a quick release wheel

20. After removing the chain, take out the split-pin and undo the outer nut on the wheel spindle

21. Do not be tempted to lever against the silencer like this, or you may dent it badly

22. Once the silencer is low enough to allow clearance, extract the wheel spindle from the hub

25. A gear sprocket may have more than one cover. This inner one carries part of the clutch mechanism

26. To remove the sprocket, first knock back its lock tabs. This one has three bolts and tab washers

27. If the sprocket turns while being undone—despite being in gear—lock it with a chain as shown

striking the wrench handle with a hammer. A couple of other methods are to lock the sprocket with a screwdriver, or wind on a sufficient length of chain to jam the sprocket within the case but go carefully! (fig. 27).

Once released, the sprocket should pull straight off the shaft. Check which way round the component fits so that the new item can be placed correctly.

As always, use a sprocket of the correct type and ensure that its securing bolt(s) are fully tightened down and the lock tabs peened over.

One particular point about replacing the sprocket cover concerns those units which have the clutch push-rod and actuation mechanism on the sprocket side. Ensure that the case is fitted 'square-on' otherwise the mechanism may jam. If in doubt, pull the push-rod part way out of its shaft, fit the operating mechanism within the casing onto the rod and push the casing home. Note however, that the sprocket cover should not go back on until after the chain has been fitted.

Chain makes

As far as conventional chains are concerned (not sealed chains) it is not strictly necessary that you fit original equipment. Indeed, there are plenty of specialist chain manufacturers around whose products are as good as if not better than original equipment. The main point to watch is that you get the right chain size and type to fit your machine and its sprockets.

Fitting the chain

If wishing to re-use a split-link it is advisable to inspect this item before fitting the chain. Split-links wear more quickly than the rest of the chain and the part to watch is the spring clip (fig. 30). If this is distorted a new link should be obtained to prevent any chance of link failure and the chain separating whilst running on the bike.

Fitting the chain is simple. Where a new chain is being fitted to original, but serviceable, sprockets and the old chain

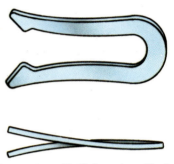

30. Check the split-link spring clip for distortion by viewing it side on as shown above

was left hanging on the gear sprocket, temporarily connect new chain to old (fig. 16) at one end with a split-link (no need to attach a spring clip). Put the gears in neutral and pull the old chain until the new one has run onto the sprocket (fig. 17).

If the old chain was allowed to run off the sprocket when dismantling, you will have to detach the gear cover to install the new unit. The procedure is then the same as it would be should you have taken the cover off previously for sprocket inspection/renewal. Hook the chain over the sprocket and run it either side of the swinging arm pivot.

If the bike has a gearbox sprocket which can be reached only after removing a primary drive, it is possible to fit the new chain as follows.

Take a length of fairly stiff wire and attach it to one end of the chain. Bend the wire a little, then feed it in over the gearbox sprocket from behind. Hook the chain on to the sprocket, using a long screwdriver, and pull the chain through by the wire.

After fitting the chain to the front sprocket, check that the rear wheel adjusters are 'off' and pull the wheel fully forward. Wrap the chain ends round the rear sprocket, then insert the split-link (fig. 18).

Always fit the split-link so that the closed end of the spring clip faces in the direction of chain rotation (fig. 31). Failure to do so may allow the chain to separate while running.

Adjusting the chain

It is most important that a chain—new or not—be correctly tensioned and the sprockets aligned. Otherwise rapid wear of all components concerned will occur. It is also important that a new chain be checked after approximately the first

23. Pull the wheel sideways to free it from the cush drive and sprocket, then pull it straight out

24. Undo its shaft securing nut and remove the rear sprocket. Note the position of all spacers

28. Another method of locking a sprocket is to wedge a screwdriver between the teeth and the casing

29. If you have a sprocket like this, the plate must be aligned with the splines before removal

31. Always fit a split-link so that the closed clip end faces in the direction of chain rotation

800km (500 miles) so that any preliminary wear can be adjusted.

A further point that you should be aware of is that an over-tightened chain will rapidly wear out and could be dangerous. The extra stress can rapidly destroy wheel and gearbox bearings.

Where the rear suspension forks have wheel adjuster marks the whole procedure is much simplified. The wheel can be adjusted back by equal amounts on either side, using the marks for reference, until the correct chain tension is achieved. By doing this, the sprockets should also be in line and the wheel securing nuts can be tightened without further trouble.

On bikes without wheel adjuster marks, accurate tensioning and alignment may prove a little more difficult.

Try to turn each adjuster the same amount and as you go along keep an eye on the sprockets to see that the chain does not come off one or the other at an angle.

Having finished chain adjustment check the rear brake action and adjust as necessary (drum type).

If your bike has a drum type rear brake with a tie-rod, check the brake adjustment once the chain adjustment and any wheel alignment procedures have been carried out. The reason for doing this is that moving the wheel backwards or forwards in the spindle forks while adjusting the chain causes the tie-rod to rotate the brake drum on the hub, thus operating the brake. (This does not happen, of course, on cable-actuated types.) So check the brake pedal travel for too little or excessive movement and adjust the operating rod as necessary.

In this chapter we have dealt with chains with detachable links. Endless chains are covered next.

Detaching rear wheel sprockets

32. A worn out sprocket is recognized by its hooked teeth, as on the left; a new sprocket is on the right

33. If your rear sprocket is held by a circlip, remove the clip using the proper circlip pliers only

34. With the clip free, pull the sprocket off the hub. This sprocket is an integral part of the cush drive

35. If the sprocket is bolted, knock back the tabs and undo the bolts. Ensure the new sprocket is seated squarely

Replacing endless chains

Three main types of drive chain are in use on bikes: split-link, endless and O-ring. Split-link chains were to be found on nearly all machines up until recent years, when endless and sealed chains came into use.

Endless chains have no detachable link and are to be found on many Japanese bikes from intermediate cubic capacity upwards. They can be removed only after detaching the rear wheel and swinging arm, or by breaking the chain.

The sealed chain is by far the most recent type and not particularly common, being found only on very large machines. A sealed chain is identical to an endless unit in all respects except that it is self-lubricating. It can be identified by the O-ring seals set between the side plates where they overlap at each chain roller. These seals serve to retain the lubricant within the chain rollers.

Checking for wear

Unlike the split-link variety, it is not practicable to remove an endless chain from the bike to check the amount of wear against manufacturer's specifications. Instead you must rely upon any wheel adjustment marks on the swinging arm forks to tell you when the wheel has reached the end of its travel and the chain is worn out.

The only other possible check is to try to insert a pencil between the chain links and rear sprocket teeth at the central point to the rear of the sprocket. This quick check may be made at any time, no matter whether the wheel has been adjusted right back or not, and is a fairly accurate guide. If you are able to fit a pencil into this space the chain must be renewed and the sprockets inspected and if necessary renewed.

Removing an endless chain

One way to remove an endless chain is to 'split' it and then detach it in the same manner as for a detachable-link chain.

To split the chain you will need a special tool called a chain or link splitter. This works by forcing out one of the rivetted pins from the chain, allowing a link to be separated.

Particularly on bigger chains you may find that a chain splitter is not strong

Harley Davidson Low Rider

Splitting an endless chain

1. To break an endless chain, first grind down the link's rivet head. Use a small grindstone on an electric drill

2. Fit the link splitter round the link and gradually tighten the tool until it forces out the rivet

147

enough. This is because modern bike chains tend to have much stronger link rivets than older bikes. In this case, first grind away part of the link rivet with a small grindstone attached to an electric drill (fig. 1), then use the chain splitter (fig. 2).

In many cases, you can replace an endless chain, should you so wish, with one of the split-link variety for simpler maintenance. If you cannot obtain a split-link chain of the right size, try to obtain a split-link on its own and fit this to a new endless chain as a conversion. Always fit a link of the same make as the chain to avoid pin diameter variations.

If you want to remove an endless chain without breaking a link – perhaps because it just needs cleaning and lubricating – the rear wheel and swinging arm will have to be completely detached from the bike. The swinging arm has to come off.

Removing a sealed chain
A sealed chain is detached in exactly the same way as an endless one – that is, you can split it to simplify removal if the old unit is known to be excessively worn.

Note, though, that a sealed chain should never have a split-link fitted to it, and that a bike designed to take a sealed chain should always be fitted with one. Therefore, while splitting the chain makes removal quicker, you will still have to undo the swinging arm pivot in order to fit the new chain. You are shown how to remove the swinging arm in the instructions following.

Removing the rear wheel
The procedure for removing the rear wheel depends on whether the wheel spindle sits in open ended forks or slotted forks. A quick release wheel may be fitted to either type, but only with slotted forms does the spindle have to be extracted.

Start by placing the bike up on its centre stand and checking the frame, if need be, to get the rear wheel off the ground.

Remove the split pins, if any, and slacken off the wheel spindle nut(s). Free the locknuts on both wheel adjusters then back off the adjusters in the required direction and remove any stop bolt and spacer block from each unit (figs. 3 to 4). On open ended spindle forks, pivot the adjusters downwards for clearance purposes.

Next, on drum brake wheels, undo the brake adjuster nut completely (fig. 5), withdraw the brake rod from the lever and hang it up out of the way (put the adjuster nut back on the rod to prevent losing it). Then undo the brake drum tie rod at the drum (fig. 6).

If your bike has a rear disc brake, you can either slacken the caliper mount and pivot the caliper free of the disc or undo and remove the unit completely from the disc and hang it up out of the way. Which method is used depends on whether there is sufficient clearance for the wheel to come out without the disc fouling the caliper – in some cases there is no need to move the caliper at all.

Removing an endless chain

3. First steps are to remove the lock pin from the castellated nut, then to extract any adjuster stop bolt

4. Slacken the adjusters next. Where applicable, pivot the adjuster down and extract the adjuster spacer block

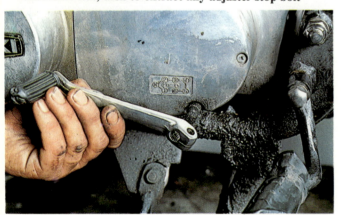

7. Slacken the rear wheel spindle nuts and unhook the chain. If the chain won't come off, detach the gear lever next

8. Remove the gear sprocket cover(s) and take the chain off this sprocket. If need be, detach the sprocket as well

Regardless of this, once the disc is free, wedge a block of wood between the caliper pads to prevent accidental ejection of the piston.

On open ended spindle forks, the wheel should now come out. So you may be able to push the wheel fully forward, slip the chain off the sprocket, then pull out the wheel. If the chain won't come off the rear sprocket at this stage, you may find it easier to take it off the smaller gearbox sprocket, as described below.

On slot type spindle forks, you will have to extract the spindle from the hub and the wheel from the rear sprocket/ push drive assembly (see page 142), as well as detach the chain, before the wheel will come out.

Removing the gearbox sprocket cover
If the chain is still on, you will have to gain access to the gearbox sprocket – in fact, you should do this anyway to inspect the sprocket.

First, the gear lever will have to be unbolted and removed from the splined operating shaft (fig. 7), and the silencer, footrest and any kickstart on that side may also have to be detached to give you the necessary clearance.

Having detached the cover, reach in and disengage the chain from the gearbox sprocket. To do this, make sure that the rear wheel is pushed fully forward in the swinging arm so that the maximum amount of chain slack is available.

If there is still insufficient clearance around the sprocket, remove the sprocket itself and draw it off the shaft with the chain still attached (fig. 8), until the two can be separated.

Undoing the swinging arm pivot
Before attempting to separate the swinging arm pivot, unbolt each lower damper mount from the swinging arm (fig. 10). You should not have any problems with this, but keep a check on the position of any nuts, bolts or spacers.

Releasing the rear suspension pivot can be the most awkward part of the job, but if your bike has plain pivot bushes the work is quite straightforward. First unscrew any grease nipples set in the pivot spindle ends, taking care not to damage them.

Next, undo the pivot securing nut (fig. 11). A spanner with a long handle, or a socket extension bar, is often best for freeing this nut as a lot of leverage may be needed.

Do not remove the nut completely, but slacken it off until its outer face is level with the spindle end. This is to prevent damage to the spindle threads, for it will usually have to be hit with a hefty mallet (not a hammer) before it moves. If the spindle seems reluctant to move when trying to knock it through, spray some penetrating oil round it and try again.

The spindle should budge after a few knocks from the mallet. When it does, and the spindle nut is flush with the frame, move to the other side, spray some more penetrating oil round the pivot and tap the spindle back.

5. On rear drum brakes back off the brake adjuster nut, using a spanner to overcome the return spring pressure

6. On a rod operated drum brake also undo the bolt securing the tie rod, then hang the tie rod out of the way

9. With the chain off at the front, it will now come off the rear sprocket. Withdraw the rear wheel from its forks

10. Undo the bolts on both rear suspension lower mounts and let the swinging arm pivot downwards

Do this a couple of times until the spindle is moving freely. The spindle nut should then be taken off and a long, soft metal drift of the correct diameter used to push the spindle through with the aid of the mallet (fig. 12). An old spindle from the same type of machine may serve as a drift. However, whatever is used as a drift, ensure that its diameter is such that it will slip easily into the pivot bore, otherwise the pivot bushes will be ruined.

Take care that the spindle does not foul the rear brake pedal as it comes out, If this does happen, you will have to depress the brake pedal sufficiently to allow clearance.

The swinging arm can now be removed from the frame, but as you do so check the number and position of any pivot end washers or sealing rings (fig. 14) so that they can be replaced correctly later on. And now – at last – the chain can be taken off (fig. 13).

Checking and renewing the sprockets
Both the gearbox sprocket and rear sprocket should be closely inspected for wear or damage (see page 147) and re-

placed as necessary with the correct type for your particular machine.

Replacing the sprockets
Sprocket replacement, similarly, is a reversal of the dismantling procedure. But it is essential that any spacers or washers either side of the sprockets are refitted in the correct positions. If this is not done, and any deviation in wheel alignment results, you cannot correct it by means of the wheel adjusters.

Fitting the new chain
To fit an endless or sealed chain, you reverse the procedure detailed above. Several points need to be watched, though. First, pay special attention to the correct replacement of the swinging arm, any washers or shims and the tightening of the pivot spindle. Second, any pivot seals should be inspected for wear or damage and replaced if necessary to prevent lubricant leaking from the spindle. Third, the pivot spindle nut must be torqued down to the correct specification or it may loosen in service. Consult a dealer if in doubt about the torque setting.

Finally, inject some grease of the correct grade through any pivot nipples after reassembly to ensure that the joint is well lubricated. Note that where only a single grease nipple is provided at one end of the pivot spindle it is advisable to lubricate the bearings before reassembly to provide thorough distribution of the grease.

Wheel alignment
Adjusting the chain tension is not the sole function of the wheel adjusters, for they have a measure of control over sprocket and wheel alignment too.

The drive chain should always run squarely off both sprockets. If it comes off either sprocket at an angle, the components concerned will wear. The simplest method of checking sprocket alignment is to sight down the top of the chain from behind the rear sprocket while tensioning the chain. So, if turning the adjusters by equal amounts still produces a bias at the rear sprocket, you should be able to see this at the point where the chain comes off the sprocket and compensate for it on the relevant

11. Take a spanner, or socket and extension bar, and remove the nut securing the swinging arm pivot spindle

12. Lubricate the pivot spindle with penetrating oil, then drive it from the bushes using a mallet and drift

13. When the pivot spindle is out, pull the swinging arm away from the frame and remove the chain from the arm

14. Note the position of any spacer or sealing rings on the pivot bushes for replacement purposes later

wheel adjuster.

Another fault which can cause sprocket misalignment is if the rear sprocket is warped. This is not a particularly common fault, but can be checked by setting up a dial gauge on the sprocket side, just below the teeth, to measure the run-out against the manufacturer's specifications. (Using a dial gauge is described on pages 189 to 190). If a rear sprocket is warped beyond limits it must be renewed.

The final role of the wheel adjusters is to align the rear wheel in the frame so that it lies in a straight line with the front wheel (fig. 15). Most modern bikes have marks stamped in the swinging arm to help with the whole chain tensioning, sprocket and wheel alignment process, but these are not always accurate. The result is that while you may have the chain tension and sprockets right, the rear wheel may be at a slight angle in the frame, causing it to 'crab' as you drive along. So it is best to check the wheel alignment in one of the following ways.

First of all, place the front wheel in the straight ahead position. If your handlebars are straight and centrally fitted in their clamps, you can check this by measuring from either bar end to a central reference point on the tank (presupposing that the wheel is straight in the front forks).

The old method of checking the wheel alignment used to be to run a length of string or elastic from the front wheel, alongside it and alongside the rear wheel, then to pull it taut. You could then sight along the string from the front wheel to see if there were any gaps between the string and either side of the rear wheel.

The drawback, though, is that the front and rear tyres of many modern bikes are of different sections, making such a check difficult. In this case pass the string down either side of both wheels in turn and check that the gap between string and wheels is the same both sides.

A more accurate method is to use a straightedge to take the measurements at the wheel rims. Before undertaking such a check, find out whether either of the wheel rims is distorted, for this will place them out of true with the wheel hubs and negate the whole exercise. A rough check can be made by raising each wheel from the ground in turn and spinning it by hand while looking for a pronounced wobble in the rim as the wheel revolves.

You can make a straightedge from a 50 mm by 50 mm (2in. by 2in.) batten slightly longer than your bike. You will also need four bolts about 150 mm (6in.) long, threaded for most of their length, and eight nuts to fit.

First, lay the timber alongside your bike so that it touches both wheels, as

high up as possible. Make a pencil mark on the timber exactly opposite both sides of both rims – that is, four marks in all.

Drill holes for the bolts at the four places marked. Insert the bolts and lock them with nuts on either side. Now adjust the bolts until their heads make a dead straight line – you can check this by placing them on a known flat surface.

This gives you a tool (fig. 15) which you can place against both wheels, first on one side and then on the other, while you check and adjust the rear wheel alignment: if one of the bolt heads fails to touch a rim, you know that something is 'out'.

Where the rear rim has a wider section than the front, divide the difference between the rim widths by two and adjust the bolts which will lie on the rear wheel by the same amount. (So that their length is shorter than the bolts for the front wheel). As before, use the tool on both sides of both wheels.

On rod operated drum brake rear wheels, the final point is to check the adjustment of the brake. Because a tie rod is fitted to the drum, each time the wheel is moved backwards or forwards in the swinging arm, it causes the drum to rotate slightly, moving the brake further on or further off. Just turn the brake adjuster nut in the required direction to give the correct brake pedal travel.

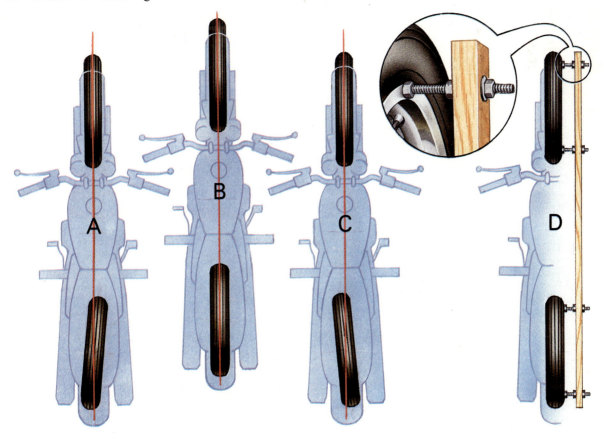

**15. Adjust the rear wheel so that it is dead in line with the front wheel as in B.
The wheel aligning tool is shown being used in D.**

Adjusting the steering head

It is all too easy to ignore steering head bearings. The regular greasing and servicing times are usually quite far apart— and it can seem a daunting job to examine them and repack them with grease. However, checking them, or even replacing them if necessary, is quite a simple job.

The manufacturers' recommended intervals of examination and greasing vary a lot, from 8,000 km (5,000 miles) to 24,000 km (15,000 miles). Practically, unless a really great distance is covered annually, it is best to look at the steering head bearings every year or 10,000 km (6,000 miles). If between greasing intervals there are symptoms of poor adjustment or damage (described below), they must be examined at once, otherwise the handling and safety of the bike will deteriorate.

Symptoms of wear and tear

Two things can affect the function of the steering head bearings. Fortunately, it is sometimes possible to tell them apart.

With any set of bearings that have to withstand the extremely tough forces of the road irregularities transmitted through the wheels and forks to the bike frame, it is no wonder that with time, the steering head bearings develop play. This play or slack can easily be taken up. It must not be confused however, with actual wear and breakup of the bearings which are cured in a different manner.

Simple wear can be identified in a number of ways. The easiest is to put the bike on the centre stand, get hold of the fork legs, and try moving them backwards and forwards. No play should be detectable. If there is, see if it comes from the forks themselves, or from the steering head. If it comes from the steering head, now try raising the front wheel off the ground and, having slackened off any steering damper, move the handlebars from lock to lock. If there is smooth movement from lock to lock with no discernable rough patches, you can assume that the bearings have only a small amount of play and are not actually worn. If there is any resistance to the side-to-side motion, or any feeling of irregularity in the move-

ment, the steering head bearings will have to be examined.

There are other signs that tell you when the bearings need attention, and they are mostly changes in the handling characteristics of the bike. It is difficult sometimes to tell what changes are caused by which part of the bike. Some of the effects of worn steering head bearings can be the same as those of a worn swinging arm bush or even of poor tyres. In fact, handling faults are some of the most difficult to pin down to any particular part of the bike, and quite often are caused by a number of things.

If there is anything unusual about the bike's road performance, the bearings can be suspected. One of the most common types of bad handling that can be caused by worn head bearings is the tendency of a machine in otherwise good condition to fall off raised road markings or to follow longitudinal grooves in the road surface. Another symptom is for the bike to give a feeling of instability on bends. It is a very vague thing to say that a bike 'feels' unstable, but with experience you will be able to tell what particular feelings indicate the general area to look for the cause of the handling defect. The machine may also weave at high speeds and have a light feeling at the front end. Perhaps the giveaway of worn bearings is that under heavy braking, as the brake is applied, a discernable clunk will be felt through the handlebars. In some cases there will even be a juddering as the brake is applied. If there is a clunk, it could possibly be caused by the fork legs, or on some older bikes by the front brake torque lug being loose, but it is a fair bet that the steering head bearings are worn, and at least need tightening if not examination.

Types of steering head bearing

The steering head bearings are located in the headstock and at both ends of the steering spindle (figs. 1 and 2), their functions are to provide the means whereby the bike's front wheel may be smoothly and evenly turned from side to side, and to support the weight of the front end of the bike under all conditions from heavy braking to stressful cornering. Also they have to withstand the battering and stress of all the bumps and road irregularities transmitted through the front forks to the frame. The next time you go over a really bad pot-hole and you feel a shock through the handlebars and the bike lurches,

Puch Maxi and Batavus Starglo

Cup and cone system

Taper roller system

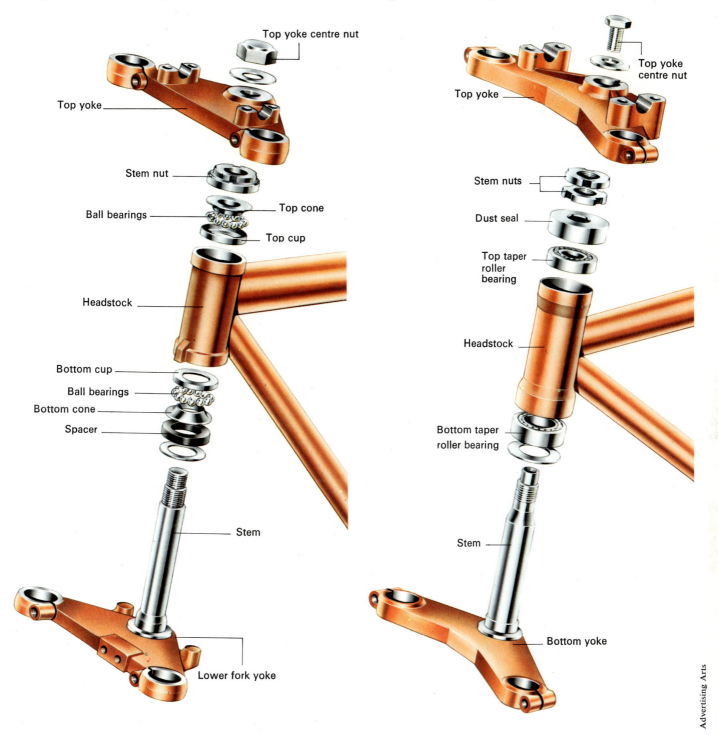

Cup and cone system labels (left):
Top yoke centre nut
Top yoke
Stem nut
Ball bearings — Top cone
Top cup
Headstock
Bottom cup
Ball bearings
Bottom cone
Spacer
Stem
Lower fork yoke

Taper roller system labels (right):
Top yoke centre nut
Top yoke
Stem nuts
Dust seal
Top taper roller bearing
Headstock
Bottom taper roller bearing
Stem
Bottom yoke

Advertising Arts

1. The head bearing arrangement on this cup-and-cone type is typical of most of the machines made today

2. The taper roller bearings used on some bikes are less prone to wear than the cup-and-cone type of bearing

think of all the stress being put through the steering head bearings which are transmitting all that energy to you. It might seem surprising that the bearings can stand up to all that force.

To cope with all the shocks, there are two common designs of steering head bearings. They are the cup and cone type, and the tapered roller type. The cup and cone type (figs. 3 to 5) are by far the most commonly used, being found on the great majority of bikes.

The tapered roller type, (figs. 6 to 7) while not as commonly used as the cup and cone type, are usually found on the larger European bikes, and lately on some of the larger Japanese machines. By nature of their design they both perform the same function, which is to provide smooth circular motion while not allowing any up or down or side to side motion.

With the cup and cone type, the two cups (fig. 4) are retained in the top and

bottom of the headstock. In these cups or races, the ball bearings are held by the cones (fig. 3). The cones are located one at the bottom of the stem, and the other at the top. It can be seen that the cup and cone together provide a housing for the ball bearings and that the balls are free to move and rotate freely between the two surfaces, without movement in any direction other than round and round.

With the tapered roller type there are

153

Types of bearings

3. The cone of a cup-and-cone type of bearing. The large metal surround is there to keep out dust

4. The cup of a cup-and-cone type of bearing. The ball bearings run in the shiny hardened ring

5. The ball bearings are retained in the cup by the cone pressing down, forcing them into the bearing groove

6. This taper roller bearing has the rollers in their cage resting on the lower taper

7. The bearing is completed by putting the upper taper on to the rollers in their cage

8. You may need a C-spanner to undo the stem nut. Make sure you use one that is the correct size for the bike

three parts, the top taper, the roller cage with bearings, and the bottom taper (figs. 6 and 7). They perform exactly the same function as the cup and cone type, but here the bearings are held in place by the cage. Usually, the two inner races are fitted around the stem adjacent to the yokes, while the outer rings are fitted into each end of the headstock. An adjuster ring or nut fits around the top of the stem when the assembly is complete.

Both types are lubricated with ordinary grease, the high melting point type being needed only where there is heat generated by fast rotation, as in the wheel bearings. They are also held under slight pressure which prevents them from allowing movement in any other than a circular manner. It is when the pressure slackens off, for whatever reason, that they have to be adjusted.

Steering head service

As no play should develop between regular services, even though the steering head bearings can be adjusted without stripping the steering head, if play does develop, it is a good idea to perform a full examination and service on the bearings.

The two types of steering head bearing are retained in machines in very similar ways, the main differences between bikes occurring in the design of the bits and pieces around the top fork yoke. All the variations in procedure are described below.

Before you start

No special tools are required apart from a C-spanner (fig. 8) if your bike has the appropriate type of stem bolt. Some ordinary tools that might be useful are a pair of tyre levers and a selection of drifts for displacing the bearings from their housings if they prove to be worn. The drifts you will need will depend on the size of the bearings in your bike, but as a general rule when dealing with bearings of any kind, any drift you use must never put any force on a part of the bearing that touches either the balls or rollers. So, it should, in the case of the steering head bearings, be as large as the outer diameter of the bearing without impinging on the face itself.

To remove the bearings from the headstock, you will need a cylindrical length of metal such as a length of plumber's pipe. It must be small enough in diameter to pass through the inner diameter of the cup or race, but

not big enough to damage the bearing when drifting it out. You will need some grease and plenty of old rag for cleaning the bearings and also, possibly, some spirit for degreasing prior to inspection.

Dismantling the steering head

On most bikes you will have to remove the front wheel before you can dismantle the steering head. To do this, remove any cables from the speedometer drive or the brake and hang them out of the way (fig. 9). Now, with the front wheel off the ground, undo any split pins on the wheel spindle (fig. 10) and either knock out the spindle or undo the spindle clamps and let the front wheel drop out. It should be possible to remove the wheel without tampering with the disc brake set-up if your bike has a disc or discs. Now, with the wheel out of the way, you can start to strip the steering head.

The secret of speedy maintenance is not to do more dismantling than is necessary. So, if it is possible to strip the steering head without removing the front forks from the lower fork yoke, and without having to remove and disconnect the headlight unit from its supports, you will save yourself a lot of time. On some large bikes, the weight of

George Wright

the forks, disc brake arrangement and the headlight/instruments may make it hard to remove them all in one. So if you are in doubt about the weight, get a friend to assist you with the dismantling and assembly. If you cannot get assistance, you might have to strip the forks out of the fork yokes to make for easier handling of the bike (pages 158 to 161).

Before you get to the forks, you will have to remove the handlebars. Undo the four bolts on the handlebar clamps and take off the handlebars (fig. 13) letting them hang on the control cables. If you have a hydraulic disc brake, be sure not to pump the lever while the bars are hanging. If you do this, you might get air into the brake system which will seriously affect the braking capability. Now undo the top fork yoke middle nut (fig. 14). On some bikes the top yoke centre nut is also the steering head bearing nut. In these cases, there is usually a pinch bolt to be undone first (fig. 11). Also, some bikes have a steering damper which you will have to unscrew and remove before you can undo this nut (fig. 12).

Now undo the two fork-top nuts that retain the top fork yoke (fig. 15). With these nuts out of the way you should be able to remove the top yoke complete with the instruments (fig. 16). Hang it out of the way on the instrument cables. If your bike is one of those that has the top yoke centre nut as the steering head retaining nut, you are now ready to remove the fork and spindle assembly. If it is not you will have to use the C-spanner on the stem nut or steering head retaining nut (fig. 17). As you undo this nut make sure that you support the fork assembly. Also if you have access to a large tray, place it under the front part of the machine to catch any of the ball bearings that may fall out if your machine has the cup and cone type of steering head. After undoing the stem bolt, take off the washers and top cone or taper (fig. 18).

Now you can remove the stem and lower yoke assembly from the headstock. If you have left the fork and headlight assembly complete, let it hang down on the various parts of the wiring system.

Inspecting the bearings
Fortunately, it is not hard to tell if the bearings are worn. You do not have to remove the races to tell if the bearing assemblies are due for replacement. Take the ball bearings off the races (fig. 19) and be sure to put them in a safe place. Some bikes have different sized balls in the top and bottom races; if this is the case, keep them separately. With tapered roller type bearings, the

Dismantling the steering head

9. Remove all cables from the front wheel. The speedometer cable on most bikes is a push or screw fit

10. If there is a split pin on the bike's wheel spindle, be sure to use a new one on reassembly

11. Some bikes have a pinch bolt that has to be slackened off before the stem nut can be undone

12. Steering dampers have to be removed. Some types are screwed through the centre of the head

13. Undo the handlebar clamp bolts and remove the handlebars, letting them hang down on the control cables

14. Undo the top fork yoke centre nut. Put it in a safe place and be sure to keep any washers with it

15. Remove the two fork-top nuts and put them to one side. Be careful of the chrome on these nuts

16. Now lift off the top yoke. If it is stuck, a light blow with a hide mallet should free it

Continued

17. Before undoing the stem nut, support the front forks. Use the C-spanner and remove the nut

18. Take off the nut, the washer or dust seal, and the top cone or taper. Catch any balls that may fall

rollers will not escape unless the cage has broken. Clean off all traces of grease (fig. 20) and examine the cups and cones for wear. If they have any traces of rust or appear to be pitted (fig. 21), they must be replaced. If there appears to be excessive grooving or indentation on the hardened bearing surface, they must be replaced. With tapered roller type bearings, the signs to look for are similar to those of the cup-and-cone type. Look for any irregularities in the bearing surface, and check that the cage of the roller bearing is not cracked or distorted.

Next, examine the actual bearings themselves. With ball bearings, clean them thoroughly with a rag, and then look at each one in turn. If you have one, it may be helpful to use a magnifying glass. If there are any flat spots on the bearing, or if it shows any signs of grooving (fig. 22), the whole set must be replaced. Steering head ball bearings are quite cheap and easy to replace, so if you have any doubt as to their state, buy a new set.

Tapered roller bearings have to be checked for flat spots along their length and excessive looseness in the cage. A good test is to place the cage back on a completely clean lower taper and try spinning the cage. If there is any resistance to the free spinning, the bearing will have to be replaced. As a complete test of the whole bearing, put all three parts of it together while they are clean and try spinning them. There should be no resistance to free spinning.

If you decide that the bearings are not worn, you can reassemble the steering head (see below).

Removing and replacing the bearings

If you have decided that the bearings need replacing, you will have to drift them out. Start by removing the bottom race. Use a drift of the appropriate size and gently tap the bearing free of the headstock (fig. 23). Now do the same to the top race. To remove the bottom cone or taper, you can use two tyre levers or other levers of similar size to prise it off (fig. 24). At a pinch, two screwdrivers will do, though be careful not to damage the bottom fork yoke.

Even if they are no good for their designed task, it is always a good idea to keep any worn or old bearings, since they make very good drifts for other sizes of bearing.

Next, being sure that your drift will not damage the face of the bearings, gently put the new races into the headstock (fig.25). If you think your drift might damage the bearings, put a piece of wood between the bearings and the drift. The bearings must be a secure, tight fit back in the headstock. If they are at all sloppy, the handling of your machine will suffer. If they do seem a bit loose, make sure that they are fully home. If they still seem loose, they will have to be removed again.

Several options are open to you if you have trouble putting the bearings back tightly enough. If there is both a lot of play and enough metal in the headstock, then the best solution is to have the headstock sleeved. If the play is minimal however, then a plastic bearing retainer such as Loctite is ideal.

The bearing on the stem is replaced in a similar manner, using a long hollow drift (fig. 26). Again, if this bearing is a loose fit you can either sleeve or replace the spindle or use Loctite.

In all cases the bearing must be correctly seated. Otherwise your work will have been in vain.

Reassembling the steering head

With the races back in place, you can now put in either the balls or the rollers. With ball bearings, the balls must be held in place on the races' grease. Liberally grease the race and

Bearing examination

19. Remove all the ball bearings from the cups and keep them safely. Keep different-sized balls separately

20. Thoroughly clean all the bearing surfaces, removing the old grease with a piece of rag or tissue

21. The bearing surface on this cup is badly worn. An irregular groove is clearly visible

22. This ball bearing has a ring scored round it. It would cause roughness when turning the handlebars

put the balls on one by one (fig. 27). When they are held in place, put on another coating of grease (fig. 28) to make sure they do not move about during reassembly. With roller bearings, all you have to do is to grease them thoroughly and put them on to the taper.

You are now ready to offer up the stem to the headstock (fig. 29). If you think that it may be too heavy for you to do it accurately on your own, get a friend to do it for you while you secure it at the top with the stem nut and top race. Offer up the stem and, with it supported in position, put back the top cone or taper (fig. 30), the washer (fig. 31) and the stem bolt. Tighten up the stem bolt so that there is no free play at the bearings but they are not too firmly held.

Now assemble the top fork yoke, the handle bars and the other components in the reverse order to assembly.

After assembly

With the bike back together again, try the side-to-side test with the handle-bars. If there is too much resistance, you will have to slacken the stem nut until there is no play in the bearings and no resistance to free movement.

Removing and replacing bearings

23. If they need replacing, drift out the races from the headstock with a suitable cylindrical metal bar

24. Lever off the cone or taper. It if is tight, gently hit one of the levers with a mallet to free it

25. Drift the cups back in with a piece of metal that will not damage the hardened bearing surface

26. The lower cone or taper has to be drifted back on with a circular hollow piece of metal

Reassembling the steering head

27. The ball bearings are retained with grease on the races. Be sure to put back the correct number of balls

28. An extra layer of grease will make sure that the ball bearings are not dislodged when you are reassembling

29. With both sets in place, offer up the stem through the headstock. You may need assistance

30. Replace the top cone on to the bearing making sure not to dislodge any of the balls from the cup

31. Put back any washers or dust seals, and then put the stem nut back on to the stem and finger-tighten it

32. The stem nut has to be tight enough to prevent play without restricting the free movement of the bearing

157

Forks and rear dampers

The suspension system on your bike is a very important factor in providing a smooth ride. Here we show how to overhaul the front forks and the rear dampers.

The front suspension on all but a few motorcycles is by means of telescopic forks, ranging from the undamped units of the moped to the sophisticated 'air' forks of the superbike.

The suspension medium in these units is usually a coil spring, but may be a combined air and spring device. All telescopic fork suspensions, bar the simple units found on some small machines, are oil damped. This chapter covers the overhaul of all types except 'air' forks.

All fork units are liable to wear after a reasonable length of service. On the undamped versions this will be internal bush wear, allowing the lower sliders (which hold the front wheel) to move sideways in the top tube. Oil-damped forks suffer mainly from bush (where applicable) and oil-seal wear.

On both types, such wear may show up as fork leg judder when applying the front brake. However, this should not be confused with judder due to play at the steering head bearings.

If you suspect fork leg play, a check can be made as follows. On the damped units each leg will have to be removed from the bike and its slider placed in a vice (see Fork removal, below). Grasp the upper tube (stanchion) firmly and try to rock it to and fro. Any movement between the two leg tubes denotes wear, and the fork legs will have to be overhauled.

This method of checking for play is not necessary on undamped units, which are easier to check while still attached to the bike. Place the machine up on its centre stand or blocks so that the front wheel is clear of the ground. Disconnect the front brake and any speedometer cable, then remove the front wheel and mudguard. Have a second person hold the steering head firmly, then pull each slider leg to and fro. If any play is felt the bushes must be renewed.

A particular wear point on damped forks is at the oil seals. A worn or damaged oil seal will allow damping oil to leak out and thus affect the fork

Overhauling an oil-damped fork

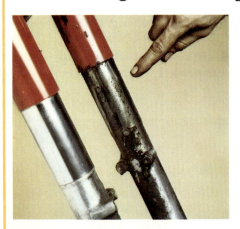

1. One fork leg on this machine is worn. Oil has leaked past the seal on to the slider shroud

2. Place the forks up and detach the front wheel. Next release the lower yoke clamps

3. This bike has no top yoke clamps. So next you undo the top end bolts from the stanchions

6. If you have not already done so, undo the plug in the fork leg and drain the remains of the old oil

7. Instead of a gaiter or dust cover, this leg type has a 'pressed on' shroud. Tap it off carefully

8. Having removed the shroud, use a pair of long-nosed circlip pliers to extract the oil seal circlip

operation. Such a fault is easily detected by the presence of oil on the stanchion and around the top seal (fig. 1). If your bike is fitted with fork gaiters, which may easily conceal an oil leak, it is advisable that they be unclipped and a check made at least at every regular service.

Undamped forks

Most simple, undamped forks have the sliders to which the wheel fixes moving inside top tubes. These tubes are invariably an integral part of the steering head assembly, but as they rarely wear or are damaged there should be no need to detach the steering head, and the sliders may be removed on their own.

Begin by lifting the machine so the front wheel is clear of the ground. Slacken off and disconnect the front brake cable, release any speedometer cable fixing from the wheel and remove the front wheel and mudguard.

At one end, the fork spring in each leg is screwed directly to the slider. The other end is fastened inside the top tube, thereby holding the fork leg together. So next undo the securing nut from the top of each upper tube to free its slider and spring.

Pull the leg dust seal off the top tube so that it slips down the slider. These seals are normally a press fit to the tube but some may have to be unscrewed instead. Each slider and spring assembly can now be withdrawn.

Overhauling the components

Before dismantling each spring and slider, make a note of the components and their relative positions.

Unscrew and detach the upper spring locating plug, along with any bump stop, then unscrew the spring from the slider. If the latter job proves difficult, place the slider in a vice with padded jaws and undo the spring.

Note that some of these springs have anti-rattle C-washers inserted in them, the Puch Maxi springs being an example, and the position of these should be checked before removal.

Next remove the bushes from the slider – the bushes on these units are often of the split nylon type with locating lugs. Prise open each one with a screwdriver until the lug clears its locating hole and slip the bush off the slider. Discard the old bushes and degrease all components except the leg dust sleeves.

Note that in some cases no bushes are located on the slider, instead a bush and spacer assembly is fitted inside the top tube and must be drifted out. Use a metal rod drift inserted through the top bolt hole to do this.

Before rebuilding the forks with new bushes installed, the other components, particularly the spring and slider, should be inspected for wear or damage.

A fractured spring must, of course, be replaced. The fork springs should also have their free length measured to see whether they are within limits (fig. 11). If a spring has softened so that its length is approximately 13 mm ($\frac{1}{2}$in.) less than the figure specified by the manufacturer, it should be changed.

If one spring has to be renewed, the other one must be, too. Always change springs in pairs in order to preserve suspension balance.

Also check the sliders to see if they are out of true. If so, they must be renewed or straightened.

The forks are reassembled in the reverse order of dismantling with plenty of LM grease applied to the bushes and springs. Ensure that the fork springs are correctly located. Do not fully tighten the top end bolts until the front wheel is secured and the forks aligned.

Oil-damped forks

Where drain plugs are provided in the leg the damping oil can be drained prior to removing oil-damped forks. These plugs are usually located at the bottom of each fork leg near the wheel spindle mount (fig. 6). Undo each plug and drain the oil into a container that will hold 0.6 litres (1pt). To improve the oil flow, pump the forks up and down until the leg worked on is empty.

If no drain plugs are provided, the oil will have to be poured out after detaching the legs.

Begin stripping out the legs by putting the bike on its centre stand or blocking so that the front wheel is clear. Detach the brake and any speedometer cable, then remove the wheel and mudguard.

4. If a leg is stiff in the fork yokes, ease the lower yoke clamp slightly with a screwdriver

5. Pull each fork leg out from below with someone else bracing the bike to stop it overbalancing

9. Next, pull the complete stanchion and spring assembly out of the slider with the oil seal still on

10. Discard the oil seal, then degrease all other components thoroughly ready for inspection

11. Lay the coil spring flat and check it for wear with a ruler against manufacturer's specifications

12. Examine the top bush on the stanchion for wear. Renew it if it is loose or scuffed

13. Check the stanchion for straightness and pitting, and also the damper/bush for wear. Renew if necessary

14. When fitting the new oil seal to the stanchion, first lubricate it with the correct grade of oil

15. Use a tyre lever to seat the oil seal within the slider before fitting the retaining circlip

If a front disc brake is fitted you may have to remove the brake caliper. If this is detached, its hose is best freed from any support bracket and the whole assembly tied up out of the way. Ensure that any rigid metal hydraulic pipe is not bent while doing this.

Once the disc is free of the caliper, any movement of the front brake lever will force out the caliper pistons. To prevent this, tape a block of wood between the lever and the bar.

The fork legs should now be ready to come out. Steering heads normally have fork shrouds with the headlamp supports and indicators attached but which do not have to be removed from between the yokes.

In some instances, however, access to the fork leg tops may be restricted by the handlebars, cables, wiring and instruments and these should be taken off. If the handlebars are in the way, just undo their clamps and tie them out of the way. If a brake hydraulic fluid reservoir is mounted on the handlebars, ensure that the flexible hose is not strained at the union.

Before you remove the fork legs, though, there are two further points to watch. First, on many bikes there are spacers and seat rings where the fork

legs attach to the yokes. The position of these should be noted if they come out while removing the legs.

Second, on those forks fitted with rubber bellows gaiters instead of slider dust caps, the top gaiter securing clip has to be unscrewed before removing each leg.

The fork legs are held to the steering head in one of two ways: upper and lower yoke clamps or a lower yoke clamp and top end bolt.

All-clamp types

With the former type, first check the positions of the fork leg stanchions in the top yoke. The top end bolts may stand proud of the yoke, may be flush with it or the stanchions may extend beyond the yoke (on some trail bikes).

Next, release the yoke clamp bolts and withdraw the fork legs. If the legs are a tight fit, the yoke clamps may be eased apart slightly with a screwdriver (fig. 4). This must be done with care as brute force can snap off the yoke ears.

If the forks still refuse to move, apply some penetrating oil around the clamps, then tap each leg out with a mallet.

Clamp-and-bolt types

Where a top end bolt is used, instead of

a clamp, to secure a fork leg to the top yoke, there are two different types. On many machines with their fork legs attached in this way, the top end bolts simply act as a locating device and undoing the bolt releases the leg from the yoke.

On some machines, many of the British bikes among them, the fork ends are a taper fit in the top yoke and have the end bolt heavily torqued down. On this type the taper joint has to be separated with force.

Undo the lower leg clamps, then slacken off the top nut one or two turns using a socket and extension bar. Place a block of wood over the bolt head and strike it with a hammer to break the joint. Ensure that the top bolt has sufficient threads in engagement to withstand the impact. With the joint broken, undo the top bolt and any damper lock nut, then withdraw the forks.

Dismantling the forks

Once the forks are out of the bike, drain them (if this has not already been done) by pouring the old oil out of the leg ends.

On those fork legs which are extracted with the top end bolts still attached, the bolts must now be undone, not only to drain the oil, but also to release the fork springs.

The bolt heads may have a standard hexagon or, on a few models, pin spanner holes. It is usually safest to hold the stanchion in a vice with padded jaws while the bolt is undone.

On a few versions you may find that the top belt is attached to a damper within the stanchion as well as to the stanchion itself. In this case, undo the top bolt, then continue to hold it in the wrench while slackening off the lock nut which retains the coil spring on the damper rod. Take the top bolt and the locknut off to release the spring from the damper rod.

Some fork legs do not have top end bolts but instead have an internal plug held by a circlip. The early Suzuki 250 GT is an example.

To release the springs from these, prise the plastic cap out of the leg end, extract the internal circlip, then force the spring retaining plug from the leg end by carefully compressing the fork. Take care not to have your face in the way while doing this as the plug tends to fly out. Some of these leg plugs are intended to be extracted using a puller and this type can be identified by the screw hole on top of the plug.

Before removing the springs from any fork type, note which way up they are fitted. Most go either way and have no extra fittings but this is not always so. In some cases, washers or spacers fit above and/or below the spring. In others, the spring is multi-wound, with more coils at one end than the other and must be assembled the right way up. With a few, two springs are used, with a collar in between.

With the spring out, the next stage of dismantling is determined by how the damper mechanism is fitted. The most common method requires the leg to be inverted and a damper-fixing Allen screw removed from a recess in the wheel spindle yoke (fig. 17). With this type it may be necessary to insert a wooden rod, or similar object, inside the stanchion to lock the damper while the fixing screw is undone.

The stanchion and damper mechanism can finally be extracted from the slider after freeing the slider top seal, although sometimes the seal will come out last of all. This is reached after unclipping or prising off the bellows gaiter or slider dust seal.

Instead of a dust seal or gaiter, some forks have a chrome shroud fitted to the top of each slider. Tool locating points are rarely provided to undo these so each one is best removed by gently tapping it off with a blunt chisel (fig. 7), taking great care not to damage the components.

The majority of oil seals are held into the slider by a circlip and can be prised out of the slider after removing the clip (fig. 21).

An alternative method of seal removal is needed when the seal is carried in a screwed ring on the slider. This ring often requires a chain wrench to undo it, but in some cases a C- or pin spanner will do the job. When using a chain wrench, wrap a section of old inner tube around the ring first to avoid damage to the alloy ring (fig. 22).

With the oil seal free, the complete stanchion and damper mechanism can be withdrawn from the slider. Damper

Oil seal renewal

16. If the oil seal only has gone on this fork type, remove the leg and pull out the spring first

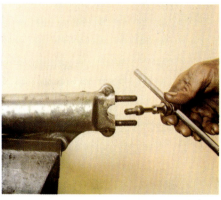

17. This type has a tube damper, so next undo the bolt in the leg bottom that holds the damper

18. These forks don't often have an oil drain plug, so drain the oil out of the damper securing bolt hole

19. The next step is to remove the stanchion from the slider. Just pull it out, complete with valve

20. Take a thin screwdriver and prise out the oil seal retaining clip from its recess in the slider

21. Lever out the old seal, then rebuild in reverse order. Lubricate all components before assembly

design varies a great deal but if not a separate unit held to the slider bottom by a screw, similar to the rod type detailed previously, it will be attached to the stanchion by circlips.

Where bushes are incorporated on the stanchion, these will also be held by circlips and are easily removed. Note that in a few instances, bushes double as damper pistons.

Cleaning and checking

Once the fork leg has been stripped, each component (except the oil seals and O-rings) must be completely cleaned with a degreaser or solvent (fig. 10). In particular, any oil passage holes in the damper should be cleared of any obstructions. If necessary use a soft wire brush as well as a degreaser. The slider legs should also be cleaned out to

22. On those forks with the oil seal in a ring on the slider you may need a chain wrench or strap wrench to undo the ring

remove any sludge or metal particles from the bore bottom.

When the parts are clean, check them for signs of wear or damage. Wear is most likely to occur on the bushes (if any), the stanchion and slider bore. These parts should be checked with a micrometer against the manufacturer's specifications. However, as such tools and specifications are not always readily available, normal practice is to inspect the component surfaces for scuffing, pitting or other damage. If difficulty is experienced in examining the slider bore surface, shine a light through the damper screw/drain plug hole.

Damper units (non-bush type) rarely wear, although the rod type should be inspected and renewed if the rod is at all bent.

All oil seals and O-rings should be renewed as a matter of course, as well as a split rubber dust cover/gaiter. Many dampers have a seal or seals fitted to the piston which should also be changed.

Measure the fork springs' free length and if they have shortened so far as to be outside limits (see details under Undamped forks), replace the springs as a pair not singly.

Reassembling the forks
Assembly and refitting of oil-damped forks is a straightforward reversal of the dismantling process.

Damper overhaul

Worn out rear dampers are easily detectable by the deterioration in handling. This is because once the dampers cease to damp, the suspension springs will continue to oscillate after they have been compressed by a bump in the road.

To the rider the bike will feel excessively bouncy, and fast cornering will become both difficult and dangerous.

Apart from damper unit failure, the suspension springs are also prone to rust. While this is largely a cosmetic fault it is possible for the rust to become severe enough to weaken the spring. And after a while the damper eye bushes deteriorate as the rubber perishes.

While spring and bush maintenance is possible for almost all damper types, a full overhaul of the dampers themselves is only possible on certain models.

Whether you are just replacing the bushes or completely stripping the dampers the initial stages of removal are the same.

Removing the dampers
Before attempting to remove the dampers, set them on their softest pre-load with a C-spanner. Then undo the top and bottom retaining bolts. It may be necessary to drift them out; if so use a hide mallet and support the rear of the bike on blocks of wood to take the load off the dampers. The dampers can then be lifted away.

Bush replacement
On most types of damper the securing bolts ran through metal and rubber bushes. In time the rubber part of these bushes perishes and the dampers become sloppy in their mounts. If this is the case the bushes must be replaced.

Damper eye bushes are often quite tricky to remove, particularly if they have been in situ for a long time. Liberal use of a rubber lubricant or Vaseline jelly is useful and a modified gudgeon pin extractor.

Removing damper springs
Most machines have rear dampers which are sealed units but on nearly all types the spring can be removed and replaced or refinished. Marzocchi and CZ dampers are, however, repairable and it is possible to dismantle them fully.

The first step is to remove the spring. This is secured by collets in a similar fashion to the means used to secure valve springs. As in that case, to remove the collets and hence the spring, the spring must first be compressed.

The best way to do this is with a coil spring compressor. These can be bought quite cheaply from most tool shops, or they can even be hired. Alternatively, you can devise a home-made compressor by drilling a hole in a plank of wood just large enough to clear the collets. Then, with the help of a friend, you should be able to press down on the wood to compress the spring sufficiently so that you can fish out the collets with a pair of

long nosed pliers. Once the collets have been removed the wood can be raised slowly allowing the spring to expand fully. Take care when releasing the wood, otherwise the spring may take matters into its own hands and shoot into the air, either causing injury or scattering parts.

The spring can now either be replaced or stripped and refinished. It is not worth painting it, however, as the spring twists as it compresses and the paint will soon crack and flake off. It is, however, worth priming it with a rust inhibitor if you intend to fit protective gaiters.

Damper overhaul
With the spring removed the damper can be given a closer examination. Look for any signs of oil leakage and check whether the rod is bent. To determine whether the damping is effective push the rod right home and then pull it back. You should be able to feel some resistance on the compression stroke but much greater resistance should be detected on the outward stroke. The rod's travel should also be completely smooth.

Koni dampers have a facility for adjustment designed to compensate for wear within the units. It is basically a means of cutting off some of the oil feeds and stiffening the internal bypass valve spring, which results in stiffened damping. To do this simply lock the damper's lower eye in a vice, compress the unit fully and then rotate the rod until it engages with the adjusting nut. You can then turn it up to two and a quarter turns to gain the necessary amount of stiffening that you desire.

If you have obvious problems with your dampers and you cannot adjust them, or if adjustment makes no difference, then you will either have to replace them or if possible, rebuild them. Obviously before proceeding you should check with your local main dealer to ensure that parts are available. A typical overhaul kit will comprise piston seals, main oil seals and sealing rings.

Using Marzocchis as a typical example of dampers which can be dismantled, disassembly proceeds as follows. Having removed the spring in the manner described above next undo the damper cap. With this undone you will be able to withdraw the damper rod, assembly and inner sleeve. Now undo the end nut with an 11 mm socket spanner. This will allow the damper assembly to be withdrawn and pulled apart. Before doing this, however, make a quick sketch on a pad and note the relative position of the various seals. Once this has been done, final disassembly can proceed and the seals replaced.

Overhauling a rear suspension damper

23. Some bikes are fitted with dampers which can be overhauled. For these you may need a spring compressor

24. On this Marzocchi damper we found it quite easy, and safe, to remove the spring and collets by hand

25. With the spring removed give it a thorough clean and inspect it for rust or any other signs of decay

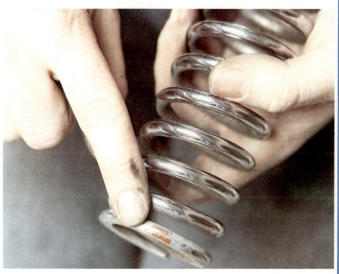

26. Dampers which have changeable springs generally have the spring rate marked on the spring with coloured paint

27. Next remove the adjuster ring which simply slides up and off the damper

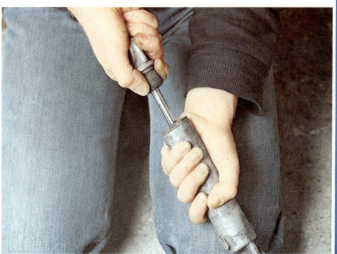

28. Now check damper action by pushing the rod in. It should go in smoothly but offer some resistance

Jake Wynter

Continued

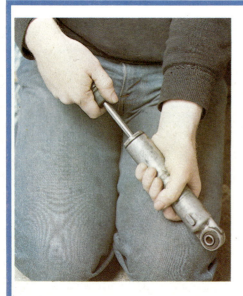

29. Pull the rod out and you should feel much greater resistance. Again the rod should travel perfectly smoothly

30. Check the damper's rubber bushes. If perished, extract them with an old socket and a universal puller

31. New bushes can be replaced in the same way but lubricate them first with a dab of Vaseline

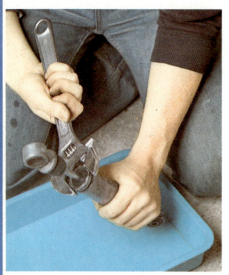

32. If from your tests you decide that the seals need replacing then the first step is to remove the cap nut

33. With the nut undone remove the damper from the body over a drip tray to catch any remaining oil

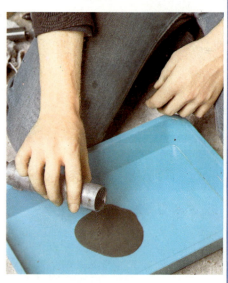

34. The remainder of the oil can then be tipped out and the damper body cleaned inside and out

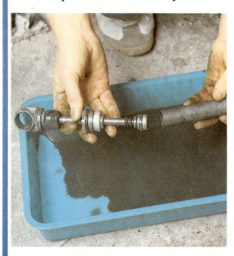

35. Now pull the damper assembly from its outer sleeve. The sleeve can then be given a thorough clean

36. With all the rod exposed you can check its surface. This one is badly pitted and needs replacing

37. Judicious use of vice grips will allow you to remove the valve at the base of the sleeve

Continued ▶

38. To dismantle the damper assembly first undo the end nut with a suitably sized socket spanner

39. With the nut removed carefully pull the components off the rod, noting their order ready for reassembly

40. Once the piston assembly has been removed you will be able to remove two washers, a spring and the cap

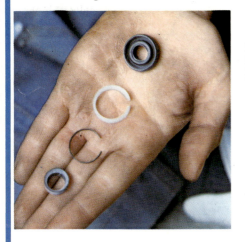

41. For Marzocchi dampers an oil seal replacement kit includes a sealing ring, piston seals and main oil seal

42. The piston seal has a nylon outer ring, held in place by an inner ring of spring steel

43. Removing the top sealing ring is simply a matter of pushing it out with your finger

44. The main oil seal is much harder to remove and may have to be partially destroyed with pliers first

45. When reassembling the damper you will have to compress the piston seal rings to fit the sleeve

46. Lastly, fill the body with the right grade and amount of oil, fit the damper and tighten the cap nut

Tip all of the remaining oil out of the damper body and give all the components a thorough clean, making sure that no grit is left in the assembly.

The damper body can then be refilled with the recommended amount and grade of oil and the damper assembled in the reverse order to disassembly.

Once rebuilt, the dampers can be refitted to the bike. If you are more interested in reliability than aesthetics then at this stage it is a wise move to fit a pair of gaiters over the springs after having given them a thorough greasing.

The gaiters can be firmly attached by means of large hose clips.

With the damper fitted on the bike, bounce the rear end a couple of times to prime them and check that they are working correctly before making a test ride.

Jake Wynter

Rebush the swinging arm

If the rear wheel lurches out of line every time you corner hard there is a good chance the swinging arm bushes are worn. Replacing the bushes will cure the problem and improve handling.

The swinging arm is the forked prong that carries the rear wheel. It is bolted to the bottom of the frame behind the engine. The arm hinges on two bushes so the rear wheel can ride over the bumps in the road without transmitting the shock to the rest of the frame, and ultimately the riders seat. To keep traction with the road the swinging arm is sprung with shock absorbers to damp arm movement.

As well as keeping the rear tyre stuck down to the road the swinging arm must hold the wheel exactly in line with the rest of the bike. If the wheel is skew, the suspension geometry will be altered and the bike may wander off line especially over bumps and on corners. This can happen during fierce acceleration or heavy braking when the swinging arm must absorb heavy twisting loads. As an aid to this, some bikes are fitted with metal struts to help relieve such forces built up under particularly heavy braking.

The arm may carry additional equipment like the master cylinder for the back brake, pillion footrests and the final drive unit used on shaft drive bikes.

It is obvious that the swinging arm absorbs a lot of punishment, the bushes have to withstand the forces of friction and the reciprocating loads caused by stresses in the arm while it is in motion. Wear from friction will be small if the bushes are kept well lubricated, but if the arm is allowed to run dry the spindle will rapidly become scored and in need of replacement.

The reciprocating load arises from a slight rocking moment set up between bushes and the pivot. The designer tries to prolong the life of the bushes by making the clearance between the mating surfaces as small as possible. In the end he chooses a bush that offers a compromise between expense and wear resistance.

There are four types of bush used in swinging arms, each tailored to the needs of the particular bike in question.

Silentbloc
Often called the rubber bonded type, this is made out of two steel sleeves with a ring of rubber in the middle.

This is an ideal design to absorb the rocking movements that do so much damage, and is cheap to manufacture. For this reason silentbloc bushes are used in nearly all mopeds and the majority of lightweight motorcycles like the Honda CB125, Suzuki GT185, and the Yamaha FS1E. Some of the larger bikes also use this type. A number of BSA models also employ them, notably the A10 and A7. Honda fit them to the 400 four.

The reason that rubber bushes are not more widely used on bikes is that modern machinery is so powerful and heavy that the life of this type of bush is too short to be worthwhile. Instead most makers fit the steel backed type of bush.

Metal-backed bush
Phosphor-bronze is traditionally used as a bushing material. It is easy to make and porous to lubricants, which means that maintenance is kept to a minimum. However, most bikes fitted with this type use steel backed bushes with phosphor bronze inserts. The steel casing keeps the inside metal rigid. The bronze layer is employed for its porous qualities. It can be impregnated with graphite PTFE and synthetic polymers to enhance its lubrication. Now bikes often use bushes with plastic inserts instead of phosphor-bronze, as they are cheaper to make.

Needle roller bearing
As an alternative to the steel back bush some larger motorcycles use the needle roller bearing. This offers greater precision and longer life, but this must be offset against the extra cost of manufacture. The rollers spin in slot machined from a circular billet, (see fig. 1). The surface to each roller is case-hardened to make the unit very hard-wearing. It still requires regular lubrication with a grease gun to keep the bearing swinging freely, but the main advantage of using this type of bearing is that it stops the arm rocking from side to side. In this respect, it has an advantage over the metal backed type of bearing. This is important on the big bikes where the cost is justified, for example they are used on the Kawasaki fours and Suzuki GS range. Here the improvement in stability and handling qualities is enough to justify the cost.

Taper roller bearing
In this bearing the swinging arm locates on two studs which are threaded into each side of the frame. The bearings slide on the stubs and form an interference fit with a conical taper machined in the arm.

Dismantling chain drive bikes
Remove chain and rear wheel as shown in the chapters on Replacing chains and sprockets (pages 140–151).

Next, disconnect the rear brake. If this is a drum type detach the brake lever by unscrewing the adjuster threaded on the end of the rod. An increasing number of bikes use disc braking on the rear wheel. To remove this assembly,

1. Replacing swinging arm bearings. Worn bearings can either be prised out with a screwdriver, or removed with a puller. New bearings are then drifted into place.

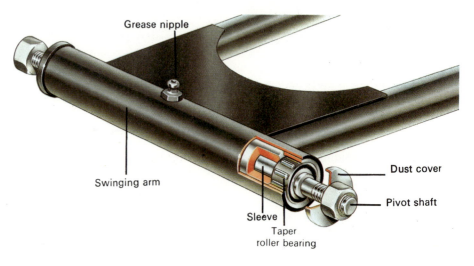

Grease nipple

Swinging arm

Sleeve

Taper roller bearing

Dust cover

Pivot shaft

Overhauling the swinging arm on a Tiger Cub

2. On the Triumph Tiger Cub drift out the old bushes and then ream the new ones to size

3. Compare the old bush (left) with the new one. Grease the back of the bush before refitting it

4. Press the new bush into place with a vice. Ensure that the bush enters the fork squarely or it will crumple

5. Alternatively, the bush can be knocked in with a suitable drift. This one is an old gearbox layshaft

6. Adjust the reamer to a smaller diameter than the sleeve. Cut the bush away until the shaft is a sliding fit

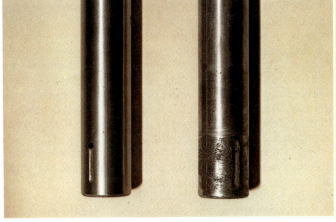

7. If the pivot shaft is worn, like the one on the right, renew it at the same time as the bushes

undo the bolts holding the caliper and ease it off the disc, it is best to tie it back to the frame, out of harms way. If your bike has a torque arm fitted, detach this at the point where it joins the hub. Avoid bending it out of the way as this will weaken the arm.

Straighten the split pin located in the end of the wheel spindle. Often it is badly corroded and you can save time by snipping the top off with a pair of pincers. If you need a new one, buy an assortment from a hardware store; they are always useful. Undo the

castellated nut on the end of the spindle. Frequently this is rusted solid, so start by cleaning up the nut and thread and spray it thoroughly with an aerosol penetrant oil such as WD 40. Make sure that the spanner or socket you intend to use fits properly, if the nut is rounded file new flats on the faces.

Knock out the wheel spindle with a hammer and drift, tap out the spacer that fits over the spindle, the wheel should now fall out from between the forks. Remove the chain adjusters, they are usually a press fit on the end of the forks. Take off the chainguard and release the shock absorbers from their mounting brackets on either arm.

The swinging arm is held to the rest of the frame by a long bolt that pins the pivot between two lugs on either side. It usually takes the form of a long bolt, or in a few cases, two small bolts, the pin being released by undoing the nut. Here again corrosion may make the nut difficult to move. Once again, use a squirt of penetrating fluid. Once the nut is off, hammer out the pivot and try to work the arm clear of the frame. Sometimes the arm is shimmed to take up wear in the frame so look out for the washers when the arm is removed. Yamaha fit shims to their range of two strokes and they are widely used on British machinery.

Shaft drive bikes
Shaft drive bikes have an additional complication as the swinging arm carries the shaft and bevel. The taper roller bearings are supported on adjustable stubs, which are secured on the frame. Put the bike on the centre stand and detach the rear brake lever if drums are fitted. This applies to all but the most recent BMW's and to the Honda CX500. The Yamaha XS750 and all BMW models from 1978 onwards use disc braking, and here the caliper must be unbolted and gently lifted off the disc. Remove the torque stay if one is fitted. It can be released where it bolts onto the hub. Now take out the wheel spindle and lift the wheel clear of the bike. The drive shaft is connected to the gearbox by a universal coupling. In normal use this is covered by a rubber gaiter. Release the hose clips holding the gaiter and slide it back out of the way. The coupling is bolted together with four bolts, slacken these in an even sequence.

Remove the caps that protect the adjusters, release the locknuts and unscrew the stub with the key provided in the bike's tool kit. The arm can be lifted out, it is not necessary to drain the oil in the final drive to do this as long as the unit is upright.

Replacing the bearings
Once the swinging arm is off the bike take the unit inside to a workbench fitted with a vice or a clamp to hold it

steady while you work on it. You will need a hammer and an assortment of drifts and chisels handy to knock out the old bushes. A hacksaw is useful for dealing with bearings which have rusted into their housing. A tin of grease will be needed for reassembly, applied with a grease gun. All bearing manufacturers recommend high melting point lithium base grease for this application such as Castrol LM or Shell Retinax A. There is no point in using a molybdenum disulphide as this is just an expensive substitute.

Metal-backed bush
This variety of bush frequently sticks in its housing in the arm. Sometimes this is due to corrosion of the metal casing but on other occasions it is caused by distortion of the casing under load. Start by removing the dust covers and oil seals which shield the bush. Slide out the inner bearings or sleeve on which the arm rotates.

If possible, mount the arm in a vice and insert a drift in the opposite end of the arm. Locate the drift on the lip on the bush you want to remove. Hammer the bush out in stages working round the edge. If this fails, thread a hacksaw blade through the bush and attach it to the hacksaw so that it cuts through the bush.

The replacement parts for this type of bush come pre-reamed to the size of the new spindle. However, on some bikes you will find it is necessary to ream the bushes to the correct size (see fig. 2 to 7). An adjustable reamer is an uncommon tool which you may be able to hire or borrow if you do not own one.

To fit a new bush into the swinging arm use a vice and two metal plates. The bush is positioned in the vice square to the casing. One metal plate is slipped behind the new bush, the other is placed behind the arm. The vice is closed up forcing the bush into the casing. It is vital that the bush is presented square to the seat or it will crumple as the vice is wound inwards.

Needle roller bearing
Needle roller bearings are usually a press fit in the swinging arm and often they can be drawn out with a pair of pliers or gently tapped out with a drift and hammer. If you can see flats on the surface of the rollers, the bearing is worn out. Once this has happened the bearing behaves like a ratchet on the movement of the arm and this causes the bike to wander off line. Fit the new bearing and thoroughly grease the rollers and the cage with bearing grease.

Taper roller bearing
This is the only type of bearing in which wear can be adjusted out and this is done when the arm is refitted. Apart from this all that is required is regular greasing.

To dismantle the bearing, remove the oil seals, withdraw the races and clean with paraffin. A toothbrush is useful here. Inspect the rollers for flats or signs of pitting. If these are present the roller must be replaced. Reassemble the bearing with plenty of grease.

Silentbloc
The replacement of this type of bush is quite straight forward, often the bushes can be pressed out by hand or with gentle persuasion by a hammer and drift. Once removed the bushes are always replaced as their cost is quite low. Inspect the pivot pin for misalignment, this can be done by checking it against a flat surface like plateglass or on an engineers' table. If it is bent it must be replaced.

This is a simple matter involving minimal expenditure and effort.

Refitting the swinging arm
Reassemble the swinging arm with new oil seals and dust covers, gently manoeuvre the arm into position between the mountings brackets. Slide the pivot shaft through the arm and tighten the retaining nuts. Now check the bushes for close fit by trying to rock the arm back and forth. If the arm can slide along the spindle this means that there is too much end float. The problem can be overcome by placing washers or shims on the end of the spindle.

This procedure is common among old British bikes, but the only manufacturer to use this method at the moment is Yamaha.

Once the arm is in place it should be thoroughly lubricated with a grease gun. Pump the grease through until grease starts to squirm out of the side. This job should be done everytime the engine oil is changed. On some models like the early Norton Commando the arm is lubricated with oil wicks.

Make sure that the rear wheel is properly aligned with the front one.

Shaft drives require a different procedure. The swinging arm is put back in the frame and an allen key is used to adjust the bearing. Start by loosening the locknuts and screwing up the adjusters. As you do this move the swinging arm up and down until you can feel the bearing beginning to drag. The arm is now correctly assembled. Finally reassemble final drive shaft.

Checking electrics

Faced with the confusing mass of lines that go to make up the wiring diagram for even the simplest of big bikes, the eyes of the average motorcyclist begin to blur. But once you have grasped the basics, even the most complex circuits can be quickly read and appreciated.

One of the problems in understanding circuit diagrams is that everyone seems to use different systems. While there is a basic European structure of symbols and notations in the German DIN standards, even BMW deviate in at least some areas from the normal terms, and the Japanese manufacturers each have their own totally different systems.

Nevertheless, all these systems operate on the same basic electrical principles and really it is only the shorthand description of the components of the circuit that is different. So there are some important rules common to all bikes that must be borne in mind when examining a wiring diagram and trying to relate it to the reality of the bike.
First of all, a basic electrical principle is that for a current to flow there must be a complete circuit.
When following the wiring on the diagram for any component then, you can be sure that you have not finished your search if you have not traced a complete circuit. As in most electrical systems the search is made considerably easier by the fact that the 'return' path very rarely has to be traced all the way along its course. Many circuits are, for

instance, 'earthed' to the body of the bike very near the component and the return path is simply via the body of the bike to the earth strap of the battery.

A second principle to remember is that all circuits need a power source. On the bike this is either the battery or the generator, and may feed the component directly or indirectly. Again you can be sure you have not acquired the complete picture if there is no battery or generator in your mental analysis.

However, unlike in many cars, the ignition switch controls all the electrical components on a bike with a battery. So unless the ignition is on, nothing works, even though few components require the engine to be running. What this means is that the ignition switch controls the power source. There is therefore rarely any need to trace back beyond the ignition switch to find the power source since the power for every component is routed through here.

The circuitry for the power supply via the ignition switch to the bike's electrical system – generator, regulators, rectifiers, battery and so on – is organized in separate circuit systems as you can see in fig. 7.

These are not covered in detail here, though it is important to know that the supply to the ignition switch is usually fitted with a fuse, which is located in the fuse box along with all the other fuses. Its function is to protect the rest of the circuit against damage by burning out easily and breaking the circuit if there is any malfunction. Since all the power to the ignition passes through this fuse, it must be able to take a higher current before burning out than the other fuses; otherwise it would burn out too easily and require constant replacement. Consequently this fuse is higher rated – typically 20A compared to 10A for the other circuits. A complete failure of the entire electrical system can often be traced to a blown power supply fuse. However, simply replacing the fuse will not cure the fault that caused it to blow in the first place.

After the ignition switch, the bike's electrical system splits into its component circuits, although not necessarily immediately: on the Kawasaki Z1000 the ignition and circuits do not separate until immediately before their respective switches. If the circuits divide directly at the ignition switch, this is usually so that the ignition switch can have multiple positions to connect up various functions. On the Kawasaki Z1000, for instance, the ignition switch has three positions: 'off', 'on' and 'park'. In the 'on' position, the supply to the ignition circuit is connected. With this connected, the bike is so wired that the supply to the lights and all the warning lights, horn and brake lights is also connected but each of these can be operated independently by their own switches. In the park position, a supply from the battery is connected to the tail light and the key can be removed to allow the tail lamp to remain illuminated when the bike is left in a dark street. With the ignition switch at 'park', the tail light is not connected to the rest of the light circuit and is illuminated independently; in the 'on' position, the tail light is connected to the lighting circuit but not directly to the battery and so is operated by the main light switch.

Other bikes have different variations in the ignition switch configuration, including such things as 'day', 'city' and 'night' but its function as the main electrical switch remains the same.

1. **Apparently a confusing tangle, each lead can be easily traced to the appropriate coloured terminal**

Using a circuit tester

A circuit tester consists of a length of wire, a bulb and a small battery connected together in a self-contained unit. It is used to test wiring or electrical components for continuity. Continuity is the unbroken flow of electricity through wires or components that is necessary for their function.

The circuit tester contains its own power supply to light the bulb so it must never be used to check components in a live circuit.

To test a fuse – fix the clip of the tester to one end and touch the probe on the other. If the fuse is not broken the bulb will light because there is electrical continuity through the fuse, completing the circuit between the terminals of the tester.

To test a length of wire – disconnect it from its terminals at either end, fix the clip to one end and touch the probe

on the other. The bulb will light if there are no breaks in the wire. To find the exact location of a hidden break in insulated wire, fix the clip to one end of the wire. Push the sharp tip of the probe through the insulation, so that it touches the wire core as close as possible to the clip. The bulb should light. Move the probe in short stages along the wire until the bulb fails to light. The break

in the wire will be between the tip of the probe and the last place it was inserted when the bulb lit up.

To test a switch – put the switch in the off position. Connect the tester clip and probe to the two terminals joined by the switch's moving contact when in the on position. Turn the switch on. The bulb will light if the switch is working properly.

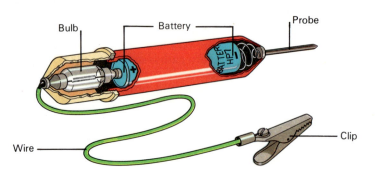

Bulb — Battery — Probe

Wire — Clip

Checking a fuse

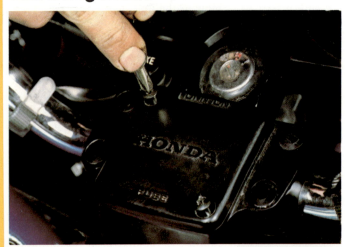

2. The fuse box on this Honda is on the steering head. On other bikes it may be found under the side-panel or seat

3. The position of each fuse should be marked on the cover. Trace the headlight fuse and remove it for inspection

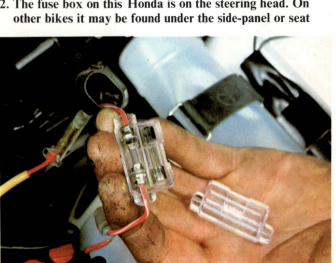

4. Where a single fuse is used to protect the electrical system it will usually be found under the side-panel

5. Test the continuity of a fuse with a circuit tester. If the tester's bulb fails to light the fuse is broken

Fuses and connectors

A. Bullet connector

B. Lucar or spade connector

C. British or Japanese type fuse

D. Bullet connector with sheath

E. Continental European type fuse

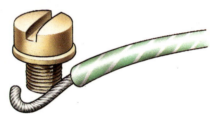

F. Screw terminal

6. For mid-lead junctions, most modern motorcycles use either bullet or Lucar connectors. Bullets cost less and take up less room but can be difficult to connect and disconnect. Lucar connectors are easy to use and also fit on to terminals readily. Not surprisingly, many people fit Lucars when rewiring their bikes despite their extra bulk

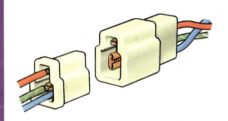

G. Multi-point connector

ponents alongside to assist identification on the diagram.

In contrast, the DIN system, although benefitting from standardization, is much less clear to the inexperienced. The symbols for components are much more abstract. A BMW circuit diagram, for instance, will show bulbs as a circle with a cross and a coil as a solid black rectangle. The mystery is further compounded by the fact that the DIN system rarely names the components on the diagram itself. Instead they are given numbers which can be decoded with the aid of a table either supplied with the diagram or a standard electrical handbook such as Bosch's. The reason for this degree of abstraction and symbolism was to save space and time in compiling the diagram but, unfortunately, the tradition has continued in many of today's workshop manuals even though the readers are quite obviously average motorcyclists rather than electrical wizards. To help you find your way through this maze, we have compiled a table of some of the more common symbols and numbers along with their Japanese equivalents (see over). British systems are again varied, but fall somewhere in between the DIN system and the Japanese in their degree of abstraction.

Often the hardest part of following a circuit through is to trace the path of a certain wire. Since the very early days, electrical wires have been given different coloured insulating covers to assist with identification. Although it has been possible to achieve standardization with the relatively simple domestic electrical system, it has proved virtually impos-

Reading the diagram

With these basic principles in mind you can begin to examine the wiring diagram to discover how a particular component is wired.

Your first task is to identify the component on the diagram. This is not always very simple because of the various symbols used to represent a particular feature of the circuit. Honda, for instance, use a pair of opposing tapered bars to represesent a spark plug, while the German DIN system uses a pair of arrow heads, and Kawasaki employ a simplistic drawing of a plug.

Generally, Japanese circuit diagrams are easier to understand than their European counterparts. This is because the components are represented more pictorially; a bulb is normally shown as a simplified drawing of a bulb (with two filaments if it has two) and a coil looks like a coil. It is also common practice with the Japanese manufacturers to write the name of major components on the diagram.

Terminal problems

When reconnecting an electrical component, you may find it difficult to decide which lead should go on which terminal. Of course, the best policy is to make your own marks before disconnection but many components have their own terminal markings to assist identification.

Some manufacturers use letters, and these are usually easy to interpret. On the coil, for instance, you may find the marking CB beside the terminal to to be connected to the contact breaker and SW beside the terminal for the ignition switch.

Most bikes built on the European continent, however, use the DIN system which has a numerical code, though letters are also used on these bikes. Here is a selection of the more common numbers.

1. Ignition coil LT: contact breaker
2. Magneto: kill switch
4. Ignition coil HT: distributor
15. Ignition switch: output
30. Supply from battery positive
31. Negative earth
49. Flasher relay: flasher switch
49a. Flasher relay output
50. Starter switch to solenoid
51. Rectifier output (DC)
56. Headlamp supply to dipswitch
56a. Dipswitch: main beam
56b. Dipswitch: dipped beam
56d. Headlamp flasher
57. Side light switch: bulbs
59. Flywheel magneto: rectifier (AC)
83. Multiple switch input
85. Relay output: earth
86. Relay input: battery
Others may be found in the Bosch Automotive Handbook.

Steve Cross; Kuo Kang Chen

sible in the more complex circuitry of the motorcycle – perhaps because the consequences of misconnection are, if expensive, rarely fatal. Lucas have their own colour coding system, so do Bosch, so do each of the Japanese manufacturers and so do many others. While a blue and white lead denotes headlamp, mainbeam and blue and red denotes dipped beam on a Lucas system, these leads are respectively red and black and red and yellow on Kawasakis.

Nevertheless, the wiring colours for any particular bike should be consistent, unless a previous owner of the machine has replaced wires with the wrong colour coding. A red wire on a Lucas system, for instance, will always denote an earth lead in a positive earth system; with a negative earth system, earth leads are black. A wire will not change colour in mid-route. If it appears to, this should be because it has been joined by another wire or because it has passed through some component. In this case its function will have changed. So to trace the supply for a particular component on the wiring diagram, you must follow the colour right from the component's terminal.

Again, because of printing costs and technology, very few circuit diagrams are actually printed in the appropriate colours. Instead, all the lines are in black and you must follow the symbols which are normally an abbreviation of the colour in the relevant language. Thus on Lucas diagrams red is R while on BMWs red is RT since the German for red is 'rot'.

Following a particular lead through on the diagram can be immensely difficult on a large diagram with all the leads represented by thin black lines. It can be particularly difficult if the layout is poor. It must be remembered that the layout of the diagram has absolutely no relationship to the layout on the bike. The diagram is laid out to portray the maximum amount of information in the minimum space, and, though not so obviously, with maximum clarity. All wires are represented by a single line drawn either vertically or horizontally. When lines cross on the diagram they should only join electrically if the crossing point is dotted, although this rule is not always adhered to.

Unfortunately clarity is usually lost for the sake of space saving or in order to locate the components in a way that represents their location on the bike. If this is the case on your diagram, take a piece of tracing paper and fix it firmly to the page. Mark a few reference points on the tracing paper – tracing, for example, the battery and ignition switch   to tell you if the paper slips, and follow the required lead through by marking its route out with a coloured pencil.

With the basics of the route established on paper, you must then apply your knowledge to the bike itself.

On the modern bike, electrical components are generally located within a few principal areas: switches and warning lights are on the handlebars, lights are, of course, at each end and the charging circuit and ignition components are either above the gear box or beneath the seat or tank. Because of this concentration, wiring can be a lot simpler on a bike than on a car, even though a modern superbike may have just as much electrical equipment. On the better-designed bikes, there can be two major electrical junctions, one in headlight and one beneath the sidepanel. A single properly bound multiple loom of wires can connect these two junctions. Connecting a component is thus a simple matter of plugging the lead into the appropriate and clearly marked sprocket. There may often be a few spare sockets for new components. Although BMW have done this for years, few others have . . . but things are changing.

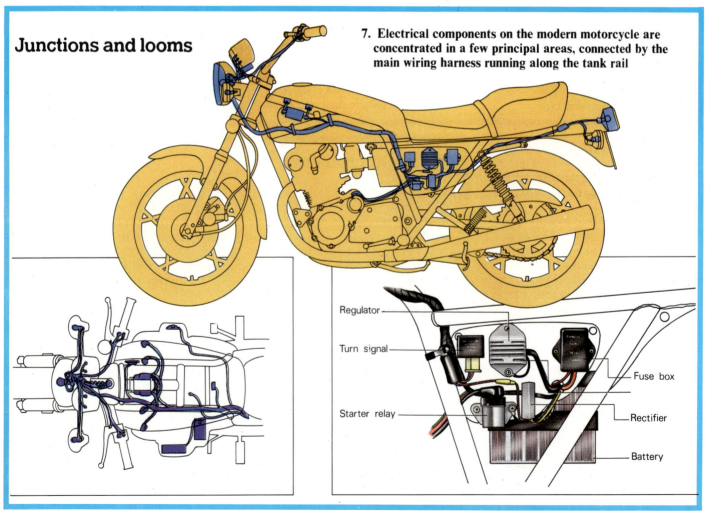

Junctions and looms

7. Electrical components on the modern motorcycle are concentrated in a few principal areas, connected by the main wiring harness running along the tank rail

Regulator

Turn signal

Starter relay

Fuse box

Rectifier

Battery

Steve Cross

Get to grips with your symbols

		DIN standard	Japanese	British
Current	DC			
	AC			
	3 phase AC			
Battery (with cell number)			Suzuki — 12V 14AH; Kawasaki — 12V 14AH; Yamaha; Honda	BATTERY 12 VOLT
Lines crossing	unconnected			
	connected			
Earth			Suzuki; Kawasaki and Yamaha; Honda	
Switch	normally open			
	normally close			
Resistor	fixed			
	variable			
Coil				
Coil with core				
Ignition induction coil				COIL
Transistor		PNP; NPN	PNP; NPN	
Semiconductors	rectifier diode		A — C		RECTIFIER
	zener diode		A — C (G)		ZENER DIODE
	thyristor		Kawasaki; Honda	
Capacitor				
Fuse			Suzuki; Kawasaki; Yamaha	
Lamp				
Headlamp (double filament)			Suzuki; Kawasaki; Yamaha	
Spark plug			Suzuki; Kawasaki; Honda	
Permanent magnet				
Starter motor (shunt wound)		M +		S
DC Dynamo		G		
Alternator		G		
3 phase alternator (with wound rotor)		G		
Flywheel magneto		G		
Cam activated switch (e.g. contact breaker)				
Horn			Suzuki; Kawasaki	
Brake light switch			Suzuki; 1. Kawasaki 2.	
Relay				
Flasher relay			Suzuki; Kawasaki; Yamaha	

Kuo Kang Chen

173

Section 3

COMMON FAULTS AND CURES

When a fuse blows

If your bike breaks down and checks show that the HT ignition circuit is in working order you should investigate the wiring circuit for any interruption such as a short circuit or poor connection.

Electrical faults can be the most frustrating problems to solve because they are so often hidden in the guise of a broken wire or a poor connection.

If you have coasted to the side of the road with a silent engine you should begin by checking if the lights and horn work. If they do the main battery fuse must be intact. If the fuse has blown and you have no spare, a piece of wire or even a piece of silver paper will suffice as a get-you-home substitute. However, whether or not you have a proper fuse to replace the broken one, you must find the cause of it blowing before proceeding. If you simply replace the broken fuse with a nail, the next item to break down may be something irreplaceable like the voltage regulator. Of course, if your bike hasn't got a fuse, current overload will simply cause the wiring to melt, or burn out. Consequently you should trace the cause of the electrical fault before going any further. This will be made much easier with the help of an improvised

1. Ideally, you should bring your bike indoors in order to check out the fuses

2. Having cured the fault that blew the fuse you can replace the broken one temporarily with some silver foil

wire and bulb tester.

To make a tester at the side of the road remove an indicator or tail light bulb and connect two lengths of electrical wire to the contacts. One piece of bared wire must be connected to the

blob of solder that forms one terminal on the bulb and the other piece must be connected to the threaded or plain body of the bulb which forms the other terminal. It is very important to make the connections well or else you will drive yourself to distraction looking for an elusive poor connection that only exists within your own tester. If you are carrying some tape solder you can make a soldered connection on the spot, if not you will have to make as good a connection as possible using tape. Solder two lengths of wire to a bulb of the correct voltage (6 or 12 volt, depending on the electrical system to be tested), and sufficient wattage (5 watts will do). The addition of small crocodile clips on the free end of the wires can make the testing process easier.

Tracking down a short
The first level of short circuit tracking should be a thorough visual check. It is likely that a short, severe enough to blow a fuse, will be quite visible once you have located the general area. Grasp all connections and pull and push them gently. Similarly examine the wires where they pass through any bodywork panels. If a visual inspection reveals nothing amiss you must continue with the second level which involves the use of a continuity tester.

Given that a complete circuit will result in some wire or component overheating you must not switch the ignition on. Consequently you must arrange a remote source of power for the test bulb. The bike's battery will suffice if a dry battery is not available. First connect one of the wires fixed to the bulb to either of the battery terminals. Then connect another length of wire to the the other terminal. The test wires are then the two remaining free wires.

To test for a short circuit place one of the free wires on the cable and the other aginst any earth point. If the bulb lights, the circuit must be complete. Having isolated the short circuit either effect a repair with some insulation tape or replace the relevant cable. In the case of a short circuit in a cable connector the cause could be dirt or grease which is conducting current. Clean the connector with solvent and dry it thoroughly before retesting it.

Circuit checks
The importance of good clean connections to all electrical components cannot be overstressed. This applies particularly to bikes because the electrical circuits are so exposed to the weather. The typical reasons for electrical problems are: corroded battery terminals, poor earth connections down

 © Marshall Cavendish

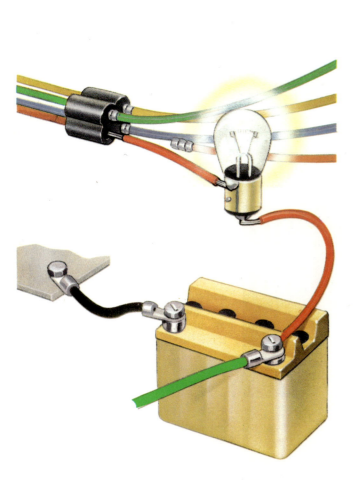

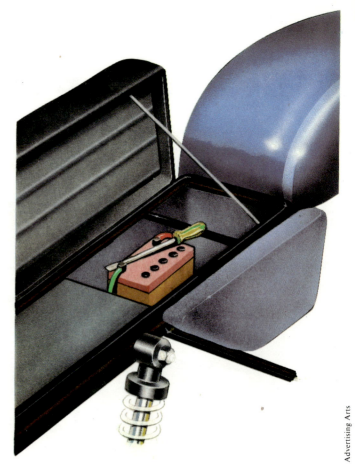

3. Connect the bulb as shown and use one lead as a probe to test wires and components for continuity

4. A screwdriver or even a badly fitted metal seat pan can effectively short out the battery

to the frame, and wire insulation that chafes due to the motion of the machine. It is sound practice to ensure that wiring is securely held in place along a fixed part. When checking wiring and electrical contacts it is well to remember that the object of the cable is to convey current to the point where it will be used with a minimum voltage drop. For example, a poor earth contact is often the reason for a flickering light bulb (the bulb, weakened by being continually switched on and off, will expire early). Similarly a speck of grease on the point where the bulb makes contact with its socket will stop the current getting through. A common area for problems is the earth strap to frame connection – if this breaks or becomes dislodged or the terminal is not clean or in good condition, the entire circuit will be affected. Checking potential shorts is just as simple if the same exhaustive type of search is employed.

Battery terminals may short if something like a screwdriver under the seat or the seat itself bridges them. But certain parts of the wiring are more susceptible to wear and tear than others. In particular the wires to the rear light which are threaded through the rear mudguard. A bent or loose mudguard or even a larger than standard rear wheel can cause the wires to chafe and come into contact with earth and so result in

Wire grading

The principle of electricity remains the same whatever the system.

The positive terminal of the generator/battery has an excess of electrons and the negative terminal has a lack of electrons. Therefore, when the circuit is complete a flow of electrons will naturally pass from the positive terminal to the negative terminal.

This electron flow, or current is carried between components by copper cables which are insulated by plastic or rubber. The cables are made up of strands of wire twisted into a gradual spiral rather than a single copper wire which would be less flexible and, therefore, more fragile. In normal circumstances the wires are capable of carrying the current required without overheating. The wires are graded according to the number of strands and the diameter of a single strand: for example, 16/0.20 metric shows that the cable in question has 16 strands each with a diameter of 0.2 mm. Cables are similarly denoted in imperial grades.

Whenever a cable is required for a particular installation the most important consideration is that the cross-sectional area of the copper is large enough to carry the current flow without overheating and that the volt drop (from natural resistance) in the conductor (wire) is small enough. The current rating and the volt drop rating is inversely related as cables increase in size. The manufacturer will use a cable which is the minimum size to do the job. And the criteria are: (a) that volt drop on full load must not be too great; and (b) that the cable heating must be within specified limits.

The current carrying ability of a wire depends on its cross-sectional size. And cable heating depends on both the cross-sectional size and the cable's heat-shedding ability. A single cable exposed to air can be used to carry a much higher current than if it were bunched up with other cables as part of a loom and shielded from passing air by being placed, for example, under the fuel tank or inside the headlamp shell. Cables that are required to carry a current for a short time only can be worked at a higher current density but in this case the deciding factor on size is usually based on the voltage drop arising from the cable's high resistance. To ignore the rules is to court disaster.

5a. The short circuit, where electrons bypass part of the circuit, resulting in build up of heat, can be seen as a leaking water pipe – where water flows out of a hole and results in a flood

5b. A poor electrical connection, where the electron flow is slowed down and results in a loss of power, can be seen as a blocked water pipe – where the flow of water is restricted

a short. Whenever you are dealing with a bike that has been modified from standard fettle you should check that all wires are sufficiently long and well secured and that wires are not joined simply by twisting them together and then just covering them with tape.

6. To insert a fuse in a circuit cut the feed supply wire, solder a fuse holder in, and cover the joint

The fuse

Electrical power essentially comes in the form of electrons flowing from the positive terminal of the battery to the negative. In rough terms the electrons which flow around the system are first stored and then discharged as a spark. And as the electrons flow around the lighting circuit their energy is converted into light and, of course, heat. The lights, horn and the ignition coils restrict the flow of the electrons and, therefore, slow it down ('triction') in the process of using the electron's energy. The current flow produces heat in the wire – the greater the current, the greater the heat produced. In normal circumstances the wire on a bike will be able to cope with the heat produced by the current flow through the various components. However, if a short circuit occurs, the current of electrons will by-pass part of the circuit and a direct flow of electrons will continue between the positive and negative terminals of the battery/generator. This unrestricted flow leads to a higher current which in turn creates greater heat and inevitably the plastic insulation covering the wire melts and burns, and the wire oxidizes with disastrous results.

The most likely cause of a short circuit is a live wire coming into contact with the earth. Another possibility is a faulty component which is not working and consequently 'leaking' power: the result is that the current flow is not sufficiently restricted and a short is consequently created. The standard wiring on a bike will tolerate an increase in the flow of power until the overload point is reached.

Although nearly all modern bikes have at least one fuse in the circuit, a few older machines do not. And in order to avoid the possibility of overheated wiring you should fit a fuse. To do this cut the positive wire from the battery and insert a fuse holder with the correct value fuse. It is best to solder the wires together. Basic soldering techniques are easily mastered. Finally, wrap the exposed portion of wire with some insulating tape. Generally a 15 amp fuse is adequate, however, the correct fuse value should be quoted in the handbook for a later model of the bike. All fear of smoking wiring can be prevented by a regular check of the likely trouble spots.

Steve Cross

Advertising Arts

Curing oil leaks

All motorcycle engines rely on oil to prevent metal-to-metal contact between moving parts. And if oil starts to leak out the result can be, at best a dirty, messy engine, or at worst, a complete seizure.

A motorcycle engine consists of a number of separate or linked components many of which contain lubricant to protect the internal components. Such compartments are often joined by removable pipes or are bolted together for easy dismantling and, therefore, incorporate some form of joint. These joints may have to be oil-tight internally, depending on the design and type of engine. But the common factor of all engines is that the external casings form the outside oil boundary through which no oil should escape.

Oil by its very nature has a 'searching' action and will find its way through tiny gaps. The usual method of ensuring that oil stays inside the engine is to use a paper, cork or composition material sealing gasket between bolted joints; and flexible sealing rings to stop oil seeping past rotating shafts. But age, wear, heat distortion or vibration can cause a seal to break down resulting in a leaking joint. The faulty seal should be tracked down and repaired as soon as possible, as a serious leak could deposit oil on the back tyre making riding hazardous, or cause components to seize-up, making an expensive re-build necessary.

Tracing a leak

Tracing a leak on the upper part of an engine is usually fairly straight forward as the source of trouble can be seen from the resultant smear or stain. But the exact source of a leak on the underside of an engine where most leaks occur may be a little more difficult to find.

Most bikes accumulate road dirt and grease underneath as this part of the machine tends to be neglected during routine cleaning. So if a leak develops, the bottom of the engine may be turned into an oily sticky mess making it impossible to see where the oil is coming from. The exact point of the leak is therefore best tracked down by removing all the dirt and oil first. Several proprietary solvent/cleaners such as Gunk and Jizer, are available to make removing thick oil and grease easy. Apply the cleaning agent to the engine with a stiff bristle brush (fig. 2), wait a few minutes for it to act, then wash it off with clean water. Dry the area off, start the engine and leave it running until it is fully warmed up. This is necessary because cold, thick oil may not be able to escape through a joint whereas hot thin oil may run out freely. If oil from the leak point does not appear immediately put a sheet of clean newspaper under the bike and leave it. Later, check the newspaper for stains – you should be able to trace a leak from the position of the stain on the newspaper.

If an internal gasket or oil seal starts to leak, several signs of the fault may be noticed depending on the site and severity of the leak. First, oil may find its way into another part of the engine causing a fault in an unrelated component. Or the added pressure of escaping oil may cause a gasket to blow repeatedly in another part of the engine. On 2-strokes,

1. **Some of the many products made to help you keep your oil where it belongs – inside the engine**

Symptom	Possible cause	Remedy
Engine leaks oil	Blown gasket or faulty flange face	Renew gasket or restore face (page 179)
	Worn oil pipe union	Re-seal or replace union (page 180)
	Leaking oil seal	Renew oil seal (page 181)
	Leaking 'O' ring	Re-seal or replace (page 181)
	Blocked breather	Clear breather vent (page 181)
	Faulty oil pressure release valve	Inspect valve components (page 182)

oils seals play a vital part in maintaining pressure in the crankcase. If, for example, a crankshaft oil seal fails, the engine will lose compression and may refuse to start. Renewing an oil seal of this type sometimes demands a partial engine strip and will therefore be dealt with fully in a later Workshop article. But oil seals that are more accessible on both 2-strokes and 4-strokes can be dealt with fairly easily.

Curing oil leaks

There are basically four types of leak. The most common is from between two mating flange faces, where the gasket or the faces have deteriorated. But oil pipes, unions or oil seals may all wear or perish and break down necessitating a repair, and some may even require a complete engine stripdown.

2. Clean off a dirty, oily engine with a proprietary solvent. This makes tracing the exact source of a leak easier

Curing a flange face leak

3. Remove the outer cover of a leaking flange face component and pull off the old gasket

4. Old gaskets become brittle and may break up on removal. So use a sharp knife to clear the faces

5. Use plate glass – a car's flat side screen will do – and grinding paste to restore a marked flange face

6. Coat the surface of the face to be ground with fine paste. Use a coarse grade first if it is badly marked

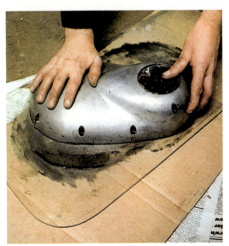

7. Place the component face down on the glass. Apply even pressure and rub it round in small circles

8. The restored face should be an even satin-grey all over when the marks have been completely ground out

Nelson Hargreaves

Leaking flange faces

The procedure for curing a flange face joint leak is the same wherever the leak lies. The crankcase halves, and its outer covers, the rocker box and cylinder head are examples of flange face joints. And the only difference in dealing with them is the amount of dismantling that may be needed to make a repair.

First unbolt and separate the leaking joint. If a gasket is fitted pull it away from the face (fig. 3). Gaskets become brittle with age and sometimes disintegrate as they are removed. Pieces of gasket and sealing material that remain stuck to the faces can be removed by careful scraping with a sharp knife (fig. 4). Try not to damage the relatively soft faces of alloy components – use gentle pressure and keep the knife blade square to the face. Finally wipe off all traces of dirt and oil.

If the faces are rough or have been marked or scratched by careless handling, oil may leak through the indentations even when a gasket is fitted. But you can restore the flange faces to an almost perfect, oil-tight mating joint by 'lapping' the faces with a piece of plate glass and some rubbing compound (fig. 5). Plate glass, and not ordinary window glass, must be used as this is manufactured with a very flat, regular surface. If you cannot buy a piece of plate glass from a glaziers use a car's flat side-window screen. You should be able to buy one of these fairly cheaply from a scrap dealer.

Smear a thin coat of rubbing compound, fine graphite grinding paste is ideal, onto the flange face of the component (fig. 6). Put the plate glass onto a flat, smooth surface and place the component to be ground face down on the glass. Apply an even downward pressure to the component and rub it on the glass with small circular movements (fig. 7). After a few minutes wipe the face clean and inspect it. If scratches or marks are still present, apply a little more paste and continue rubbing. Do this until the face has a regular, dull grey satin finish all over (fig. 8). Repeat the operation on the other mating face of the joint. But if this component part cannot be conveniently stripped from the engine to be put on the glass you will have to hold the glass and rub it on the face.

The joint can now be remade. But first remove all traces of grease and rubbing compound with petrol or a proprietary solvent. If a gasket should be fitted between the faces make sure that a new one is used, never try to re-use an old one.

If the gasket for the joint you want to seal is unobtainable, you can make one

Making a new gasket

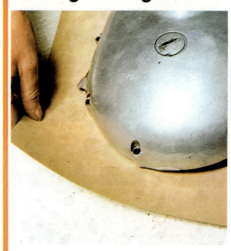

9. If a gasket for the joint you want to seal is unobtainable, make one from a sheet of gasket material

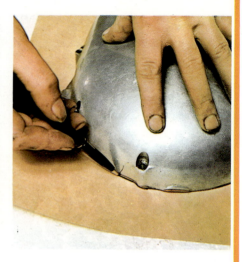

10. Place the cover face down on the sheet and mark round its outer edge with a felt-tipped pen

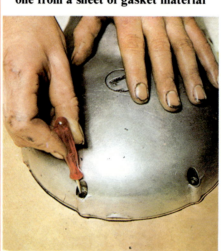

11. Before removing the cover from the sheet, push a sharp tool through the bolt holes to mark their positions

12. Remove the cover and sketch in the inner edge of the gasket. Make it a little wider than the flange face

Nelson Hargreaves

Continued

from a sheet of gasket fibre material (fig. 9). Place one of the joint faces on to the gasket material and mark round it with pen (fig. 10). Before lifting the component away, push a sharp instrument through the bolt holes to mark their position on the gasket. The inside edge of the gasket which corresponds to the depth or thickness of the flange face can be roughly sketched on the sheet (fig. 12). The gasket can then be cut out.

To make a good seal with a gasket, first cover one face of the joint with a jointing compound, such as Hylomar (fig. 14). Wait a few minutes for the compound to become tacky, then place the gasket carefully on the flange face (fig. 15). Smear a light coat of compound on the other face and offer up the two parts together taking care not to dislodge the gasket. The joint can then be bolted up.

An alternative seal to a fibre gasket

and jointing compound can be made with 'instant' gasket material. This is a silicone based material supplied in a tube (such as Loctite or Hermetite). It is resistant to heat and oil and is applied directly to one face of the joint (fig. 16). This method offers the advantage of speed and simplicity and is particularly useful if a repair has to be made when a gasket is not available.

Leaking unions

Threaded oil pipe unions may leak after prolonged service. Replacing the piping and the unions as an integral component can prove expensive. If the piping itself splits it is not advisable to make a repair – it should be renewed. But if a union leaks because the threads are worn it can be repaired. Similarly a repair can be made to other threaded unions if they weep or leak, such as the tacho-

Oil pressure warning light

Many 4-stroke bikes have an oil pressure warning light fitted to the instrument panel. This is activated by a pressure sensitive switch located on, or near, the oil pump. It is designed to detect a drop in oil pressure below the engine's working minimum. The warning light may come on immediately the engine is started but should go out after a few seconds when the oil pump has built up the pressure.

If the warning light should come on when the bike is running normally, stop the engine as soon as possible. This usually signifies a very significant loss of oil or a major internal failure.

Check the engine and look particularly for a blown crankcase cover gasket, blowing head or base gasket, or plug that has come loose or even disappeared. This could cause the loss of the entire oil supply. Under no circumstances start the engine again until the leak or fault has been rectified.

ped out of the groove, or it is not seating properly. Check the ring by dismantling the component and inspecting its seating. Take the ring out and renew it if it is damaged.

Blocked breather
A breather is a hole or vent in a casing. It allows pressure that builds up when the engine is running to escape. But only 4-strokes are fitted with a crankcase breather though 2-strokes sometimes have one in the gearbox. If the breather is partially blocked an increase in temperature in the engine builds up air pressure, and this can cause oil to be forced out through the hole.

Check your bike for a breather. There may be several and the location is often obscure and varies widely from bike to bike. But the breather hole will usually be located at, or near, the highest part of an engine casing. Check with the manufacturer to find out where they are.

Clear the breather by unscrewing the

meter drive union. A special thin tape (PTFE tape) can be used to wrap round union threads to give them an oil-tight fit (fig. 18). The tape is commonly used by plumbers and can be bought from a plumber's merchant.

Where a pipe is a push fit on to a metal union pipe (fig. 20) it can be sealed if it has become slack. Use a pipe line sealer such as Loctite. Apply the paste to the metal union (fig. 21) then push the oil pipe over the union and secure it with a hose clip. Ensure that surplus paste does not find its way inside the pipe or it may get blocked when the sealant hardens.

Leaking oil seals
Oil is prevented from leaking past a rotating shaft, which passes through a casing, by an oil seal. The seal is a flexible ring containing a circular spring which is fixed to the stationary component, or casing which surrounds the shaft. Most oil seal leakages are caused either by wear in the shaft or the bearings on which it runs. Such wear allows the shaft to whip sideways and run eccentrically and this eventually distorts the seal. Age hardening of the seal also allows leakage. Before renewing a seal, the shaft and its bearings must be checked for true running otherwise the seal may fail again.

To renew a seal, hook or prise the old one out with a screwdriver. Before refitting the new seal, make sure that its recess in the casing is perfectly clean. Fit the seal with its lipped side facing the direction from which the oil is to be contained. Lightly lubricate the outer and inner faces of the seal, this will prevent the delicate lips from burning or tearing when the shaft starts to rotate. Press the seal squarely into its recess. This is best done with a soft drift, such as a piece of wood, and a mallet.

Leaking 'O' rings
An 'O' ring is a ring of rubber-based

material often used as an oil seal where two bored surfaces are pressed together to stop oil leaking to the outside; for example where some types of oil filter canisters fit directly into the crankcase.

The ring sits in a groove and sometimes causes a leak because it has hop-

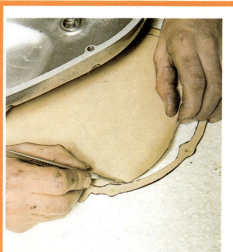

13. Cut the gasket out of the sheet. A sharp knife is better than scissors, especially for the bolt holes

14. To re-seal a gasket joint, coat one face with a jointing compound such as Hylomar

15. Place the new gasket carefully on the face, line up the holes, then coat the gasket with compound

16. An alternative seal to a gasket can be made with an 'instant' paste such as Hermetite or Loctite compound

Nelson Hargreaves

Sealing a threaded union

17. If a component leaks oil through a union, such as this tachometer drive, first undo it and clean it off

18. Worn threads of the union can be made oil tight with plumber's PTFE sealing tape

19. Cut off a piece of tape the same width as the threads, then bind it tightly round them

cap (if one is fitted) and cleaning it out, or poke a piece of stiff wire in the vent hole to clear it.

A breather sometimes blows out oil in a fine mist consistently, even if it is not blocked. This can cover surrounding components and make them unsightly. But you can put the escaping oil to good use, or direct it away from the bike with a simple modification.

Connect a short length of metal tube to the engine casing over the breather vent. To save drilling and tapping a threaded tube into the engine you can use a powerful adhesive such as Araldite to fix it in place. Push a length of plastic pipe over the tube and secure it with a hose clip. Now route the pipe through the bike to wherever you want the oil directed.

For example, the pipe can be clipped to the frame and positioned so that the end of it hangs over the lower run of the chain. The regular drips of escaping oil from the pipe will provide your bike with an automatic chain oiler.

Alternatively, route the pipe so that oil is chanelled away from the bike.

Faulty pressure release valve

Dry sump lubricated 4-stroke bikes are sometimes fitted with an oil pressure release valve. This is a spring-loaded ball bearing seal which fits into a seat in the top side of the crankcase. The spring is made to a predetermined rate and will only compress if pressure in the crankcase rises to a higher level than it is capable of holding. When the spring is compressed the ball seal lifts off its seat alowing oil to escape. This prevents a dangerous build-up of pressure in the

crankcase assembly.

If the spring loses its tension through prolonged service, it will allow oil to escape past the ball even when pressure is normal or low. This results in a continuous stream of oil being thrown out of the valve. The spring should, therefore, be renewed.

Remove the release valve assembly by unscrewing it from the crankcase side. There are usually hexagon flats for a spanner on the domed cap of the unit. Withdraw the spring from the valve body and check its length against a new spring to see if it has worn. At the same time examine the ball bearing. If it is

pitted or has a shoulder worn onto it, replace it. Finally re-assemble the unit. A gasket is sometimes fitted round the threads of the valve so renew this and apply some jointing compound to make a good seal.

If it is the threads that have worn, the only cure is retapping the hole in the crankcase, and fitting a new valve with a matching thread. A good stopgap repair is to wrap some threads of waxed string around the threads on the valve, and very carefully refit it to the crankcase. This will only last a short time, and a full repair should be done as soon as possible.

Sealing an oil pipe union

20. Oil pipe joints sometimes leak at their unions. Undo the pipe clip and pull off the pipe

21. Clean all traces of oil from the pipe and union. Then coat the inner pipe with sealing compound

Nelson Hargreaves

Fixing a faulty exhaust

Exhaust systems on standard production bikes are designed to give optimum performance from an engine and yet reduce its naturally noisy operation to a minimum. If the exhaust develops a leak then both engine performance and rider comfort can suffer from the escaping gas.

An exhaust system is a relatively simple component consisting of a separate or integral pipe and silencer. But its simple construction is based on very complex design factors which take into account the exhaust's many functions.

The exhaust must channel away hot, poisonous gas produced during combustion, so that the engine is not damaged by the heat nor the rider burned nor stifled. The gas must also escape freely enough to prevent the engine choking on its own fumes, but without infringing the law by allowing the full bellow of its escape into the open air.

While doing this, the exhaust system has to stand up to a severe battering from inside and out. Internally, the hot, high-speed gas, its corrosive acid by-products and moisture from condensation eat away the metal. Oil and carbon carried out of the engine with the gas get deposited along the system, clogging it up. Externally, the exhaust faces corrosion and damage from poor weather conditions, while vibration from the engine shakes the system continually.

Eventually, a well-maintained exhaust will break down completely under the constant stress and must be renewed. But long before this stage is reached, an exhaust system is likely to suffer local rusting and damage, or shake loose its mounting brackets and clamps. If this happens, exhaust gas may be able to find its way out of the system other than at the end of the silencer. And the result will be a leaking and (illegally) noisy exhaust which can have an adverse effect on both the machine and the rider.

Leaking exhaust

If an exhaust system leaks, two things will become immediately noticeable. First, depending on the severity of the leak, engine performance will fall below its usual standard. The shape and size of an exhaust system plays an important part in determining the performance characteristics of an engine, particularly on 2-stroke machines. Acceleration may become sluggish and the bike will seem generally under-powered.

Second, the sound of the exhaust will change. Under normal conditions the exhaust gas resonates in the system to produce a distinctive exhaust note. But if gas can escape before reaching the end of the system, the gas flow, and therefore the sound, will change. Increased noise usually points to a leak in the exhaust or a faulty baffle tube.

Any leak in the forward part of the exhaust system can also be very dangerous. Poisonous carbon monoxide fumes may be directed towards the rider and inhaled, instead of blowing away behind the bike. The cause of a leaking exhaust should therefore be traced and repaired as soon as possible.

Exhaust systems

There are two types of exhaust system, single-piece and two-piece. On single-piece exhausts, the pipe (header pipe)

1. The component members of a complete two-piece exhaust system

Checking a baffle

2. Undo the baffle retaining screw through the hole in the silencer

3. Withdraw the baffle tube from the end of the silencer with pliers

4. Inspect the tube for damage, wear or corrosion

Symptom	Possible cause	Remedy
Noisy or leaking exhaust	Worn out or defective baffles	Replace baffles or silencer (page 183)
	Hole in exhaust	Repair or replace (pages 184–185)
	Leaking pipe/silencer joint	Tighten clamp (page 186)
	Loose or broken header clamp	Tighten or replace (pages 187–188)
	Blown header gasket	Replace gasket (page 188)

Using exhaust bandage

5. **The exhaust bandage repair kit consists of bandage, a length of fine wire and a piece of metal foil**

6. **To repair a hole, first roughen the area with a file. This will help the bandage grip to the smooth chrome**

7. **Wet the bandage, remove the protective backing and then position the piece of foil over the leaking area**

8. **Wrap the bandage round the silencer at least three times. Mould it over contours by rubbing it with your fingers**

which connects to the cylinder head is integral with the silencer and cannot be separated from it. Two-piece systems (fig. 1) incorporate a removable silencer but are otherwise similar to one-piece types.

Tracing a leak
An exhaust leak can occur almost anywhere along the exhaust system, especially if it is caused by a rust hole or accident damage. But the most common leaks are usually due to defective joints at the exhaust manifold and between the pipe and silencer.

The source of a leak will usually be obvious when the engine is running, as gas can be seen blowing out of a joint or hole. An oil stain or smear from the gas may also mark the place. But if the source of the leak is not readily visible, you can make a simple check to find it.

Run the engine and press your foot, or a thick piece of rag, over the end of the silencer. If there is a leak, the build up of gas under pressure will force the gas through an alternative escape route. If you have a multi-cylinder bike with exhaust pipes which run into a common expansion box, or are joined together

9. Use the wire provided to wrap round the repair bandage. Twist the wire tightly with a pair of pliers

10. The finished job should look neat and tidy. The wiring will hold the bandage securely until it has hardened

with a balance tube before the silencers, cover all the silencers at once. Otherwise the exhaust will simply re-route itself through the other pipes and a leak will not show. As an added check put your hand close to the pipe and silencer and move it along. You will feel the gas at the point where it is blowing out.

If no leaks are apparent but the exhaust is excessively noisy, the silencer baffles are probably faulty.

Defective baffles

Baffles are fitted inside a silencer to bear and absorb impact of the exhaust gas as it leaves the cylinder. If the baffles break down or rust away, the gas will have a relatively unrestricted passage to the open air causing a noisy exhaust.

Most 4-stroke bikes use a silencer with integral baffles. If they become faulty then the whole silencer must be replaced. If a removable baffle is fitted it will be very similar to the 2-stroke

type described below.

Two-stroke silencers, because of the oily nature of their exhaust, usually contain a baffle tube which can be removed for cleaning. It can therefore be removed and inspected for damage.

Baffle tubes are usually screwed into the silencer or retained by a single screw or bolt, accessible either through a small hole in the silencer (fig. 2) or at the end of it. Remove the screw or bolt and withdraw the baffle (fig. 3). Examine the tube for corrosion. If wire gauze is used in the tube as a sound deadening material, make sure that it has not disintegrated. Renew the whole baffle if it is faulty.

If the baffle is intact, but the silencer or pipe is leaking and noisy due to a hole, you may be able to repair it.

Holed exhaust

A holed silencer or pipe can be repaired effectively and easily as long as the rest

of the system is generally sound. Local rust holes and punctures or splits can be covered to prevent exhaust gas escaping and the repair should last for the life of the system. Although a repair may not look particularly attractive it will certainly save the great expense of renewing part, or all, of the exhaust system.

Two types of material are available to repair a holed exhaust – a heat-resistant filling paste and an exhaust bandage kit. Both materials harden with the heat of the exhaust so you should only make a repair when the exhaust system is cold.

An exhaust bandage kit (fig. 5) is useful for covering large holes or splits in either the pipe or silencer. To repair a hole in, for example, a silencer first clean the area around the hole with a wire brush. Then roughen the same area with a file (fig. 6). This is necessary to provide a keyed surface so that the bandage will grip on the hard, smooth chrome. Carefully measure out the

Using repair paste

11. Exhaust repair paste can be used to seal small holes or cracks in the pipe or silencer

12. Apply a thick blob of paste over the hole and the surrounding area to seal the tank

13. Rub your finger over the paste to smear it into a smooth, even coat. Exhaust heat will harden the paste

length of bandage needed to wrap around the silencer at least three times. Remove the protective backing, then lightly dampen the bandage in water. A piece of aluminium foil either attached to the bandage at one end or supplied separately is included in the bandage kit. Position the foil over the hole (fig. 7), then wrap the bandage around the silencer. The bandage can be moulded to follow any contour and the layers will blend together when rubbed to form a solid seal. Use the wire provided to bind the bandage securely in place (fig. 9). After a few minutes start the engine and run it until the exhaust pipe becomes hot. The heat will cause the bandage to shrink slightly and harden, forming a permanent seal.

Sealing paste can be used to seal small holes in a pipe or silencer (fig. 11). Smear a thick blob of paste over the hole and rub it over with your finger to form a smooth coating (fig. 13). Heat up the exhaust pipe and leave the paste to harden.

Leaking pipe and silencer joint
On two-piece exhausts the pipe and silencer joint may leak. This can be dealt with without disturbing the pipe header clamp and manifold joint.

The joint is made by the exhaust pipe fitting into the slightly larger bore of the silencer. A pinch clamp is usually used to close the two parts together, though a rubberized sealing ring is sometimes fitted into the silencer and the two parts are a tight push fit. Alternatively the pipe and silencer may screw together (fig. 14).

Check first for slackness in the joint. If a clamp is fitted, make sure it is screwed or bolted up tight. If the clamp is fully tightened, but the joint still leaks, the pipe or silencer may need to be replaced. But before renewing any parts separate the joint and inspect it as you may be able to make an inexpensive repair.

To separate the joint, first slacken, but do not remove, the silencer mounting bolt. If the joint is of the clamp type, slacken the bolt or screw fully. Now free the silencer altogether and carefully pull it backwards off the pipe.

If a seal is fitted in the silencer, prise it out with a screwdriver. There is little point in trying to repair this type as a new seal is inexpensive and easily fitted back into the silencer. However if the new joint is still slack due to slight ovality of the pipe, it can be sealed with an exhaust joint paste (such as Fire Gum). Smear a thick coating of paste on to the pipe then push the silencer back in position and secure it. Wipe off surplus paste and start the engine. This type of paste hardens by the heat of the exhaust in a similar way to the repair paste described above. But the seal it makes is not permanent – it can be broken fairly

Packing a joint

14. This pipe and silencer joint is held by a threaded ring. You will need a C-spanner to undo it

15. Position the jaw of the C-spanner in one of the ring's castellations, then twist the ring to undo it

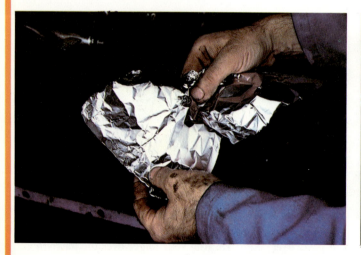

16. Aluminium foil can be used to pack the pipe joint. Tear off a piece wide enough to be folded several times

17. Fold the foil into a tight strip. The thickness of the foil can be adjusted by further folding or unfolding

Continued

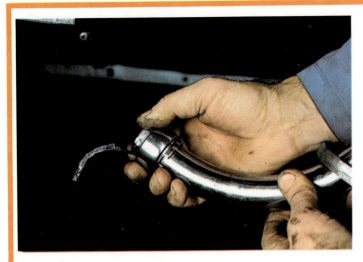

18. Wrap the foil strip tightly round the outside of the pipe and cut it so that the ends overlap

19. Hold the strip in place and twist the pipe into the silencer so that the strip is not pushed out of position

Types of header clamp fixing

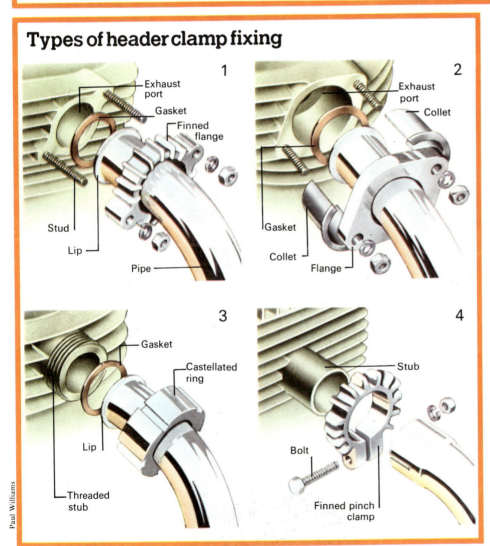

Paul Williams

20. Common types of header clamp fixing. (1) A finned flange fits over studs in the cylinder head. When the nuts are tightened, the lipped pipe and gasket are drawn to the exhaust port. (2) A plain flange over the pipe draws the pipe and its two sealing collets into the bore of the exhaust manifold. (3) A castellated ring over the pipe screws to a threaded stub on the exhaust port. (4) The slotted header pipe fits over a stub on the exhaust port and a finned pipe clamp closes the pipe tightly on to the stub

Wrap the foil tightly round the pipe (fig. 18) and push the silencer back over the pipe. Twist the silencer so that it screws itself over the foil strip and prevents the strip from being pushed up the pipe. Joint paste can be smeared over the repair as an added precaution. Now re-tighten the clamp. The packing should ensure that the clamp presses the silencer firmly around the pipe to seal the joint.

Loose header lamp
The header clamp is the device which holds the first section of exhaust pipe on to the exhaust manifold in the cylinder head. If the clamp is broken or loose, vibration will break the gasket seal between the parts and cause a leak. To cure a leak at this joint the clamp must be undone and the pipe pulled off the manifold.

Several types of header clamp are fitted to modern machines. Nearly all are similar to, or slight variations of, the four basic types shown in figure 20.

A header clamp holds the exhaust pipe in position in one of three ways: first, it may be bolted to studs in the cylinder head; second, it may clamp the

easily the next time you need to remove the silencer.

Clamp and screw joints can be repaired by packing out the joint to make an effective seal. Ordinary aluminium cooking foil is ideal for this as it is heatproof and easily shaped. To pack a joint, first cut off a piece of foil from a sheet long enough to be wrapped once around the exhaust pipe (fig. 16). And make sure that the foil is wide enough to be folded several times. The number of folds you make determines the final thickness of the packing. This can be adjusted by further folding or unfolding of the foil. The finished folded strip should be at least 20 mm (about 1in.) wide to ensure a good seal.

pipe over a stub on the exhaust manifold stub. To remove the latter type you may need a C-spanner to grip the castellations on the retaining ring. Alternatively, the ring can be tapped round with a mallet and a soft metal drift. If the ring is finned and has no provision for a spanner it may have to be undone by hand. Wrap a piece of rag over the fins and twist it loose to unscrew it. On no account hit the fins with a hammer to loosen the ring. They are very brittle and may snap off.

On other machines, such as some Triumphs, a finned header clamp fits around the top of the exhaust pipe but does not hold the pipe in position. The clamp is fitted purely to enhance the appearance and the pipe is a tight push fit into the exhaust manifold. A bracket further down the pipe prevents it from shaking loose. Remove this first to pull out the pipe.

To remove the exhaust pipe and inspect the gasket, undo the header clamp bolt, flange (fig. 21) or ring and slide it along the pipe out of the way. But before the pipe can be pulled out of the manifold you will have to disconnect some other part of the exhaust depending on the type of system fitted.

On one-piece types the silencer must be freed from its mounting so that the pipe can be removed. On two-piece types, the pipe and silencer joint clamp or ring must be fully slackened off. If a balance pipe is fitted between the exhaust pipes to connect them together, then this too must be disconnected. They are usually held together by a simple pinch bolt clamp.

The pipe can now be pulled from the manifold. Push-fit pipes may be difficult to remove so try tapping out the pipe with a soft hide mallet. As the pipe comes away, look for two collets which are sometimes fitted over the end of the pipe like a sleeve. These are sometimes fitted instead of a gasket. Notice which way round the collets locate and make sure they are returned in the same positions when re-assembling.

The gasket, where fitted, is usually recessed in the manifold port. Prise this out with a screwdriver (fig. 23). Manifold gaskets are usually the copper and asbestos sandwich type and after prolonged use or overtightening may become crushed and lose their sealing properties. Inspect the gasket and if it looks blackened or burned replace it. Smear joint sealing paste on the clamp flange or exhaust pipe on re-assembly (fig. 24). This should ensure that the joint remains gas-tight.

There is nothing worse than a noisy exhaust. Not only does it make a lot of unpleasant noise but that noise can get you in trouble with the law and mean a costly fine. Regular checks on the mountings and condition of the exhaust system should keep things quiet.

Checking the header joint

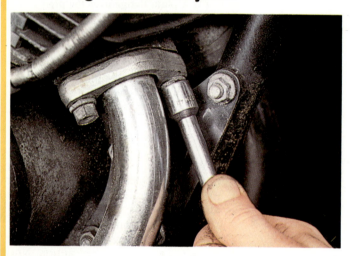

21. To inspect the header clamp joint undo the pipe flange retaining bolts and pull the flange clear

22. Pull the pipe away from the manifold. Inspect the pipe for cracks in the lip and defects in the mating faces

23. If a gasket is recessed into the manifold port, prise it out with a screwdriver and renew it if necessary

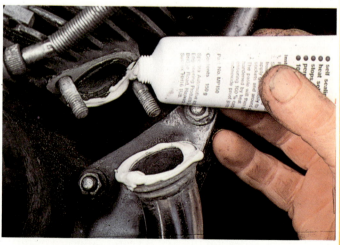

24. Before re-assembling the joint coat the mating faces with a sealing paste to ensure a leak-proof seal

George Wright

Fixing a faulty brake

A bike's front wheel brake should slow the machine down from high or low speed to a quick, smooth stop. If instead the bike judders to a halt, there is likely to be a fault in the brake disc or drum.

Inspecting disc brakes

1. A front disc brake caliper. This one is fixed to a plate which bolts on to the lower fork slider

2. Ensure that the bolts are tight and fitted with a shake-proof washer. A loose caliper could cause judder

3. A badly scored disc. It will have to be re-worked or renewed to maintain full front brake efficiency

4. Use a micrometer at several points on the disc friction area to check for thick and thin conditions

5. A dial gauge with a mounting bar attachment. It is used to test the disc for alignment or run-out

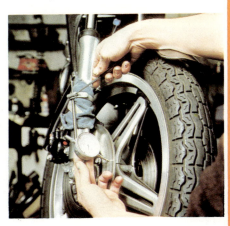

6. Clamp the dial gauge rigidly to the fork leg with a hose clip. Use a rag to protect the leg from scratches

Nelson Hargreaves

Continued

Such trouble usually occurs when vibrations, caused by brake pads or shoes grabbing or biting intermittently on the friction surface, pass through the front braking system and forks. The brake lever may also vibrate or pulse when held on, or the fault may simply cause the braking effect to be intermittent in time with wheel rotation.

A pulsing brake lever may help positively identify the problem as a brake fault. But very similar juddering often occurs at the time of braking when the fork head bearings are worn or out of adjustment.

If you are unsure whether it is the front brake or the forks that are causing the trouble you can make a simple check. Put the bike on its centre stand and support the frame so that the front wheel is off the ground. Facing the bike head-on, grasp the bottom of each fork leg and try to move the whole fork backwards and forwards. If you detect the slightest movement, the fork head bearings are probably at fault and will need to be inspected. This is dealt with fully in another article. If, however, no free play is evident the front disc or drum brake should be checked for faults.

Two main faults cause the distortion or wear of discs or drums which, in turn, causes juddering. Overworn pads or linings usually cause severe scoring or marking of the brake friction surface. And heat stress, to which all brakes are subjected (especially already worn ones), can cause distortion of the disc or drum.

During normal braking about two-thirds of the braking force is taken by the front brake. The heat build-up from the friction usually dissipates quickly through the disc or drum as the designers intended. But if the bike is subjected to prolonged heavy braking abnormally high temperatures will occur. Even under normal road conditions repeated heating and cooling of the brakes may lead to eventual distortion. Distortion may also be caused by accidental damage to a disc, or when a drum-backed wheel has spokes repaired or simply overtightened.

Disc brakes

Disc brakes, more easily cooled than drums, are used for the front braking system on most modern machines. The disc brake (fig. 18) consists of a flat metal disc made usually of stainless steel or cast iron. The disc is bolted to the front wheel and surmounted by a caliper containing the friction pads. The caliper is rigidly mounted on the front fork either in front of or behind the

Symptom	Possible cause	Remedy
Bike judders when the front brake is applied	Front disc/drum worn or distorted	Inspect and replace (pages 190–193)
	Fork head bearings out of adjustment	Adjust or replace bearings
	Wear in fork legs	Repair fork legs

slider. Twin discs are set up in the same way, one on either side of the wheel.

Inspecting the brakes

To inspect a disc brake, the front wheel can be left in place but put the bike on its stand and support it so that the wheel is free to rotate.

A loose caliper could cause a juddering effect, so first check that the caliper mounting on the fork is tight. Two or three bolts may be used to fix the caliper directly to the fork (fig. 1). Alternatively a mounting plate on the caliper body may connect it to the fork. If you have the manufacturer's torque figures, tighten the bolts to the recommended setting. If not, make sure the bolts are properly tight, but do not tighten further without a torque wrench.

Checking for wear

Whether you need to remove the disc for testing will depend on whether you have a dial gauge (see below). But first make a visual check of the friction surface anyway. It should be flat, smooth and free from ridges. Ridging or scoring on the surface may not, by itself, directly cause brake judder. But it will certainly impair the efficiency of the brakes and could lead to juddering.

If the surface is deeply marked or scored (fig. 3), the disc must be replaced or re-surfaced. Disc re-surfacing is a service offered by some specialist engineering firms, who skim a thin layer of metal from the friction surface to bring the disc back to a flat, true condition.

Whether re-surfacing is worthwhile

or not depends largely on the minimum working thickness of the disc. Manufacturers make discs of varying thicknesses and even discs on the particular model and make may vary slightly. So check with one of these specialists, or with a main dealer, whether the job can be done on your bike and what the minimum thickness of your discs should be. The problem is that some manufacturers produce discs thick enough to be re-surfaced without impairing braking. Others advise that a maximum of about 1 mm (0.04in.) of metal, or less, be removed either by wear or skimming. As a significantly worn disc would probably need at least 1 mm of metal removed to achieve an acceptable surface, the disc would be virtually 'worn out' if you had it skimmed.

7. Position the gauge plunger so that it rests on the disc. Then turn the dial until zero is indicated

8. Rotate the wheel slowly. Any run-out will show as a fluctuation of the needle on the gauge

9. To remove a disc caliper, undo the main mounting bolts which hold it to the fork leg

10. Carefully lift the caliper off the disc and tie it out of the way. Try to avoid straining the brake pipe

11. Insert a small wedge of wood in between the brake pads to prevent the pistons accidentally coming out

12. To remove a front wheel held by spindle clamps, undo and remove the lower part of the clamps

Continued

13. With the clamps removed, carefully manoeuvre the wheel out of position between the fork legs

14. Unbolt the disc from the wheel hub. This disc has a dished carrier cast as an integral part of it

15. The disc can now be re-worked or replaced. Replacement is a reversal of the removal procedure

If too much metal has been removed, the disc will be unable to dissipate heat as fast as intended. It could distort under heavy braking. So use a micrometer to measure the thickness of the disc (fig. 4), taking several measurements at various points round the disc in case wear has been uneven. If the disc is found to be less than the manufacturer's specified minimum thickness, it must be replaced.

If the disc is not scored, marked or thinner than recommended, make the same check with the micrometer to test for high and low spots on the disc. A bump or depression of as little as 0.1 mm (0.004in.) could cause judder when the brake is applied. If only very small differences occur, it may be worth having the disc lightly skimmed to correct the high and low spots.

Checking for run-out
If the disc surface is shown to be perfectly smooth and regular after measuring, the next step is to check for run-out. For this you will need to hire or buy a dial gauge (fig. 5).

The disc should rotate in exactly the same plane relative to the disc friction pads and the wheel hub with no side-to-side or twisting movement.

Run-out occurs when the disc, because of accident damage, wear or distortion, runs out of true to its intended plane.

To check for run-out, the dial gauge must be set up accurately and rigidly against the disc face. For the best results fix the dial gauge to a fork leg with a clamp or magnetic attachment (fig. 6). Do not set up the gauge independently of the fork, or the slightest movement of the steering will affect the reading.

Now, move the needle of the gauge carefully into contact with the disc face. Set the gauge to zero and turn the front wheel slowly so that the disc rotates with it (fig. 8). Look for any fluctuations in the needle reading and note the amount. Repeat the operation on the reverse side of the disc. If the total run-out on both sides of the disc exceeds 0.1 mm (0.004in.), then the disc will probably have to be replaced. But, before scrapping it, try removing it, giving it a quarter-turn or half-turn and replacing it. This can sometimes compensate for disc misalignment and bring run-out within acceptable limits.

Replacing a disc
To replace a disc the front wheel must be removed. If the speedometer is driven from the wheel, disconnect the cable by undoing the knurled nut.

Unless twin disc brakes are fitted, you will not have to remove the disc caliper to take out the wheel. But if they are, at least one caliper will have to be removed. Undo the mounting bolts and lift the caliper away (fig. 10). Usually, flexible hydraulic piping is used for the entire brake line and this can be bent quite safely when the caliper is lifted from its mountings. But on some bikes a short length of rigid metal pipe is supported in a bracket; the bracket will have to be removed so that the caliper can be pulled away from the disc. This avoids the need to disconnect the brake line and saves bleeding the system later. While the caliper is removed you should take the opportunity to inspect and, if

Inspecting drum brakes

16. To inspect a drum brake, first undo the threaded lever arm adjuster on the end of the brake cable

17. Pull the cable away and allow the brake lever to spring into a fully off position

Continued

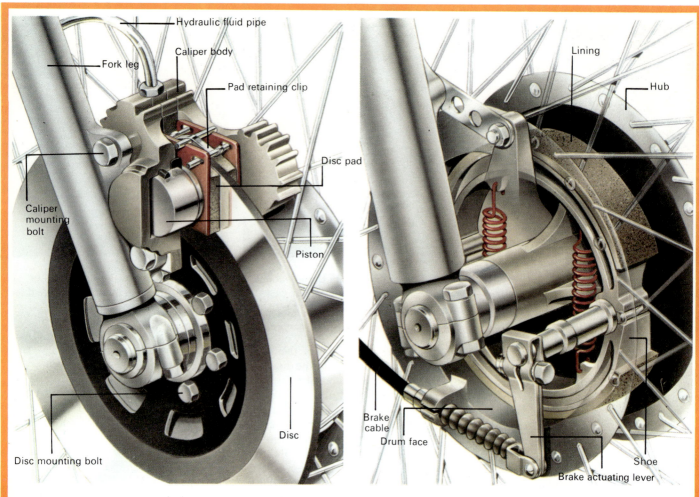

18. A front disc brake. A steel disc bolted to the wheel hub is surmounted by a caliper containing the friction pads

19. A single leading shoe front drum brake. Under braking the linings are forced against the inside of the hub

necessary, replace the brake pads. Full details on this are in an earlier chapter, pages 67 to 72.

Wedge a piece of rag or a chock of wood between the pads in the caliper so that accidental pressure on the brake lever will not cause the pistons to pop out (fig. 11).

Now the wheel can be removed. Undo the castellated nut and withdraw the wheel spindle, or unbolt the spindle clamps. Then carefully manoeuvre the wheel out of the forks (fig. 13).

Brake discs may be bolted directly to the wheel hub or, alternatively, bolted or rivetted to a carrier which in turn bolts to the hub (fig. 14). Tab washers are usually used to secure the bolts, so bend these out of the way before undoing the bolts. The replacement disc is fitted by a reversal of the above procedure.

Drum brakes

A drum brake (fig. 19) is usually cast as an integral part of the wheel hub. A separate plate, housing the brake shoes and linings, locates into the drum from one side of the hub. This type of

brake is almost invariably mechanically operated.

Drum brakes are prone to overheating because of their enclosed position. To gain access to the drum for inspection, the wheel must be removed as described. But any components attached to the brake must be taken off first.

Slacken off the brake adjuster fitted to the handlebar lever and/or the brake plate. Next undo the cable from the shoe actuating lever and remove it completely (fig. 16).

The brake plate is usually secured in position and prevented from rotating with the drum and wheel in one of two ways—by a torque arm, or by an anchor block. A torque arm is a short, sturdy piece of plate which bolts to the fork leg at one end and to the brake plate at the other. The arm must be undone before the wheel can be removed. An anchor block is simply a groove or protrusion on the brake plate which slides into a corresponding part on the lower fork leg (fig. 21).

With the wheel off the machine, lift the brake plate out of the drum complete with the brake shoes and actuating

mechanism (fig. 22). Notice the position of any spacing shims or washers so you can replace them on reassembly. Wipe out any dust with a damp cloth. Avoid inhaling the dust as it contains dangerous asbestos particles.

Checking for wear

Check the condition of the brake linings. If they are worn down or scored, replace them. This is detailed fully on pages 59 to 61 of an earlier chapter.

The most common cause of judder on drum brakes is when the linings grab intermittently on and off the drum. This is usually caused by inadequate or even a complete lack of chamfering on the leading edges of the linings.

On a single or twin leading shoe front brake, both ends of each lining can be chamfered to prevent grabbing. The shoes need not be taken off the brake plate to do this.

Carefully rub down the linings with emery paper or a fine file to a chamfered edge (fig. 24). If the linings are already chamfered, rub them down a little more. Now check the brake drum for wear and distortion.

20. If the speedometer cable is driven from the front hub, remove it by undoing the knurled retaining nut

21. Pull the wheel out of the forks. Notice the slotted anchor block on the brake plate

22. With the wheel on a work surface, carefully lift out the brake plate from the hub

23. The complete braking mechanism is mounted on the brake plate. It need not be dismantled for inspection

24. Use a fine file to cut a chamfer on the lining edges. Protect the brakes with a rag while doing this

25. The finished chamfer should slope at about 45 degrees and will help prevent the brakes from juddering

26. Make a visual inspection of the hub and drum face. If it is badly worn it must be re-worked or replaced

27. Test a drum for ovality by opening calipers across its diameter. Take measurements at several points

28. Any difference in diameter can be measured by slotting a feeler gauge between the calipers and drum face

First look for visible signs of wear such as scoring or a deep wear ridge on the lining contact area. In cases where the drum is badly damaged it can usually be reworked in the same way as a disc (see above).

As a brake drum is an integral part of a spoked wheel, it should not be dismantled from the rim for truing or it may distort once more when rebuilt. A wheel-building specialist should have a large lathe in which the whole wheel can be mounted for this operation.

Bike manufacturers rarely supply ready-built wheels across the counter.

And the cost of a new drum, especially if it is made of magnesium, can be greater than the cost of reworking and rebuilding. So unless you can buy a second-hand, ready-built wheel in good condition it is usually cheaper to have the drum re-worked.

In the absence of any obvious signs of wear, check the drum for ovality, as this can cause juddering. (Make this check also on a second-hand drum in a built wheel before you buy it.)

To do this, you use an internal micrometer or measuring calipers and check the diameter at several points across the drum (fig. 27). If using calipers, differences in diameter will show as a gap between the drum face and the measuring caliper arm. Measure the gap with feeler gauges. A difference of 0.1mm for each 100mm of the drum diameter (one thou. per inch) is an acceptable limit of ovality. Thus a 210 mm (8in.) drum can be up to 0.210mm (0.008in.) out of true before it needs reworking or replacing.

When you have made a full inspection of the brakes and are satisfied that any faults have been rectified, try the bike again. It should now stop smoothly.

Puncture repairs

Few things are more irritating than getting a puncture while riding a bike. Not only do they frequently happen when it is raining, but when they do there is usually nothing else to be done other than start walking. So it is well worth taking all the precautions you can to avoid a puncture in the first place, as well as knowing how to deal with those you do get.

Punctures vary in degree from the slow, where a tyre loses air gradually over several days or weeks, to the blow-out which occurs when riding. All types of puncture, however, can have their frequency of occurence greatly reduced by regular and careful tyre maintenance.

Whilst most bikes on the road today have tubed tyres, an increasing number have tubeless tyres. The basic pro-cedure for maintaining tyres is, how-ever, the same no matter what type of tyre your bike has.

The first and simplest job is to make a weekly check of your tyre pressures to make sure that they are correct. The tyre pressures should be based on the manufacturer's recommendation but taking into account the type of riding, and amount of weight, the bike is subjected to. Obviously a light rider will find the recommended tyre pressures a little hard for general use although they would be ideal for high-speed motorway riding.

Maintaining your tyres at the correct pressures is essential, as not only do incorrectly inflated tyres create handling problems but they also increase the possibility of puncture. Too low a pressure in a tyre results in a greater area of rubber meeting the road than when the tyre is correctly inflated. This increases the chance of the tyre picking up sharp objects and the low pressure will allow them to penetrate the cover easily. Damage to the tyre wall is also likely to occur if a tyre is ridden on while under-inflated. And the battering

Removing the tyre

1. You should make periodic checks of the tread and remove any sharp objects which might work through the cover

2. An old slotted dust cap can be made into a very handy valve key by screwing it on to a suitable bolt

5. To remove a punctured tyre, let out any remaining air and then push the beads into the well of the rim

6. Removing the beads from the rim is a lot easier if you lubricate the beads with soap or liquid detergent

Nelson Hargreaves

the cover receives in addition to the heat generated can ruin a tyre very quickly.

Try to avoid riding up kerbs or over pot-holes whenever possible, as this throws a massive strain on the walls of the tyres and can cause a rupture of the sidewall support cords. Eventually this type of treatment will lead to the complete breakdown of the tyre structure and totally ruin it. If you have any cracks in the tyre wall, however small, you should replace the tyre at once. In fact any type of repair, even a temporary 'get you home' one is illegal in Britain.

Driving over puncture-provoking objects such as glass from a shattered windscreen is sometimes inevitable, however carefully you drive. So periodically you should inspect the tread for tiny fragments of glass or sharp stones as over a period of time these will work their way through the cover. Any

suspicious objects found in the tyre should be prised out with a screwdriver. Take special care to examine the tyres after riding in the rain. Rain water present on the road lubricates sharp objects like nails and allows them to slide into the tyre more easily.

Proprietary puncture 'Sealants'

Apart from the usual routine tyre maintenance, one further step which can be taken to help eliminate the possibility of a puncture is the use of a liquid rubber sealant. This is a fluid which, once injected into the tyre through the valve, remains liquid and helps balance the wheel. If the tyre is subsequently punctured the sealant immediately plugs the hole before any serious loss of pressure can occur.

Even though the seal may seem permanent, a regular check should be made for traces of damage and any suspect puncture repaired or the tube renewed.

Tracing puncture causes

If, after all the precautions described above, you still get a flat tyre then the next step will be to identify the cause. A lot can be guessed about the source of the leak by the way the tyre went flat. If the tyre went down very suddenly then a large and obvious puncture should be suspected. A slow leak may well indicate a faulty valve. The valve should be checked first anyway in your search for the air leak as it is the easiest check to make.

Checking and replacing a valve

Checking and replacing a valve is a simple and straightforward procedure. First, make sure that the valve dust cap is fitted as it not only keeps out dirt and grit from the valve core mechanism but acts as an extra seal if the valve is leaking slightly. Then remove the dust cap from the valve stem and put a droplet of saliva on the end of the stem.

3. If you suspect that the valve is leaking then you will have to remove it for inspection

4. Check the valve core for dirt (which can hold the valve open) and wear—if in doubt simply replace the valve

7. Next insert two tyre levers either side of the valve and gently prise out the top bead of the tyre

8. Then, using a third lever, prise out a little more of the bead and work progressively around the rim

Continued

If air is escaping the saliva will show it by bubbling.

If it does, check the tightness of the valve core. A special key is required for this. This is simply a small slotted bar and is occasionally incorporated into the design of the dust cap. If your dust caps are not of this type, then the key can be bought inexpensively at most accessory shops. Insert the key into the valve stem so that it locates in the core. Then turn the key clockwise to screw the valve up and anti-clockwise to unscrew it.

If the core is to be removed for inspection or replacing, do not forget that you will need an air supply to re-inflate the tyre. The core can be removed without removing the wheel, but make sure that the bike is firmly supported before you let the air out of the tyre. Never let the tyre down when the machine is on the sidestand or not firmly supported.

Unscrew the core and make a quick visual inspection (fig. 4). Look for dirt or grit stuck in the mechanism causing it to stick open. If it appears dirty, wash it in water and, if possible, direct a high-pressure jet of air at it to blow away dirt. Often, however, it is worth replacing the core anyway for it is both easy to obtain and inexpensive.

After replacing a valve, re-inflate the tyre and road test it to check that the fault has been cured. If the tyre still goes flat then a puncture must be suspected and the tyre will have to be removed.

Mending a puncture

Most punctures occur, or are noticed, while the bike is being ridden. This means that you are usually a long way from home when you realize you have a flat. If the puncture is slow, you may be able to 'garage-hop' your way home, re-inflating the tyre a little at each stop. A more severe leak, however, will require another solution. The simplest is the use of a proprietary aerosol which both inflates and seals a punctured tyre. These aerosols are available at most bike accessory shops and can be used in both tubed and tubeless tyres, although if you have a tubeless tyre which has gone completely flat and the beads have moved away from the rim, then the aerosol will prove useless as only a high-pressure air supply will reseat the beads.

All you do is first remove the cause of the puncture and then connect the nozzle of the aerosol to the valve. The tyre should then inflate and the puncture seal.

If the puncture has been caused by a nail, piece of glass, or some similar foreign body which has made a clean hole in the tread, another type of repair may be possible. This is by using a rubber plug. With the cause of the puncture removed the plug can be slid into the hole with a special bodkin. When the tool is withdrawn the plug will be left in the tyre. The 'tail' of the plug can then be snipped off close to the face of the tyre. The puncture should now be satisfactorily sealed and the

9. Once enough of the bead has been levered out of the well you should be able to remove the rest by hand

10. With all of the top bead free, the valve's locknut can be removed allowing the inner-tube to be pulled out

13. You should also check the condition of the rim tape and make sure that none of the spokes are projecting

14. If the puncture is too small to see or feel, simply immerse the tube in water and watch for the bubbles

Nelson Hargreaves

tyre ready for re-inflation. Again a high-pressure air supply is essential to reseat the beads on tubeless tyres.

It must be stressed that these two forms of tyre repair are strictly temporary. Once such a repair has been carried out the bike should be ridden very carefully and not faster than 80 km/H (50mph). Once home you should make a permanent repair at once and not give in to the temptation to leave it a while. Exactly what you can do in the way of making a permanent repair will depend on whether your tyre is tubed or tubeless. It is not possible to repair a puncture in a tubeless tyre without vulcanizing equipment, the cost of which cannot be justified by the odd puncture you may have to repair. So if you have this sort of tyre you should take it to a professional for repair.

A tubed tyre on the other hand can be mended, in much the same way as you would fix a punctured tyre on a push-bike, a standard procedure.

Patching a tubed tyre

Before you can patch a punctured inner-tube the wheel and tyre must first be removed (pages 140–146, 189–193). Tyre removal is often dodged by the DIY mechanic but is basically quite simple as long as you carefully follow the steps given below.

Before starting to remove the tyre, try to find the source of the puncture as this will save a lot of time later.

Once you have done this, deflate the tyre by removing the valve core. Make a mark on the tyre adjacent to the valve so that the tyre can be replaced in exactly the same position and maintain the wheel's balance. Also draw an arrow on the tyre to show its direction of rotation, again to aid correct refitting.

With the tyre completely flat, push the bead of the tyre into the well of the wheel rim (fig. 5). Make sure all the bead is forced into the centre or you will have difficulty levering it out. Once you have done this, free the valve by removing its locking nut. Next, starting close to the

valve, insert a tyre lever (fig. 7) and lever the tyre's bead over the rim. If your bike has alloy wheel rims, do this very carefully as they damage easily. With part of the bead over the wheel rim, levering out the remainder of the top bead should present no problems (fig. 9).

At this stage the inner-tube (fig. 10) can be removed for patching. If you want to remove the tyre as well either for vulcanizing or replacement, the next step is to turn the wheel over. You then have to insert a tyre lever under the bead in the centre well and with the edge of the lever against the lower rim lever the whole tyre away from the wheel.

With the inner-tube out of the tyre, the next job is to locate the leak. If you managed to find the hole in the tread and have marked it, this should not be too difficult. If you could not find the source of the puncture in the tread, you will have to locate it in the tube. A small leak is best found by re-inflating

11. Most modern tyres are so flexible that they can be removed

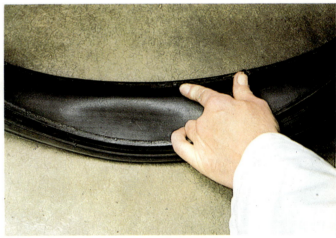

12. To check the cover for sharp projections, hold the tyre upright and push down so that the lower part is flat

15. With the puncture located and marked, make sure that the tube is dry and then rough-up the area to be patched

16. Next apply a coat of rubber solution. When the glue is dry apply another coat and wait for it to become tacky

Continued

the tube and then placing it in a bowl of water (fig. 14). Once the tell-tale air bubbles have located the leak, mark its position and then deflate the tube. The tube should now be dried thoroughly.

With a piece of sandpaper or a rasp, lightly scour the tube around the puncture so that the surface of the tube will accept an adhesive, and cover the area to be patched with rubber solution from a proprietory puncture repair kit (fig. 16). Choose a patch which covers the puncture with room to spare and, when the glue is dry, peel off the protective layer and smooth down the patch. A screwdriver handle is useful to roll the patch and squeeze out any air bubbles which may be trapped between patch and tube.

The adhesive goes off almost immediately and the final check to ensure that the patch is firmly located is to peel off the top protective layer. The patch should remain in position. If it shows any sign of lifting, repeat the rolling process for a minute or two. End by dusting the patch and its surrounding area with french chalk or talcum powder to prevent the tube sticking to the inside of the cover.

Before refitting the repaired inner-tube, check the inside of the tyre cover (fig. 12) for any tiny sharp projections which could puncture the tube again. Make a visual inspection first and then, if you cannot see anything serious, lightly run your fingers round the inside of the cover. Once you are sure that the tyre is free from projections, partially inflate the tube and start pushing it into the tyre. Now place the tyre on top of the wheel so that the valve can be slotted home, taking note that your chalk marks are correctly positioned. With the valve in place, partially lock it by screwing down its securing nut a few turns.

Working on the side of the tyre opposite to the valve, push the lower bead into the wheel. Work progressively round towards the valve. The last part will be the trickiest to seat. The job can be made a lot easier if the beads are kept well lubricated. Soapy water is ideal for this and copious amounts should be on hand.

Once the first bead is seated in the well of the rim, start work on the other, again from the side furthest from the valve. This must be done as carefully as

possible to avoid trapping the inner-tube. When you come to the final piece of bead near the valve, push the valve up into the tyre. This should save the tube from being nipped by the last piece of bead as it goes home.

The last few centimetres of tyre will take the form of a straight line across the arc of the wheel (fig. 20) and it is often thought that this is the most difficult part of the replacement operation. In fact it is not. All that has to be done is to slip two tyre levers under the bead about 50 mm (2in.) each side of the valve and gently force it up and over the rim. The two key factors to remember are to keep the bead well pushed down into the well all the time the cover is being fitted, and to keep the bead well lubricated.

If the fitting process becomes really difficult at any point, never resort to brute force or you will simply end up damaging the wheel. Usually the fault lies in the bead not being pushed far enough down into the well.

Once all the cover is on the wheel, check that the inner-tube is not trapped at any point. Then inflate the tube. Nearly all tyres have a thin line or rib on both walls which can be used to see whether the tyre is evenly seated around the rim. If it is not, rolling or bouncing the wheel should do the trick.

With the tyre correctly seated and inflated to the recommended pressure, the wheel can be put back on the bike and the job is complete.

The final check is to road test the bike. Ride slowly at first just in case the repair does not hold and the worst happens.

If all goes well then the repair can be considered permanent, for a patched tube should, in theory at least, be as strong as an unpatched one. Even so, if a tube has been patched several times then it is perhaps a wise move to replace it with a new one before any long tours are undertaken.

Fitting new covers

If the cover was severely damaged by the puncture or is badly worn, then it should be replaced. When buying and fitting a new cover there are a couple of points worth remembering.

Firstly always fit the correct replacement. Any move away from the recommended tyre size or rating could have a disastrous effect on the bike.

Secondly, when a new tyre is bought it is often still partially covered with a waxy release agent used by the manufacturer to free the tyre from its mold. Therefore it is a wise precaution to ride cautiously for the first few kilometers and take bends particularly slowly.

17. When the solvent has evaporated, peel the protective cover from a patch and stick it down

18. Smooth the patch down to remove any trapped air and then remove the patch's top protective layer

19. With the tube inside the cover, fit the valve into the rim and push as much cover onto the rim as you can

20. To seat the last piece of cover use two levers to force it over the rim while securing the rest with a knee

Nelson Hargreaves

How to fix fuel line faults

A bike engine that coughs, splutters, lacks power and finally stops is probably suffering from fuel starvation due to a fault in the fuel line or carburettor.

Beginning at the filler cap, the fuel line includes the petrol tank, the tank or tap filter, lengths of connecting fuel pipe and the carburettor.

When dealing with a fuel-line fault it is best to work methodically through the system from tank to carburettor. This means that you first reach the faults that are more common and easier to rectify.

Throughout all checks and work on fuel system, keep lighted cigarettes or naked flames well away from the area. Petrol is highly inflammable.

Blocked tank breather

The first check – so obvious it is often overlooked – is to see that there is fuel in the tank. The next is to see that it can get out.

As fuel is used up, the space left behind in the tank has to be filled, otherwise a vacuum forms. If air cannot enter, gravity cannot draw the petrol from the tank. The result: fuel starvation at the carburettor.

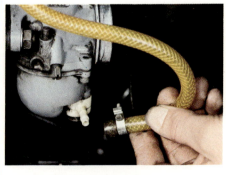

1. Two types of fuel tank filler cap with different air breather systems. Make sure that the holes are clear

2. To remove the carburettor fuel line, unscrew the hose clamp and pull the pipe away from its union

George Wright

On nearly all bikes this problem is overcome by the fitting of a breather in the tank filler cap (fig. 1). The breather is a fine capillary passage which acts as a simple valve running through the filler cap. Air can enter the tank through the breather hole, but petrol cannot escape through it in significant quantities.

Tiny particles of dirt or grit in the breather are enough to stop petrol from leaving the tank. So poke out any dirt with a piece of fine wire then blow through it to make sure it is clear. Finally, flush it out with clean petrol.

If the breather is clear, check that petrol is reaching the carburettor. The first step is to check the feed pipe running from the tank to the carburettor. Most feed pipes are made of a transparent synthetic material, but if the feed pipe is coloured or opaque you will have to disconnect it from the carburettor to see if fuel is being passed through.

First, make sure that the petrol tap is switched off. The pipe is usually fixed to the carburettor by a tight push fit over a stub tube and secured with a small hose clip. Unscrew the clip and ease the pipe off the stub with a screwdriver (fig. 2). Hold a rag over the end of the pipe to catch any fuel that may escape, then switch on the tank tap. If petrol pours out, the tank and fuel pipe are obviously clear and the fault probably lies with a blocked carburettor. If no fuel comes out, the fault is most likely to be a blocked tank filter or fuel pipe.

Blocked tank filter

The tank filter is the main filter device in the fuel line of almost all modern machines. Its function is to trap dirt or rust which finds its way into the fuel tank and to prevent it from entering and damaging the carburettor.

A high concentration of dirt on the tank filter screen will prevent fuel from passing through. The filter must therefore be removed and cleaned.

There are two types of tank filter, the bowl and tube types. Both filter units are integral with the fuel supply tap on the base of the tank.

If twin fuel taps are used, one on either side of the tank, be sure to check both. There may be a filter on each of them and either could be blocked.

The bowl filter with which most modern machines are fitted (fig. 3) is usually screwed to the lower part of the tap and contains a wire or nylon gauze screen. To remove and clean the filter you will not normally have to drain the fuel tank. The tap usually interrupts the fuel supply before the filter bowl so, as long as the tap is switched off, no fuel can escape.

Disconnect the fuel pipe from the tap, then unscrew the bowl. Some types have a hexagon bolt head on the base of the bowl (fig. 5); others are unscrewed by hand. As the bowl comes away, look for a fibre gasket or rubber sealing ring and renew this on reassembly.

The filter screen is usually a flat, circular or crescent shaped piece of gauze which locates either in the bowl itself or on the lower part of the tap. Some filters of the latter type are retained in position by a single screw; others are push fit. Remove the filter and brush it clean with fresh petrol. Wipe round the bowl and tap with a rag to clear out any sediment.

If a filter screen is not found when the bowl is removed, the bowl itself is a sediment trap. The filter will most

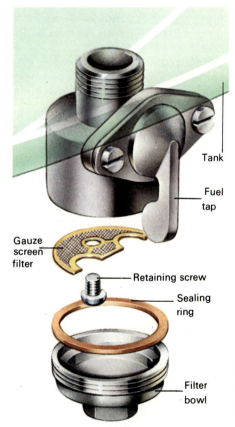

Tank

Fuel tap

Gauze screen filter

Retaining screw

Sealing ring

Filter bowl

Advertising Arts

3. A tank tap with an integral bowl filter. The crescent-shaped filter is held in place with a screw

Symptom	Possible cause	Remedy
Engine splutters, lacks power and fades	Tank breather blocked	Clear breather (page 199)
	Tank filter blocked	Clean filter (pages 199–202)
	Fuel pipe blocked	Clear pipe (page 200)
	Carburettor blocked or water in carburettor	Clean carburettor filter, needle valve and jets (pages 200–202)

likely be of the gauze tube type (fig. 4) which projects into the tank from the tap. In this case the tap must be removed from the tank in order to clean the filter.

To clean a tube filter the tank must be drained of fuel. This can be done with the tank in place but is often easier if the tank is removed.

Fuel taps are attached to fuel tanks in two ways, by screws or by a threaded union. The most common method employs a flange on the tap, secured by two screws to the base of the tank. Where a sediment bowl is used in conjunction with a tube filter, access to the screws can be gained by first removing the bowl.

Taps with a threaded union use a hexagon union nut above the tap. Undo this to free the tap (fig. 8).

Carefully withdraw the tap from the tank, taking care not to damage the wire or nylon filter on the sides of the hole. Use clean petrol to wash dirt from the filter and renew the sealing ring or washer if it shows sings of perishing. Reassemble the parts and check the fuel flow again.

Blocked fuel pipe

It is unusual for the fuel pipe to become blocked, but check it if the fuel supply is still restricted. You can see through the clear plastic type of pipe, but coloured or rubber types must be removed completely. Flush petrol down the pipe and blow through it to make sure it is clear.

After prolonged service, petrol pipes lose their flexibility and become hard and brittle. So take this opportunity to replace the pipe if it shows signs of cracking or hardness.

The final checks for a fault in the fuel line are made at the carburettor.

Blocked carburettor

There are three main areas in the carburettor which may be affected or blocked by dirt carried in with the fuel. These are the float needle valve and seat; the jets; and the fuel inlet filter.

Nearly all motorcycle carburettors are of the variable-jet (variable-choke)

type in which a sliding needle controls the main jet opening. Variable-jet carburettors such as those made by Mikuni, Kei-hin, Amal, Dell'Orto and Bing comprise two main parts, the upper mixing chamber and the lower float bowl. Most modern types are based on a concentric design so that the main internal components all surround the central main jet inside the float chamber. Close design similarities between the major makes of carburettor mean that the general checking and dismantling procedures are virtually the same on every type.

On all carburettors of this type you may have to remove the carburettor from the engine, though only the float bowl assembly needs to be dismantled to deal with possible blockages. But where an external carburettor fuel filter is fitted, remove and inspect this first.

Filters are fitted to few modern carburettors though some Amal, Dell'Orto and Kei-hin types are exceptions. Most of these filters are of the banjo union type (fig. 10) and are located where the fuel pipe union joins the carburettor. This may be on the side of the mixing chamber or on the bottom of the float bowl. To remove the filter, disconnect the fuel pipe and undo the single central bolt holding the filter cover (fig. 12). The nylon or wire gauze filter screen

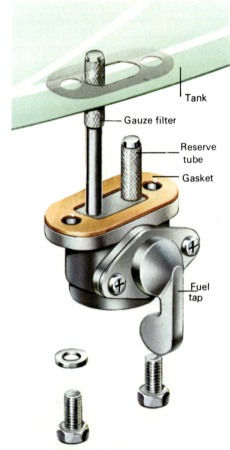

4. A fuel tank tap with two gauze tube filters. One is the main filter; the other covers the reserve fuel feed

Inspecting a bowl filter

5. To inspect a bowl filter, unscrew the lower part of the tap so that the filter bowl comes away

6. Carefully clean out any sediment in the bowl with a rag. Then remove the filter and wash it in petrol

7. To remove and inspect a gauze tube filter, first undo the petrol feed pipe from the tank tap union

8. Use a spanner on the upper hexagon nut to unscrew the tap and filter unit from the base of the tank

9. Carefully withdraw the tap from the tank. Use clean petrol to wash off any dirt from the filter tube

should pull away with the cover. Wash the filter clean with petrol and wipe out any dirt from the cover.

Some Kei-hin carburettors, as fitted to small capacity machines, have a similar filter to that described above but it is found inside the float bowl and can be inspected only after the float bowl is removed.

Taking the float bowl off a carburettor usually involves removing the carburettor from the engine. This is a simple operation on single and twin-cylinder engines. On multi-cylinder machines, where the carburettors are all mechanically linked together, the

procedure is a little more difficult. But such carburettors are often fitted to a common inlet manifold. You just remove the manifold and its clutch of carburettors; there is no need to separate each carburettor from the manifold.

The float chamber cover is held to the main body of the carburettor in one of three ways, by a single central bolt, four small screws or a spring clip. Invert the carburettor and remove the cover. As it comes away, notice the position of the gasket and replace it on reassembly if it is damaged (fig. 16).

The float is hinged by a single through pin to a point on the side of the chamber. To check that it is operating freely, turn the carburettor the right way up and push the float up lightly with your finger. It should drop down smoothly when it is released. At the same time, notice if the float needle which is operated by the float drops downwards too. If either the needle or the float sticks, fuel will be prevented from entering the chamber and so cause fuel starvation. Dirt or grit in the needle valve could also cause fuel supply problems.

To remove the float, pull out the hinge pin with your fingers (fig. 17) or press it out with the tip of a screwdriver. It is unlikely that the float itself is damaged but it can be checked for punctures by immersing it in petrol. If the float shows signs of leaking it must be replaced.

Next, pull out the float needle from its valve seat (fig. 18) and check the point for wear or pitting. Most needles are hardened metal and wear only slowly but some are made of plastic or nylon which wears rapidly. The latter are particularly prone to lipping where they locate on the valve seat. And this can cause the needle to stick. If the needle point is anything but perfectly smooth, replace it.

Some needles are retained in place by the valve seat unit and cannot be taken out until the valve is removed.

Valves may be screwed directly into the carburettor or held by a small clip (fig. 18). Remove the valve and inspect the fuel inlet orifice (fig. 19). Blow

10. A typical carburettor filter. This one from an Amal is of the banjo-union type

- Float bowl
- Filter
- Filter cover
- Cover retaining bolt

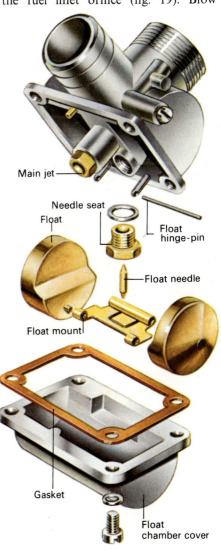

11. The main float chamber components of a concentric design carburettor found on most modern machines

- Main jet
- Needle seat
- Float
- Float hinge-pin
- Float needle
- Float mount
- Gasket
- Float chamber cover

Inspecting a carburettor filter

12. Remove a carburettor filter by undoing the single central bolt that holds the cover in place

13. Pull the cover, with the filter, away from the carburettor. Take note of any gasket or seal

14. Separate the nylon filter from the cover and clean it. Make sure that all fuel feed holes are clear

through the valve to clear any possible obstruction, then flush it out with petrol.

The final carburettor check involves removing the jets to make sure that they are clear. There are usually three: the main, the needle and the pilot jets.

The main jet on nearly all carburettors is a slotted or hexagonal-headed brass screw located in the middle of the float chamber. Unscrew the jet (fig. 20) and examine it.

The jet orifice is tiny and the slightest speck of dirt could block it. Blow through the jet, preferably with a high pressure air line, to clear it. On no account poke wire or anything else into the jet. The orifice size and profile are critical and any change will ruin it.

The needle jet is usually situated under or adjacent to the main jet, and may be a push or screw fit into the body of the carburettor. Most are removed from below just as the main jet,

but others must be pushed upwards through the mixing chamber. In the latter case, the needle slide must be unscrewed from the top of the carburettor to allow the jet to come out.

The pilot jet is recognizable as a small brass-headed screw found close to the main jet.

Remove and clean both jets as described above.

Finally, reassemble the components and try the machine again.

Cleaning float chamber components

15. The float chamber cover on most concentric carburettors is removed by undoing four small screws

16. Pull the float chamber cover away from the upper carburettor body. Renew the gasket on reassembly

17. Remove the float by withdrawing its hinge-pin from the mounting posts on the side of the chamber

18. Invert the carburettor so that the float needle drops out of its seat. Notice the seat retaining clip

19. Unscrew the needle seat retaining clip and pull out the seat. Blow through the seat to clear it

20. Unscrew the main jet from its seat and clean it, but do not poke wire or anything else into the jet hole

George Wright

202

When the engine won't start

If your bike won't start there is no point in punching the tank; better to look inside and see if there is any fuel. Then check the systems in a methodical way.

Four conditions are necessary for your engine to run properly: the engine must be in good mechanical condition, fuel must reach the combustion chamber, air must mix with fuel in the correct ratio and a spark must arrive at the spark plug on time. If the bike develops a fault which fails to satisfy any one of these conditions, then the engine will probably fail to start.

If you have no reason to suspect a fault in one particular area, locating the cause of the problem can pose a formidable task. Hours can be wasted if fault finding is approached in a haphazard fashion.

An important factor in the whole investigation process is the circum-stances of the machine's failure to start. If, for example, you have just adjusted the carburettor and the bike won't start, it is quite likely that the fault lies in the carburettor. Similarly, if you have fitted new points to the machine and it won't start, your investigation should begin with the points and ignition timing.

Knowing your machine is crucial to the fault finding process. If, for example, only one cylinder runs on a Honda CD175, the fault cannot be with the carburettor because, on this bike, a single carburettor feeds both cylinders. Similarly one faulty cylinder on an in-

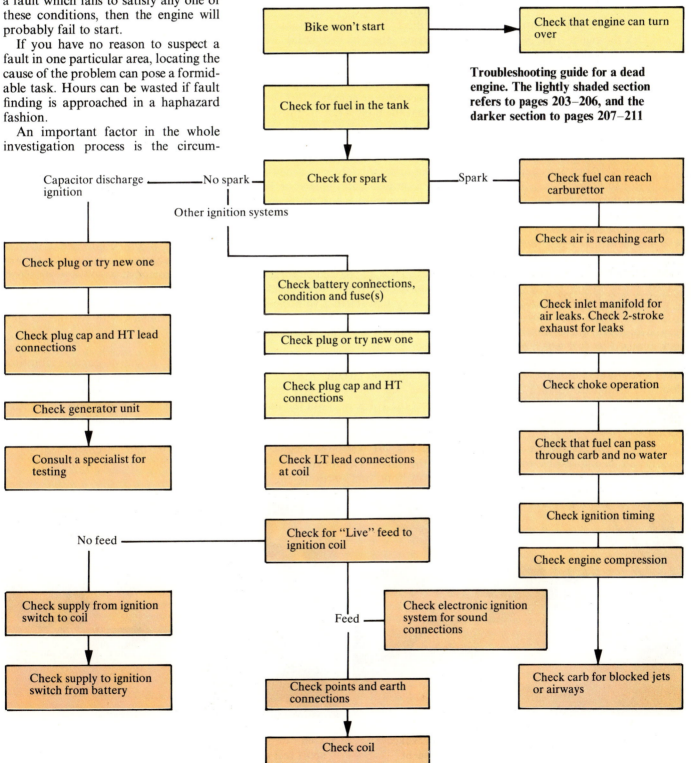

Troubleshooting guide for a dead engine. The lightly shaded section refers to pages 203–206, and the darker section to pages 207–211

Bike won't start → Check that engine can turn over

Check for fuel in the tank

Capacitor discharge ignition ← No spark ← Check for spark → Spark → Check fuel can reach carburettor

Other ignition systems

Check plug or try new one

Check plug cap and HT lead connections

Check generator unit

Consult a specialist for testing

Check battery connections, condition and fuse(s)

Check plug or try new one

Check plug cap and HT connections

Check LT lead connections at coil

Check for "Live" feed to ignition coil

Feed → Check electronic ignition system for sound connections

No feed ←

Check supply from ignition switch to coil

Check supply to ignition switch from battery

Check points and earth connections

Check coil

Check air is reaching carb

Check inlet manifold for air leaks. Check 2-stroke exhaust for leaks

Check choke operation

Check that fuel can pass through carb and no water

Check ignition timing

Check engine compression

Check carb for blocked jets or airways

Bernard Fallon

1. Hold the spark plug against the head and kick the engine over. No spark indicates an ignition fault

line Honda 4 cannot be due to faulty points because each set operates two cylinders. So, with a knowledge of the bike, allied to a systematic checklist covering the bike's mechanical state, ignition system, fuel line and carburation (see troubleshooting chart on page 203), you can concentrate your efforts on locating the fault quickly.

Engine won't turn over

A machine which feels 'locked solid' when the kickstart or starter button is pressed may have either broken or misplaced parts inside the engine or a crankcase flooded with petrol.

Do not force the starter if any resistance is felt, there may be a 'fluid lock', caused by fuel which has leaked from the tank into the crankcase. It takes a substantial amount of petrol to flood the crankcase to such an extent, and the fault will only really occur if the bike has been left standing over a long period.

Petrol in the crankcase naturally presents an incompressible force to the descending piston, and is strong enough

to bend a con-rod.

Check for a flooded crankcase by removing the drain plug (if fitted) (fig. 2). Allow the crankcase to drain – the presence of petrol in the oil will be self-evident. Then investigate the fuel supply system (see pages 199 to 202), paying particular attention to the fuel tank tap, the float needle valve and float assembly in the carburettor(s). Flush the engine out with flushing oil and refill with fresh lubricant.

On 2-stroke machines, such as the Yamaha RD400, which has no crankcase drain plug, remove the spark plug(s) and operate the starter to empty the crankcase.

If there is no fuel present in the crankcase the 'locked solid' feeling must be due to broken or misplaced parts inside the engine' First try turning the engine over by pushing the bike with second gear engaged, just to make sure that the fault is not confined to the kick start or electric starter mechanism. If the engine is definitely 'locked' (possible faults are broken rings in the port, broken or seized valves, jammed pushrods, jammed cam chain or seized piston(s)) it will have to be dismantled step by step until the fault is found.

If the engine turns over but fails to start, see if there is any fuel in the petrol tank (fig. 3). Few bikes sport fuel gauges so it is all too easy to forget that you have no fuel. Now check the ignition system starting with the spark plug. When you are trying to identify a fault, always work in an orderly way as described here.

Faulty ignition circuit

Remove the spark plug(s) and re-connect the HT lead. With the ignition switched on, and the plug electrode earthed against the cylinder head or barrel (fig. 4), turn the engine over with the starter. Do not spin the engine over without first earthing the plug,

because the spark may break down the internal insulation in the coil. Hold the plug cap with a pair of insulated pliers rather than your hand, between 10,000 and 20,000 volts are developed across the gap, enough to give you a nasty jolt. If the plug is in good condition, you should see a bright blue spark jump between the centre electrode and the ground electrode, and hear a loud crack as the plug fires. If all seems well with the spark plug then the ignition circuit must be working and the fault must lie in the fuel line, compression system or the ignition timing. These faults are dealt with in the dark brown boxes on page 203. Before leaving the spark plug, check that water has not collected in the spark plug well. This can cause current passing into the plug to discharge through the water around its metal base rather than at the electrodes inside the combustion chamber. If, however, there is no spark or it is very weak, you should check the ignition system in the following sequence. Bikes with capacitor discharge ignition require a slightly different procedure. This is dealt with on page 209.

No spark at the plug

Begin by checking that the battery leads are firmly connected to their respective battery poles. If the leads are tight but corroded on to the posts, clean them off. Remove any white 'furry' deposits with a wire brush and coat the battery terminals with petroleum jelly (Vaseline).

Next, check the main fuse. A short circuit or excessive engine vibration will cause the fuse to break. Replace the fuse with one of identical wattage. Switch on the ignition and if the fuse blows again there must be a short circuit. Trace the short by checking the wiring loom and its component parts for continuity using a circuit tester (see page 170).

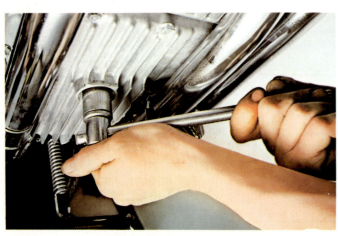

2. Remove the drain plug to check for a flooded crankcase. The presence of petrol in the oil will be self-evident

Rupert Watts

3. Don't forget to check the fuel tank for petrol. Few bikes sport fuel gauges and it is easy to run out

4. If the spark plug has a metal cap hold it to the cylinder head with a pair of insulated pliers

5. First check the battery by a visual inspection. A good battery will show a clear electrolyte and plates

6. A poor battery will have white deposits on the plates and a sediment in the bottom of the electrolyte

7. Check the battery condition with a hydrometer. Squeeze the bulb to fill the tube. The float indicates condition

7a. The components of an ignition circuit. In this case the energy transfer type

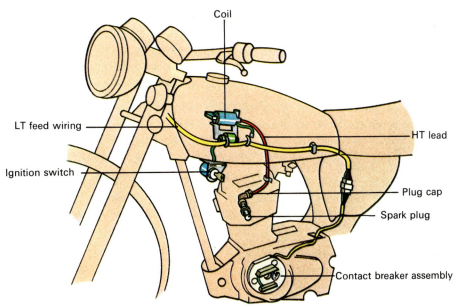

about 1.280. If neither tool is available connect a headlight bulb directly between the terminals (fig. 8). If it lights up brightly the battery should be good enough to start the bike.

Faulty spark plug

Unscrew the spark plug and examine the electrodes. A light brown coloured insulator shows that the motor is healthy and the plug is the correct grade. But thick deposits on the electrodes could lead to a weak spark. White deposits or a rounded earth electrode indicate a hot running engine – a sure sign of a weak mixture. Black deposits or 'oiled up' electrodes show that the engine is running too cold – a sign of a rich fuel mixture. As with all rules of thumb this guide is not totally comprehensive. Modern engines run very weak, with high combustion temperatures, so white plugs are inescapable, especially on a hard ridden bike.

If the fuse is intact, examine the state of the battery. First check it visually. A healthy battery will display a clear electrolyte and clean plates (fig. 5). A poor one will have white deposits on the plates and excessive sediment in the bottom of the electrolyte (fig. 6). If the battery appears good check it either with a battery condition meter or a hydrometer (fig. 7). The meter must naturally indicate a good condition, the hydrometer a specific gravity reading of

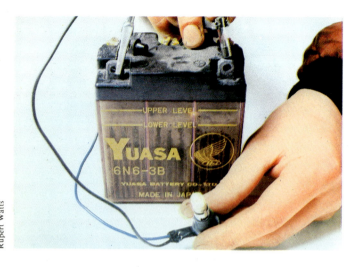

8. Connect a bulb directly between the battery terminals. If it lights up brightly the battery can start the bike

9. Check the spark plug gap with a feeler gauge and if necessary adjust with a gapping tool

10. Hold the HT lead against the cylinder head with a pair of insulated pliers and kick the engine over

11. Check the continuity of the HT lead either with an ohmmeter (as shown) or a simple continuity tester

Conversely engines always run rich at low revs to provide instant 'pick-up'. A rider who 'potters' around, therefore, will find black deposits on the plug with nothing being amiss.

Next, check the plug gap with a feeler gauge, and if necessary adjust the gap by bending the ground electrode with a spark plug gapping tool. Clean the plug or replace it and test again for a spark. If a spark is still not evident, examine the plug cap and HT lead connections.

Broken plug cap or HT lead

A damaged spark plug cap will usually only cause trouble in the wet. In damp conditions a damaged plug cap can cause the current from the HT lead to discharge before reaching the plug electrode. Although a combination of dirt, water and oil is only slightly conductive, a high voltage always takes the shortest route to earth; and if that route does not include the spark plug there will be no spark to ignite the fuel mixture.

Metal plug caps are most likely to cause trouble in the wet, and the best

remedy is to change the metal cap for one of the plastic encased types. Plastic caps rarely cause problems but they may develop a fine hairline crack through which water may seep.

HT leads, like the plug caps, require good insulation to prevent water acting as a leak conductor. The water attracts the current from the lead to earth before it reaches the spark plug. Check that the HT lead is firmly connected to the plug cap and to the coil. An excessively stretched or bent HT lead can result in the breakage of the internal core. Unfortunately, the more common self-suppressing leads have a carbon core which is rather less flexible than the traditional wire-cored leads.

To check an HT lead, remove it from the plug cap and hold the bare wire next to the cylinder head (fig. 10). Turn the engine over and check for sparking. As before, hold the lead with insulated pliers rather than your hand. If a spark appears between the end of the HT lead and the cylinder head, the plug cap is probably broken and must be replaced. If there is no spark then suspect the HT

lead. Remove the HT lead from the coil (if possible) and check its continuity either with a purpose-built circuit tester, or one made up from a bulb, bulb-holder, battery and length of wire. If there is no continuity replace the HT leads. On many Japanese machines, however, it is not possible to separate the HT lead from the coil. Refer to page 159 for the method of testing this type of HT lead. If the lead is found to be faulty, cut off the broken section and fit a length of new lead by joining the pieces with an in-line suppressor. If the bike still fails to start the next item for investigation is the low tension side of the coil.

In the remainder of the chapter from page 207, fault-finding continues with a check of the low tension ignition circuit from the coil through the points to earth if there is a 'live' feed to the coil, or a check from the coil back to the battery if there is no feed. There is also the sequence of checks necessary for bikes with flywheel ignition and CDI ignition systems and the correct sequence for fuel and compression systems.

LT ignition checks

12. Check LT wiring for 'live' feed. Connect one terminal to the ignition supply wire and the other to earth

13. Check for 'live' feed to the coil. Connect one terminal to the supply tag and one to earth

14. Check for continuity through the points. Connect one terminal to the 'feed' side and one to earth

Checking the LT side of the ignition circuit involves testing for electrical continuity from the battery through the ignition switch to the coil and finally the contact breaker points. At this stage, differences will become apparent between those bikes with conventional electro-mechanical ignition and those with electronic ignition systems.

There are three types of electronic ignition system and each has its distinguishing features. All systems feature a 'black box' amplifier which is fitted between the coil and the trigger device.

Transistor-assisted systems, such as the inductive discharge unit made by Boyer-Bransden, retain the points but feature an amplifier to boost the spark.

'Point-less' systems, such as the magnetically triggered system made by Lucas and Boyer Bransden, and the optically triggered systems made by Lumenition, Piranha and Martek, retain the coils but dispense with the conventional contact breakers.

Capacitor discharge ignition systems (CDI) are fitted as standard to many modern machines such as the Kawasaki KH(S) models and Ducatis; this system is similar to both on types fed with higher voltage by special windings in the generator.

Continuity checking procedure is identical for transistor-assisted and point-less systems as well as conventional coil and contact breaker systems. But CDI types demand a different procedure and this is dealt with on page 51.

Given that there is continuity on the HT side of the coil and that the spark plug cap and lead are working, you should test the LT circuit by checking for an unbroken live feed from the battery to the ignition coil. The feed from the battery to the coil is interrupted by the ignition switch. Start by checking the colour coding of the wires between components, from your circuit diagram.

Coils are always connected with the same polarity as the bike's battery; if the battery is 'positive ground' (positive terminal connected to the frame) the coil's positive (+) terminal is the one connected to the contact breaker. On some coils the terminals are labelled SW (to switch) and CB (to contact breaker). Get out the circuit tester and test for continuity between the ignition coil feed wire and earth (fig. 13). If there is no continuity check the supply from the ignition switch to the coil.

If a kill-button is fitted test the wires between the ignition switch and kill-switch and the coil. Replace any wire which is broken or 'shorting' out. If there is no continuity through either the ignition switch or the engine kill-switch, water or dirt may be causing a 'short'. Squirt some moisture dispersant fluid such as WD 40 into the switches and try the connections.

Replace the ignition switch if there is still no continuity – most cannot be serviced. Rather than dismantle the ignition kill-switch, remove it from the handlebar, fill it with sand and operate it several times, then clean it out with white spirit. If there is still no continuity replace the switch, or wire it out of the circuit by joining the wires together.

If the bike still won't start, check next the supply to the ignition switch from the battery. Trace and replace a faulty section of wire or bad connector where you find the continuity interrupted.

If there is continuous feed to the ignition coil(s) next check for the continuity through and out of the coil to the contact breaker and ground. Look for the ground terminal on the coil or the one marked CB. Using a tester, check for continuity of the wire connected to that terminal. Replace the wire if it is broken or 'shorting'. Next, expose the contact breaker points (see page 41) and close them by turning the engine over. Test for continuity between the contact breaker feed wire and the static point (fig. 14). Clean the points by rubbing them carefully with a fine emery board. If they appear pitted or burnt, replace them. Badly pitted or burnt contact points indicate that a capacitor has broken down. Test for a suspect capacitor by substituting it for a known good one. A dud capacitor alone, however, will not stop the bike from starting. If the bike still won't start check all the earth connections of

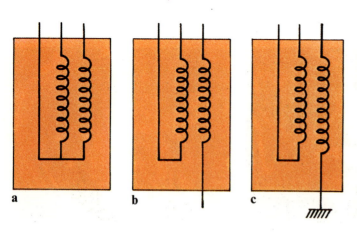

15. Three different types of internal coil windings. Your bike's circuit diagram will indicate which type you have

16. Pull the fuel supply pipe off the carburettor and turn on the tap to see if fuel is reaching the carb

the ignition circuit. These being the static contact point, the coil(s) and the spark plug.

Faulty low tension circuit

You will already have checked the spark plug earth at the beginning of the procedure so concentrate on making sure that water or dirt are not stopping the LT current from reaching earth after being fed to the coil(s) or contact breaker. Remove all traces of grease with a wire brush and wipe the connections with a dry cloth. If the bike still won't start examine the coil(s).

Faulty earth

Coils are usually located on the frame spine and access to them may require the removal of the petrol tank. Faulty coils must be renewed as they are of sealed construction and not serviceable. It will already have been established that current can reach and leave the coils by the tests described above, so it remains to check the coils for continuity through the windings inside.

There are three different types of internal coil winding arrangements. However, as all three types are externally identical, with two LT terminal connections and one HT connection, you will have to refer to a circuit diagram for your bike to find which type is fitted. Low tension terminals are connected to the normal 12V type wire whilst the high tension terminals are connected to much thicker HT lead.

In the first type (fig. 15a), check for continuity between any two terminals, then use a multimeter to test resistance between the LT and HT terminals. The meter should show a moderate (midway) reading on the ohm scale. Make sure that there is an infinite resistance (an open circuit) between each terminal and the coil casing. If the multimeter registers any resistance, replace the coil.

In the second type of coil (fig. 15b), check for continuity between the two LT terminals and then between the two HT terminals, an open circuit between all the terminals and the coil casing, and then between the HT and LT terminals.

In the third type of coil arrangement (fig. 15c), check for continuity between the two LT terminals, an open circuit between the LT terminals and the HT terminal, continuity between the HT terminal and the coil casing, and for an open circuit between the LT terminals and the casing.

If after completing the check sequence on the ignition system the bike still won't start there must be a fault in the fuel system. This is dealt with on pages 210 to 211. A systematic check will find the fault.

Checking flywheel ignition system

Flywheel ignition systems are fitted as standard to many bikes, such as the Honda step-through range, all single cylinder Hondas and the Yamaha XT500. Two types are used: one with the ignition coil within the flywheel, called a flywheel magneto; and one with a separate ignition coil, usually under the tank, called the energy transfer system.

Look at the HT lead to see which type your bike has. If it comes from behind

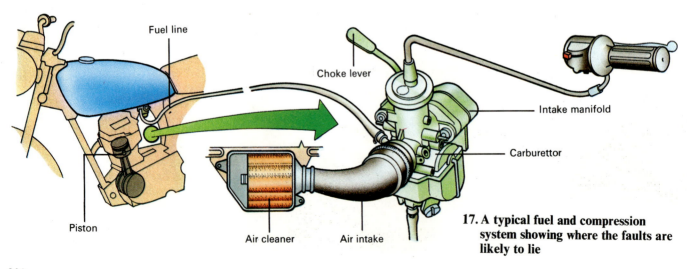

17. A typical fuel and compression system showing where the faults are likely to lie

the cylindrical cover on one side of the engine, it is a flywheel magneto system (found usually on lightweights and singles). If it comes from a mechanical device which is part of the engine or from within the engine castings, it is a magneto (found usually on older machines). Because both types of flywheel ignition do not require a battery to produce a spark the ignition checks are simplified.

The ignition switch and kill switch on this sytem simply earths out the 'live' supply. Disconnect them to check if they are malfunctioning. Disconnect any coil fitted under the tank, wedge a piece of paper in the points gap and test for continuity between the points. Remove the paper, disconnect the capacitor and test again for a spark. If a spark is produced, the capacitor is shorted internally and must be renewed. If there is no spark then either the coil is shorted out or the HT windings are faulty.

Another possible fault could be that the rotor had become demagnetized. To check this, turn the lights on and kick the engine over with the spark plug removed. If the headlight glows brightly the rotor is properly magnetized. If the headlight does not glow the rotor is demagnetized and must be replaced. If all seems well then the timing must be incorrect. To check and adjust the timing see pages 40 to 41 and 49 to 52.

Checking CD ignition system
Capacitor discharge ignition systems are fitted as standard to many modern bikes, such as the Kawasaki KH(S) series, the Suzuki GT250X7 and Honda's CX500. Exercise extreme caution when examining this ignition system because it is self-generating and the 'black box' amplifier/transducer unit

can hold a charge of up to 400V. Because of the complexity of the testing procedure and the inherent dangers of inexpert tampering you should not attempt any more than a visual check of the device, leave it to a qualified mechanic.

Begin by checking the spark plug(s) as described in the earlier checks for conventional ignition systems. Make exactly the same check as previously described for the spark plug cap and HT lead connections.

Next remove the cover of the generator unit and check the soundness of the visible connections and the security of the components. If the visual check reveals nothing amiss you must take the bike to a dealer.

Before checking the fuel system, examine the spark plug for clues as to where the fault lies. If the engine is being started from cold it needs a rich fuel/air mixture to promote combustion and the chances are that it is not getting one. Remove the plugs and look at the electrodes. If the electrodes are dry, there may be a fuel system fault such as a sticking or blocked starter jet, a fuel blockage, or too low a fuel level in the float bowl. If the electrodes are very wet, or if neat fuel comes out of the exhaust, the carburettor could be flooding due to too high a float bowl fuel level, a loose jet or some other fault (ignition timing, compression system or fuel system) which is preventing the engine from igniting the fuel. A sooty black plug indicates a rich mixture or too much slow running and may be shorting under compression. An oily plug will display the same conductivity effect and points to broken or worn piston rings, worn valve guides, too much oil in the fuel or wrong 2-stroke

oil pump settings. A sooty or oily plug can also mean too cold a plug. If the spark plug offers no clues follow the checking sequence as shown in the sequence below.

Blocked fuel line
First make sure that fuel is reaching the carburettor. Begin by removing the carburettor fuel line (fig. 16). On most Japanese bikes the fuel pipe can be pulled from the carburettor by removing the spring clamp from the pipe coupling with a pair of pliers. On bikes with a reinforced plastic pipe the connection may be parted by loosening a screwed pipe clamp. If, when the fuel tap is switched on, no fuel comes out or it merely trickles out, there must be a blockage in the tank filter, the fuel pipe itself or in the tank breather. Try the reserve position; this may be clear and allow you to start the engine to confirm there is no other fault. Fuel line faults and their remedies are dealt with on pages 199 to 202. If the fuel line is clear, check for air starvation next.

Air starvation
Without air the carburettor cannot produce a combustible mixture for the engine. Check that the air inlet is clear. On many bikes the tool tray lies directly behind the air inlet filter and it is all too easy for a rag, or something similar, to foul the inlet filter completely. Check the air inlet tube by carefully pushing a thick piece of wire, such as a suitably straightened coat hanger along it towards the carburettor. Before doing this, however, wrap the end of the wire with a piece of inner tube, or similar rubber to protect the carburettor slide and body from scratches.

If petrol and air are reaching the

18. It is easy for a rag carried in the tool tray to find its way into the air intake and completely choke the motor

19. Check the operation of the starter unit by moving the lever to see if the plunger rises and falls

209

carburettor and the bike still won't start check the inlet manifold for air leaks. Examine the joints between the carburettor and the inlet stubs and between the stubs and the cylinder head. An air leak substantial enough to make starting impossible will be evident from a visual inspection. Inspect the inlet stubs for any signs of an air leak. You may also be able to hear a sucking noise as the starter is operated. If the inlet stub is rubber examine it for splits and replace it if it is damaged.

Blockages in the exhaust system of a two-stroke bike will also make starting impossible. Check for a blockage by feeling for puffs of escaping gas at the exhaust whilst kicking the engine over.

If there is no pressure refer to pages 183–188 for the right way to deal with a blocked exhaust. If plenty of pressure is felt when kicking the engine over continue the checking sequence by investigating the choke operation.

Faulty choke

On most modern bikes the choke operating lever is fixed directly to the carburettor(s). In this case check for the correct operation of the lever and the actuating mechanism. Where the choke is of the slide or flap type, listen carefully for the sound of its movement inside the carburettor. Where the carburettor features a plunger type mechanism, watch to see if the actuating mechanism is operating the plunger (fig. 19). This is all that can be done without actually removing the carburettor from the bike but unless you have positive grounds for suspecting the choke, proceed to check the carburettor float bowl for petrol.

Fuel not reaching float bowl

Many bikes have carburettors with accessible drain screws which can be undone without removing the carburettors (fig. 20). Unscrew the drain plug and see if fuel comes out. If you find that no fuel comes out of the float bowl, remove the carburettor and check it for blocked jets or a faulty float needle. On some bikes however, the float bowl is inaccessible or not fitted with a drain plug. This type of carburettor often has a tickler button. Hold the button down and see if fuel escapes from the tickler location. However if there is no tickler, first check the ignition timing and engine compression in preference to disturbing the carburettor which should be done only as a last resort.

Blocked carburettor jets or airways

To check the carburettor for blocked jets or airways, first remove it from the bike and dismantle the float bowl components. Details of this procedure are shown on pages 89 to 90.

Take care when removing the jets; they are brass and can easily damage the soft alloy body of the carburettor.

20. Some carburettors have a drain screw in the float bowl. Remove it as shown to see if fuel is reaching the bowl

21. Some carburettors have tickler buttons. Hold it down to see if fuel is reaching the float bowl.

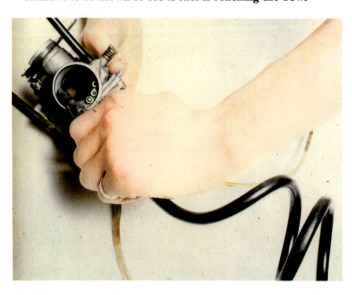

22. Blow through all the carburettor air ways and jets with an air line or bicycle pump

23. To check the timing, watch the timing marks and see if the points open at the correct position

Similarly, exercise care when replacing the jets. Do them up finger-tight and then using only moderate force tighten them.

With the jets removed from the carburettor flush out any particles of grease or dirt with petrol. Then blow through it with an air-line or hand pump (fig. 22). If you find it impossible to dislodge a jet blockage you should replace the jet. There is no point in trying to dislodge a blockage with a piece of wire as you will undoubtedly enlarge the jet orifice and ruin it. So, blow through all the airways in exactly the same way, feeling for a free flow of air through the jets with your fingertips. If fuel can get into and out of the float bowl, check the ignition timing.

Ignition timing out

Incorrect ignition timing means that a spark at the plug will be produced when the combustion chamber is either just filling with fuel/air mixture or as it is being emptied. The result is a combustion explosion which partially escapes through an open inlet or exhaust port rather than presenting a force to the piston to continue the combustion cycle. Ignition timing and point gaps must, therefore, be checked or reset to restore correct firing.

To gap the points and set the ignition timing, refer to pages 40 and 49. If you have one of the electronic ignition systems, such as the Lucas Rita or Boyer-Bransden system, fitted to your bike, refer to their manuals for the correct timing procedure. If your bike is fitted with a capacitor discharge electronic system you must time the engine dynamically. In this case, first check the compression system and then the carburettor jets and airways. If the bike still won't start, the ignition system must be suspect and you will have to consult a dealer as the checks require specialized equipment.

Compression system failure

If the ignition timing is correct there may be a fault in the combustion system.

To bring about combustion, the fuel/air mixture must be relatively hot and compressed. If the mixture is able to escape from the combustion chamber before being properly compressed, it will not heat up or ignite. This principle is explained on page 13. There are three escape routes that the mixture can take once it enters the combustion chamber; through the spark plug hole, the inlet and exhaust valves (on 4-strokes), past the piston, the decompressor on some 2-strokes or through a faulty head gasket.

A simple compression test can be made by removing the spark plug(s) and placing your thumb over the plug hole while turning the engine over. If compression is at a healthy level your thumb will be forced out of the hole however hard you hold it there. For an accurate test, however, you will need a compression tester. These are widely available and easy to use.

You can buy a universal type tester with a rubber cone connector from most car or bike accessory shops. To test engine compression remove the spark plug and press the tester firmly into the spark plug hole. Press the tester down hard and turn the engine over two or three times (fig. 24). Remove the tester and read off the compression indicated by the needle against the scale. You should get a reading of at least 8.5 kg/cm² (120psi) on a 4-stroke machine and at least 7 kg/cm² (100psi) on a 2-stroke machine. If you find the reading is substantially below these values or if you are able to hold your thumb over the spark plug hole while turning the engine over, there must be a compression fault.

24. Press the compression tester into the plug hole and turn the engine over with the starter

25. Poor compression may mean that the bore, rings or piston (as shown) are worn or damaged

Possible compression faults can arise from badly seating spark plugs, badly seating or incorrectly timed valves (on 4-strokes), or worn or broken piston rings or damaged cylinder bores or gaskets.

Badly seating spark plugs are a result of a crossed thread on the plug and in the cylinder head. The fault will be obvious from a visual inspection and there will be sooty deposits around the outside of the plug and its hole indicating a burnt air/fuel mixture blow-by. If the plug is wrongly inserted, as well as replacing the spark plug you must also restore the spark plug hole threads, either with a tapping tool or thread or heli-coil insert.

Badly seating valves can result from either loose tappets or excessive burning. To check the valve clearances refer to pages 99 to 103. If the clearances are correct, check the valve timing as shown on pages 111 to 116. If you can find nothing wrong with the valve gear the piston rings must be badly worn or broken, or the head gasket may be damaged.

To check for a blown head gasket examine the joint between the head and the barrel for sooty deposits, puffs of air when the engine is turned over and a dry squeaky noise. This may be caused by stripped or under or overtightened head bolts, or deterioration of the gasket. If you suspect a blown head gasket you must remove the cylinder head. This is detailed on pages 111–116 and 117–122.

To check the piston rings the cylinder barrel must be removed. Barrel removal and piston ring replacement procedure is shown on pages 134 to 138. Once you have removed the barrel, look at the piston rings and their grooves in the piston. Broken rings will be self-evident. Unbroken rings can be inspected for wear by pushing them squarely into the cylinder bore one at a time. Push the ring first about 2.5 cm (1in.) down the bore and measure the gap between its ends with a feeler gauge. The correct gap will be specified in your bike's handbook. Take another measurement with the ring about half way down the bore and a final one with the ring at the bottom of its travel. Measurements should be consistent at all points.

If the gap is in excess of specifications you will either need new rings or a cylinder rebore. You can either buy new rings and make the same test again or hire an internal micrometer to measure the diameter of the bore. If either check reveals the cylinder to be worn excessively the cylinder must be rebored by a specialist, since the job requires professional skill.

Index

Glossary

Accelerator pump Device fitted to some modern carburettors to give a richer mixture for acceleration. Usually a diaphragm pump squirts a fine jet of petrol into the inlet tract as the throttle is snapped open.

Advance Amount by which the ignition spark precedes the position of maximum compression at Top Dead Centre. Can be measured in millimetres of piston movement or degrees of crankshaft rotation (eg 5.5 mm BTDC or 36° BTDC). The actual amount depends on many factors including the engine speed (rpm); many engines need much less advance at low engine speed than at high. The difference between the two settings is the advance range (eg 10° at 1,000 rpm, 36° at 5,000 rpm, advance range 26°).

AF Across-flats, distance between opposite sides of square or hexagonal nuts and bolts.

Air lever Control lever, usually handlebar mounted, giving some control of the air-fuel mixture. On many carburettors until recently, extra air could be supplied to weaken the mixture and give more economical running. The name is still used for a carburettor control even if the action is to give a rich mixture for starting purposes.

Alternator Electrical generator which produces alternating current. On motorcycles the current is produced in the stator by a rotating magnetic field. The magnetic field may be from a ring of permanent magnets or an electromagnet with several poles (an 'excited field').

Ammeter Electrical instrument indicating the amount and direction of current flow, usually as charge or discharge of the battery, in amps.

Armature Rotating part of an electric motor, dynamo, or magneto. By convention, the term is usually applied to windings which rotate, not to the rotating magnets of a simple alternator, or flywheel magneto.

Automatic advance unit Mechanical device with bob-weights and springs, in which centrifugal force causes an ignition cam to move round on its spindle as engine speeds rise, thus altering the amount of advance.

Baffle Plate used inside a silencer to deflect the gases, or fixed inside a petrol tank to prevent the fuel sloshing about when the tank is part-full.

Balance weight Mass of metal added to a design to counterbalance other moving parts. Acorn-shaped balance weights are used on wheels; many modern engines have balance weights driven by the crankshaft to reduce vibration.

Banjo Junction between a flexible pipe and a fixed component in which a drilled banjo-bolt retains a cylindrical union with a side connection. Soft washers are fitted each side to seal the joint.

Battery Collection of cells for the storage of electricity. Normally a motorcyle battery consists of 3 or 6 lead-acid cells, with a voltage of 6 or 12 volts.

Battery acid Mixture of sulphuric acid and distilled water used for lead-acid batteries. The specific gravity should be 1.26–1.28; this strength can be bought from a garage or made up by a chemist.

Bearing Circular support for a rotating or pivoting component.

Big-end Bearing forming the lower end of the con-rod and joining this rod to the crankshaft. Plain or roller bearings are used.

Bleeder nipple Small screw fitted to hydraulic components to allow bleeding to be carried out. A hole beside the inner end is connected to a central drilling to allow air to escape; they are easily broken.

Bleeding Process whereby a hydraulic system is purged of trapped air. Also, fault occuring when spraying over a strongly coloured surface in which the original colour stains the new surface. Common when spraying white over red.

Boost port Additional smaller port in a 2-stroke, usually arranged between the main transfer ports, and serving not only to allow more mixture to be transferred but to aim the scavenging flow up the back of the cylinder.

Bore Diameter of the cylinder of an engine; the term is sometimes also used for the inner surface of the cylinder, or the hole itself. The bore of an engine is always given in millimetres.

Bottom Dead Centre (BDC) Position of the moving engine components when the piston is at its furthest from the cylinder head. The opposite of Top Dead Centre, TDC.

Breather Means by which excess pressure built up inside a chamber is vented into the atmosphere. Usually a simple spring and ball bearing valve is set to open at or above a pre-determined pressure load.

British Standard Fine (BSF) Fine thread series used on many British machines especially in the sizes $\frac{1}{4}$ in., $\frac{5}{16}$ in., $\frac{3}{8}$ in.

British Standard Whitworth (BSW) Thread form of coarse pitch often used for threads in light alloy components on British machines.

Brush Carbon block used to conduct electric current to and from a rotating part.

Burnt valve A condition where excessive combustion temperatures normally result in the exhaust valve becoming damaged by heat with a consequent loss in compression.

Butterfly Valve used for throttle or choke in a carburettor. A spindle passing across the air tube carries a circular flap and can be turned to open or close the passage.

Caliper Measuring instrument with two bent legs (like a blunt pair of dividers) used to compare internal or external diameters. Also that part of a disc brake assembly which fits around the disc carrying the friction pads and pressure cylinders.

Cam Device for turning regular rotational motion into irregular linear motion. Cams often consist of egg shaped projections on a rotating shaft. They are used to open valves in four-strokes and to open contact breakers in ignition systems. Double cams are often used in drum brakes.

Cam follower Component moved up and down by a cam. Cam followers can be pivoted at one end or in the middle, or slide in a bore; the part contacting the cam may be flat or curved or fitted with a roller.

Capacitor Electrical device capable of storing electricity and used in many ignition systems. Two strips of metal foil are separated by paper or other material, usually rolled up like a Swiss roll. Also called a Condenser, but this term is no longer recommended.

Capacitor discharge (CDI) Ignition system in which the spark is produced by allowing electricity stored in a capacitor to discharge suddenly through an ignition coil. The capacitor is usually charged up to around 400V and discharged by an electronic switch instead of contacts.

Carburettor Device which provides the fuel air mixture to the engine, which also has a valve allowing the rider to control the amount of mixture supplied and thus the engine output.

Chain tensioner Device allowing the slack in a chain drive to be controlled. Rear chains are tensioned by screws moving the wheel spindle or by an eccentric drive. Some cross-country machines also have a spring loaded tensioner pad acting on the lower run of the chain.

Choke Carburettor system designed to produce a rich mixture (more fuel than normal) for cold-starting purposes.

Circlip Spring ring fitting into a groove in a recess or around a shaft, used to prevent or limit axial movement. They can be pressed from sheet steel (Seeger circlips) or bent from spring steel wire or strip.

Clearance fit Two components have a clearance fit when one slides easily over the other on assembly.

Clutch Device fitted between the engine output and the rear wheel by which drive may be transmitted or released, allowing the drive to be engaged progressively. Most clutches rely on friction between plates of different materials.

Clutch drag A fault revealed by the failure of a clutch to free properly when required, making gear changing difficult and causing the machine to creep along when waiting in traffic. Usually due to incorrect adjustment or buckled plates.

Clutch slip A faulty condition in which a clutch is unable to transmit all the torque supplied to it. At large throttle openings the revs will rise without a corresponding rise in speed, often because of wear, incorrect adjustment, or contamination with lubricant.

Coil Component of helical form. A coil spring has turns of spring steel wound like the turns of a thread. An electrical coil has insulated wire wrapped around an iron core. An ignition coil has two such windings.

Collet Small collar of metal fixed round a component to hold it in place. Normally a pair of semi-circular collets is used, for instance to hold the spring retainer to a poppet valve or suspension unit.

Commutator Cylinder built up from strips of copper each connected to one end of an electric motor or dynamo rotor winding; Carbon blocks called brushes rub on the strips to pass current in or out; as the commutator rotates electricity passes through each winding in turn.

Compression ratio The ratio between the internal volume of an engine cylinder with the piston at TDC and the volume at BDC. As the volume at BDC can be difficult to measure the ratio is calculated as $CR = \dfrac{S+D}{D}$ where S is the swept volume or capacity and D is the dead space or clearance volume.

Connecting rod The component joining the piston to the crankshaft and serving to transmit forces from one to the other. Each end has a journal bearing; at the piston end is the little end or small end bearing, the big end bearing or eye encircles the crankpin. Often abbreviated to con-rod.

Contact breaker A pair of electrical contacts held together by a spring but opened by a rotating cam to break or switch off the ignition circuit to produce sparks. Also called contact points or just points.

Cotter pin Split pin used to prevent a nut on a cotter from loosening. The term is also applied to the cotter itself.

Crankpin The cylindrical portion of a crankshaft around which the big end turns. The term is applied in particular to built up cranks; in a one piece crank the term big end journal is more usual.

Crankshaft The part of the engine which is driven round by the connecting rod. The crankshaft rotates on bearings called main bearings fixed in the crankcase.

CV Constant velocity.

Damper Device which controls movement by converting knietic energy into another form, usually heat. Dampers are built into suspension and steering systems and instruments, to limit repeat oscillations.

D.C. Direct current.

Decompressor Manually operated device which allows the rider to release some of the pressure in the cylinder, making starting easier. On a 4-stroke the mechanism lifts the exhaust valve slightly off its seat; 2-strokes have a tiny poppet valve fitted in the cylinder head.

Desmodromic A system of operation in which positive motion occurs in both directions without relying on springs. Most poppet valves are opened by cams and closed by springs; desmodromic valve gear has an extra pair of cams arranged to close the valves instead of springs, and enables high engine speeds and fierce valve operation to be achieved without valve bounce or spring surge.

Diode Simple electric device which allows current to flow in one direction but not in the other. Modern diodes are usually made of silicon or germanium, and they are used in rectifiers which convert AC to DC for battery charging, and in many electronic devices.

Distributor On some multi-cylinder machines with coil ignition, one coil is used, and the distributor is the device used to direct the spark to each sparking plug at the correct time. They are common on motorcars but rare and obsolescent on motorcycles. The term is also applied to devices which resemble distributors but which serve only to carry contact breakers (for instance, on Moto Guzzi 850 models).

DOHC Double overhead camshaft.

Dry sump Lubrication system in which the oil is kept in a tank, and pumped into the engine from which it falls into the sump to be returned to the tank by a separate pump.

Dwell The period during which the contact points remain closed as the operating cam rotates. It can be expressed in degrees or as a percentage. A dwell of $180° = 50\%$. Many dwell meters are designed for 4-cylinder cars and are calibrated only from 0–99°; to find the dwell for a motorcycle this reading should usually be multiplied by four.

Dynamo Generator of direct current. An armature carries windings and a commutator, and it is driven round inside a magnetic field provided by field coils and controlled by a vibrating-contact regulator.

Electronic Electric drive which relies solely on the changes produced in semiconductors and associated devices by electric currents. The term is applied particularly to devices which use such effects to replace a mechanical assembly, such as voltage regulators and ignition systems in which electric currents are controlled by transistors, thyristors, etc.

Expansion chamber Specially shaped tube used as part of the exhaust system for silencing purposes or to encourage or stifle resonance, especially on 2-stroke engines.

Firing order In a multi-cylinder engine this indicates the sequence of combustion.

Float Buoyant metal or plastic component which helps determine the level of fuel in a carburettor or similar device. The float operates a float needle within an enclosed space called a float chamber, thus cutting off the fuel supply when the float reaches a predetermined level.

Flywheel Circular mass of heavy metal fixed to and turning with the crankshaft of an engine to give smoothness and help low speed running. The same effect is often obtained by using full circle crankwebs, themselves called flywheels.

Four stroke Internal combustion engine design in which a power stroke occurs every four strokes of each piston.

Four stroking Common fault that occurs in 2-stroke engines when the engine misfires each alternate revolution.

Gasket Sheet or film between two surfaces to keep fluid in or out. Often found between crankcase halves or under engine covers to keep oil in the engine. High pressure gaskets between cylinder and head retain combustion gases.

Gearbox A system of gears that converts the rotational speed of the input shaft to a different speed at the output shaft. By changing gear a selection of gears are used and a different ratio of input to output speed is obtained.

Gear In general, a hardened steel wheel with teeth around its circumference which engage with teeth on another gear wheel.

Gear ratio The ratio between the different speeds of gear wheels when their differing diameters are meshed together. The number of teeth on each wheel determines the ratio.

Gear selector forks Components which bear on the gears and move them along the shaft out of and into engagement.

Generator Device which produces an electrical current by rotating a coil through lines of magnetic flux.

Grommet Small piece of rubber or plastic that either fills a disused hole or acts as a protective around the edge of a hole where wire or cable passes through.

Hairpin spring Helical spring with two long parallel arms at right angles to the coil.

Hot spot Point in engine, cylinder head, or piston which attains especially high temperature.

HT High Tension as in HT lead connecting spark plug to ignition coil.

Idler Gear or sprocket used to space out a system or take up slack, but not used to drive any component directly.

Ignition The lighting of the mixture in the cylinder.

Ignition advance As the flame takes a certain time to pass through the compressed mixture the moment of ignition is arranged slightly before the piston is at top dead centre. This ignition advance may be expressed in terms of piston movement (in mm) or in crank rotation (degrees).

Ignition coil Source of high voltage (HT) used to give a spark for ignition; two coils of wire are wound on an iron core and encapsulated in plastic or sealed into an aluminium canister.

Ignition system Electrical parts required to produce sparks for ignition.

Ignition timing The details of ignition advance required for a particular engine. Timing is often set by moving a contact breaker or by changing the position of a trigger coil. Point-less electronic ignition, in use on many modern machines, has a preset timing which should not vary in normal use.

Injection Instead of a carburettor, some engines have the fuel squirted in under pressure. Petrol injection can give improved power or economy but is complex and expensive. Fuel injection is a necessary feature of diesel engines.

Jet Brass tube with a carefully calibrated hole used in carburettors to control the flow of fuel, air, or mixture. Similar parts are used to restrict oil flow in some lubrication systems.

Journal The cylindrical portion of a shaft around which a bearing is fitted. A journal bearing is normally intended to take radial loads only.

Lap Metal tool with a surface impregnated by a fine abrasive used to improve the surface finish of flat or cylindrical parts. The term lapping is also extended to cover the use of fine abrasive paste on poppet valves and seats, petrol tapes, float needles etc, to mate the surfaces exactly together.

Leading shoe In a simple internal expanding brake, one shoe is in front of, or leading, the pivot, and the other is behind, or trailing it, considered from the point of view of wheel rotation. The leading shoe is much more powerful in its effect because of its servo action; some brakes are designed to take advantage of this fact by reversing the trailing shoe and using two cams to give a two leading shoe brake.

Liner Sleeve inserted in a component to give a hardwearing surface. Cast iron liners are often fitted to light alloy cylinders.

Little-end The end of the connecting rod which forms the bearing around the gudgeon pin. Also called the small end.

Long stroke Engine term meaning that the length of the stroke is greater than the bore diameter; the same as undersquare.

Low tension The low voltage feed to the primary windings of an energy transfer or coil ignition system, as opposed to the high tension fed to the parking plug.

Mag dyno Device common on motorcycles

made between 1930 and 1960 in which a magneto and dynamo were combined. Usually the magneto was driven directly and carried a cylindrical dynamo driven through a pair of gears.

Magneto Self contained device, containing magnets and coils, and driven by the engine, which delivers the high voltage to the spark plug for ignition. In most magnetos, the coil rotate between the poles of a fixed magnet, but in some types the magnet rotates between the end of yoke carrying the coil, and in flywheel magnetos the magnets rotate around the coils.

Main bearings The bearings which carry the crankshaft of an engine.

Main jet The carburettor jet which meters the fuel passing into the engines at full throttle.

Mainshaft The gearbox shaft which is driven by the engine and in turn drives the layshaft or output shaft.

Manifold Pipe assembly connecting one carburettor to two or more cylinders, often (wrongly) used for a single inlet pipe. The same term is also used to indicate a multiple exhaust connection.

Manometer Device for measuring pressure differences such as manifold depression.

Master cylinder The hydraulic cylinder that is lever-operated by the rider to activate the slave cylinders which work the brakes.

Mixture Short for fuel air mixture; a rich mixture has too much for proper combustion, a weak or lean mixture has too little.

Needle roller bearing Rolling bearing with small cylindrical rollers much longer than their diameter. The rollers may be completely loose, held in a flanged cup, or separated by a cage.

Octane Hydrocarbon found in petrol, with the formula C_8H_{18}. It is particularly resistant to knock or detonation when used as a fuel.

OHC *see* Overhead camshaft.

OHV *see* Overhead valve.

Ohm Electrical unit of resistance, found by dividing the voltage applied across a component by the current flowing through it. Symbol Ω.

Oil Liquids which are not very reactive, are fairly viscous and not volatile, and most often used as lubricants. Most lubricating oils for vehicle use are based on mineral oil from petroleum, but vegetable compounds, such as castor oil, and animal products, such as sperm oil, have also been used.

Oil control rings Piston rings fitted below the compression rings in a 4-stroke engine. The ring groove is drilled or slotted to allow lubricant scraped from the bore to escape into the interior of the piston.

Oiled up Fairly common problem on 2-stroke engines where, for a number of reasons, the oil in the compressed mixture is not burnt often during combustion. The resultant wet oil on the spark plug electrodes inhibits spark production and gives rise to poor ignition.

'O' ring A seal of rubber or synthetic band that is fitted between two mating surfaces, normally in a groove.

Overhead cam (OHC) Engine design in which the overhead valves are operated by a camshaft which is also carried in the cylinder head. Drive to the camshaft may be by chain,

toothed belt, shaft and bevel gears, eccentric straps, or a train of spur gears.

Overhead valve (OHV) Engine design in which the valves are fitted to the cylinder head, either parallel to the cylinder axis or at an angle. The term normally refers only to engines in which the valve operation is by push-rods and rockers, as distinct from overhead cam designs.

Overall gear ratio The ratio of the engine rpm in any gear to the rear wheel rpm; the same as saying that the number of times the engine goes round for each revolution of the rear wheel in a given gear.

Petroil Mixture of petrol and oil used as a fuel in may 2-stroke machines.

Pilot jet The small petrol jet provided in a carburettor to control fuel mixture when the throttle is closed or only slightly open. The pilot system also includes drillings and a pilot screw so that fine adjustment of mixture can be made.

Pinion A small toothed wheel which engages directly with a larger wheel. The term is also extended to mean any gearwheel.

Pinking The high pitched tinkling noise heard in an engine when detonation is occurring. It is reminiscent of piston slap and the noises made by diesel taxis, but is a serious indication of engine malfunction.

Piston The component in an engine which forms one face of the combustion chamber and can move in the cylinder transmitting power to the crankshaft. The sliding seal is provided by piston rings in grooves around the top of the piston, and below this a hollow gudgeon pin fits in bosses and joins the piston to the connecting rod. Pistons are usually cast from aluminium alloys but forgings are used in many high speed engines; in the past cast iron and steel pistons were used.

Piston rings Steel or cast iron rings of rectangular or tapering section used to seal the gap between the piston and cylinder. A gap in each ring allows it to spring outwards; the seal is perfected by oil on its surfaces, and by the gas pressure which acts between the ring and its groove.

Piston slap Audible contact between the piston and cylinder often due to excess clearance or overadvanced ignition, but inevitable in some engine designs, particularly high performance air cooled 2-strokes.

Play Slack movement in a system, which can be deliberate like the clearance between a rocker end and the valve, or due to wear like the movement which can develop in a swinging arm bearing if neglected.

Plug cap The part between a spark plug lead and the plug itself. It is usually covered to suppress radio and TV interference caused by the sparks.

Plug lead A carton or metal-stranded lead carrying the current to the spark plug.

Points Common name for ignition contact breakers, although they have not been pointed since about 1905.

Power band The range of engine speed in which the engine produces considerable power. Not an exact term.

Pre-ignition Ignition of the compressed mixture in an engine before the ignition spark occurs. It can be due to red hot particles, the wrong grade of spark plug, or a badly seating exhaust valve, for instance. While pre-ignition

on its own is not harmful, it can lead quickly to detonation which is extremely damaging.

Pushrod The component which transmits force in an overhead valve engine between the cam follower in the timing case and the rockers above the cylinder head. Most modern pushrods are made of light alloy tube with steel end caps.

Rake The angle between the steering pivot and the vertical, necessary to make the steering self centring and auto stable. Sometimes the term is applied wrongly to the angle from the horizontal. The word is also used for the angle between the top surface of a lathe tool and the top cutting face, or a similar angle in other cutting tools. Too much rake makes the edge weak, too little absorbs power.

Ram effect When gas is travelling down a pipe, it possesses inertia and will continue to flow for some while after the pressures equalize. This ram effect can help get more mixture into a cylinder.

Reach The length of thread on a spark plug, which must match that provided in the cylinder head block.

Rectifier Device which turns alternating current into direct current, normally incorporating one or more diodes.

Rocker A lever pivoted near its centre and used to change the direction of a push or pull, especially in overhead valve mechanisms. The rocker gear of an engine includes the valve rockers, the rocker spindles, the supports for the spindles and any adjuster devices. The rocker box is the cover or part of the head casting which contains the rocker gear, and the rocker feed is the pipe or hole through which lubricant is supplied.

Roller bearings An antifriction bearing in which the rolling members are cylindrical or conical solid steel rollers rather than balls. They are often used for engine and gearbox bearings and for other purposes on motorcycles.

Rotary valve This term can apply to any valve in which parts revolve, but specifically it is used for inlet and exhaust valves in place of the more common reciprocating designs. Disc valves are used on many 2-stroke inlet systems; cylindrical and conical valves have been used on both 2- and 4-stroke designs for inlet and exhaust.

Rotor The rotating parts of a magneto, alternator, oil pump, or similar device. Normally around the rotor rotates within or around a fixed stator.

Rpm Revolutions per minute; revs.

Running in The process in which the rubbing parts of an engine are made to mate exactly by a gradual increase in load and speed over the first 1,500 km (1,000 miles) of use.

Running on Fault in which an engine continues to run when switched off; often due to incandescent particles in the combustion chamber, or a faulty ignition switch. If the switch is not the cause, the engine should be decarbonized.

Runout Eccentricity or wobble in a rotating or circular component, such as a thread or wheel rim.

Scavenge The process by which burnt gas remaining in the cylinder of an engine towards the end of the exhaust phase is removed, usually by providing a flow of new mixture to sweep away the old.

Servo effect The self acting or amplification effect found, for instance, in drum brakes. The rotation of the drum helps to increase the force holding the lining of the leading shoe against the drum, and thus amplifies the braking effect.

Shim Thin, hard metal washers and similar components, in various exact thicknesses used as packing or to reduce play. The material is called shim shock and the process of adjustment is shimming. Also, the thicker metal discs used similarly to adjust valve clearances with bucket followers on many DOHC models.

Shock absorber Common term for an elastic component in a transmission system such as the rubber vane device used in some rear sprocket mountings, and (wrongly) for a suspension damper. In fact the spring absorbs the shock but the damper dissipates the energy.

Short stroke Engine design in which the bore dimension is greater than the stroke. Such engines tend to have better power to weight ratios than long stroke designs, but are usually less efficient.

Silencer Metal box through which the exhaust gases from an engine pass, in order to reduce the noise. The American term, muffler, is a more accurate description of the silencer's function and role.

Slave cylinder A hydraulic cylinder operated from the master sylinder; the term is applied to clutch cylinders but brake cylinders are more usually called wheel cylinders or caliper cylinders.

Sleeve Thin-walled cylinder usually of cast iron forming the bearing surface for the piston of a reciprocating engine. When a thicker than normal sleeve is fitted to an engine to reduce the capacity it is said to be sleeved down.

Sludge An accumulation of insoluble substances in a lubrication system resulting from breakdown of the oil, and contamination from wear particles and combustion products. Many such particles are so small that they will pass through a filter.

Snailcam Plate with a spiral outer edge, sometimes notched, used for rear chain adjustment. Plates on each end of the wheel spindle are turned progressively against locating pegs and the spindle moves back as the radius of the cam increases.

Splenoid Heavy duty electrical relay, usually causing mechanical movement as well as closing contacts when it is operated; in a pre-engaged starter system a solenoid is used to move a gear into mesh and then connect the starter motor.

Spark plug Threaded fitting fixed in a combustion chamber, with a pair of electrodes across which a spark can pass for ignition.

Spindle The rod or tube around which a component rotates.

Splines Alternate grooves and ridges along a cylindrical shaft and within the bore of a mating part, allowing axial movement and transmitting rotary motion. Fine splines are often called serrations.

Split pin Locking device consisting of a length of half round wire doubled up and with an eye at one end. It is passed through holes inadjacent parts, and the two ends are spread out so the pin cannot fall out.

Sprag A bar of metal or similar tool used to lock a component, such as a crankshaft or clutch drum, so that fixing nuts can be turned.

Sprocket Toothed wheel driving or driven by a chain, especially a roller chain.

Stator The fixed part of an electrical machine, around or within which the rotor turns.

Steering damper One fixed to the front forks of a machine to help reduce steering wobble.

Steering head The part of the frame which carries the bearing in which the front forks turn.

Steering lock A key operated device fitted to fix the steering of a machine so that it cannot be ridden. The term is also applied to the degree of steering angle.

Stroboscope Lamp designed to emit a bright flash of light at the instant that the ignition spark occurs; it can be directed at a rotating component to check ignition timing.

Stroke The distance moved by the piston between TDC and BDC, normally quoted in millimetres. An engine which is 'stroked' is modified to increase the stroke thus increasing the swept volume.

Subframe Assembly of tubes and brackets forming part of a structure. Some machines such as many BMW models have a subframe holding the seat and rear suspension; trail bikes often have the headlamps held in a subframe formed by brackets.

Sump The space at the bottom of an engine unit into which the oil drains. A wet-sump engine uses the sump as the oil reservoir, a dry sump is emptied continuously by a scavenge pump feeding a separate oil tank.

Suspension The system whereby a road wheel is allowed to move up and down over road surface imperfections with little effect on the main part of the vehicle or the rider. Three different requirements are: controlled movement, springing and damping. A suspension unit comprises a hydraulic damper combined with a coil or pneumatic spring and acts between fixed and moving part.

Swarf Metal filings and turnings produced in machining operations.

Swinging arm Rear suspension design in which the rear wheel is carried on an arm or arms pivoted at the front end and attached to suspension units towards the rear. To be strictly accurate almost all modern machines have a swinging fork comprising two swinging arms but the term arm is often used for the whole assembly.

Tachometer Correct term for any instrument which measures speed, normally used for engine speed in place of the term rev-counter, although the tachograph fitted in commercial vehicles records road speed not engine revs.

Tapered roller bearing Rolling bearing in which the inner and outer races, and the rollers, are conical, excellent at resisting a combination of radial and axial loads and often used in pairs for wheel bearings, swinging arms, and steering heads.

Tappet Cam follower used in many side valve and overhead valve engines – a mushroom shaped or cylindrical component, slides up and down in a bore in the timing case, under the action of the camshaft. The term is sometimes extended to cover all types of cam follower, especially where an adjustment is provided. Setting the tappets means correcting the valve clearances, even on an engine which properly speaking has no tappets.

Telescopic forks Front suspension in which the wheel is carried in a pair of tubular slides, which can move within or around tubular stanchions carried on the steering head.

Three phase When maximum output is required from an alternator in a given space, three separate windings are arranged so that the voltage in each rises to a maximum in turn rather simultaneously. The output is rectified by a device containing at least six diodes.

Throttle A valve in carburettors that controls air flow and the power of the engine.

Thrust bearing One designed to resist axial load, often used, for instance, in clutch operating mechanisms.

Timing chain or gears The mechanism by which the camshafts are driven.

Torque The twisting effect produced in a shaft or similar part when power is transmitted along it: or an indication of the tightness of a threaded fastener or the output of an engine at a particular speed. In ordinary use, 'good torque' means good output at low speed, although in fact whenever an engine produces power it exerts torque.

Total loss Lubrication system in which a small quantity of oil is fed to the engine at regular intervals but no means of recirculating used oil is provided. All 2-stroke motorcycles and most speedway machines have total loss systems.

Transfer port Passage provided between a 2-stroke crankcase and the cylinder wall through which mixture is transferred when the piston is around BDC.

Transmission The system by which power from the engines is passed to the driving wheel.

Two leading-shoe Drum brake design in which both shoes are leading shoes; this gives improved self servo effect but increases the tendency to fade.

Two-stroke Internal Combustion engine design in which a power stroke occurs every two strokes of each piston.

Vacuum gauge Instrument for measuring the vacuum pressure in an engine when the throttle is opened. It is usually calibrated in inches of mercury or water.

Valve bounce Condition in which a poppet valve seats so rapidly that it rebounds.

Venturi The central tube in a carburettor through which the air passes.

Viscosity index The viscosity index is a scale which indicates how much thinning occurs when an oil is heated.

Volt Unit of electromotive force that bears an amp of current against an ohm of resistance.

V-twin Engine design in which two cylinders are fixed on the crankcase so that they form a V.

Wankel Engine in which a three-sided rotor spins on a crank rotating within a two-lobed space.

Wet sump Lubrication system in which oil carried in the sump is circulated by splash or, more recently, an oil pump, and returns to the sump by gravity.

Wheelbase The distance between the front and rear spindles of a machine.